Embeddedness
& Corporate Change
in a Global Economy

PETER LANG
New York ○ Washington, D.C./Baltimore ○ Boston ○ Bern
Frankfurt am Main ○ Berlin ○ Brussels ○ Vienna ○ Oxford

Embeddedness & Corporate Change in a Global Economy

Edited by
Rueyling Tzeng
and Brian Uzzi

PETER LANG
New York ○ Washington, D.C./Baltimore ○ Boston ○ Bern
Frankfurt am Main ○ Berlin ○ Brussels ○ Vienna ○ Oxford

LIBRARY OF CONGRESS CATALOGING-IN-PUBLICATION DATA

Embeddedness and corporate change in a global economy /
edited by Rueyling Tzeng and Brian Uzzi.
p. cm.
Includes bibliographical references and index.
1. Organizational change. 2. Strategic alliances (Business).
3. International economic integration. 4. International business
enterprises—Management. I. Tzeng, Rueyling. II. Uzzi, Brian.
HD58.8 .E45   658'.049—dc21   00-020418
ISBN 0-8204-4986-5

DIE DEUTSCHE BIBLIOTHEK-CIP-EINHEITSAUFNAHME

Embeddedness and corporate change in a global economy /
ed. by: Rueyling Tzeng and Brian Uzzi.
—New York; Washington, D.C./Baltimore; Boston; Bern;
Frankfurt am Main; Berlin; Brussels; Vienna; Oxford: Lang.
ISBN 0-8204-4986-5

Cover design by Nona Reuter

The paper in this book meets the guidelines for permanence and durability
of the Committee on Production Guidelines for Book Longevity
of the Council of Library Resources.

© 2000 Peter Lang Publishing, Inc., New York

All rights reserved.
Reprint or reproduction, even partially, in all forms such as microfilm,
xerography, microfiche, microcard, and offset strictly prohibited.

Printed in the United States of America

Table of Contents

List of Figures vii
List of Tables and Charts ix
Acknowledgments xi

Introduction: Embeddedness Perspectives on the Change
   of Institutions, Interfirm Networks, and Labor Markets
      Brian Uzzi and Rueyling Tzeng 1
1. The Local and the Grandiose: Method, Micro and Macro
   in Comparative Studies of Culture and Organizations
      Mats Alvesson 11

Part One: Embeddedness and Organizational Transformation in Various Societies

2. Societal Transformation and Enterprise Change in Eastern Europe:
   A Comparison of Hungary and Slovenia
      Richard Whitley 49
3. Networks, Transaction Costs, and the Persistence of Interfirm Ties:
   The New York Apparel Industry, 1985 to 1995
      Michael Alan Sacks and Brian Uzzi 79
4. The Transformation of Family Firms in Taiwan
   under Initial Public Offerings
      Yunshi Liu and Kuang S. Yeh 105
5. Corporate Responses to the Issue of Sexual Harassment
   in the Workplace in Taiwan—Lessons from the United States
      Cing-Kae Chiao 131
6. The Political Economy of State-owned Enterprises
   in Foreign Investment: The Case of Taiwan
      Hsing-Chou Sung 169

Part Two: Embeddedness and the Co-evolution of Markets
  7. Business Globalization and Local Embeddedness:
     The Case of Foreign Investment in Taiwan
     Rueyling Tzeng 211
  8. Foreign Companies and the Transformation Processes in Poland:
     The Role of Western Financial and Human Capital
     Hedwig Rudolph 239
  9. Immigrant Firms and Transnational Embeddedness:
     Chinese Entrepreneurs in Los Angeles
     Yen-Fen Tseng 263
  10. Transnational Entrepreneurs and Regional Industrialization:
     The Silicon Valley-Hsinchu Connection
     AnnaLee Saxenian 283

Bibliography 303
List of Contributors 343
Index 345

Figures

Figure 6.1 The Source of Challenges to State Legitimacy............................ 187
Figure 6.2 The State's Alternative Strategy for Maintaining its
           Legitimacy 188
Figure 6.3 The FDI of Taiwan's SOEs: An Explanatory Model................ 191

Tables and Charts

Tables

Table 2.1	Late State Socialist Institutions in Hungary and Slovenia	52
Table 2.2	Enterprise Characteristics in Late State Socialist Hungary and Slovenia	58
Table 2.3	Major Institutional Changes in Hungary and Slovenia	68
Table 2.4	Expected Enterprise Changes in Hungary and Slovenia	73
Table 3.1a	Random Effects Panel Probit Estimates of the Probability of Switching (1) versus Sticking (0) with an Exchange Partner: Better Dress Apparel Manufacturers and Contractors, 1985–1994	97
Table 3.1b	Random Effects Panel Probit Estimates of the Probability of Switching (1) versus Sticking (0) with an Exchange Partner: Better Dress Apparel Manufacturers and Contractors, 1985–1994	99
Table 3.1c	Random Effects Panel Probit Estimates of the Probability of Switching (1) versus Sticking (0) with an Exchange Partner: Better Dress Apparel Manufacturers and Contractors, 1985–1994	100
Table 4.1	Time Impact on the Degree of Family Control of the Board	122
Table 4.2	Type of Board Pre-IPO and Post-IPO	123
Table 4.3	Type of Board: Pre-IPO, Post-IPO, and Current	124
Table 4.4	Proportion of Non-Professional Directors: Pre-IPO and Post-IPO	125
Table 4.5	Proportion of Non-Professional Directors: Pre-IPO, Post-IPO and Current	126
Table 6.1	State-owned Enterprise (SOE) Foreign Investment before 1990	176

Table 6.2	State-owned Enterprise (SOE) Investment in Various Countries	177
Table 7.1	Contributions of Foreign Investment to Taiwan's Economy	220
Table 7.2	Private Foreign Investment in Approvals by Area	222
Table 7.3	Distribution of Foreign Firms in Taiwan by Industry in 1993	230
Table 7.4	Zero-order Correlation between Variables	233
Table 8.1	Financial Aid for the Transformation: Selected Donors	245
Table 9.1	Pre-migration Background among Chinese Business Owners	271
Table 9.2	Number of High-Technology Business Owners in Los Angeles County, Chinese versus Total Population, 1990	274

Chart

| Chart 8.1 | Foreign Direct Investment in Central Eastern Europe, 1989–1995 | 247 |

Acknowledgments

This volume originates from an international conference, Social Structure and Social Change: International Perspective on Business Firms and Economic Life, sponsored by and held at the Institute of European and American Studies, Academia Sinica, Taiwan, on May 9-10, 1997. After the conference, all authors revised their papers in light of commentary by the two conference discussants, who are experts in different disciplinary areas, as well as comments from the floor. The revised papers were then sent out to two anonymous experienced social scientists for review, one from Taiwan and the other from abroad, in order to obtain a wide and balanced view. When the two reviews had contradictory opinions, we sought a third review. In other words, the collection in this volume is a subset of papers that were originally presented at the conference and have since undergone a series of revisions.

We would first like to extend our great appreciation to the Institute of European and American Studies, Academia Sinica, Taiwan, for its abiding and enthusiastic support of this invaluable academic project. The director of the institute, Dr. Cheng-Yi Lin, has been most keen and supportive in seeking an international publisher for this volume. The deputy director, Dr. Chyong-Fang Ko, as well as the head of the Division of Social and Economic Studies, Dr. Shih-Yu Kuo, and her division members, all lent themselves to this project. In addition, we must not forget to mention the valuable contributions of the former director, Dr. Jia-You Sheu, and the former division head, Dr. Jiun-Han Tsao, to the course of the conference that resulted in this volume. Several young, diligent, and wonderful research assistants, including Andy Lin, Sylvia Huang, and Shih-Fang Chen, to name just a few, have assumed various tedious tasks, first in organizing a successful and joyful conference and then in transforming it into a fine printed work. We especially would like to thank Ching-yi Lee for her delicate typesetting work for this volume.

It is simply impossible to list all the persons who have contributed to this project at various stages, so it must suffice to list the roles they played: audience members, discussants, and moderators in the conference, and anonymous reviewers for the papers in this volume. We greatly appreciate their substantial input. We would especially like to mention three global managers who delivered stimulating speeches distilled from their daily managerial practices and had practical and insightful discussions with the floor, although their speeches are not included in this volume in order to maintain a coherent format and style. These gentlemen are Mr. Bruce Fredric Berkman, president of Productivity Asia Limited; Dr. Morris Chang, chairman and CEO of TSMC; and Mr. Jean-Francois Di Meglio, head of Asia Pacific Corporate Banking, Paribas. As editors, we would like to extend our appreciation to all the authors of this volume, who have remained patient and cooperative throughout this long process. Finally, we thank the editors and staff at Peter Lang Publishing, Inc., who have helped us greatly in making this volume possible.

Rueyling Tzeng and Brian Uzzi

Introduction

Embeddedness Perspectives on the Change of Institutions, Interfirm Networks, and Labor Markets

Brian Uzzi and Rueyling Tzeng

This volume presents analyses of how different forms of business organization have changed under a globalizing economic system using an embeddedness approach. The embeddedness approach offers an understanding of how economic exchange is mediated by formal and informal social structures that shape how organizations evolve differentially under similar economic changes. In this introductory chapter, we describe the nature of changes that are associated with globalization, discuss the components of an embeddedness approach for organizational change, and summarize the ways in which the papers in this volume offer a comparative perspective on organizational change and are linked through an embeddedness perspective.

Global Capitalism, Embeddedness, and Corporate Change

The past decade saw unprecedented economic changes on an international scale. Financial capital became easier for organizations to access as banks no longer monopolized financial intermediation and venture capital industries sprang up outside the U.S. (Ohmae 1990; Davis and Mizruchi 1999; cf Mintz and Schwartz 1985). Deregulation removed long-standing regulations over prices and competition in the U.S., Europe, and Asia. This lowered many entry barriers and allowed new competition to arise—bringing with it new forms of organization. In Western nations, there was also a new mixing of private and public models of organizing. Many public sector services and products as mundane as garbage collection or as important as education were outsourced to private sector enterprises that had few regulatory restrictions on how to organize their production or delivery of services—creating quasi public-private enterprises (Harrison 1994; Pfeffer 1998). Similarly, labor market arrangements in Europe and the US were liberalized as permanent jobs were externalized at an unprecedented rate and formal labor contracts that had locked labor-management relations into stable exchanges were eliminated (Harrison 1994; Davis-Blake and Uzzi 1993; Uzzi and Barsness 1998). In Eastern Europe, similar changes were injected through statewide privatization programs and the construction of Western-style market institutions of capitalism (Schleifer 1998). Asia became an international economic and financial power and a model for alliance capitalism, despite its financial distresses of the late 1990s, from which Asia is now gradually recovering. Yet, on the other hand, the heterogeneous, disparate world markets were transformed into somewhat tightly coupled fields of common economic practices and regulations by trade agreements such as the European Union, the North American Free Trade Agreement, Asian Pacific Economic Cooperation Forum, and the World Trade Organization (WTO), which delimited the free flow of goods, capital, and people across national boundaries only within the regional economic and trade blocs.

In the economic sphere of life, "globalization," as contended by neoclassical economists, is conveying the message that the world that we live in is being made into a single place, a global economy, an economy conceived of as essentially the same in all its parts. At the level of the nation, more countries are becoming capitalist societies that pursue a price market rather than a state-regulated market or an informal network market. At the transnational level, a globally integrated capitalist market economy is emerging where boundaries between countries are disappearing and the locality is not important.

As Portes and Sensenbrenner (1993) point out, embeddedness provides a very useful standpoint from which to criticize neoclassical models;

therefore, it definitely should not be omitted from the present heated debates on globalization that are usually dominated by the neoclassical models. Sociologists have recently been exploring the comparative structuring of organizations within capitalist economic systems—systems of economic exchange that are distinctive in their universal reliance on the price mechanism and private ownership of assets (Hamilton and Biggart 1988; Campbell, Hollingsworth, and Lindberg 1991; Stark 1996; Whitley 1994). An important theme in the literature concerns how the organizational changes under similar economic and technical factors are shaped by the social structures within which they are embedded (Kahn and Zald 1990; Stark 1992; Nee and Ingram 1998; Fligstein 1996; Fligstein and Mara-Drita 1996; Putnam 1993). Contrary to the neoclassical economists, they suggest that the development of the capitalist system is divergent across different countries. Hollingsworth and Boyer (1997: 434) further argue that too much coordination by markets may trigger global instabilities and this is especially the case with financial markets, as the crashes of 1929 and 1987 clearly demonstrate. At the transnational level, Hirst and Thompson (1996) contend that MNCs are not becoming footloose with global capital, and globalization warrants not less but more regulation and better governance in the economic sphere.

While embeddedness has long been an important area of scholarship in sociology, its recent resurgence in sociology is shared by neighboring disciplines that have found new insights in the approach—indicating the broad-minded interest and appeal of the embeddedness approach for understanding economy and society. Arrow (1998: 97) argued that new attention to social structure economics would reveal a "general principle—that beliefs and preferences may themselves be the product of social interactions unmediated by prices and markets." Ian Macneil (1999), a pioneer in the area of relational contracting law, goes even further to suggest that all contractual transactions are embedded in complex social relations and that "a surer and more rapid understanding of any transaction is achieved by contemporaneous examination of those relations than by focusing initial inquiry on the transaction itself." Similarly, prominent political scientists view embeddedness as an understudied and important new area of research (Putnam 1993; Grief 1994; Hardin 1998). Political scientists argue that social embeddedness offers a new model for understanding civic society and business organizations because it is "features of social organizations such as networks, norms, and social trust that facilitate coordination and cooperation for mutual benefit" (Putnam 1995). Consequently, the time has come for a collection of studies to be assembled on how the embeddedness of economic activity in social structures shapes the internationalization of markets and management.

If asked to contemplate how forms of business organization would evolve under these recent changes, how would you approach your analysis? The conventional, market-based wisdom would have you begin by examining how market conditions instigate competition, how the State enforces property rights, and how human capital is developed and deployed. In such models, markets are typically assumed to be composed of actors with narrow personal goals and depersonalized ties; they act simultaneously but autonomously (Evans 1995; Nee and Ingram 1998; Arrow 1998). States play the role of neutral third parties that establish and ensure protection over property rights and provide the infrastructures for business that private sector actors would otherwise not invest in because of the coordination problem of restricting access to public goods (North 1990; Fligstein and Freeland 1995; Fligstein 1990). Lastly, this approach looks at how the internal capabilities of actors, be they nations, firms or persons, shape their ability to adopt new practices or remold old practices to new market demands (Porter 1990). Based on these assumptions, a core prediction is that organizations that have experienced common economic constraints of globalization will converge upon the same universal response to problems of organizing (Jensen 1989).

You probably would have been successful if you had taken conventional wisdom and turned it upside down. The record on how globalization has affected organizational change suggests that similar market and State conditions produced different outcomes and that similar outcomes arose in economies that shared few commonalities in market conditions, labor skills, or State governance (Hollingsworth et al. 1994; Berger and Dore 1996; Crouch and Streeck 1997). In Eastern Europe, the privatization of State-owned businesses that shared similar State institutions and a common labor pool did not lead to a single form of hierarchy or market governance, but to a plurality of forms. Similarly, large firms in Taiwan have not arisen to supplant small firms despite an under-developed financial market and system of law, which should make small firm transacting costly. The U.S. economy was sharply deregulated in an effort to intensify individualistic competition yet has become a leader in adopting interfirm arrangements that blend cooperation and competition among rival firms (Hollingsworth and Boyer 1997; Podolny and Page 1998). Our point is not that conventional analysis should be discarded but to note that these cases show that governance is not determined simply by markets or States. All of the above cases share the recognition that organizational change in an economy is shaped by the social structures within which forms of economic exchange and business organizations are embedded.

Forms of Embeddedness

Mark Granovetter's article, "Economic Action and Social Structure: The Problem of Embeddedness," marked the emergence of a New Economic Sociology (Swedberg 1997). Building on classic sociological work by Polyani, Weber, and Durkhiem, Granovetter articulated a programmatic statement of research that was based on the observation that economic action is not a separate sphere of activity that operates under a logic of action distinct from the logic that the same actors use to govern other activities. Rather, he argued that each transaction is a social event, embedded in a set of socially defined attitudes, preferences, and norms that impinge upon individuals through their involvement in social networks and institutions.

The initial focus on institutions and social networks was further articulated by Zukin and DiMaggio (1990), who identified four types of embeddedness: political, structural, cultural, and cognitive. Political embeddedness refers to how power relations within society and institutions shape economic exchange and stratify rewards among economic actors. This work views organizations as coalitions of opposing actors that adopt practices and strategies for self-gain, often at the expense of market efficiency (Evans 1995; Fligstein 1996). It also sees social relations as embedded in the State, particularly the law, and social class differences that exist within nations and through the increasing spatial division of labor in internationalizing markets. Patent and tax law, government procurement policies, and labor regulation are all forms of political embeddedness that embody the distinctive institutional logics of action that shape the organization of industries and markets (Hirsch 1975; Whitley 1994; Scott 1998). Thus, this approach views organizational change as a suboptimal political market solution to problems of property rights, governance, and rule making, where particular theoretical emphasis is put on an analysis of how classes of actors enter, capture, and construct organizations based on their political capital. Powell (1996) observes that new research in this area will begin to tackle issues of how outsiders gain power, how institutional structures balance social, political, and economic restraints, and how endogenous and incremental change in an institutionalized system is linked to exogenous and discrete structural changes outside a system.

The structural embeddedness thesis states that transactions take place through complex social relations that shape individuals' opportunities for value creation by affecting not their human capital but their social capital, viz., the level of trust, information access, and norms of compliance they share with their exchange partners. Research has focused on how networks promote mutual advantages by embedding commercial transactions in social relations that offer extra-contractual, self-enforcing governance mechanisms and facilitate information transfer and resource pooling (Macneil 1978). While this work has been most unified in its concentration on networks as a descriptive and analytical tool, a fruitful area of research promises to tease out the differences and similarities among different variations on the network theme. For example, Granovetter (1973) and Burt (1992) focus on the benefits of weak ties and network bridges for brokering information, Abolofia (1997) and Powell (1990) focus on the collaborative benefits of embedded ties, and Baker (1990) and Uzzi (1996; 1997; 2000) focus on dual mode networks that synthesize the benefits of both embedded and weak ties.

Cognitive embeddedness refers to the ways in which actors deviate "normally" from the strict psychological rationality needed to produce the clear calculating of economic models. While much work waits to be done in this area in sociology, where an understanding of the psychology of decision making has been weak, the basic material for it has existed for decades in social-psychology under the rubric of behavioral decision theory (Kahneman and Tversky 1982; Lewin 1996). This work builds on the original and familiar insight of Simon's notion of bounded rationality, i.e., that the cognitive limitations of decision makers prevents them from dealing with complex problems of exchange in the manner hypothesized by neoclassical theory (Lewin 1996). Since Simon's seminal work, psychological research has shown why and how human actors systematically deviate from rationality within the dimensions of information gathering, processing, and retrieval (Bazerman and Neale 1983; Thompson et al. 1995; Messick and Sentis 1983; Murnighan 1994). The goal of future work in economic sociology is to show how these deviations in rationality are amplified or diminished by attributes of social structure that trigger heuristic biases and that vary with market and organizational contexts (DiMaggio 1994; DiMaggio 1997).

Cultural embeddedness refers to the role played by collective beliefs and expectations in shaping economic strategies and goals. The distinctive effect of culture is that it exists at the level of taken-for-granted assumptions. Therefore, cultural embeddedness limits decision makers' ability to act in a fully calculative manner because alternatives to current practices are typically not even imagined. Guillen's (1994) in-depth analysis of how the national contexts of the U.S., U.K., Germany, and Spain shaped managerial ideologies amply exemplifies how cultural embeddedness injects taken-for-granted assumptions into business discourses and decisions about what practices are justifiable ways to organize, especially when actual outcomes are uncertain or contested. Hamilton and Biggart (1988) presented similar cultural embeddedness arguments and evidence regarding the organization of firms in Japan, Korea, and Taiwan. Perhaps the most striking example is McGuire, Granovetter, and Schwartz's (1993) analysis of the U.S. electric utility industry. They show that cultural and political factors promoted the adoption of an industry structure built around centralized power-generating plants and that other equally or more economically viable options, such as decentralized in-home electric generators, were ignored. Current work in this area is attempting to understand not only how cultural embeddedness facilitates the adoption of different economic orders but also how it can be used strategically to enhance national economies, firms, and labor that have become transnational and transcultural (Dacin et al. 1999).

While the various themes of the embeddedness approach demonstrate its breadth and suggest that there is no current prospect for theoretical closure within or between particular themes, the "theoretical umbrella" of embeddedness appears useful for generating creative and diverse research on change in social and economic orders. Baum and Dutton (1996) estimate that Granovetter's seminal paper has been cited over 5000 times, making it the most cited work in the history of the *American Journal of Sociology*. Similarly, Dacin, Ventresca, and Neal's (1999) review of the literature on different forms of embeddedness indicates that the embeddedness approach is unifying work on institutions, social networks, and economic change. Moreover, opening a dialogue between sociologists, the pioneers of the embeddedness approach, and researchers in cognate disciplines suggests that we are entering a new phase in embeddedness research (Powell 1996; Lin and Cook 1998; Collins 1999). Whereas the early ideological energy of the embeddedness approach centered on critiquing neoclassical theory, the current work in economics, political science, and sociology demonstrates that a new generation of work is being built from the synthesis and refinement of original principles rather than the rejection of standing principles.

Consistent with this new round of empirically enriched and conceptually complex studies, the works of the authors in this volume examine two key questions regarding how embeddedness shapes organizational change in an economy in transition. The scholars of one set of papers examine whether capitalism materializes in different countries in a convergent or divergent manner. The authors of the papers on this topic analyze why different forms of organization have arisen in Eastern European, Asian, and U.S. economies in response to similar forces of globalization, particularly the processes of privatization, trade barrier deregulation, and trade block and stock market creation. The writers of the second set of papers examine the changing significance of location and national boundaries in global economies. These papers examine how greater connectivity among economies and businesses in separate regions (such as the U.S., Taiwan, and Eastern Europe) changes key practices that promote the internationalization of organizations. In particular, these scholars focus on how entrepreneurs' social connections in the nations that educate them, and in the nations that offer them production and marketing channels, provide unique opportunities for making markets and founding international businesses through institutional and social embeddedness. In regard to both questions, these papers provide two companion arguments regarding embeddedness. One argument is that a nation's configuration of networks and institutions facilitates or derails the effectiveness of generic modes of organizing (e.g., small versus large firm strategies of growth, competitive versus collaborative interfirm ties, high or low levels of state regulation) by affecting trustworthiness, knowledge transfer, and norms of appropriateness. Consequently, an understanding of what types of structures produce what kinds of outcomes offers insight into what models of organizing are likely to furnish high levels of prosperity. The second argument is that embeddedness is a filter that influences how entrepreneurs and state planners interpret the subjective and intangible value and consequences of different organizational forms, which in turn promotes or inhibits the adoption of particular practices.

Synopsis of the Volume

We organize the chapters under two topic headings: (1) Embeddedness and Organizational Transformation in Various Societies and (2) Embeddedness and the Co-evolution of Markets. In the first group of papers, our authors examine how different cultural, social, and institutional factors in formerly non-capitalist societies have shaped firms during the transformation to a capitalist society. Contrary to conventional arguments, Whitley's paper shows how Hungary and Slovenia's institutional changes in political democratization and market liberalization in the early 1990s did not prevent the late state socialist legacies from moderating radical change in either countries' enterprises. Whitley also points out a paradox for state-centered theory—since market liberalization is the key feature of capitalism, the state's role is self-minimized. In contrast, Sung shows that in the case of Taiwan, privatized state-owned enterprises are still under state control. Some of the remaining state-owned enterprises in Taiwan have even expanded their investment in Southeast Asia in the 1990s in order to guide private firm divestiture from China to Southeast Asia and to reinforce the political legitimacy of the Taiwanese State. Finally, Tzeng's analysis also challenges the typical notion of how a state affects globalization and shows how the state is not disappearing but reconfiguring its central role, even if it is experiencing strong pressure toward financial market liberalization. She finds that Taiwan's protective but favorable policy towards foreign investment suggests that the Taiwan State has played a crucial role in effectively integrating Taiwanese business into the global production and global capitalist market.

Liu and Yeh also focus on how Taiwanese firms are adapting to globalization in their demonstration that organizations are not inevitably transforming via consolidation into big firms but are developing their own version of Taiwanese capitalism. They illustrate how the so-called "public firms" in the stock market in Taiwan have been predominantly owned and managed by families. This suggests that the western institutional setting of the stock market, which involves professional and legal processes, has not yet uprooted the traditional values of family, kinship, and trust cherished by Taiwanese (although the stock market is very slowly "professionalizing" family firms in Taiwan). They also indicate that the stock market is currently creating a potential financial crisis for Taiwanese firms and the economy.

Another instance of the effects of social embeddedness on the evolution of firms concerns the way in which new social expectations are introduced into firms and the relationships that arise between firms and organizations that govern the adoption process. In Asia, a critical set of social expectations that promise a sea change revolves around gender and sexual harassment issues at work. In the U.S., sexual harassment at work is the legal responsibility of the firm, the personal liability of individual managers, and punishable as job discrimination. In contrast, the Taiwanese have historically considered sexual harassment a private sexual offense between employee and employer, a condition that has historically released businesses of any responsibility for their managers' behavior. However, market internationalization has prompted an outcry for more U.S.-style sexual harassment law. In a careful comparative study of Taiwanese and American law, Chiao proposes a scrupulous transplant of American law onto the Taiwan Gender Equality in Employment Law to avert sexual harassment at work and promote affirmative business action on sexual harassment issues.

Examining the opposite process—the removal of laws governing interfirm exchanges—Uzzi examines how deregulation of trade barriers affects interfirm relationships in the U.S. apparel economy—a prototypical global industry with over 200 nations involved in trade. Uzzi sheds light on how interfirm exchanges are embedded in social structures, even in a market that is presumed to be regulated by prices with no interference from the State or other forces. It is usually assumed that the U.S. lacks traditional community ties and, therefore, provides pure markets that are usually associated with short-term action and exchange rather than long-term enhancement. In contrast, Uzzi's research on New York's apparel industry demonstrates that the so-called free market in the U.S. is not operated by one-time transactions in a perfectly competitive market, but is shaped by ongoing ties among a few firms. His argument focuses on the stick-or-switch decision, the basic choice that firms face in remaining in a repeated game with their current exchange partner or switching to a new one.

Our chapters on embeddedness and the co-evolution of culturally and geographically separate markets are concerned with how social networks can create the international ties that facilitate knowledge transfer and the importing and exporting of models of organizing across national boundaries. Alvesson presents a conceptual framework for analyzing how "cultural traffic" across and within national borders can develop new global cultural manifestations. Both Tseng's and Saxenian's papers demonstrate how ongoing ties help the emigrant Chinese set up transnational firms in Taiwan and the U.S. that facilitate the economic co-development of both regions. Similarly, Rudolph finds that western multinational corporations use emigrants' transnational networks to send *Polonia*, emigrated Poles, to their subsidiaries in Poland. The resulting phenomenon of the global capitalism brought by immigrants and multinational corporations is the co-evolution of business organizations on three continents: the Californization of Hsinchu described in Saxenian's paper, the enclave of Chinese businesses in Los Angeles described in Tseng's paper, and the westernization of Poland described in Rudolph's paper.

Chapter 1

The Local and the Grandiose: Method, Micro and Macro in Comparative Studies of Culture and Organizations

Mats Alvesson

Introduction

The world gets smaller, we are repeatedly told. Internationalization and globalization mean that societies interact and loose some of their separate, distinct characters. The global village and the world system are terms or slogans repeatedly heard. Still, the intensified traffic of technologies, information, goods, ideas and meanings does not mean that cultural uniformity results. There seems to be widespread agreement about the extensive nature of cross-national variation in terms of how businesses and organizations function (Clegg 1990; Clegg et al. 1990; Redding 1994; Whitley 1994). Cross cultural or comparative studies of management and organizations are broadly considered as increasingly significant research topics.

Comparing and understanding management and organization across diverse macro settings—such as societies, regions, industries, nations or large organizations—far too often means that the local and dynamic aspects of a culture are neglected. While the intent of this analysis is not to prioritize the latter, I will argue that both need to be taken into account in order to understand culture. The critique of neglect of the local can also be made of a great deal of studies on organizational cultures (Alvesson 1993). In these studies, culture is turned into something uniform, abstract, and static; it is essentialized and reified when reduced to a few variables and when it is assumed that it is possible to compare across a variety of internally homogeneous units. For many researchers, this may—at least when reformulated in a more positive light—represent the virtue, indeed the core, of "science." However, the critique of this approach is massive and rapidly expanding. Arguably, some kind of micro anchoring is necessary in order to avoid turning "culture" into an abstraction bearing little or no relationship to the level of meaning shared by a group of people as the central element in social action.[1] Is it possible to combine an interest in variation across diverse macro settings with an orientation to culture as a way of understanding management, companies, and organizations at the level of shared meaning expressed in specific situations and actions in companies? This is the central question of this paper.

The paper originates in two themes. The first relates to recent developments in methodology questioning empiricism, the data-theory distinction, and the view of language as a mirror and, based on this, calls for a more reflective approach. The second relates to debates and developments in cultural theory, calling for a more sophisticated use of the concept of culture in interpretive work. The major bulk of this paper is of a general methodological-cultural character, with a focus on cross-cultural or comparative organizational studies. Methodology here is understood on an overall, intellectual level. It concerns applied philosophy of science and research strategies, rather than techniques and procedures. Methodology thus structures the field in terms of vital issues and traps to consider; it facilitates informed choices and a high degree of consciousness and reflection, and it guides interaction with the empirical field.

The paper is comprised of three parts. It begins with a critical discussion of conventional ideas of science and knowledge, raising questions about the ideal of abstract, generalized, accumulated knowledge. The paper then proceeds with a discussion of culture in the context of cross-cultural organizational studies. Finally, it ends with some suggestions regarding the need to combine attention to local culture with an interest in comparison across macro settings. This last issue may be referred to as a multi-layered approach to culture in organizations. The paper argues for the need in cultural studies to take seriously the looseness and fluidity of boundaries, cultural diversity, the significance of power, and representations of the other that are constructed in contrast to ones self.

Rethinking Methodology

The Problem of "Grand Storytelling"

In social science, the dominant tradition has encouraged us to take a particular stance, to tell a grand story in which the stance and its components (assumptions, logic, vocabulary, a set of variables/distinctions constructing/freezing social reality in a particular way) appear as the superior explanation, or source of understanding, and are backed up by empirical evidence. Language is viewed as reflecting a social, economic, political and psychological objective reality "out there." Objects of study are fixated through operational definitions. The use of variables allows comparisons and abstractions and makes possible generalizations across settings and time (at least, so it seems). The objective is to discover laws or law-like patterns, or to describe and explain a wide-ranging empirical terrain.

Of course, these assumptions can and indeed have been radically challenged in recent years. Critics have argued for a less a priori/elitist approach and a more open/emergent one (to use the vocabulary of Deetz 1996). They have drawn attention to the nature of language (performative, contextual and metaphorical) and the problems of using it (and thus science) as a mirror of reality, as well as to its virtues in other respects, including its productive capacities. These scholars have also pointed out the historical, unstable nature of social phenomena: the status of diversity, ambiguity and fragmentation as crucial features of social reality; the risks prioritizing order and patterns at the expense of processes, fluidities and modes of ordering and organizing; and the risks of essentializing and reifying the social world. (Deetz 1996; Law 1994). An important part of this critique, sometimes expressed in rather extreme ways, has been raised by postmodernists (Chia 1995; Rosenau 1992; Sarup 1988), but there are also many other forms of post-empiricist or post-rationalist critique (Alvesson and Sköldberg 2000; Denzin and Lincoln 1994; Gergen 1978; Steier 1991) that raise similar issues.

There is a trend away from abstract, general categories and efforts to standardize meaning and towards an increased focus on local patterns, where cultural and institutional contexts and meanings are developed by participants (or jointly by participants and researchers), rather than one-sidedly, indeed, in an authoritarian manner (elitist/a priori) by the researcher (Alvesson and Deetz 2000; Gergen 1978; Shotter and Gergen

1994). This trend results in a favouring of a more open or emergent kind of study in which social relations and processes are treated as complex and varied, which calls for attention to specific circumstances. The appearance of an increasing number of organizational ethnographies is perhaps the most salient manifestation of this development (e.g., Kunda 1992; Van Maanen 1991; Watson 1994). These studies avoid unrecognizably transforming social phenomena through the application of standardized measures and abstract categories, which turn diverse phenomena into numbers that, as a result appear quite similar. This approach downplays grand theories, in which a limited number of variables and causal relations are considered relevant for explaining phenomena. Instead, the researcher takes seriously the ambiguity of the terms to be interpreted (such as "leadership," "formalization," "network," "woman," "satisfaction," and "business group"). Such terms, when employed to reveal an essence stemming across complexity and variation, normally cover a wide diversity of actions, feelings, thoughts, relations and social processes while the merits of applying the favoured term as an interpretive device are seldom self-evident.

According to Sandelands and Drazin (1989), the vocabulary of organization studies often glosses over substantive actions: the literature's frequent use of performative verbs results in the blending of process and outcome (accomplishment). To understand this is to care about how the vocabulary is applied and to show respect for the contextual character of language and meaning. This move requires intimate knowledge of the phenomenon under study and depth of understanding, at the expense of abstraction, generalization, and the artificial separation of theory and data. As an alternative to the use of vocabulary crudely related to context and situation, scholars should carry out research that is *language-sensitive*. This call is not, however, one for precise definitions and operationalizations, as in conventional research. Instead, it is a call to take seriously the ambiguities, contextual and constructive character of language (Deetz 1992; Potter and Wetherell 1987). For language cannot easily transport meaning across the local settings in which statements are made. To some extent, this fact is inherent in the interpretive character of inquiry. This point, however, goes beyond that basic fact. As Deetz (1996) explains, "conceptions are always contests for meaning. Language does not name objects in the world; it is core to the process of constituting objects. The appearance of labeling or categorizing existing objects is derived from this more fundamental act of object constitution through language." Further, it is important to recognize that the outcomes of qualified interpretations can only be with care and pain compared or aggregated according to a logic of knowledge accumulation. This is a consequence of the local, context-dependent nature of language use.[2] This increased awareness of the need to take language seriously in organization studies has been reflected in recent work focusing on talk, narratives and other aspects of discourses in organizations (e.g., Gronn 1983; Alvesson 1994; Deetz 1994, Grant et al. 1998).

Related to this point is the recognition of the *theory-laden* nature of empirical work. Empirical observations are informed by, and dependent on, a framework which makes the meaningful structuring of what is perceived possible. Thus, everything that is observed or emerges as data does so from a particular perspective. The significance, as well as relativity, of the paradigms and root metaphors within researchers which work have been strongly emphasized by Burrell and Morgan (1979), Morgan (1980, 1986) and others.

Related to this problem of language and the contextual nature of meaning, is the importance of stressing the local as opposed to the universal. It is not only the ambiguities and hanging circumstances of language, but also the ambiguities of social and cultural conditions that motivate a trend from grand theory and explanation to local theory and context-sensitive understanding. The *historical and cultural* character of social phenomena motivates agnosticism to the grand theory project of developing universal theory and general explanations. Even though universal concepts such as manager, owner, planning, authority, business group, and hierarchy may appear to make quite different phenomena comparable, they do so at the expense of suppressing diversity and counteracting rich understanding. (On these issues, see Fraser and Nicholson 1988; Lyotard 1984). If universalistic concepts are to be used—and there are often social and symbolic rather than empirical reasons for this, as Astley (1985) points out—local grounding is necessary. Social phenomena subtly (and not so subtly) vary over time and place and with context on a variety of levels. Meaning is related to micro as well as macro context. The use of any non-trivial term varies from sentence to sentence when used in a meeting, a talk or an interview. But also economic and material contexts, socialization patterns and produced self-identities, ideologies and generalized meaning patterns differ heavily between different historical periods, between different societies and industrial sectors, and also between different organizational sites in the same period. In cross-cultural studies, of course, the context-dependence of language and meaning must be taken seriously and care must be taken before comparisons can be made.

Another important aspect of social studies concerns the significance of considering *diversity, ambiguity and fragmentation* as crucial features of social reality. It is too easy, or at least too tempting, to constitute social reality as a neatly structured single order. Giving priority to order, patterns and regularities is done at the expense of disorder, contradiction, change and variation. Processes, fluidities and multiple modes of ordering/organizing also belong to what is far too often sacrificed in social science that is directed at explanation and searches for correlations and causalities (Chia 1995; Linstead and Grafton-Small 1992; Martin 1992; Meyerson and Martin 1987). The latter often involves a strong inclination to essentialize and reify the social world: cultures are described as robust entities made up of a few basic attributes, emptied of qualities, and reduced to seemingly uniform variables. This is the case, for example, in the definition of cultures as either collectivist or individualist.

All of these points have radical implications for research, including for how the researcher approaches the object of study and produces texts. Traditionally, a research project and a subsequent text are arenas in which the researcher establishes him or herself as an *authority*. The researcher, empowered with skills, intelligence, an image of rationality, methods, readings of the literature and certain, persuasive standards of writing, engages in the enterprise of convincing the reader that she or he should think as the researcher-authority claims the world looks. In this context, successful research means that the reader adapts to the researcher's opinions and arguments and refrains from independent thinking or deviating from the researcher's agenda. Agreement is indicative of success, signs of enduring disagreement are, if not failure, at least sources of worry. The style in situations of espoused disagreement—and these prevail in social science—is normally one of convincing the reader that others are wrong while oneself, or the like-minded, are correct. The idea is to show that one's opinion (theory, explanation) is the correct one, as one's own data have, or future research will, show.

Research results may, however, be presented in a less authoritative or elitist manner in which a *conversational* understanding and style is developed.[3] Central to this technique is the idea of "the dialogical character of rationality," and "the situated, embodied, practical-moral knowledges it involves" (Shotter and Gergen 1994: 27). These knowledges are "accountable to an audience" rather than "provable within a formal system."

This mode of study aims for an interpretive, historical, language-sensitive, local, open, and non-authoritative understanding of the subject matter (Alvesson and Deetz 2000). Dissention may be productive, while consensus may make dialogue uninteresting and lead to a low level of scholarship. This approach is the anti-thesis of the dominant positivistic line of study, which appears to be particularly unsuccessful in comparative management and organization studies. As Redding (1994) argues, "the bankruptcy of empirical positivism... has sent the subject round in circles for thirty years" (p. 345).

The methodological suggestions above are of general relevance as well as of specific importance in cross-cultural work, where the difficulties of translation and the context-dependence of language add complexity and where a researcher's own parochial frameworks color expectations and results.[4]

Divergence as an Outcome of an Increase in Studies

Traditional social science aims at building valid knowledge and theories by testing hypotheses. One would expect that over time and with an increase in the number of well-carried out empirical studies, this work would result in the accumulation of more and better knowledge. Increasingly sophisticated, empirically strongly confirmed theories should have been produced and sanctioned by consensus in the research community. It is interesting to note that the logic sometimes appears to be the opposite of what would be expected by the dominant conception of social science: the more studies, the more disagreement. This is not just the case across paradigmatic/theoretical borders (to the extent there are clear such borders), but also *within* a certain research orientation. The experience of social science appears often to be the dis-accumulation of knowledge.

A good example of this trend is found among leadership studies, which are characterized by a high level of conformism and a strong dominance of positivist values and rules. In addition, the field is heavily U.S. dominated, which rules out some of the problems of cross-cultural variation in both researchers' credos and empirical phenomena. Despite the fact that thousands of studies have been conducted, an optimal condition from an accumulation position, the outcome of these enormous efforts has been meager. There are varied opinions as to whether one can talk about this as a failure or not. One review of the research concludes that "the only point of agreement is that existing approaches have largely lost their usefulness for the further development of the field" (Andriessen and Drenth 1984: 514). Another reviewer claims that "...progress continues in developing better understanding of leadership traits, behavior, power, and situational factors" (Yukl 1989: 254), but also concludes that the field:

> ...is presently in a state of ferment and confusion. Most of the theories are beset with conceptual weaknesses and lack strong empirical support. Several thousand empirical studies have been conducted on leadership effectiveness, but most of the results are contradictory and inconclusive. (p.253)

While some review authors do think that real progress has been made (House and Aditya 1997), others think that a basic change in methodology is called for (Bryman 1996).

Also, within other areas where a large number of studies have been conducted, the accumulation of studies points towards divergence and confusion rather than agreement and certainty. In gender studies, different empirical studies indicate rather different results in terms of, for example, women and leadership style, discrimination against women in employment, evaluation and promotion situations, and effects of an increase in the number of women in a specific work field on pay (for a review, see Alvesson and Billing 1997). In terms of leadership, for example, some reviewers of the literature say that there are no significant differences between men and women, while other authors conclude that there are (cf. Powell 1988; Eagly and Johnson 1990). In another case, two studies of British managers arrived at radically different conclusions regarding the experiences of this group (reviewed in Watson 1994). The results of Lincoln and Kalleberg (1985) and Near (1989) indicate lower levels of organizational commitment and work satisfaction among Japanese than US workers, which runs against impressions and claims made by a large number of other researchers (e.g., Wilkinson and Oliver 1990). Their results may be read as the punctuation of myths—common beliefs are perhaps partly contingent upon overgeneralization from some leading Japanese companies to Japanese working life as a whole—or the data may simply be misleading.[5]

Of course, there are also research fields where studies tend to support each other and point in the same direction. For example, Hofstede's influential work (1980) tends to be confirmed, according to Søndergaard (1994). But the overall track record of research examining similar themes or testing theories indicates that there are reasons to be skeptical of the idea that the accumulation of empirical studies will lead to truth. Rather than "homing in" on the phenomenon under study, a multitude of studies and methods lead to the "homing out" of it (Potter and Wetherell 1987). It sometimes seems as if the more researchers there are that dig into the subject matter, the more variation there seems to be in terms of not only theoretical viewpoints and lines of argumentation, but also in terms of where empirical material seems to be pointing. What Mueller (1994) notes about empirical material on the globalization-societal effect on organizations, namely that "the evidence available is very ambivalent. For every example of globalization, counter-examples of national differentiation can be provided" (p. 416), is probably valid for many other areas as well.

Variations and divergence in research results may be explained in different ways. We live in a world that exhibits great variation and changes over time, meaning that "the truth" is, at best, bounded in space and time. We also live in a world where social researchers vary in their pre-structured understandings, vocabularies, research agendas and choices, thus producing research results differently. If we to this add the impossibility of mirroring an external reality in research procedures and measurements, there is no reason to expect research results to converge on the same truth.

I read all this as supporting an epistemology different from the dominant neo-positivist one and embracing somewhat different ideals than those directed towards arriving at law like, abstractly generalized, repeatedly, context-independently confirmed hypothesis, theories and empirical claims. Such ideals may include learning from specific cases and developing local theory, i.e., covering a limited area of application.

A Case for Caution in Large-scale Truth-telling

The great difficulties social science has in its goal of arriving at theories, explanations or hypotheses which will receive broad and uniform support may be read as implying relativism—either in the crude and very seldom espoused idea that all statements are equally true, false or of equal value, or in the idea that all statements are a reflection of the position and framework of the researcher—but this is not my point. I do believe that all observations are theory-laden and that we cannot step outside our prestructured understandings and look objectively, perspective and theory-free, on matters. However, I also assume that cross-paradigmatic interaction is possible and that empirical studies may inform critical debates across positions—at least as long as the positions are not too dissimilar. Empirical material may be seen as offering arguments—rather than firm evidence—for certain claims.

The viewpoints presented here may encourage research that is somewhat more modest, but more delineated and more precise in terms of theoretical and empirical aspirations. Many efforts to make bold statements about the true character of mass, extremely complex and varied phenomena—such as the organizational commitments of US and Japanese workers (Lincoln and Kalleberg 1985), the styles of Indian and British managers (Tayeb 1994) or the differences in inter-corporate relations among East Asian countries (Hamilton et al. 1990)—may, upon reflection, be seen as too large to handle very well. US workers, Indian managers and Taiwanese business groups are in themselves labels covering highly diverse (and theoretically debatable) phenomena. Comparing these constructions with corresponding constructions easily becomes a colossus on clay feet. With a focus on a level of aggregation highly remote from specific phenomena that are observable or that exist at the level of meaning (in connection with experiences or actions), empirical claims and explanations may be only, at best, loosely connected to more concrete empirical phenomena. At the very least, the uncertainties and arbitrariness involved are considerable, meaning that empirical claims risk becoming as shaky as they are wide-ranging.

Even if one does not accept the idea of a radical incommensurability between different cultures (or theoretical paradigms) proposed by Winch (1958), Lyotard (1984), etc., but adheres to the idea that expansion of understanding across one's initial horizon is possible (Bernstein 1983), this is certainly a difficult, complex and uncertain project, calling for careful work involving many steps (Tayeb 1994). The plurality, variety and heterogeneity of members of different societies and subgroups within them is one problem to deal with; the same qualities that characterize the different research contributions one has to work with, and from, represent another challenge. Trans-societal and trans-theoretical meanings are thus crucial to address in all comparative research work (Sztompka 1990).

To illustrate this point, we examine Lincoln and Kalleberg's (1985) large study of workforce commitment in the USA and Japan. The sample included 8,000 subjects. The design and analysis seem to be well thought through, but one may be skeptical of the possibility of measuring and comparing work satisfaction and organizational commitment across wide groups. Despite efforts to produce precise statements to respond to, ambiguity and meaning variation across people, groups and situations is difficult to avoid. A question such as "I am willing to work harder than I have to in order to help this company succeed" may be seen as a reflection of commitment. But it may also reflect an externally imposed work level. If it is low—due to technical conditions or limited social pressure—the willingness to work harder than I "have to" is presumably greater than if one has to work hard. While group pressure may force people to work hard and such pressure may reflect organizational commitment, a negative response (low score) to the claim "work harder than I have to" may not necessarily, as intended in the study, indicate a low degree of commitment, but can also mean the opposite. Questions such as "how satisfied are you with your job?" and "there is a lot of variety in the kinds of things I do in my job" are very vague and different people may ascribe different meanings to them. They may also do so on different occasions. Any experience of how satisfied one is may vary during a typical workday and with how the question is framed, what the purpose behind it might be, and so on. One may go further and question the very idea of there being something out there in the minds of people being mirrored as a fixed entity labeled "job satisfaction" or "commitment."

Lincoln and Kalleberg themselves are hesitant to accept their finding that US workers are more satisfied and committed than Japanese workers, thinking that the cultural pressure in the countries make Americans exaggerate positive aspects while the Japanese may express a downward bias. In addition to the difficulties in translating between languages, language use always works in a cultural context, which means that the questions reflect cultural meanings of words such as "satisfaction" and "work hard." The subjects of the study vary not just according to nationality and language system, but also in other ways, such as region, company, gender, age and education. In the study women are indicated to respond more positively, while educational level is negatively correlated with satisfaction and commitment. These results are viewed as an outcome of expectations. Women's lower and the well-educated's higher expectations for job rewards and status make them respectively more and less satisfied, it is argued. But an equally plausible explanation is that the cultural differences between the genders and the high- and low-educated means that there are different interpretations and rules for language use. Variations in the cultural meaning of questionnaire statements and norms for expressing oneself, as much as "objective" variation in experiences or attitudes, may thus explain the bulk of the results. Normally, the effects of cultural meanings and language codes on "data" go undetected as the logic of questionnaires and the rules for data processing (including those characterizing "rigorous" qualitative approaches emphasizing codifications) typically hide these effects.

For example, most of the US sample answered the questionnaires during the workday. In those US companies where the subjects were not allowed to complete questionnaires on company time, the response rate was very low. Despite the fact that the Japanese subjects completed the questionnaires on leisure time, their response rate was 80 per cent, in itself a sign of high commitment, as Near (1989) remarks. Perhaps this high response rate gives a better indication of commitment than exactly which squares the subjects put their X's in.

Without denying that the study produces interesting results, some degree of skepticism as to the popularity and status of this kind of studies within mainstream social science is called for. Wide-ranging, generalizable results stand on rather shaky grounds, to some extent camouflaged by rhetorical powers of techniques, procedures, numbers and tables.

Of course, this applies to the general problem of the possibility of measuring nontrivial phenomena and the critique is valid for all "dataistic" research, including a great deal of qualitative studies. The problem is, however, magnified the more diverse the groups under study are. Meanings vary depending on the nuances of language and the cultural context offers guidelines for how questions are interpreted and should be answered. The more varied language codes and cultural contexts are, the less sense the idea of straightforward comparisons from measures makes.

Many social researchers (although not in the area focused on in this paper) have, as a response to the problems mentioned, moved towards a rather extreme micro orientation, focusing on language use as the only accessible target for empirical work. Potter and Wetherell (1987), convincingly demonstrating that the idea of a fixed and stable "attitude" is highly questionable, suggest that we study discourses, i.e., language use in practical situations. Others view conversations as a proper object of study (Silverman 1985, 1993). In studying these limited topics we have accessible empirical material, can avoid all speculative ideas about interview statements, questionnaire responses or public statistics reflecting objective reality "out there" or even people's "genuine" beliefs, attitudes or whatever. As Mills (1940) remarked in his classic piece, vocabularies of motives rather than "real" motives are possible to study. Discourses and conversations may tell us something about the institutional contexts in which they take place. A specific focus for social science could be meetings—a crucial part of corporate reality (Alvesson 1996; Schwartzman 1987). The study of situations, delineated in time and space, in which actors and actions are visible but still clearly related to institutional context and thus to macro concerns, offer a potentially fruitful approach (Knorr-Cetina 1981). Of course such empirically rich, but narrow material is preferable to a thinner and generalization-oriented study.

Ethnography lies somewhere in the middle in terms of depth and scope. A longer time period of participant observation and interviewing, and the gathering, structuring and interpretation of other types of empirical material indicating lived experience appears, as the far most ambitious enterprise. But also, ethnography has received a fair amount of critique and its current popularity (even though it is more often preached than practiced, Rosen 1991) is accompanied by an emphasis on the problems of representation and the constructed, fictional nature of ethnography (Clifford and Marcus 1986; Van Maanen 1995), which makes it a promising approach. Virtues of anthropology, beyond the representation of objective cultural reality "out there," have been emphasized: insights, new ideas, multiple readings, the aesthetics of the text, pragmatic results, etc. Producing a good text that encourages active readership—not just passive consumption of authoritative results—is sometimes seen as more valuable than trying to "mirror" social reality.

Nevertheless, ethnography, compared to other methods, offers the possibility of offering a rich, detailed understanding of the subject matter. It could be argued that the only way of getting beyond superficiality in the study of cultural meanings is to rely on ethnographic material. Commentators on the limited progress of cross-cultural studies of management (e.g., Redding 1994; Tayeb 1994) often point at the lack of deeper studies in which the meanings and logic of the people being studied are appreciated.

Where does all this leave us? There are strong reasons for a less grandiose storytelling than the one dominating social science: abstract, universalistic statements describing and explaining great chunks of social reality too easily domesticate, impose order, essentialize and reify "too much." Some ingredients of these qualities may be helpful, indeed unavoidable. Yet, too much means that the fictional qualities take the upper hand in relation to contact with and some grounding in observations of social practices and carefully interpreted accounts of lived reality. A more general criticism is that the adherents of this approach often adopt inappropriate research procedures ("positivism") and that their language is only tenuously related to the real world it describes, at best glossing over the underlying reality and ignoring the fact that micro-events are the empirical reality of human actors.[6] Even though the generalization-local dimension is not exactly the same as the macro-micro, there is a strong overlap.

On the other hand, there are also strong reasons for going beyond concentration on a narrowly focused piece of the social world and relating specific phenomena to a wider context. Addressing micro issues simply leaves too many vital and interesting aspects of life unexamined. An interesting question is if, and if so how, a focus on specific, concrete phenomena can be combined with a systematic exploration of macro aspects ("society", nation, region, corporation, industry)?[7]

I will try to address this question based on a cultural approach to business and organizations. I will begin with a brief account of culture, then go on to describe a view of culture capable of dealing with some of the problems sketched here. First, however, let me briefly summarize the argumentation of the first part of this paper

Summary

Broad and increasingly powerful trends in the social sciences have raised doubts about conventional views on methodology. Problems of representation, authority and the legitimacy of the traditional route to knowledge follow from insights about the nature of language as constructing rather than mirroring reality, the impossibility of separating theory and data and the multiple nature of social realities. While such awareness has far reaching implications for all social research, it is especially the case for what may be labeled "grand storytelling" in comparative work on macro units (societies, complex organizations). A move towards research that is sensitive to language and language use and to the study of how paradigms, metaphors and theoretical ideas impregnate all empirical material and how research objects, the researcher and the research act are historically, culturally and politically situated is recommended. Such research resists privileging patterns, order, regularities and essences. A more local focus allows these virtues to guide research.

Rethinking Culture

On Culture

As with all popular concepts in social science, culture is used in a rich variety of ways (Alvesson and Berg 1992; Keesing 1974; Ortner 1984). On a very general level, culture may be used as an explanatory variable or as a framework for understanding, as a definable object "out there," or as a theoretical lens for illuminating significant aspects of social reality (Alvesson 1993; Smircich 1983). In cross-cultural comparative studies, culture is often used in a rather vague, all-embracing way and it's meaning is not explored (e.g., Clegg et al. 1990; Wilkinson 1996). The term thus lacks interpretive depth and analytic bite.

Following Geertz (1973), Schneider (1976) and other anthropologists, culture may seem to be a system of common symbols and meanings. In this understanding, culture is placed on a conceptual level that is not primarily "inside" people's heads, but somewhere "between" their heads and their bodies where symbols and meanings are general, collective phenomena. These phenomena can be seen in human patterns of action—in work group interactions, story telling and in board meetings.

Geertz' concept of culture means that culture governs the understanding of behavior, social events, institutions and processes. Culture is the setting in which these phenomena become comprehensible and meaningful. In Geertz's view, good cultural analysis does not subordinate social conditions to cultural factors, nor does it regard culture as a reflection of an overall social structure, instead it makes a clear analytical distinction between the social and the cultural system. The latter may be analysed in relation to the former, but clearly the culture researcher's primary task is to interpret culture, i.e., symbols and meanings. The distinction between culture and social structure implies that the former is regarded as a cohesive system of meanings and symbols, in terms of which social interaction takes place, while the latter is regarded as the patterns which the social interaction itself gives rise to. In the former case (culture), then, we have a frame of reference of beliefs, expressive symbols and values, by means of which individuals define their environment, express their feelings and make judgements. In the latter case, that is to say at the social level, we have a continuous process of interaction. As Geertz (1973: 145) states, culture is the creation of meaning through which human beings interpret their experiences and guide their actions, while social structure is the form which action takes or the network of social relationships which actually exists.

This means that culture and social structure represent different abstractions of the same phenomenon. Culture describes social action as depending on the meaning it has for those involved, while social structure describes social action from the point of view of its consequences on the functioning of the social system. This understanding permits treatment of the tension arising between culture and social structure. A reasonable assumption is that culture and social structure do not necessarily have well-integrated and harmonic relationship (i.e., not best defined or analyzed in terms of integration and coherence). Discontinuity between social and cultural structures can occur, for example, when there is a change in social institutions (e.g., formal rules, social practices) which is not matched by a change in cultural patterns.

Despite the emphasis on culture set forth by Geertz and others as an ideational phenomenon, cultural analysis is, of course, not limited to studying the minds and ideas of people. Cultural analysis may be applied to all forms of social action and all types of institutions, including the economy, technology and production. The point is that abstractions of a certain type, which involve meanings anchored and transmitted in a symbolic form, constitute the level of analysis which this form of culture research deals with. As a description of how people understand and relate to their world—they create and are guided in thinking, feeling and acting by cultural meaning—it is difficult to argue that culture is not important. (It may be argued that culture denotes something too vague and broad to be very useful, but cultural analysis may be more delimited and precise.) Of course, sometimes culture is viewed as residual and/or as something other than economics, technology, social institutions, power, politics and so on. When culture is viewed as a set of freely floating values and orientations having nothing to do with more tangible social phenomena, rather working "outside" of them, then its significance is obviously debatable. Alternatively, culture may be seen as a medium, a way in which experiences and knowledge are organized through the aid of meaning and symbolic patterns. Culture is then seen in terms of language, interpretative filters, cognitive categories and ordered systems. Culture presents the framework in which an understanding of reality can be built up. This does not necessarily imply consensus or homogeneity: groups and individuals may relate to a (loose) framework in a variety of ways.

The rich interpretive capacities of culture can only be utilized if its study is open-minded, careful, locally oriented and close to social practices and meanings in organizations. This is then the opposite of questionnaire-based, generalization-oriented research that cannot go beyond "thin description" (the inverse of Geertz's concept of thick description). Broad and abstract cultural explanations in which a variety of nations are captured under an overall cultural label—for example, "Confucian values" (Bond and Hofstede 1990)—also suffer from this weakness and have received considerable criticism (Clegg 1990; Wilkinson 1996). Brief, abstract characterizations of core variables are often problematic. American culture is, for example, often described as "individualistic" (e.g., Biggart 1990). Even if repeated questionnaire studies confirm this description, it is not self-evident that it says more than that people in the U.S. are inclined to put their X's on questionnaires in a particular way, perhaps reflecting a historical myth about "individualism" which affects the level of the espoused more than the level of being. The myth may, of course, very well have "truth effects," but hardly so that there is a pervasive, consistent inclination for people to exhibit indications on "individualism" in all sectors of life. U.S. group experiments (Milgram, Sherif, etc.) indicate a strong inclination towards subordination to groups and authorities (Asplund 1980). In the context of business, Jackall's (1988) excellent case studies shows how bureaucracy effectively stream-lines cultural rules for conduct and thinking and provides rather limited space for "individualism" among US managers.

Depth-oriented cultural research studies culture in the context of material, economic, political and social conditions—thus stressing the internal relation between cultural meanings, ideas and values, and their "surface" manifestations (behaviors, artifacts).

A Dynamic Concept of Culture

A productive concept of culture avoids temptations to reify, personify, essentialize, unify, idealize, consensualize and otherize. In other words, thinking culturally means that one is hesitant to treat "culture" as a thing; as something that acts or does things (causal factor); that is reduced to a few essential, basic qualities; that it is strictly bounded and well integrated with firm borders; that it is free from contradiction and conflict; and that is set-up in order to offer a straightforward contrast with "ourselves"(i.e., something radically different from the researcher and his/her audiences' culture or between two alien cultures). Most uses of the concept of culture in organization and, in particular, in cross macro setting/comparative studies, leave much to be desired in these regards (Alvesson 1993).

On Unifying and Diversifying. Keesing suggests that cultural theory should make "no assumptions about closed boundaries within which cultural meanings hold sway: 'a culture' as a bounded unit would give way to more complex conceptions of interpenetration, superimposition and pastiche" (1994: 310). There are corresponding doubts concerning the appropriateness of talking about distinct, separate societies. Ahrne, for example, believes that, "It was probably meaningful to divide the world of two hundred years ago into separate societies. Today, however, it is not possible to tell where one society ends and another begins" (Ahrne 1990: 66). For this reason considerable openness and flexibility are needed when deciding what is a productive identification of a macro-setting. I prefer this term to "societal culture" or "nation," as it is less definitive about what is a meaningful terrain for a macro cultural analysis. A nation may not be a nation: almost overnight the Soviet Union and Yugoslavia ceased to be possible objects of study. As Schneider (cited in Mueller 1994) puts it, "many nations are multicultural and many cultures are multinational."

The above remark is also valid for organizations. In organizational culture studies, an assumption that organizations form unitary and unique cultures is—or used to be—as common as it is now questionable (Alvesson 1993; Van Maanen and Barley 1985). Marcus and Fischer (1986) propose that ethnographic description move away from a "self-contained, homogeneous, and largely ahistorical framing of the cultural unit toward a view of cultural situations as always in flux, in a perpetual historically sensitive state of resistance and accommodation to broader processes of influence that are as much inside as outside the local context" (p. 78). This is not easy to accomplish: as Keesing (1994: 302) notes, postmodernist anthropologists like Marcus and Fischer occasionally invoke radical alterity in the same ways they hope to avoid. Operating with some notion of distinct cultural entities corresponding to societies, nations or parts of the world (e.g., continents or parts thereof) is to some extent unavoidable in comparative studies across macro settings. However, it is possible to work with a "weak" notion of separateness and distinctiveness, recognizing the constructed, fluid, interactive, internally heterogeneous nature of cultural settings, whether these are continents, regions, industries, companies or even work groups.

On Ordering and Essentializing. Quite often it is assumed that the social scientist "has to order what is already ordered, to map what is already mapped, and to interpret what is already interpreted" (Sztompka 1990: 48). The search for regularities is often seen as the self-evident guideline and objective for social science (Huberman and Miles 1994). This is not wrong, but a bit one-sided. Is it so clear that social reality is already ordered, mapped and interpreted once and for all? Perhaps the researcher should take an interest in (what is already) disordered, fluid and confusing? Or, in a deconstruction-inspired manner, explore how ordering, mapping and interpretation rely on highly shaky foundations. Normally we associate culture with tradition, inertia and gradual change, but also with a dominant set of meanings that may change radically and unexpectedly, as the developments in many former communist countries have illustrated. Researchers drawing attention to diversity, fragmentation and ambiguity certainly point to aspects far too important to be treated as noise and nuisances to get rid of through rigorous data analysis which too often means imposing an order.

There is a risk that in searching for cultural patterns, we blind ourselves to contradictions, conflicts and everything else that does not fit. But what is there to say that what we are dealing with is one pattern or one structure? Against such concepts that hope to capture wholeness and consistency, we should set the analysis of contradictions, inconsistencies, splitting and dissonance. Perhaps it may then become evident that the world of thoughts and beliefs is characterized primarily by disintegration, by more or less demarcated elements that do not cling together (Ehn and Löfgren 1982: 68).

Culture and Power. Culture may also be related to power, politics and conflict. This refutes a common orientation within organizational culture studies in which culture is viewed as implicating mainly consensus and harmony, culture is seen as shared values (e.g., Hofstede et al. 1990; Schein 1985). Sometimes culture is treated positively because the concept is seen as standing for harmony and consensus (Schein 1985), sometimes culture is rejected as an explanation for the same reason (Wilkinson 1996).

A more sophisticated understanding is reluctant to see culture as grounded in "genuine," organic consensus. Culture is thus not seen as standing for the consensual, collective, coherent and integrated, but may also be interpreted in terms of contradiction and conflict, dominant ideologies, class and gender bias, and so on. As Wolf (1994) writes, "power is implicated in meaning through its role in upholding one version of significance as true, fruitful, or beautiful, against other possibilities that may threaten truth, fruitfulness or beauty" (p. 226). A focus on meanings rather than values is therefore preferred. Cultural ideas and meanings may be seen as an instrument, as a means to power or as a defensive weapon. When used defensively, culture is referred to as counter-culture (Ehn and Löfgren 1982). Struggle and antagonism between various groups are to some extent considered to have a cultural expression: a conflict is a question of the validity, the legitimacy and the dissemination of various competing pictures of reality. Symbols, rites and signs are used as a means of persuasion and propaganda. How meanings are developed, changed and used may then be read in terms of power, politics and sectional interests. Cultural meanings are loaded with various social and political implications (Frost 1987; Knights and Willmott 1987; Rosen 1985).

Cultural themes do not then work autonomously or automatically, but always in relationship to specific circumstances and through their role in forming a basis for (but also being put in action by and consciously or unconsciously utilized by) various agents. "[I]n organizational terms culture works through framing the assumptions that agencies are able to cooperate with. It frames and it enables; it enables and it constrains" (Clegg 1990: 150).

Beyond the Essence of the Other. A basic problem with much talk about culture is that it traditionally had, and still does have, a ring of "bounded universe of self-reproducing structures...for our creation and evocation of radical diversity" (Keesing 1994: 301). Talk of culture and other concepts such as society and nation often means an emphasis on difference and the idea that "cultures" are put in separate compartments and characterized in essentialist terms. Rather than putting forth comparisons in which simplifications coming close to stereotypes are demanded in order to create easy contrasts, the perspective-contingent nature of description is emphasized. The researcher may follow a hermeneutic approach and use her prestructured understanding in a conscious way[8] or use a range of cultural points of reference in order to illuminate that the other cannot easily be frozen and described in terms of a few essential traits.

Beyond Culture as a Thing-like Force. Culture is easily ascribed a thing-like and agent-like character, as if culture was something homogenous "out there" that can be measured through a couple of variables or was capable of acting and accomplishing something. Culture is, for example, seen as the force making people do certain things, for example, working according to certain values. Following Geertz (1973), among others, culture is better understood as a sense-making device—a frame and interpretive repertoire for the development of situation-specific meanings. Cultural meaning guides people in their constructions of organizational reality and in their ideas about the organizational world and what exists "outside" it.

Summary. Some guiding principles for the study of culture could be:
1. Viewing any object picked out for cultural analysis as loosely bounded: cultural borders are non-distinct, floating and changing; recognizing that borders are constructed by the researcher and not natural
2. Recognizing the organic and processional nature of cultural ideas, meanings and values
3. Paying attention to heterogeneity, diversity and ambiguity
4. Considering culture as a medium in politics and power; recognizing contradiction and conflict as well as the political engineering of (seemingly) shared values and ideals
5. Viewing culture as fused with—and as a crucial dimension in—economic and institutional conditions
6. Anchoring cultural understanding to the level of social practice and meaning
7. Providing the reader with an intimate feeling for the culture at the level of social action and experience

Cultural and Other Approaches

Culture is one major concept and approach for illuminating cross-national differences in business and organizations, among other issues. It thus competes with culture-free organizational structure theory. The competition is less a matter of explanatory power than one of understanding (if, as argued here, culture is not seen as a "factor" or variable but as a mode of understanding). It also competes with economic organization theory, for example transaction costs analyses which emphasize the exchange of markets and hierarchy-based solutions for the efficient ways of coping with bounded rationality and opportunism (Williamson 1975). Some scholarly works offer a synthesis of transaction cost and culture ideas, through emphasizing "clans" as an effective means of regulating transactions in complex exchange situations in which neither markets nor bureaucracy work very well (e.g., Wilkins and Ouchi 1983). Another approach is more purely sociological, emphasizing the "social embeddedness" of economic life and organizations and stressing the significance of social relations and structures (Granovetter 1985). Still another, increasingly significant, approach is institutional theory (Powell and DiMaggio 1991; Scott 1987). Institutional theory seems to refer to "everything"—handshakes and families as well as formal organizational structures, laws and markets are "institutions"—but with an emphasis on stabilizing social arrangements of a sociocultural and behavior-directing character. All these approaches are mainly consensus-oriented. A more power and conflict-oriented approach emphasizes the significance of interest, options, agents, strategic action, politics and coercion (Wilkinson 1996).

Apart from viewing these perspectives as points of departure, one may also consider viewing cultures in terms of the relative significance of efficiency, tradition, legitimacy and utilitarian types of meanings (Ebers 1995). Cultural meanings may thus be understood by taking into account the aspects advocated by other perspectives, but at the level of cultural meaning rather than "objective," non-symbolic reality "out there." The significance of culture for explanation or understanding, depends on what the concept refers to. It is important to avoid an all-embracing as well as a too narrow use of the term. If culture is seen as including all beliefs, ideas, values, norms, cognitions and feelings characterizing a collective, then of course it is crucial. If it is viewed as having nothing to do with economics, customers, politics, law, organizational structure, technology, etc., then it appears as a less significant phenomenon. Culture is, however, as mentioned above, best utilized to interpret the dimension of shared meaning central for all human, organized life. The trick is, as Geertz (1973) says, to cut the concept down in size so that it covers less and reveals more. The meaning of organizational structure—i.e., how work and social relations are regulated—cannot be understood without consideration of cultural issues. Tayeb (1994) notes how structural dimensions such as specialization and decentralization cannot be conceived without understanding cultural context. Alvesson (1995) shows how organizational structures are symbolically processed: the meaning of being a managing director and of organizing business in subsidiaries is central to the regulation/organizing of relations between superior and subordinate and between different units in the company.

Issues that may appear to be purely technical or economical may also be understood in cultural terms. Computers and information may, for example, often be seen as carriers of symbolic value (Feldman and March 1981). Chinese firms often rely heavily on capital provided by networks and involve banks to a relatively low degree. Finance thus becomes partly a cultural issue. Successful investments sometimes are facilitated by similar cultural understandings amongst the parties. Taiwanese venture capital invested in non-Chinese-American high-tech companies in the 1980s was, generally, unsuccessful due to language barriers and inefficient information flow. Investments in Chinese firms in the USA were seen as more successful, partly due to better communication and the establishment of informal relationships between capitalist and entrepreneur (see Chapter 9). According to one Swedish executive, he and his colleagues were appreciated for replacing labor with technology in a way that even changes leading to a questionable financial result were evaluated positively. The positive symbolic value of new technology and rationalization took the upper hand. Thus, there is always a meaning and value context guiding seemingly economically rational behavior. At the same time, culture cannot be understood on a purely idealistic level, as a set of free-floating ideas and values, but needs to be anchored in social and economic institutions and practices.

Multiple Cultural Configurations

Geertz (1973) makes a useful point for cultural studies when he says that anthropologists do not study villages, they study in villages. Of course, this does not mean that sets of meanings and symbolism are contained within a specific, isolated village. The study in a village may be an excellent point of departure for broader cultural phenomena. The problem, in the context of comparative management/cross-national organizational studies, is how to combine the strengths of a focused ethnography which emphasizes specific, micro grounded phenomena, with some interest in illuminating cultural macro configurations (or factors that appear across a variety of micro situations). The attempt to seek commonalities and uniformities among variety should thus be done in a way in which trends as well as diversities receive careful attention.

One ingredient here may be to think culturally or to study the cultural (Keesing 1994), rather than study one or several cultures as objects. One may also concentrate on cultural organizing processes—actions, events, situations—in which shared meanings and, thus, the basis for coordinated social action, are accomplished, reinforced or drawn upon. This would lead one to discover not just neat and single-level patterns but also the frictions, ambiguities and multi-level operations of different cultural groupings and themes. The objective would be to recognize the uniqueness and specificity of the individual case, while raising oneself above the specificities and saying something of a broader relevance that would illuminate cross-cultural variation.

A possibly helpful concept or framework here is what I call multiple cultural configurations (Alvesson 1993; cf. Martin 1992). It assumes that organizations can be understood as cultural sites which shape local versions of broader societal and global, as well as locally developed (intra-organizationally originated), cultural manifestations. These manifestations selectively form local collectives in a multitude of ways. Organizations are then understandable not as uniform wholes, nor as a stable set of subcultures, but as a mixture of different ideologies and other cultural manifestations existing on different levels and forming different kinds of collectives and groups dependent on the issues and topics concerned. People have more than one type of cultural belongingness: they are connected in different degrees to organization, sub-organizational unit, profession, gender, class, ethnic group, nation, continent, etc, all of which may provide a social space for the development of meanings and understandings. Cultures, then, always overlap in an organizational setting and are rarely manifested on the organizational level in "pure" forms across all members.

It is especially important to note the existence of cultural traffic; that neither organizations nor the societies in which they exist are cultural islands nor stable cultural patterns that exist independently of the issues at hand. Rather, values, ideas, meanings and understandings are affected by the societal level and have different kinds of origins and are clustered around different social categories depending on the issue concerned. There are several aspects to consider here. There is traffic associated with the moves of groups of people: organizations employ young people from schools, immigrants and people from new occupations. Between Taiwan and California there is, for example, a steady flow of Taiwanese people working for or founding Californian companies and then going back to Taiwan and/or forming steady links between the two places. In some areas, there is even talk about the "Californization of (parts of) Taiwan" (see Chapter 10). There is also traffic associated with the distribution and changes in fashionable ideas driven by mass media, higher education, management books, consultants, green and feminist movements, and so on. Related to these multiple "cultural movements," but of great significance in itself, are the groupings and regroupings around various issues that trigger different social constellations and cultural orientations. We can thus talk about dynamic cultural repositionings, fueled by the multitude and dynamics of social and ideational sources of meanings, ideas and identifications. This is the core of cultural traffic and something that has powerful theoretical and methodological implications for the study of organizational cultures, including comparative work.

A few empirical examples may illustrate my point. The first case is a Swedish university department which is, compared to most organizations, extremely homogenous. In some respects, people shared organizational-level understandings of social relations, but in other instances the social fields to which they belonged meant significant variation. The ideas and values of those oriented towards "soft," interpersonal, emotion-oriented therapy was very different from those engaged in "objective" experimental research (Alvesson 1993). In the case of the Women's Bank, a feminist ideology was broadly shared and had some influence, but on certain issues there were no broadly shared commitments, and ideologies which were not organization-specific informed different organizational members' understandings (Martin 1987). Thus, cultural configurations vary according to the issue and the ideology to which they are related. Such is the case not only in average sized business companies employing a variety of occupational groups and characterized by far reaching horizontal and vertical division of labor, but also within small and, in many respects, less heterogeneous organizations. Variation is not only an outcome of local diversity, but also related to how macro-level, environmental and cultural diversity affects different segments of the organization. In complex organizations, there are shared meanings, ideas and values to which environmental norms and values are central (e.g., ideas on ecology and gender equality). In addition, technical performance conditions (e.g., where productivity is easy to measure and crucial for competitiveness) play a major or a minor role for different parts of, and issues in, the organization (Ebers 1995).

Any specific cultural manifestation identified—an example of symbolism, an idea, belief or value expressed in a specific situation—thus originates in a multiple of cultural configurations, from local group interaction to occupational/industrial subfield orientations to macro cultural traditions and meaning patterns. Any specific manifestation is thus a possible source of insight on several levels. That is, several levels must be worked through in terms of interpretive powers before the researcher decides what is a reasonable interpretation pointing at a specific level of analysis.

There is no definitive relation between various issues. When for example Hofstede (1980) identifies a variable that is seen as indicating an interesting distribution of cultural values across countries, we can not run out the chance that the variable could be divided up or constructed in other ways and other value distributions would be produced. Hierarchy may, for example, be "de-essentialized" and seen as varied and contingent upon whether one addresses public or private/informal manifestations of asymmetrical behavior, managerial circles, or blue-collar-foreman-lower manager groups; whether it is a matter of strict work-related issues or concerns going beyond what is specified in job descriptions; and whether competence on a specific issue breaks with formal hierarchy or not.[9] Hierarchy is an element in social relations that varies with circumstances, not a fixed property.

The multiple cultural configuration view differs from the differentiation/subculture view in organization studies. It does so in emphasizing the diversity of groups in organizations (Frost et al. 1991; Martin 1992; Martin and Meyerson 1988; Van Maanen and Barley 1985) in at least three distinct ways: (a) it focuses partly on extra-organizational origins of local cultural manifestations without reducing these local manifestations to only reflections of broader patterns; (b) it pays attention to overlapping cultural configurations in the organization; and (c) it views such configurations as changing depending on issue (e.g., hierarchy, performance, training, wage, job security, customer relations).

Considering multiple cultural configurations means that clear, isolatable origins and manifestations of cultural phenomena do not exist, but that any cultural manifestation is "overdetermined" by the dense interplay of local and distant social sources of cultural issues. Instead of societal, globalization and MNC organizational effects, all manifestations may be investigated in terms of these contexts. Specific phenomena are never "free from" nor reducible to a specific level. Rather, they allow interpretations addressing all levels.

A Note on Work Methodology

The multiple cultural configurations approach motivates a case approach, in which what is treated as a case is given careful consideration. Awareness of the artificiality of all boundaries is important. Neither societies defined as nations nor formal organizations are "natural" or necessarily particularly fruitful units for cultural analysis. Sociological fact-sheet variables should be treated as less significant than how the people being studied see their world. A case may be constructed in a variety of more or less creative ways. Often it is better to address carved out cultural terrain in order to say something interesting, allow for a delimited theoretical theme, and encourage local theory and micro-anchored empirical material. One formal organization may be the site of several cases.

Real events and situations may be a fruitful starting point for tracking meaningful boundaries. The idea is to study cultural manifestations rather than cultures. Possible focus could be on events interpreted as rituals, certain kinds of interactions (e.g., between juniors and seniors) or talk about particular themes (customers, strategies, goals, technology). A case may be the workday of a senior manager, the carrying out of a task of a work group (e.g., project), a decision making process, etc. Based on tape-recordings of the interactions of a school principle over the course of two days, Gronn (1983) chooses three events for scrutiny: one example each of, respectively, corridor talk, office talk and staff meeting talk. Thick description and the offering of a rich feeling for the carved out, focused cultural terrain are important. It should not be so narrow, however, that only one cultural constellation emerges in the case.

Given the purpose of facilitating understanding across macro settings, one may either use a traditional anthropological approach or rely on more than one case. A researcher studying an alien culture may in an anthropological manner produce interesting knowledge through the systematic use of the confrontation of a new, foreign cultural context with the cultural knowledge inherent in the prestructured understanding of the researcher. The emergence and solving of breakdowns between the original cultural framework and that of the natives being studied may be the cornerstone of the project (Agar 1986). The expectations and perspectives of the researcher should be acknowledged and used, not hidden as if an alien or different social terrain could be explored in a "culture-free" or standpoint-independent way.

Relying on several cases increases the likelihood of saying something of relevance for cross macro setting understanding—or being seen as trustworthy in this enterprise. According to the position of this paper, cases should not be treated in a reductionistic way (reified, essentialized) in order to facilitate comparisons, nor be treated rigorously in terms of dimensions and variables. This inevitably leads to thin description and contradicts the ideals mentioned above. Comparisons must be "soft," i.e., indicate broadly similar or different qualitative patterns among diverse and complex cultural manifestations, bearing in mind the difficulties transporting meanings outside their specific contexts. Cases may, of course, come from the literature. The context and perspective guiding the telling of the case stories must also here, of course, be born in mind. The construction of alterity (the other) of other authors may differ radically from one's own. The use of several cases may show a mix of tendencies and variation within a macro setting allowing indications of macro patterns to emerge without falling into too much essentialism and alterity.

An Illustration

Let me try to illustrate some of the themes above, including: (a) some of the problems of straightforward comparisons en masse; (b) the need for micro anchoring and situating cultural concepts; (c) how a manageable chunk of organizational reality may be carved out; (d) how the patterns/diversity issue can be handled through narrowing/broadening the scope (different kinds of zooming in); (e) how micro anchoring and the use of ideographic results may be combined with broader, cross-macro setting comparisons; and (f) the perspectival and alterative character of cultural description may be treated. Space restrictions as well as the methodological rather than substantive nature of this paper allow only a brief treatment of the subject matter.

The comparison concerns the issue of hierarchy in US and Swedish companies. It explores this issue based on case studies treating specific cultural manifestations of relations between formal superiors and subordinates. To say something universal about US companies is not easy, nor perhaps very meaningful. US society is large and heterogeneous. One may assume, however, that General Motors and Pepsi Cola are relatively typical for large-scale US businesses. Two studies that I have come across emphasize their hierarchical and ritualistic nature at least in the spheres of senior management.

> GM had many rituals that supported the core value of deference owed to authority. For example, subordinates were expected to meet their superiors from out of town at the airport, carry their bags, pay their hotel bills, and chauffeur them around day and night. The higher the status of the superior, the more people would accompany him on the flight and the larger the retinue that would wait at the airport. (Martin and Siehl 1983: 57)

A ritual among the top marketing people in Pepsi Cola, described by the former vice president John Sculley (1987), also illustrates hierarchy and strict rules for conduct.

> Like other meetings, this one was a ceremonial event. We marked it on our calendars many weeks in advance. Everyone wore the unofficial corporate uniform: a blue pin-striped suit, white shirt, and a sincere red tie. None of us would ever remove the jacket. We dressed and acted as if we were at a meeting of the board of directors. (p. 2)

People entered the room in hierarchical order. First came people from the marketing investigation consulting company, then junior and subsequently senior managers arrived in order corresponding to their ranks. Corporate formality dictated where people sat. The company's top officers gravitated to the front of the table, the junior execs toward the back. When the president has arrived, Sculley went to the chairman's room and informed him that everybody was present. The chairman entered and the meeting started. The core of the meetings was the monitoring of results. According to Sculley's story, the meetings were often harsh:

> These sessions weren't always euphoric. Often the tension in the room was suffocating. Eyes would fix on Kendall (the chairman) to capture his response at every gain or drop in every tenth of a market share. An executive whose share was down had to stand and explain—fully—what he was going to do to fix it fast. Clearly in the dock, he knew that the next time he returned to that room, it had better be fixed.... Always, there was another executive in the room, ready to take your place. (p. 4–5)

These empirical illuminations of hierarchical (and a few other) aspects of relations between senior managers in large US companies tell us a very selective and partial story about a segment of a couple of US companies. But they presumably still tell us something of the situation of large scale, machine bureaucratic, US companies having adopted a specific style of management/organization. The point is that specific empirical examples are not just simply and straightforwardly US (national, societal), but that they are always the fusion of a variety of contexts and contingencies, patterns and idiosyncrasies. Carving out and abstracting a specific dimension is appropriate if it is not uncoupled from observable social practice and if one takes great care in generalization.

When trying to establish such qualities, the relative nature of social phenomena must be born in mind. As I said, hierarchy is not a simple attribute that can be determined on an absolute scale. Hierarchy is always something perspectival, something that emerges in the context of explicit comparison or implicit expectations. These examples are selective and relative to something else in a complex manner. I selected them to prove a particular point. They are also selected—both in terms of the example chosen and how the cases are accounted for—by the authors to whom I refer. Sculley (1987) uses a particular version of Pepsi as a contrast to Apple, the company he worked for after leaving Pepsi and which employed him at the time of the book's production. Martin and Siehl (1983) also use their example as a contrast between a particular corporate culture (GM's) and a counter culture that is ascribed to a division headed by J. Delorean, who was dismissed by GM. Nevertheless, at least from a Swedish (academic) viewpoint—but presumably also from many others—the two case descriptions appear to be highly exotic.

Compared with, for example, Taiwanese relations in organizations, US people sometimes appear as relatively non-hierarchical (Tzeng 1996). In Tzeng's case study of a Taiwanese-owned and run company in USA, the US workers expressed much less respect for the owner and management of the company than did their Taiwanese colleagues. The slightly different impression from this study compared to the glimpses of GM and Pepsi mentioned above, may illustrate several lines of interpretation: a) the cases illustrate variety in US companies—it may be impossible to say anything general about US organizations; b) the impression of US employees as non-hierarchical is relative to the point of comparison: from another position, originating in other expectations/framework for comparison, the picture may be more hierarchical; or, c) there may be substantive differences between various strata/classes in companies; hierarchical relations among the higher and lower echelons may be very different. The point here is not that one should sort out which of these interpretations is the best, but that these themes should always be on the agenda, as part of what comparative work always has to struggle with. Progress in the field is then a matter of developing increasingly insightful, reflected struggles, not a final solution on terms of finding out "how it is."

Compared to my experiences with Swedish organizations, the impression is rather different. I shall briefly refer to two ethnographies of Swedish companies. A Swedish computer consulting firm, a young organization employing 500 persons, provides a useful contrasting point (Alvesson 1995). Corporate policy downplays formal hierarchy and emphasizes equality. This is, among other things, expressed by the fact that all office interiors are standardized from presidents on down to secretaries, and that top management is located on the bottom floor, close to the reception. All newcomers, whether they are managers, consultants or secretaries participate in the same, week-long introduction course. There are also more or less institutionalized ironic expressions about "Giant directors" in the company, which aim at demystifying and de-hierarchizing the managerial role. Thus, many clearly visible material, action and verbal symbols reduce hierarchy and inequality. This relatively egalitarian company policy is of course not contradiction-free, but the lack of visible status-symbols is worth highlighting. To say something definite about hierarchy (hierarchical distance) is not easy but one may point to the existence of hierarchy-downplaying social practices.

This example may be complemented with an account of a ritual in a Swedish industrial company (Alvesson and Björkman 1992). This organization is also primarily populated by men, most of them engineers or marketing people with an engineering background. Every third month there is an informational meeting for the forty or so managers in the division. (All are men, with the exception of the female personnel manager and the secretary.) Gustaf, the divisional manager stands at the door and welcomes all the participants. During the introductory speech he gives a "soft" impression, his jacket is unbuttoned. The agenda is characterized by several speakers and the divisional manager holds a low profile. The manager could have done some of the presentations himself, but chooses to let someone else take the center stage. The atmosphere is informal and friendly. Sometimes the manager jokes with people and sometimes he is the object of their jokes. During his presentation of results, the controller uses the manager's picture aimed at showing changes in results on different markets in a pedagogical manner:

> "Now we go over to Gustaf's own picture, the quantum physics diagramme."
> (Everybody laughs)

After some comments, Gustaf asks the audience:

> "Everybody laughs at me and this diagramme. Do you find it unclear? I think it is rather revealing." Some people reply:
> "At first glance it looks quite difficult (laughter), but when you have looked at it some time..."
> "It is easier for me who is color blind." (More laughter)

During the break, the divisional manager serves coffee together with his secretary and the personnel manager. The overall impression from the meeting is one of community rather than formalism and hierarchy.

The two Swedish case studies have not been developed for the purpose of comparison. The two cases were published as separate case studies. The absence of explicit comparisons of course do not prevent implicit comparisons, for example between the cases and ideas about normal or average patterns. However, we can broaden the picture of the last case company somewhat by directing attention not only to the division but to the next hierarchical level and the social relations involved here. The secretary of the divisional manager, Herbert, provided the following account, referring to senior managers in corporate and business unit management:

> They are sitting a bit isolated in large rooms with closed doors. You don't go into them without a good reason. It is a bit of a different world. Rather quiet corridors. They don't run down here and talk with people. They meet their immediate superiors, they never go down and sit here. The personnel here has wanted that to happen. Everybody has said: imagine that he could come down here and walk around, and pick up the habit of walk in sometimes and sit down instead of only sending after people. For example, Herbert always had to go up. Bert (his boss, business sector manager) never came down.

Other empirical material indicated similar opinions among the unit's employees. Senior managers are absent, they rule from distance, are anonymous, their styles strongly differ from those of lower managers, interviewees say (ibid). In particular older employees bemoan this, saying that some years ago things were different. Senior managers were known personally by low-level employees ("now they are only names"), there was a feeling of community in the company. Through adding this example, the picture of a limited hierarchical distance is complicated somewhat. Illuminating the varied character of organizational cultures and subcultures prevent us from the unitary and unique fallacy.

In broader comparisons, for example Hofstede (1980), US people score slightly higher on power distance than Swedes (40, 31 points respectively). This may tell us something, but if power distance is only treated as people's responses to some questionnaire items, it gives us little of indication of what "power distance" may mean in corporate practice. Through comparing examples of managerial rituals in diverse corporate settings and illuminating how various dimensions are involved, we get some indication of how national/societal cultural orientations may put their imprints on—as well as be constructed through—corporate social processes and practices. Case material showing "real" actions or events is, of course highly selective, but the richness and relevance of the material may well compensate for the lack of measurement and generalizability—the latter quality being of questionable value to the extent that it is contingent upon abstract, arbitrary and thin empirical material. If one takes the many faces of cultural manifestations seriously, showing patterns as well as diversities (something inherent in the concept of multiple cultural configurations), then the risk of overgeneralizing is limited.

In the studies reviewed, public cultural manifestations—rhetoric, rituals and material arrangement engineered by management so that they are broadly visible—support hierarchy, authority and career aspirations in the US cases, community, across-level communication and a favorable work climate in the Swedish cases. Expressions of hierarchy and distance across levels in one of the Swedish cases are hidden, possibly non-intentional. They are not intended for public consumption in the organization, but remain, from a managerial point of view *vis-a-vis* subordinates, in the cultural background of unfocused meanings. It is hardly possible to generalize from this observation, but it may provide an interesting clue for unpacking hierarchy and power distance as misleadingly equivocal dimensions.

Conclusion

This paper has argued for an approach to cross macro-setting study of organizations that takes recent critiques and developments in methodology and culture theory seriously. Freezing culture by capturing values or other cultural items as a particular score on a measure may tell us something and facilitate comparison, but the understanding reached is often shallow, the re-presentations of cultural themes standing in an uncertain or remote relationship to specific values, ideas, symbols and meanings expressed in concrete organizational situations and social actions.

The mode of study suggested aims for an interpretive, historical, language-sensitive, local, open and non-authoritative understanding of the subject matter. Soft comparison—thoughtful, interpretive comparative work—is then to be preferred to the comparison of measures of variables. Recognizing complexity, diversity and the importance of giving rich glimpses of cultural manifestations as expressed in "real" settings means that comparisons become less straightforward and that comparative work becomes more empirically anchored, less cumulative and generalization-oriented. It also means that more modest projects than the grandiose explaining of wide-ranging empirical terrain are promoted. Instead, the carving out of a manageable chunk of organizational reality is suggested. Rather than aiming for an abstract world of pattern variables, local theory accounts for how a particular empirical terrain is put together, normally as a melting-pot of a multiplicity of cultural configurations, concentrating on "real worlds of human activity and distinctive cultural meanings" (Hamilton et al. 1990: 109).

The paper also argues for the use of a more reflective concept of culture than is common in organization studies and comparative management. Cultural interpretation then avoids excessive temptations to reify, personify, essentialize, unify, idealize, consensualize and otherize. In particular, it is important to avoid equating cultural boundaries with formal or legal ones, as implied by terms such as corporate culture or national culture. Instead, the suggested approach: (a) relates the cultural to specific events, situations, actions and processes; (b) treats it as a network of meaning guiding feeling, thinking and acting rather than an external force; (c) views meanings as complex and situated and not as a fixed essence; (d) is sensitive to variation and contradiction, the action—and practice—related nature of cultural manifestations, and is reluctant to treat culture as an abstract system of values, presumed to have a general impact; (e) recognizes how power operates in dominant meanings and the asymmetries of social relations work behind established cultural order; and (f) acknowledges and is reflective about one's own pre-structured understanding, the relativity of all claims about cultural manifestations and is explicit about the interpretive and analytic moves behind the formulation of clear contrasts that often mask an "us" vs. "them" approach (the problem of otherness or radical alterity).

Recognizing that the tremendous difficulties of conventional ideas on methodology (often unrecognized, as the cultural meanings and language codes so central for the responses are effectively camouflaged behind "data"), and recognizing the complexities of culture, go hand in hand. Conventional methodology tends to freeze and reify culture, while a local, interpretive, language-conscious understanding of culture facilitates the application of a more sophisticated concept of culture and thus a more nuanced and deeper exploration of organizations. Of course, even though conventional methodology obstructs the use of a qualified cultural theory, there is no intrinsic relationship between the methodological ideas suggested above and culture theory. However, the possibilities and tendencies for the two to support each other are strong. A qualified understanding of culture is, for example, crucial for methodological awareness as there are no "culture-free data" (if human subjects are involved). To evaluate empirical material calls for considering the material as cultural expression and appreciating how cultural meanings and rules are constitutive of all empirical material produced by human subjects. This is valid for all social research, but it becomes central for cross-cultural comparative work.

Given the problems of comparison following from the local and unstable nature of language and the variety of cultural codes and rules for language use, one may conclude that comparative work within radically different macro contexts unavoidably rest on shaky foundations (at least when it is focusing on complex, ambiguous phenomena) and that it may be wise to instead devote one's energy to more productive fields. Methods reliant upon similarities in terms of meaning construction and language codes for the possibility of simple comparison, e.g., through quantitative indications, may actually only be appropriate—if ever—for the study of a homogenous group. There are, however, strong reasons for engaging in comparative work of organizations and culture across macro settings: we certainly need to understand highly different organizational practices, and confrontation with foreign cultures may challenge parochialism and taken for granted assumptions about organizational and social life. Seeing national or even western organizational arrangements and theories as exhaustive of how we can think about organization is clearly narrow-minded, practically, as well as theoretically. Comparative work aiming at such understanding must be realistic about the problems of language and meaning contexts and respond to these with theoretical-methodological awareness and sophistication, not with an emphasis on techniques and procedures. This means the opposite of a fixed a priori design: it means an appreciation of the complexities and a tolerance for the ambiguities of melting-pot like cultural organizations as well as all statements claiming to represent "reality." It means intensive interpretation in which careful appreciation of the situatedness of all empirical material is central and all knowledge products—vocabularies, theories, hypothesis, earlier research—upon which one draws are used in a critical and sensitive manner. Research then becomes a reflective rather than a pre-designed project.

Notes

1. The argument for micro anchoring is valid for social and organization studies in general (Sandelands and Drazin 1989). I am using comparative studies of culture and organizations as a focus and example.
2. Of course, non-ambiguous phenomena such as physical length, number of people, turnover, etc. may often be compared rather straightforwardly, but almost all interesting organizational phenomena are too complex to fit into a view of language as a context-independent, transparent medium for the transport of meaning.
3. See Calás and Smircich (1988) for an exploration of authority-creating moves in a research text.
4. On parochialism in international studies of management, see Boyacigeller and Adler (1991).
5. The authors express some doubts themselves whether the comparison really works across the two samples. I will come back to this example later.
6. "Our lives are micro. Whatever human experience is, high points, low points and every other existential dimension, it happens to us in micro-situations" (Collins 1988: 244).
7. I use the term macro in a relatively loose way, as it is important to be open about how a macro context should be identified. The arguments used here are in no way restricted to cross-national comparisons.
8. Compare with the idea of "confessional" styles of reporting, as described by Van Maanen (1988).
9. For an account of the complexities of senior-subordinate manager relations in some large US companies, see Jackall (1988).

Part One:
Embeddedness and Organizational Transformation in Various Societies

Chapter 2

Societal Transformation and Enterprise Change in Eastern Europe: A Comparison of Hungary and Slovenia

Richard Whitley

Introduction

As the differences between varieties of capitalism are further explored, the institutional embeddedness of economic systems is becoming increasingly recognised (see, for example, Gerlach 1992a; Hollingsworth and Boyer 1997; Lazonick 1991; Whitley 1992a). Major differences in the sorts of economic activities that are coordinated through ownership and authority relations, and in how these activities are coordinated, have developed as the result of significant differences in processes of industrialisation and in associated institutions. This is particularly true of differences in the structure and policies of the state and the nature of the financial system. The kinds of institutional arrangements governing the establishment of interest groups and how they compete and collaborate in gaining access to key resources have clearly made significant differences to the sorts of firms and organizations that have become established in European, East Asian and North American capitalist societies (Kristensen 1997; Lilja and Tainio 1996; Campbell et al. 1991; Whitley 1992a). As a result, a number of distinctive systems of economic coordination and control—or "business systems" (Whitley 1992b)—have become established in the industrialised capitalist economies.

This interdependence of economic systems and societal institutions implies that where institutions change radically, as they did during the Allied occupations of Germany and Japan after 1945 for example, then so too should major characteristics of firms and their interrelations. Thus, the radical transformations of the dominant political and economic institutions of Eastern Europe in the early 1990s, coupled with the sharp losses of traditional markets in the Soviet Union, would be expected to have had major consequences for enterprise structures and actions during this period. The Eastern European case therefore provides an ideal opportunity to examine how changing institutional arrangements structure firm type and behaviour.

Because the legacies of the state socialist period—and indeed of pre-war societies—differed significantly in a number of important respects among Eastern European countries, the types of enterprises that dominated these economies also varied. These variations affected their responses to the transformed institutional environments. Thus, the sorts of economic systems that are developing in Eastern Europe can be expected to diverge quite considerably where the state socialist legacies differ and where the structures and policies established in the 1990s also vary significantly. The ways in which institutional changes are linked to developing characteristics of firms and market organization—and thus to the establishment of distinctive business systems—can, then, be particularly sharply observed in this region.

The contrasting consequences of different state socialist legacies for enterprise development are especially marked when comparing the countries that were integrated into the Council for Mutual Economic Assistance (CMEA), on the one hand, with the countries of the former Yugoslavia, on the other hand. The important differences in the nature of these state socialist regimes generated different sorts of enterprises that pursued distinctive policies and practices during and after the late state socialist period. They therefore provide a useful contrast for exploring the relationships between institutional contexts and systems of economic coordination and control.

In this paper, I outline some of the ways in which the state and its policies varied most significantly between these regimes and explore their consequences for the kinds of enterprises which have developed in the 1990s. I examine these changes in two countries: Hungary and Slovenia, formerly part of Yugoslavia. Because the nature of state socialism differed considerably in the 1970s and 1980s in these two territories, processes of political-economic transformation also differed, and have led to the institutionalisation of contrasting kinds of market economies. My primary purpose here is to show how these differences in enterprise environment have led to the development of different kinds of enterprises with different types of behavior in the 1990s. Initially, I summarise the key differences in the late socialist regimes of these societies and then explore their effects on enterprise development in the 1970s and 1980s. Next, the key changes in their environments in the early 1990s are highlighted and the consequences of these changes for enterprises in Hungary and Slovenia are outlined.

Dominant Institutions in Late State Socialist Hungary and Slovenia

Table 2.1 summarises the dominant institutions of the late state socialist period (the 1970s and 1980s) that affected the nature of enterprises in Hungary and Slovenia. While many of the features listed in Table 2.1 are similar to those used to compare market economies (Whitley 1992b; Whitley and Kristensen 1996, 1997), increased attention is paid here to state structures and policies, given their dominant role in the economy under state socialism. The key differences can be considered under the headings "the values and norms governing trust, authority and loyalty relations," "the state," "the banking system" and "the labour system." While these features were all part of the party-state regime in state socialist societies, it is useful analytically to separate them since most market economies institutionalise these activities and agencies as distinct arenas, albeit to differing degrees.

Values and Norms Governing Trust, Authority and Loyalty Relations

Authoritarian and totalitarian regimes usually generate low degrees of trust in formal procedures and institutions as these are subordinated to the interests and wishes of regime leaders. In late state socialism, the subservience of the legal system and related procedures for regulating economic relations to the party-state limited trust in formal institutions (see for example, Crawford 1995; Hall 1995; Lampland 1995; Sajó 1994) and there seems little evidence that Yugoslavia differed much from Hungary in this respect (Lydall 1989). In general, the legacy of the selective modernisation carried out by the state socialist regimes in most East European societies has resulted in a form of ethical dualism in which a

Table 2.1 Late State Socialist Institutions in Hungary and Slovenia

	Hungary	Slovenia
A. Cultural Conventions		
Trust in formal institutions and procedures	Limited	Limited
Authority relations	Low legitimacy of formal positional authority	Low legitimacy of formal positional authority
Collective loyalties	Low beyond nuclear family	Strong local attachments
B. State Structures and Policies In 1970s And 1980s		
State autonomy and cohesion	High but becoming more fragmented	Decentralised to republics and communes, declining central cohesion
State direction of enterprises and subsidisation	Considerable but indirect and declining in mid-1980s	Considerable at the local level, but managers more autonomous in Slovenia when profitable.
State control of imports and exports	High but declining in mid-1980s	Medium
State control of foreign exchange	High	Delegated to trading companies
State coordination of inputs and outputs	High, but declining in 1980s	Limited
State control and guarantee of demand	High for most large enterprises	Limited
Formal state decentralisation of power to local workforce	Negligible	Considerable
State control over allocation of surpluses and investment funds	Considerable	Limited
Predominant pattern of industrialisation	Rapid, extensive, heavy industrialisation in urban centres	Polycentric after early 1950s.
C. Banking System		
State control of banks	High	Shared with enterprises at republic and commune level
Dominant role of banks	Instrument of state control	Enterprise and local development
D. Labour System		
State regulation of wages	High	Intermittent
Role of Unions	Political control and welfare services management	Political control and welfare services management
Training system	Extensive school based system	Extensive school based system with firm scholarships
Labour mobility	Indirectly restricted by the state	Low

strong regard for the law is coupled with an unwillingness to be personally bound by it and a limited degree of trust in others' obedience to it (Marody 1997).

While systemic trust may have been slightly greater in post-reform Hungary than in some other East European societies, such as Poland (Swaan 1993), the extensive political control over the legal system and the high level of discretion and lack of accountability of officials in managing the society and economy are unlikely to have led people to put much faith in formal procedures for resolving disputes and enforcing agreements, especially when these involved state officials. Rather, bureaucratic bargaining and personal networks of obligation and influence seem to have been the primary means of dealing with problems.

Formal authority derived from incumbency in leadership positions is also unlikely to be regarded as legitimate in societies where such positions are tied to party membership and loyalty rather than to expertise or more traditional criteria. Cynicism about the party leadership and the whole state socialist project seems to have been widespread in most state socialist societies by the 1970s (see, e.g., Lampland 1995). This was accompanied by an increased emphasis on formally certified expertise that resulted from the expansion of state training systems in the 1970s and attempts by some party élites to bolster their fading authority with technocratic expertise (cf. Szelenyi 1989).

The focus and strength of collective loyalties, however, developed quite differently in Hungary and Slovenia. In Hungary and most of the CMEA countries, forced industrialisation in the 1950s resulted in rapid urbanisation and migration from the countryside to heavy industry based company towns and capital cities. Often, local ties and loyalties were severely disrupted and weakened in this process, so that individual nuclear families became the primary unit of identity and commitment and social relationships became quite atomised (Csepeli and Orkeny 1992: 5; Lampland 1995: 1–4).

In Slovenia, in contrast, industrialisation and economic development were much more polycentric and less concentrated in the major cities of Ljubljana and Maribor (Konjhodzic 1996). Together with the tradition of local house building and ownership and high levels of political, financial and economic decentralisation in the 1970s and 1980s, this encouraged considerable local loyalties to particular localities and inhibited geographic and labour mobility. Consequently, enterprise and local dependence and loyalties have tended to be much greater in Slovenia than in Hungary (see, e.g. Jaklic 1997; Svetlicic and Rojec 1996).

State Structures and Policies

The major differences between these two economies, though, concern the degree of centralisation of state control. Despite the post 1968 reforms in Hungary which delegated some control of enterprise activities to top managers (particularly after 1984), the degree of political and economic central control by the party-state remained considerable, although the division of powers between the party, the government, trade unions and other agencies became more evident and more fragmenting in the 1970s and 1980s (Berend 1990; Revesz 1990; Swaan 1993).

In contrast, constitutional reform in Yugoslavia in the 1970s greatly decentralised political power to the provincial republics and local communes. Many of these took on significant governmental functions (Smidovnik 1991). At the same time, the large vertically integrated enterprises that dominated many parts of the domestic economy were decomposed into Basic Organizations of Associated Labour (BOALs) which were the smallest economic units capable of producing tradable commodities (Lydall 1989). While many of these subsequently recombined into larger Work Organizations (WOs) and Composite Organization of Associated Labour (COALs), the political emphasis on workers self-management at the smallest feasible organizational units ensured that these latter groupings were rarely fully integrated into a coherent managerial hierarchy (Dyker 1990; Jaklic 1997).

Thus, although the "state" in both economies remained the dominant agent in economic coordination and control, in Hungary it was centralised in Budapest while in Slovenia the central Yugoslav state in Belgrade was less significant for many activities than provincial and commune governments. Correlatively, the degree of central state support of loss making enterprises in Slovenia was less than in Hungary given the Serbian domination of the Yugoslav bureaucracy and the considerable delegation of powers and responsibility to the provincial republics. The geographical and ethnic distance of Slovene enterprises from Belgrade meant that they were both more autonomous from the central state and received less support from it than their Hungarian counterparts (Whitley et al. 1999). While both enjoyed "soft budget constraints" (Kornai 1986), state support in Slovenia was much more localised and less directive than in Hungary.

The CMEA system itself contributed considerably to the central control of enterprise policies in Hungary. Even after the 1968 and later reforms, many large Hungarian enterprises were tied to long term contracts for the whole CMEA market which were negotiated by governments rather than by managers. This encouraged high levels of enterprise specialisation and dependence on state authorities and on the former USSR (Csaba 1993; Daviddi 1993). In contrast, since many Slovene enterprises were oriented to OECD markets and were outside the CMEA system, they had to adapt to shifts in demand and could not rely on planned allocations of customers. They did, however, have the not inconsiderable benefit of a protected domestic market, although their share of this was not guaranteed by state authorities. Additionally, Hungarian enterprises often had to accept centrally decided deliveries of key inputs with major restrictions on imports from OECD countries. While the shortage economy was often circumvented by informal inter-enterprise connections in practice, the formal control of inputs by the central state was much greater than in Slovenia (Konjhodzic 1996).

The Banking System

Similar differences characterised the banking systems of these two economies. In most CMEA economies the state bank(s) were conduits for channelling investment funds to enterprises without any autonomy over leading decisions or ability to recover assets following delays in payments or defaults. Even after the introduction of the two tier banking system in Hungary in 1987, which was supposed to separate the commercial banks from the central bank, dominant state ownership and central control of the banking system remained (Kemme 1994; Várhegyi 1993; cf. Bonin and Schaffer 1995).

In Slovenia, on the other hand, while many banks were politically controlled, they were also decentralised to the commune level and were often established to channel funds to "their" local enterprises by coalitions of local politicians and managers. They were not then simply agents of the central state or part of the central bank, but rather integral units of local economies and under joint local political cum enterprise ownership and control (Lydall 1989: 155–157).

The Labour and Skill Development System

Finally, considering the ways in which skills were developed certified and made available to enterprises, both economies had quite extensive secondary school systems for developing practical skills. These were typically state controlled, funded and managed. They produced a considerable number of skilled workers in a wide variety of occupations. However, there was usually not much enterprise involvement in the definition and certification of skills. Although a number of the larger organizations did develop training schools and offer work placements, the actual amount of time spent in practical work inside enterprises tended to be quite low compared to that spent in state schools, especially in the four year vocational secondary schools (Halasz 1993).

The financial returns to these skills were, however, quite restricted in Hungary by the wage regulation system. Despite the reforms of the late 1960s and 1980s, this system restricted managers' ability to reward high performing workers and effectively maintained centralised control of labour management strategies and practices (Horvath 1977; Hethy 1983). Inflationary tendencies and mounting external debts, among other factors, ensured that delegation of control over the total wage bill and delegation of other aspects of labour management to enterprise managers was quite limited in Hungary (Berend 1990: 180–182).

On the other hand, in Yugoslavia the political and economic decentralisation of the 1970s and the ideological commitment to self management restricted central control of wages and other rewards, despite a number of attempts to regulate wage increases and keep some control over inflation (Lazarevic 1994). Especially in the 1980s, managers formed coalitions with the unions and self-management leaders to maintain the managers' positions, often at the price of conceding considerable wage increases (Kovac 1991; Kraft et al. 1994). Although such inflationary tendencies may have been lower in Slovenia than elsewhere in Yugoslavia, the lack of effective central control over enterprises' reward policies meant that managers in Slovene companies had much more autonomy in their labour management practices than their Hungarian counterparts and greater incentives to develop enterprise specific strategies in cooperation with local workers' representatives (Jaklic 1997).

Additionally, although the official unions in both state socialist regimes were instruments of party control, the greater decentralisation of the Yugoslav system, coupled with the self-management ideology, meant that unions there were more enterprise focused than those in Hungary. Despite their association with the party-state in both countries, some appeared to develop a limited degree of autonomy in the 1980s, with local shop stewards attempting to represent employees' interests at the enterprise level in some sectors (Stark 1989). This local role gained some of these official unions a limited degree of legitimacy (Kuzmanic 1994; Lado 1994).

Finally, labour mobility between enterprises was limited both in Hungary and Slovenia, but for different reasons. Central control over wages in Hungary involved restricting workers' ability to move between enterprises in order to improve their pay and benefits, as well as standardising wages across employers (Bonifert 1987; Kollo 1993). While the weakness of such central control in Yugoslavia prevented such administrative limitation of mobility in Slovenia, the self management system and pervasive local loyalties inhibited workers' willingness to change employers, even within the same town (Jaklic 1997; Svetlicic and Rojec 1996). In general, the political importance of "social ownership" and "self management" in Yugoslavia, although limited in practice, meant that manager-worker interdependence was much more consciously recognised and institutionalised than it was in Hungary.

Enterprise Characteristics in Late State Socialist Hungary and Slovenia

These contrasts in the nature of late state socialism in Hungary and Yugoslavia (Slovenia) generated significantly different kinds of enterprises in the two economies. Their major features in the 1970s and 1980s are summarised in Table 2.2 and will be discussed under three headings: enterprise type, inter-enterprise relations and work organization and control. The analysis of these themes will take a similar form as discussions of business systems in market economies (Whitley 1992b, 1996). It will be argued that differences among these three characteristics particularly reflect the variations in state structures and policies summarised above, as well as the much stronger attachments between enterprises, managers and workers and their local communities in Slovenia.

Enterprise Type

The combination of a shortage economy with uncertain supplies, arising in part from the central coordination of inputs and outputs, and soft budget constraints which rarely penalised inefficient producers as long as central targets were achieved, encouraged most large industrial enterprises in the CMEA economies to integrate backwards into component production as a means of assuring the availability of supplies of the

Table 2.2 Enterprise Characteristics in Late State Socialist Hungary and Slovenia

	Hungary	Slovenia
A. Enterprise Type		
Extent of backward integration into component manufacturing	High	Considerable in some COALs
Product range	Very narrow in large SOEs	Limited to one sector or product type per BOAL or WO
Innovation	Low	Incremental
Dominant objectives	Target fulfilment, growth in size, export earnings	Employment growth, export earnings
B. Inter-Enterprise Connections		
Coordination of production chains	Informally by state, extensive informal links between managers	Within COALs, local informal links, market based transactions.
Collaboration between enterprises within sectors	Informal and personal	Low outside locality
Collaboration across sectors	Negligible	Very limited
C. Work Organization and Control		
Centralisation of decision making	High	Limited in COALs, varied in BOALs
Organizational integration of subunits	High	Limited in COALs
Employer-employee interdependence	High	High
Employer differentiation	Low	Low
Task specialisation	Formally high, in practice rather limited for skilled workers	Limited
Superior control over work processes	Limited	Low
Supervisor distance	Low	Low
Supervisor discretion over rewards, work allocation, etc.	Limited	Limited

required quality (Frydman and Rapaczynski 1993; Grancelli 1995a; Kozminski 1995; Myant 1993). Large vertically integrated combines were thus characteristic of most Eastern European states, especially where state planners themselves directly encouraged such sector centralisation and integration (Amsden et al. 1994; Hirschhausen 1995). In these respects, Hungary was quite similar to other CMEA countries.

In Slovenia, on the other hand, the much greater availability of imported supplies and the post 1974 break-up of the vertically integrated COALs, encouraged greater horizontal specialisation among the BOALs and increasing reliance on market contracting for supplies. In both economies, though, product ranges were narrow. The CMEA system encouraged high levels of production specialisation, whereby a very small number of producers were expected to supply the whole CMEA market with, say, buses or computers, and thereby reap considerable economies of scale (cf. Amsden et al. 1994). For example, *Ikarus* in Hungary concentrated on making three basic types of buses for the entire former Soviet Union and Eastern Europe—and nothing else. The BOALs in Slovenia were similarly focused on making a very small range of marketable commodities since they were specifically designated as the smallest organizational unit capable of producing separate tradable outputs, although the larger COALs were more diversified.

The CMEA planning system and central target setting discouraged enterprise innovation since changes to products and processes tended to create both difficulties with suppliers and short term disruptions to production runs, which in turn threatened target achievement and, often, managerial bonuses (Filtzer 1992). Additionally, producing new products without a centrally guaranteed demand for them in the CMEA system ran the risk of being penalized for missing targets. As Revesz (1990: 98) puts it: "Following a course dictated by the market was risky (in Hungary) because the regulators might alter the rules of the game overnight...confusion arose from the fact that taxation, wage regulations, credit and the like were controlled by different agencies, each issuing rules and granting exceptions from them." The formal move to indirect regulation of the economy in Hungary did not result in substantial delegation of decision making to enterprise managers, however, because of the combination of the wage regulation system, Comecon export targets and convertible currency targets. Enterprises continued to focus on bargaining with state agencies since these both generated and controlled the greatest uncertainty and access to resources, despite the apparent decentralisation of control over the economy (Berend 1990; Revesz 1990). Target achievement and growth in resources controlled to improve bargaining power thus remained dominant objectives in the late state socialist period (Batt 1988: 253–254; Swaan 1993).

The greater involvement of Slovene enterprises in OECD markets and their greater autonomy in selecting suppliers and customers in the 1970s and 1980s meant that product upgrading and improvement were both feasible and encouraged. Markets were more competitive than in the CMEA system and localities promoted the success of "their" enterprises in the protected Yugoslav market (Lydall 1989: 78–79). Managers had to maintain local employment and remain profitable if they were to retain both the respect of the community and autonomy from political interference (Whitley et al. 1999). Some product improvement and innovation was necessary to maintain demand, since losses invited intervention by local politicians and union leaders, as well as the loss of one's local reputation as a good manager. Decentralisation and some limited competition between enterprises and communes thus encouraged incremental improvements and a concern with employment growth modified by a weak profitability constraint.

Inter-enterprise Connections

Continuing de facto state control of the economy and enterprises in Hungary after the 1968 reforms meant that branch ministries, and their successors in the Ministry of Industry after 1981, exercised considerable formal coordination powers over inputs and outputs in production chains and greatly limited enterprises' abilities to select suppliers and customers. At the same time, the inflexibility of the CMEA system and the shortage economy necessitated managers developing informal connections to obtain the required inputs. As a result, highly personal networks of obligations and favours between large enterprises were established (Frydman and Rapaczynski 1993). Because of the disruptive consequences of changing suppliers and customers, and the resultant effects on target achievement and state evaluations, these connections tended to be quite stable and long term, although those with smaller suppliers were less significant and long lived (Berend 1990; Laky 1992).

Similarly, the continued importance of state connections and bargaining in Hungary meant that vertical links were more significant than horizontal ones and that enterprises competed with those in other sectors to obtain investment funds and exemptions from rules and taxes. Inter-enterprise relations outside the supply chain were, then, predominantly adversarial and little if any collaboration developed. This pattern was reinforced by the union structure that was—and remains—sectorally based.

In Slovenia, in contrast, inputs and outputs were more coordinated through market transactions outside the vertically integrated COALs, although communes and other local bodies encouraged enterprises to obtain their inputs locally and thus develop considerable economic autarky at the local level (Lydall 1989: 79). Unlike Hungary, though, the SME (Small and Medium Enterprises) sector in Slovenia—but not necessarily elsewhere in Yugoslavia—did develop some longer-term linkages with large enterprises (Dyker 1990: 149) and inter-enterprise connections were more flexible.

However, connections across regions were—and remain—less developed, with considerable reluctance among Slovene firms to develop close ties to firms in other parts of the republic. Even within some regions, the highly enterprise-focused loyalties and commitments encouraged by the self-management system limited cooperation between them. This was encouraged by the success of many Slovene firms in the protected domestic Yugoslav market which encouraged the belief among many managers that they could compete effectively on their own (Konjhodvic 1996). Thus, significant variations between Hungary and Slovenia in inter-enterprise relations resulted from differences in central state control and local commitments.

Work Organization and Control

The high level of enterprise dependence on the state in Hungary encouraged an equally high degree of centralised decision making in most Hungarian organizations. Typically, all significant issues were decided by the enterprise director, the party secretary and the trade union leader, together sometimes with the party youth leader (Hethy 1983). Similarly, most organizational units were strictly controlled by the bureaucratic hierarchy and factory managers were subservient to functional directors at the Head Office. The dominant organizational form was functional with long hierarchies between shop floor operation and top management (Dobak and Tari 1996).

Decision making in the BOALs of Slovenia was shared between the top managers, workers representative and local politicians, although the more successful managers were able to dominate these organizations in practice (Dyker 1990; Lydall 1989; Jaklic 1997). The COALs were less centrally integrated than the large Hungarian combines because of the separate nature and rights of their constituent BOALs, which usually sought to increase their autonomy. With political support however, COAL top managers were often able to redistribute surpluses between sub-units and to centralise foreign trading and training.

In both countries managerial and worker mobility was low and managers had to rely on workers' cooperation to meet targets and deal with crises (cf. Kollo 1993). However, their ability to reward good performance was greater in Slovenia, although wide differentials were regarded unfavourably in Yugoslavia (Dyker 1990: 180). This dependence on workers' goodwill—or acquiescence in the need—to manage shortages and poor quality of inputs, as well as machinery failures, generated considerable shop floor autonomy in many Hungarian enterprises, as Burawoy and Lukács have so graphically described (1985, 1992). This autonomy limited task specialisation and Taylorisation of work processes (Nagy 1989).

Although the shortage economy does not seem to have been anywhere near as significant in late state socialist Slovenia, considerable de facto worker independence and flexibility in how tasks were carried out seems to have been the norm in many plants, not least because of the self management ideology and representation system. (Jaklic 1997). Similarly, supervisor-worker distance was low in both countries, partly because of the quite strong egalitarian ethos and partly because of the limited powers of supervisors. In general, their discretion over performance evaluation and rewards were quite restricted, because of centralised personnel administration and the wage regulation system in Hungary and the self-management system in Yugoslavia. Variations in enterprise autonomy and the importance of labour representatives, then, had significant effects on the prevalent work systems in these economies.

Institutional Changes in the 1990s

The major institutional changes in the early 1990s were the Democratization of the political system, the Liberalization of markets and, later on, privatisation. Essentially, the state withdrew from the active management of enterprise strategies and also became more responsive to emerging interest groups. At the same time the CMEA system collapsed, together with much effective demand for Eastern European products. In both Hungary and Slovenia, these changes, together with the break-up of Yugoslavia, meant that managers had to simultaneously deal with the loss of state support and of state coordination of economic activities, as well as with the loss of many or most of their paying customers. Enterprises became much more isolated and left on their own to deal with a much tougher business environment and hard budget constraints.

These changes were less radical in Slovenia than in Hungary because it had been outside the CMEA system and was more oriented to western markets (although firms were, of course, severely affected by the loss of the domestic Yugoslav market). While both states moved from soft budget constraints and considerable enterprise support—whether at the national or the local levels—to much harder regimes which severely reduced risk sharing, Slovene enterprises were more used to operating as quasi-autonomous organizations separate from the state and were not quite so accustomed depending on state agencies for targets and assistance. Slovene firms, therefore, had more experience managing commercial risks and were more able to respond proactively to the loss of domestic markets. In this, they were considerably assisted by state support in funding early retirements of their older and less skilled workers and, in general, appear to have managed much of their reductions in employment through such means (Whitley et al. 1999). Unemployment rose in both countries in the early 1990s, but at a slower rate than many expected.

Considering institutional changes in Hungary and Slovenia in more detail, it is important to bear in mind that these countries are still undergoing considerable change and the nature of the new "rules of the game" remains to be firmly established. Dealing with Hungary first, the key point is that the state's indirect—but nonetheless dominant—role in coordinating economic activities had been greatly reduced completely by the early 1990s. However, the state as a whole remained the only collective agency capable of carrying out large scale societal transformation and was both leading the transformation processes and being transformed by them (Csaba 1995; Holmes 1995; Whitley 1996). Despite being weakened and fragmented by the Democratization and Liberalization of Hungarian society, it was still the central agency coordinating social and economic change. Its responsibilities remained considerable, despite a considerable reduction in its legitimacy, competence and cohesion.

In terms of the separate elements of the state and the political system, the executive (i.e. the cabinet) was relatively stable in Hungary and dominated both the bureaucracy and legislature for most of the Antall government and the subsequent socialist period. The bureaucracy was weakened by the loss of many élite members to private sector posts or retirement and by its low legitimacy from the past domination of party placement (Dabrowski 1994). Although the legislature was obviously more powerful and politically significant than its predecessors, it remained less important than the executive for most of the 1990s, except as an arena for the major political factions to compete for control.

Additionally, the factionalised nature of the political parties, and their often personally based groupings, has meant that the cohesion and integration of the political executive have been much more obviously limited than in the past. Conflicts and debates over transformation policies have been both factional and personal, and have involved the mobilisation of parliamentary groups within the governing parties (Agh 1996; Cotta

1996). Thus, economic and social policies have been more publicly decided and changed through bargains, trade-offs and interest group pressures, and have involved more kinds of collective actors than before. Policy making and implementation have thus been more overtly political and more obviously the focus of conflicting pressures than under state socialism. As a result, policies have also been rather varied, unpredictable and subject to sudden changes (Henderson et al. 1995).

In particular, policies concerned with the management of enterprise debt, privatisation and loss making enterprises have been the subject of considerable disputes and conflicts. Both leading personnel and decisions have been rather unstable following the early decision to avoid Polish-style "shock therapy" and rapid, discontinuous change (Kornai 1996). Relative political stability in terms of the governing parties and leadership in Hungary has thus been accompanied by the considerable instability and uncertainty of economic policies concerned with enterprises and microeconomic management (Bunce and Csanádi 1993; Swaan 1993).

One of the key policy areas for all governments in the former state socialist societies has, of course, been privatisation and changes in enterprise control and funding. In Hungary, the general approach has been incremental rather than radical, with various methods and structures being tried. After the brief period of "spontaneous privatisation" at the end of the 1980s, in which top managers were able to direct the restructuring and partial or total sale of many enterprises largely by themselves (Voszka 1992, 1995), the state recentralised control over the major enterprises and attempted to retain strategic decision making powers for much of the early 1990s. This resulted in considerable political disputes over how, when and what to privatise, as well as frequent personnel and organizational changes (Szalai 1994).

By 1995, the result was extensive foreign ownership of the largest enterprises (Figyelo 1995), not least because of the strong pressures to raise money to service the large foreign debt which had been inherited from the previous regime and the related significant influence of the IMF and World Bank. Voucher sales and similar methods of ensuring domestic ownership and control of large enterprises were, on the whole, less widespread and significant than elsewhere in Eastern Europe. In terms of state-enterprise relations, the state played a significant role in determining large enterprise strategies and their leading personnel in the early 1990s, but this had declined considerably by 1995 and 1996

In contrast, the new state of Slovenia has been less dominated by the political executive and the legislature had greater control over policy choices. Governments in Slovenia have changed more frequently since 1991 and are more fragmented in terms of ruling coalition membership and turnover. The bureaucracy is limited in its powers and capabilities because of the greater influence of parliamentary factions and their leaders, as well as the brain drain to the private sector (Rus 1994). This has meant that central control over the economy has, on the whole, been lower in Slovenia than in Hungary, not least because of the continuing strength of local government and identities.

Furthermore, the ability of many enterprise managers to mobilise support against political control over organizational restructuring and their own appointments/dismissals—which has resulted in considerable delegation of control over privatisation to managers and workers—has decentralised control over the economic transformation process to firms to a greater extent than in Hungary (Kraft et al. 1994; Rus 1994). Because of this, the transfer of ownership and control to private shareholders has been relatively slow in Slovenia and most enterprises of any size remain effectively controlled by internal coalitions of managers and other employees (Whitley et al. 1999). Where state ownership remains significant—as in many loss-making firms—it is usually vested in the Development Fund of the Republic of Slovenia which is responsible for restructuring and subsequently selling state enterprises.

The withdrawal of the state from economic coordination in Slovenia, and from direct state ownership, has, then, been less dramatic than in Hungary because it was not as directly involved beforehand and because the withdrawal process has been more decentralised. While state support for severely loss-making enterprises has continued, especially in the area of sharing redundancy and early retirement costs, enterprise dependence on the state has been lower than in Hungary and managerial autonomy considerably greater.

An additional reason for the continuance of substantial internal control of most Slovene enterprises has been the relatively low external debt burden, and the correspondingly limited role of the IMF and World Bank. The Slovene economy was the richest of the former state socialist societies in 1990 and inherited proportionately limited foreign liabilities—although it has had to assume responsibility for a significant part of the former Yugoslav central bank's debts. This comparatively healthy macro economic position, and the later success of the Bank of Slovenia in reducing inflation and managing the new national currency, the tolar, has meant that external pressures for radical stock therapy have been weak and largely ignored. On the whole, the enterprises have been left to cope with hard budget constraints and market loss on their own without also having to restructure radically their ownership and control relationships before the mid-1990s.

Turning to consider the banking system, the high levels of enterprise and bank debt in both countries, and its often poor-to-bad quality, meant that most banks could not simply be privatised as viable organizations before much of this debt was reorganised in one way or another. In both countries, a considerable proportion was effectively taken over by the state in exchange for government bonds and many banks were reorganised and merged, especially in Slovenia. Despite various debt consolidation programmes and a general restructuring of the financial sector, many banks have remained weak in terms of capital and assets, particularly in Hungary (Abel and Bonin 1994; Bonin and Schaffer 1995), and are unable or unwilling to engage in substantial new lending for industrial investment or to support new firms. Hungarian banks have also preferred to invest in high yielding and low risk state bonds when they have had access to funds. In early 1996 the Hungarian government initiated a large sale bank privatisation programme and by the end of that year control over the largest commercial banks had been sold to foreign ones.

In Slovenia, on the other hand, the previously very close connections between local banks and enterprises may have been reduced by bank reorganization, but personal ties remain and, anecdotally, seem to bypass, formal rules and procedures. Foreign competition has become more significant in both countries, and foreign ownership has recently grown considerably in Hungary, but most firms continue to have substantial borrowings from domestic banks and have not developed close connections to foreign ones. On the whole, financial institutions in Hungary and Slovenia have remained state owned and/or controlled, continue to have substantial outstanding loans to many enterprises and have been reluctant to finance major new investment. This reluctance, or inability due to lack of capital, has been mirrored in many cases by managers' unwillingness take on major liabilities during a period of political and economic uncertainty.

The labour system has also been the focus of many reforms in both Hungary and Slovenia. New legislation has considerably facilitated dismissals, restricted political connections to workplace organizations, limited the role of unions, particularly the formerly privileged communist/socialist party based unions, and generally liberalised labour markets. Education and training systems have also been restructured, but obviously it will take some time before these changes have significant consequences for firms.

At the same time, though, the state in both countries continued in the early 1990s to: (a) limit wage increases through taxation, (b) elicit the cooperation of unions in managing transformation processes, and (c) restrict large scale redundancies by imposing high costs through compensation payments and sometimes assisting employment reductions through other means. Additionally, the reformed and reorganised socialist unions have remained by far the largest and most important representatives of labour interests in the large firm sector, with most of the "new" and "independent" unions gaining little support outside narrowly defined interest groups such as professional white collar workers and other occupationally defined groups which are especially notable in Slovenia (Luksic 1994).

As a result of these contradictory pressures and interests, the dominant institutions governing labour supply and management have by no means radically liberalised the labour systems in either Hungary or Slovenia. While managers unquestionably have much more discretion in managing work and employment relations than in pre-1980 state socialism, they still have to deal with significant union strength in the large firm sector—and with works/enterprise councils—and with continued state intervention in wage policies. They also, of course, remain embedded in established conventions of fairness and appropriate standards of behaviour, especially those concerning supervisor-subordinate relations and wage differentials.

The major difference between Hungary and Slovenia in these respects is the greater importance of enterprise-based unions and councils for managers' ability to implement changes—and, indeed, ensure their own survival—in Slovenia. Close cooperation between top managers and workers representatives has thus been crucial in achieving effective reorganization in Slovene enterprises, although it certainly has not been absent in Hungary.

This brief discussion of some of the major features of the transformation processes and institutional changes in the first half of the 1990s is summarised in Table 2.3. It can readily be seen that the major differences between the two countries concern the power and control of the central state, particularly the government, over enterprise privatisation processes and over local government, coupled with the different connection between local banks and firms and the greater role of the

Table 2.3 Major Institutional Changes in Hungary and Slovenia

	Hungary	Slovenia
A. State Structures and Policies		
State executive dominance over bureaucracy and legislature	Declining but still significant	Low
State cohesion	Declining	Low
State control over enterprises	Declining but still significant	Limited
Central state financial control of local government	High	Medium
Extent of foreign debt and dependence on IMF and WB	High	Limited
Prestige and capabilities of bureaucracy	Limited	Limited
Power of the legislature	Limited	Considerable
Control of privatisation	Centralised in government	Substantially delegated to enterprises
Dominant mode of privatisation of large enterprises	Trade sales to foreign firms	Internal buy-outs plus investment funds and small external shareholders
Liberalization of imports and exports and of internal competition	High	High
B. Banking System		
State ownership/control of banks	High until sale in 1996	High
Bank-Enterprise links	Becoming more remote	Formally weakening but still close in many cases
Bank willingness to fund new large investments	Low	Limited
C. Labour System		
State regulation of incomes	Continuing, but more corporatist and less rigid	Continuing, but more corporatist and less rigid
Labour market reforms	Significant easing of restrictions on hiring and firing, weakening of official unions and of controls on differentials.	
Role of unions	Liberalization of controls on unions, growth of new unions, revival of reformed socialist unions.	
Recognised power of enterprise labour representation	Limited	Considerable
Reform of training system	Significant in both countries but little involvement of employers in curriculum development or credential assessment.	

workforce in both privatisation changes and firms' strategies in general in Slovenia. It can also be seen that the extent of radical change in all aspects of the enterprises' institutional environments in the late state socialist period has been somewhat less than might be expected. The implications of these changes and differences for enterprise type and behaviour will now be outlined.

Enterprise Change in Hungary and Slovenia in the First Half of the 1990s

The Liberalization of the economy and Democratization of the political system in the former state socialist societies can be expected to affect enterprises in three major ways. First of all, the intensification of competition in domestic and foreign markets and the imposition of hard budget constraints encourage enterprises to search energetically for new customers—sometimes at any cost , simply to keep cash coming in—and, eventually, to develop new products and processes to attract and keep customers. Such innovations do, though, require resources, both technological and human, which are typically in short supply in many state owned enterprises (SOEs), especially in the light of the speed with which CMEA markets collapsed. Thus, the common response to market loss and the withdrawal of state support in the former CMEA countries was to seek customers for existing products rather than develop new ones, as well as to try to reduce employment and other costs where feasible and/or gain state help for keeping surplus staff employed. The plurality of political parties and factions sometimes enabled managers to gain political help in the search for state support, as was the case in one Hungarian enterprise we studied in the early 1990s (Whitley et al. 1996a).

Secondly, the increased availability of domestic and foreign supplies—and the improvements in their quality—could be expected to encourage vertically integrated enterprises to close down or sell their subunits producing components to cope with the shortage economy. Again, though, this disintegration may be limited by the desire to keep the workforce employed during the market turndown, and limit redundancy costs. It may, in effect, be cheaper to retain such subunits than to close them and search for new, untried suppliers, at least in the short to medium term (Swaan 1993).

Thirdly, the withdrawal of state support and of state guidance of enterprise activities has meant that managers and workers have had both more autonomy in dealing with economic crises and more responsibility for doing so on their own. In principle, then, managers have had much greater independence and discretion in deciding what to do. However, in practice this has been much more the case in Slovenia than in Hungary, where the state has retained more control over the privatisation and restructuring processes. Slovene managers in the more successful firms have developed coalitions with employee representatives to manage their "privatisation" and retain substantial internal control over strategic choices. Hungarian SOEs, in contrast, have been more state dependent and the state typically has continued to exercise ownership rights quite directly (Whitley et al. 1996a), although managers have of course had more commercial autonomy than before. Where they have been sold to foreign firms or investors, Hungarian enterprises presumably have become integrated into their international organizational structures with limited strategic autonomy— although such integration has not happened very quickly in a number of cases (Whitley and Czaban 1998b).

Considering how this variable increase in managerial independence can be expected to affect decisions about the direction and organization of leading enterprises in more detail, the first point to emphasise is that they are greatly affected by the availability of resources for modernising production facilities and introducing new products. The "decapitalisation" of many plants in the 1980s meant that new investment was widely required in the 1990s, and yet domestic resources were difficult to obtain. Survival was thus a dominant goal in many large enterprises in both countries, but especially in Hungary. Radical change in technologies, products or markets was additionally unlikely given the high dependence on skilled workers to keep machinery working and the common specialisation of managers and workers in one industrial sector, if not indeed a single enterprise. In this situation, we might anticipate attempts to improve product quality to meet OECD customers' demands, and some product upgrading and/or incremental innovation where resources were available, but not substantial discontinuities in economic activities or organizational capabilities given the lack of a market for corporate control and the only gradually developing external labour markets.

Substantial manager-worker interdependence remains in both countries and is likely to restrict both growth by acquisition and radical changes in markets or technologies, while encouraging growth goals (Whitley and Czaban 1998b). This concentration on internal growth has been especially prevalent in Slovenia where the legacy of the self-management ideology and formally recognised participation of the workforce in the appointment of top managers has encouraged employees to consider "socially owned" enterprises to be "theirs" and to see themselves as having some rights to decide over their disposal. In particular, managers have been able to mobilise employee support against outside owners, particularly the investment trusts, on the grounds that they will demand higher dividend payouts and so prevent necessary investment in firms. Such claims are obviously more convincing when enterprises are relatively successful and can offer employees a viable future in their present industry with current resources. It is in the more profitable firms in Slovenia that little change in products, markets and technologies is to be expected. In contrast, depending on the purpose of foreign firm takeovers, we could expect Hungarian firms owned by foreigners to have improved their production processes, introduced new products and sought new markets to a greater extent than other types of firms in either country.

A further difference between some Slovene enterprises and many Hungarian ones concerns their size, which in turn is related to product specialisation. The delegation of control to managers at the end of the 1980s and in the early 1990s in Slovenia extended down to the BOALs and their successor organizations and not just to the COALs. This enabled the more successful firms to secede from their "parent" organizations and become fully-fledged autonomous firms that could keep their surpluses rather than have them reallocated to the less effective subsidiaries of the COAL. As a result, many, if not most, of the conglomerates in Slovenia broke up and the typical Slovene "firm"—or at least those that were profitable—became smaller and focused more narrowly on a limited range of products, often very narrow, such as *Iskra Emeco* which manufactures electricity supply meters.

In contrast, Hungarian enterprises which remained in state hands—or under state tutelage—had every incentive to remain large, or even to grow, since this made them more powerful in bargaining with politicians and the bureaucracy, and more able to dominate the domestic market which was still significant for many SOEs (Swaan 1993; Whitley and Czaban 1998b; Voszka 1995). Generally, the larger the enterprise, the greater the rewards for managers and the more central the firm was to the economy, especially if it did not have large losses. Thus, those which were breaking even or making profits could be expected to remain large, while heavy loss makers—or "crisis SOEs"—and foreign firm owned Hungarian firms would be more likely to reduce employment and the range of economic activities in line with market expectations. This highlights the variable nature of "firms" in emergent market economies, and the importance of state socialist legacies in determining their key characteristics.

These broad expectations for changes in enterprise type are summarised in Table 2.4. It can readily be seen that most are incremental rather than radical, and in many cases extend the pattern already developed in the late state socialist period rather than generating totally different ones. This is partly because the institutional transformations in both societies have not been quite as systematic, discontinuous and all embracing as some would have liked, nor have they been achieved in dramatically short time periods. It also, though, reflects the high level of general political and economic uncertainty in the former state socialist societies in the early 1990s that inhibited significant changes in structures and strategies (Bunce and Csanádi 1993; Rus 1994; Swaan 1993).

While the previous "rules of the game" governing enterprise behaviour and rewards had been largely discarded by the end of the 1980s, new ones were still being developed and strategic decision making has consequently been even more difficult than usual. Not only has it been unclear how to evaluate the likely results of different actions, but the exceptionally fluid political and social environment have made it difficult to pinpoint the crucial interest groups and collective actors which were likely to influence outcomes. This has been especially so with respect to privatisation and state policies on debt management and personnel changes. Given this uncertainty for both enterprises and top managers, there has been little rational basis for making major decisions and eliciting support for them from particular people and organizations. Incremental developments through trial and error were therefore to be expected more than large-scale radical shifts in enterprise type and behaviour. Even in the foreign firm owned and/or controlled Hungarian enterprises, changes have been quite slow in being implemented (Whitley and Czaban 1998b) and firms have sometimes reverted to previous patterns (Mako and Novoszáth 1995).

Similarly, limited changes can be expected in inter-enterprise relations. In the case of Slovenia, of course, the extent and impact of liberalization has been less radical than in the CMEA countries, although the loss of most of the protected Yugoslav market has required many Slovene firms to reorient their sales policies. On the whole, though, established patterns of coordination and collaboration (i.e. limited to local regions and often market based) can be expected to continue in the absence of effective state policies to encourage longer term cooperation between Slovene firms, as well as the continuation of highly localised loyalties and institutions.

In Hungary, on the other hand, the Liberalization of supply and demand relationships, the loss of predictable CMEA markets and decline of branch

Table 2.4 Expected Enterprise Changes in Hungary and Slovenia

	Hungary	Slovenia
A. Enterprise Type		
Backward integration through ownership	Reduced	Reduced
Product range	Broadened where funds available but still limited	Limited
Size	Stable SOEs remain large	Smaller
Innovation	Limited and incremental, dependent on profits	Incremental
Dominant objectives	Survival, finding new markets, growth	Survival, increasing market share and internal growth
Managerial Independence	Greater, but limited in crisis SOEs and foreign owned	High
B. Inter-Enterprise Connections		
Coordination of production chains	Personal links in SOEs, market contracting in foreign owned	Informal links within localities, market contracting
Collaboration within sectors	Reduced	Low
Collaboration across sectors	Low	Low
C. Work Organization and Control		
Centralisation	High but should decline in private firms in medium term	Power shared with employee representatives
Integration of subunits	High but reduced	High
Employer-employee interdependence	Reduced	High
Employee differentiation	Growing	Limited
Task specialisation	Increasing for semi-skilled workers, reduced for skilled workers	Low
Supervisor control	Increasing over semi-skilled workers, less so for skilled workers	Limited, but increasing
Supervisor distance	Increasing in NSOEs	Low
Supervisor discretion	Increasing in NSOEs	Low

based state coordination might be expected to lead to a reshaping of supply networks around market based contracting and declining informal collaboration between firms within production chains. This should be especially noticeable in consumer goods industries where alternative sources of relatively standardised supplies are more readily available and demand changes are more immediate and radical, and in foreign firm owned enterprises that have to fit into already established networks and relationships. While some changes along these lines do seem to have occurred by 1993–94, the predominant impression of many large Hungarian enterprises is of considerable stability of their most significant suppliers and customers up to the mid-1990s, especially among those firms still domestically owned and/or controlled (Whitley et al. 1996b; Whitley and Czaban 1998b). The larger, more capital intensive firms have continued to rely on many of their larger suppliers and have also retained some of their larger customers.

Similar differences in the degree and rate of change between Slovene and Hungarian firms can be expected in the area of labour management and work organization and control. Although both countries implemented quite similar changes in the institutions governing labour relations and organization, their impact on enterprise policies and practices in Slovenia has been weaker than in Hungary because of the greater autonomy of Slovene firms in the 1980s and the continued high level of manager-worker interdependence there. Thus, the liberalization of labour markets and the weakening of unions, while increasing managerial control over work processes and labour management in general, has not radically altered manager-worker relations in most Slovene companies. Despite—or perhaps because of—the high level of interdependence of managers and workers in most Slovene enterprises in the early 1990s, those with financial and/or market difficulties seem to have been able to implement considerable employment reductions (Whitley et al. 1999). As mentioned earlier, this has been greatly aided by generous early retirement schemes.

Furthermore, where expansion has taken place, this has often involved hiring workers on temporary contracts or other forms of flexible employment, despite some unhappiness among labour representatives. Similarly, some of the more successful Slovene firms have been able to implement more flexible working practices and production processes with the support of the unions—as they were already beginning to do before 1990—as long as established supervisory practices and norms continue. Foreign firms practising more "top down" and quasi-Taylorist management styles, on the other hand, have had considerable difficulties in making them effective, as Renault has found out (Globokar 1997).

In Hungary, the changes were more significant because of the greater extent of central state control over wages and unions. However, the resurgence of the reformed socialist unions in the large firm sector has limited the extent of managerial autocracy, and the state has continued to try to control the rate of wage increases throughout much of the first half of the 1990s. In general, employee numbers have been quite markedly reduced in the severely loss making SOEs and many of the privately owned firms, but not nearly so much in the more stable SOEs (Whitley and Czaban 1998b). Compared to Slovenia, reward differentials and the separation of managers from workers have increased in the 1990s, although managers' bonus payments were already growing quite fast in the late 1980s.

The limited extent of state delegation of control to enterprise managers has yet to encourage substantial decentralisation of control within organizations. This is partly because the state recentralised control over privatisation procedures in the early 1990s and still retains quite strong ownership rights and controls over "its" firms, especially those making losses. In the privatised firms, top management control similarly remains strong as the new owners and controllers establish procedures they can trust before delegating day to day decision making and, often, seek to make significant changes. Given the uncertain business environment and, in many cases, ignorance of exactly how these enterprises function, it is not surprising that highly centralised decision making and control was characteristic of many foreign firm controlled companies in the early 1990s (Whitley et al. 1996a; Whitley and Czaban 1998a, 1998b). As new control systems became established and top management's confidence in their understanding of organizational operations grows, we would expect decentralisation to increase.

Turning to consider work systems, we might expect a move to greater managerial control of work processes as pressures to cut costs and impose productivity increase, as well as, perhaps, a reorganization of production processes in a more flexible and responsive manner. Because of the greater influence of employees in Slovenia we would expect radical reorganization of work systems and greater managerial power to be more limited in Slovene firms than in foreign owned Hungarian ones. However, greater employee interdependence and commitment, given the low degree of labour mobility and strong local attachments, could also be expected to facilitate moves to enhance flexibility and the development of multitask, integrated jobs, as happened in one company we studied near Ljubljana (Whitley et al. 1999). Thus, overall in Slovenia we would not expect greatly increased supervisory control of work processes or performance evaluation, but might anticipate increased flexibility of production processes and willingness to trust skilled workers to manage changes in these and improve them.

In Hungary, on the other hand, greater differences between SOEs and private firms can be expected, especially between those SOEs breaking even or better and foreign firm controlled companies. Given the history of over-recruitment of skilled workers and little differentiation between them and less skilled employees in large Hungarian enterprises in the 1970s and 1980s (Czaban and Whitley 1998), together with quite loose supervision practices during the shortage economy (Burawoy and Lukács 1992), we would not expect major differences in the treatment of skilled and semi-skilled workers in the more "stable" SOEs in the 1990s. Neither, would we expect to see a move to much more directive and directly controlling supervisory styles in these enterprises.

In contrast, the foreign firm owned and controlled companies are quite likely to have differentiated between workers on the basis of their skills and contribution and to be more directly concerned with increasing work efforts and output. Because they have access to a range of other ways of managing production and are able to invest in technological restructuring, foreign controlled companies are quite likely to implement changes in production processes and to insist on greater supervisory control in order to gain a significant return on their investment. Supervisors in these firms will therefore be under pressure to improve productivity and act as managers rather than as promoted chargehands. Additionally, managers here will be more likely to allocate the more routine and predictable jobs to less skilled staff while reserving complex and uncertain tasks to the more highly skilled workers and rewarding them accordingly. Greater differentiation of task type and stronger links between task complexity and skills are thus more probable in foreign controlled firms, as is increasing supervisor distance from workers—especially the semiskilled—and discretion over work performance evaluation (Whitley and Czaban 1998a, 1998b).

Conclusions

This brief discussion of the institutional transformations and associated changes in enterprise type and behaviour in two former state socialist societies, Hungary and Slovenia, suggests four main conclusions. First, the extent and consistency of institutional changes in terms of their consequences for enterprises have been rather less radical than was expected by many in 1990. While generating considerable political upheaval and uncertainty, many changes tended to accelerate processes already begun, especially in Slovenia, and did not amount to a wholesale and discontinuous transformation of all the key institutions that affect corporate structures and activities. Furthermore, as we have seen, liberalising and decentralising policies were not infrequently contradicted by political recentralisation and party attempts to exercise control over key assets and positions.

Secondly, the impact of these institutional changes on enterprises varied according to the legacy of the state socialist period, and therefore between countries, and especially according to the extent of the economy's integration into the CMEA system and of the state's decentralisation of control over economic activities. In Slovenia, the transformation of the political system and related institutions has had limited impact on firms' structures and policies because of the considerable decentralisation of control over economic activities already achieved; the firms' considerable experience of, and involvement in, OECD markets; and the slow pace of privatisation and extensive insider control of firms. Transformation had more impact in Hungary because of the greater role of the central state in coordinating the economy. However, contradictory state policies and considerable uncertainty over privatisation procedures similarly limited the extent of enterprise change in the early 1990s and it is arguable that the loss of CMEA markets had at least as significant an impact on firm behaviour, particularly in the short term.

Third, the effects of institutional changes on organizations clearly vary according to the specific situation of each organization and industry. In particular, the financial position and economic viability of an enterprise in these economies had major effects on how their managers and workers responded to these changes. Major loss makers were both more dependent on the state for survival and less attractive to potential purchasers. They were thus unlikely to change their products and technologies and more likely to survive by large-scale cost cutting and state support, retaining essentially the same structure on a smaller scale. Less threatened enterprises remaining in state hands also were not likely to innovate significantly because they usually lacked resources, including skills, for substantial product and technology upgrading, and could not easily obtain them from an indigent state. As long as sufficient surplus was made to service any outstanding loans and to provide working capital, incremental development was the safest policy for managers of these companies.

Finally, it is clear from this discussion that complex organizations do not radically change overnight as the result of institutional transformation, nor do they respond in a single manner to each particular change in their environment or ownership. No doubt the changed contexts in which Hungarian and Slovene firms operate, and the changing nature of the groups and interests controlling them, are altering their natures and behaviour. However, such alterations take time and vary according to specific circumstances and the groups involved.

Furthermore, contextual changes interact so that anticipated deterministic relations between one type of change, such as ownership, and managerial behaviour are too simple given the variety of additional factors intervening and the variability in managers' perceptions of their situation and abilities to act on them. This is especially so when much of the "rules of the game" have yet to be established and both managers and unions, as well as other groups in the process of becoming constituted as collective actors, are able to influence their development. As comparative analyses of industrialisation indicate, the nature and roles of key interest groups during institutional transformation vary significantly between countries and these variations continue to affect patterns of social and economic organization for a considerable period after the initial changes have occurred (Kristensen 1997; Whitley 1992a, 1997).

Chapter 3

Networks, Transaction Costs, and the Persistence of Interfirm Ties: The New York Apparel Industry, 1985 to 1995

Michael Alan Sacks and Brian Uzzi

Sociology is increasingly interested in how social relations influence economic development. Early sociological work examined how institutions, culture, and law create and sanction different economic systems (Swedberg 1994). Recently, the new economic sociology, rooted in the concept of embeddedness, has begun to examine how social relations shape economic behavior in ways not addressed by the seminal theorists or modern economic theory, seeking to directly explicate how social structure affects economic action (Granovetter 1985; Coleman 1988). The promise of this work has been two-fold. First, it has shown that embeddedness is an important feature of economic exchange that enables particular economic outcomes better than competing forms, especially atomistic market exchanges. Secondly, through its use of network analysis and organization theory, this new research has rescued sociology from the absolute sway of the neoclassical paradigm.

This paper attempts to add to research in the new economic sociology by examining the dynamics of tie structuration between firms. Consistent with Gidden's (1984) notion that "the fundamental concept of structuration...[is] repetitiveness...," I analyze structuration with a focus on whether exchange partners repeat contract with one another or dissolve their tie by switching to another exchange partner, a decision I refer to as the stick or switch decision.

The study of the repeat versus switch decision is significant to the study of embeddedness and sociology in a broad sense because of the differences in opinion about the purpose and outcomes of structuration. One line of research considers the study of structuration to be important because of its effect on economic transacting, both positive and negative. Much sociological and policy research views ongoing ties as a key aspect of organizational effectiveness and development (Coleman 1988; Larson 1992; Saxenian 1994; see chapter 10). This literature is replete with references to how "trust develops over time," "ongoing exchanges reinforce reciprocity," "social capital accrues with repeated contact," and "embedded ties permit access to exclusive resources that collect with time." For example, Powell, Koput, and Smith-Doerr (1996) found that long-term ties enable learning-by-doing. White (1981), Baker (1990), and Abolafia (1996) reported that stable ties shape price setting. Romo and Schwartz (1995) found that long-term interfirm relationships condition organization migration decisions. Uzzi (1996b, 1997a) showed that ongoing ties promote organizational adaptation, Pareto-Improvements and economies of time, while Kranton (1996: 846) concluded that "...personalized relationships... significantly affect...the gains from trade. Further study of these interactions is likely to lead to a better understanding of the emergence, disappearance and efficiency of different organizational forms."

Institutional theorists similarly hold that ongoing ties are a mechanism by which firms control their environment, manage critical resource flows, and tap into strategic information (Mintz and Schwartz 1985; Palmer et al. 1986; Stearns and Mizruchi 1986; Fligstein 1990). Finally, population ecologists view organizational inertia as a consequence of successful adaptation to environmental demands (Hannan and Freeman 1989) and they assert that forms of institutional and structural embeddedness boost the survival chances of firms in competitive industries (Baum and Oliver 1992; Amburgey et al. 1993).[1] In contrast, some approaches argue that structuration impedes efficiency and segregates actors. For example, the standard economic view is that efficient markets may "...function [only] without any prolonged human or social contact between parties. Under perfect competition there is no room for bargaining, negotiation, remonstration or mutual adjustment and the various operators that contract together need not enter into recurrent or continuing relations as a result of which they would get to know each other well" (Hirschman 1982: 1473). Standard economics also views behavior ongoing relations with hostility and suspicion because they can shield actors from competitive market forces or interfere with the price system (Goldberg 1980: 50–51). In sociology, Burt (1997) contends that closely-knit networks promote informational constipation, character assassinations, and other organizational malignance.

Another line of research views the study of repeated ties as important because the decision of whether to stick or switch raises questions about the boundaries of organizations as well as markets (Coase 1937; Williamson 1975; Powell 1990; Uzzi 1997b). Williamson (1975), for example, was the first to revive the Coase-ian question of organizational boundaries and to draw attention to the transaction cost factors that influence the decision about buying a product in the market or making the product in-house. This question is important because it not only speaks to the efficient limits of organization, but also helps demarcate the features of the environment over which the firm has jurisdiction. The basic thrust of the argument is that the more an organization can reduce transaction costs by absorbing the other organizations it transacts with through acquisition, merger, or joint venture agreement, the more it can efficiently control its environment.

While transaction cost economists have focused on the formal contractual mechanisms needed to expand or contract firm's boundaries, sociologists took notice of the many informal relationships between firms in markets (Perrow 1993). Here the issues did not concentrate on how formal agreements protect transactors against opportunism, but on how networks of social ties between and among firms mitigate motives for malfeasance and change both the boundaries of the firm and the market (Uzzi 1997a). Networks of firms are legally independent organizations whose absence of arm's-length bargaining and long-term ties distinguishes them from both markets and hierarchies (Lazerson 1995). The boundaries of the firm change because networks enable trust to develop as a governance mechanism and firms to gain privileged access to interfirm resources (Powell 1990; Portes and Sensenbrenner 1993). Similarly, networks blur the boundaries of markets by changing the logic of the exchange process. Thus, whether one approaches the stick or switch boundary question from the perspective of formal ties between and among firms or from the perspective of informal social connections, the issue of whether firms stick or switch becomes important for understanding the boundaries of the firm and the market.

Given the above issues, this analysis has two aims. First, it examines the social structural mechanisms that influence sticking and switching. Secondly, it fleshes out the arguments of embeddedness, a concept which succeeds in critiquing current economic theories, but which only recently has begun to furnish its own concrete account of economic action. In undertaking these tasks, I compare two major theoretical approaches that make predictions about the stick or switch decision: the embeddedness approach (Granovetter 1985; Portes and Sensenbrenner 1993; Romo and Schwartz 1995; Uzzi 1996a, 1996b, 1997a, 1997b) and the transaction cost economic approach (Williamson 1985). These approaches offer different explanations that make their comparison useful to theory development in this area. I do not aim to conduct definitive competing tests of the theories; that is beyond the reach of one analysis. Rather, I aim to illustrate the unique properties of different perspectives and to form a basis for sharpening the embeddedness perspective.

I focus the analysis around the effects of two constructs that have been ascribed a key role in both approaches as well as operationalized in similar ways, although they are called different things in each theory. The first concept is concerned with the level of bilateral exchange between two transacting parties. It is referred to as relationship density in the embeddedness approach and asset-specificity in transaction cost economics (Joskow 1996; Uzzi 1996a). The second concept is network size in the embeddedness approach and small-numbers bargaining in the transaction cost approach. These constructs are similar in that the number of exchange partners used by the focal firm operationalizes both constructs (Pisano 1990). The concepts differ in that each approach predicts that a different set of processes will follow from these structural constraints. Thus, the important differences in these constructs do not reside in their measurement but in how these structural features facilitate or derail processes that increase or decrease the probability of switching.

In the following section, I outline the predictions from both theories, paying special attention to the mechanisms by which these constraints affect the probability of switching. I follow the lead of empirical studies that have employed the above operationalizations in order to maintain a basis of consistency with the current literature rather than attempt to flesh out new empirical manifestations of each concept. I then present the results of a random-effects panel probit model that examines the probability of switching out of a relationship. I close with a discussion of the results and their implications for future work on embeddedness and the boundary question.

Transaction Costs Economics

The transaction cost economic approach presents a framework for understanding problems of contracting and the conditions under which firms shift their organizational boundaries. One line of research within this approach has focused on how governance structures develop and the consequences they have for efficient organization. Another line of research has concentrated on how organizations adapt to the changing nature of their interfirm transactions and the problems of transacting in markets. With regard to the latter question, the transaction costs economic explanation of the boundary question has focused on two major factors: asset-specificity and small-number bargaining (Walker 1994; Masten 1996).

Asset Specificity

Williamson has noted that asset specificity is the big engine of transaction cost economics. While asset specificity has been difficult to define, it has been broadly conceptualized as any specialized asset that would lose value if it were redeployed to other uses or used in conjunction with a different transacting partner. In this sense, asset-specificity can create value that is idiosyncratic to a transaction, but it also creates asymmetric switching costs that in turn create incentives for the more powerful party to bargain unfairly.[2]

There are two propositions on how assets become specialized. In one view, the buyer requires specific assets from the start of the exchange. In the second, which Williamson calls the Fundamental Transformation, a supplier's assets are not specialized in the beginning but become so through idiosyncratic investments, which are often measured by the level of bilateral exchange. For example, Joskow (1996: 105) uses the quantity of coal supplied by a supplier to a coal plant to measure the level of asset-specificity in the relationship.[3]

> Williamson's conceptualization of dedicated assets implies that the importance of this factor in structuring coal supply relationships should vary with the quantity of coal.... The larger the annual quantity of coal that is contracted for, the more difficult it is likely to be for the seller to quickly dispose of unanticipated supplies (if the buyer breaches) at a compensatory price, and the more difficult will it be for

a buyer to replace supplies at a comparable price if the seller withdraws them from the market.

The key transaction cost argument is that increasing asset-specificity creates high-powered incentives to act opportunistically (Lazonick 1991; Lazerson 1995). This occurs because the member of a dyadic relationship with lower switching costs can dicker opportunistically without concern about retaliation from the more constrained partner.

> According to transaction cost theory, when exchange involves significant investments in relationship-specific capital, an exchange relationship that relies on repeated bargaining is unattractive. Once investments are sunk... 'hold-up' or 'opportunism' incentives are created ex post,...[that] make a socially cost-minimizing transaction privately unattractive at the contract execution stage (Joskow 1996: 168).

Once opportunism obtains in the relationship, the propensity to dissolve relations via exit or vertical integration increases as the more vulnerable actor attempts to avoid injury, potential lock-in, or higher monitoring costs. "[W]hen asset specificity is high, outside suppliers are more likely to exercise their self-interest at the buyer's expense. Therefore, when asset specificity is high, in-house suppliers will perform better than outside suppliers" (Walker 1994: 584).[4] These arguments suggest that the higher the level of asset-specificity, the more intensive are the incentives to act opportunistically, and therefore, the higher the probability is that the relationship will dissolve or end in vertical integration.

Small-numbers Bargaining

Small-numbers bargaining is the second major factor in transaction cost economic explanations of organizational boundaries (Pisano 1990). Small numbers bargaining refers to those situations in which an organization has a limited number of partners that can supply it with a critical resource. Transaction costs economic theory argues that as the number of transacting partners for a particular resource declines, "a large numbers bidding condition at the outset is effectively transformed into one of bilateral supply thereafter" (Williamson 1985: 61). Williamson reasoned that this change should have pervasive effects on the motivations of the transacting parties because, once a small-numbers bargaining situation obtains, a buyer cannot credibly threaten to switch to another supplier with the relevant expertise, which in turn creates an incentive for the seller to bargain opportunistically. Under these conditions, the buyer can either withdraw from the exchange to avoid opportunism or absorb the seller(s) through vertical integration. In the context of sponsor (buyer) firms and R&D suppliers, Pisano (1990: 158–159) summed up the relationship between small numbers bargaining and the probability of dissolution of the relationship:

> "...a pharmaceutical company that contracts with an outside supplier has limited options should the supplier bargain opportunistically during one of the renegotiation cycles. Because the sponsor could not credibly threaten to switch partners, it would be stuck in a small-numbers bargaining situation, *which itself creates an incentive for the R&D supplier to bargain opportunistically.* [This] suggests that the costs of market governance for a biotechnology R&D project are related to the number of R&D suppliers.... These hazards provide an incentive for internalization" [or switching]. (Italics added)

These arguments suggest that there should be a direct relationship between small-numbers bargaining situations and the dissolution of the relationship through exit or vertical integration.

While the relationship between the number of suppliers and the hazard of continuing the relationship lead to a clear hypothesis, another line of transaction cost economic logic argues that small-numbers bargaining situations promote opportunism but only in the presence of asset specific investments. This is because a buyer can credibly threaten to exit a relationship with a supplier if there are no asset-specific investments that create bargaining asymmetries in the favor of the supplier (Williamson 1985: 61). Statistically speaking, this proposition is formally an interaction effect between asset specificity and the number of suppliers. It suggests that small numbers bargaining has weak or no effects on continuity at low levels of asset specificity but strong negative effects on the continuity of the relationship at high levels of asset-specificity.

In summary, the transaction cost economic approach builds arguments about the stick or switch decision based on strong assumptions about self-interest seeking with guile and bounded rationality, individual interests and motives that are set in motion by the particular structural conditions of high asset-specificity and small-numbers bargaining. Both conditions are relevant over the course of transacting. In the case of asset-specificity, high levels of asset specificity create incentives for the partner with lower switching costs to bargain opportunistically, thereby driving the other firm to dissolve the tie through exit or vertical integration. In the case of small numbers bargaining, small number bargaining situations create similar incentives for the party with more exchange options to bargain opportunistically, thereby driving the other firm to dissolve the tie through exit or vertical integration, especially when the level of asset specificity is high.

Structural Embeddedness Approach

The structural embeddedness approach extends the work of Weber, Polanyi, and Schumpeter and combines it with advances in organization and social network theory (White 1981; Granovetter 1985; Powell 1990; Portes and Sensenbrenner 1993; Romo and Schwartz 1995; Uzzi 1997a). The basic argument is that the nature of relationships between and among firms and the overall structure of the network within which the firm is embedded influence individual firm behavior as well as the behavior of the entire network. The type of network in which an organization is situated defines the potential opportunities available to it, while its location in the network and the quality of its relationships with other actors demarcate its capacity to access those opportunities.

The embeddedness approach assumes that actors' interests and motives are variable and follow predictably from social structure parameters (Granovetter 1985). These differences in the microbehavioral foundations of embeddedness and the macro structural conditions of exchange are what distinguish the unique logic of embeddedness from other approaches.[5] A key feature is that actors operate under a logic of exchange that results from the distinct social structure of organization networks. This logic has been referred to as the "logic of embeddedness" because ongoing social ties shape actors' expectations, motives, and decision-making processes in ways that differ from the logic of market behavior (Uzzi 1997a). In this logic, actors use heuristic decision rules rather than intensive calculation to make decisions, and aim to cultivate cooperative ties rather than narrowly pursue self-interest. Rationality appears to be neither the super rationality of game or agency theories, nor the bounded rationality of transaction cost economics, but expert rationality (Prietula and Simon 1989). Expert rationality suggests that decision-makers are more heuristic than super rationality posits, yet less boundedly rational because the rate and degree of knowledge transfer is increased and information unevenness between network partners is reduced by the social qualities of the embedded tie (Uzzi 1997a).

In sum, three main notions distinguish this logic and explain the dynamics of the stick or switch decision:
1. Collective rationality as opposed to individual rationality (selfishness interests).
2. Pareto-improved solutions motivate action rather than zero-sum solutions (opportunistic motives).
3. Reciprocity, as opposed to calculativeness, defines the rules of exchange.

The embeddedness approach explicates how the substance of ties, as well as the network of ties in which an organization is embedded, sets in motion the above logic of exchange. The decisive factor is that particular types of social ties can mitigate opportunism, increase resource pooling, and motivate actors to seek positive sum Pareto-improved outcomes rather than selfish gains.

Uzzi (1997a) illustrated this logic using several cases grounded in fieldwork in the New York apparel industry. One case, for example, described a clothing manufacturer that was permanently moving operations from New York City to Asia. Having private information about its intention to relocate, the manufacturer was faced with the dilemma of whether or not to inform its contractors of the relocation. On the one hand, if the manufacturer informed its contractors of its impending move, it put itself in a vulnerable economic position: the contractors might shirk on quality or raise prices because they knew that the manufacturer would be hard pressed to find substitute contractors on short notice. On the other hand, if the manufacturer did not disclose its plans to move, it would seriously and irreparably injure its contractors because they would lack the time needed to adapt to the loss of business.

This case illustrates differences in transaction costs and embeddedness approaches by bringing into focus the point at which rational actors should have strong incentives to act in self-interest and there are no formal constraints (e.g., hostages) that make opportunistic behavior costly. The history of the relationship or the social relationship should play no role in the decision (Williamson 1985). Uzzi (1997a) showed, however, that when particular social structural relationships exist, they set in motion the logic of embeddedness and mitigate opportunistic acts even under those conditions in which they should be most likely to occur.

Consistent with embeddedness predictions, he found that the manufacturer notified those contractors with whom it had a social relationship of the move months before departure in order to help them adapt, while those contractors with whom the manufacturer had maintained an arm's-length relationship were not informed. The manufacturer affirmed that this dichotomy of responses was generated by differences in the social ties between it and its embedded and arm's-length ties. In this case of embedded ties, the history of interaction, the closeness of the personal relations, and the organizations' mutual dependence created a basis of trust and obligation that made disclosure feasible and rewarding.

Conversely, the contractors that received notice of the manufacturer's departure were motivated to reciprocate because of the good intent the manufacturer had showed to them in past transactions and in the current situation. In the case of the manufacturer's arm's-length ties, none of these social structural conditions existed and consequently the logic of market exchange obtained. As one manufacturer stated of arm's-length ties, "It's the opposite [of a close tie], one hand doesn't wash the other. They're the one shot deals. A deal in which costs are everything." Other interviews also focused on the lack of social content in these relationships: "They're relationships that are like far away. They don't consider the feeling for the human being." "You discuss only money."

Thus, while the manufacturer's non-disclosure of his move to arm's-length ties is consistent with transaction cost formulations, the decision to inform his "embedded ties" is difficult to explain. This is especially true because the manufacturer's divulgence of confidential information for the benefit of his close ties actually puts him at an even higher risk of malfeasance by those arm's-length ties that might learn about the move by accident or rumor.

Other noteworthy features of the logic of embeddedness that are exemplified in this case relate to (a) the use of collective rationality and (b) motives to search for Pareto-improved outcomes. Collective rationality refers to microbehavioral decision-making processes that are based on collective rather than selfish interests. This does not mean that persons ignore their independent interests but rather that persons attempt to improve the welfare of others by giving up gains that cost others or by being altruistic. In the above case, the manufacturer considered the effect of his move on the welfare of his embedded ties, even though it was likely to put his interests at risk, because he wanted to help them adapt and because their history of contact generated indebtedness. Typical kinds of responses illustrating collective rationality that were reported by Uzzi (1997a) were: "It is hard to see for an outsider that you become friends with these people—business friends. You trust them and their work. You have an interest in what they're doing outside of business." Another interviewee said, "They know that they're like part of the company. They're part of the family." Dore (1983) and Larson (1992) demonstrated similar outcomes in the examination of Japanese supplier relationships and in the formation of interorganizational ties in the US respectively.[6]

The case also illustrates how embeddedness can generate individual motives for the search for Pareto-improved outcomes. In typical economic based models, individual motives are thought to be opportunistic in nature (Ghoshal and Moran 1996). This case demonstrates that social structure can motive actors to find Pareto-improved solutions to transacting problems that make at least one player better off without making any player worse off. Because the contractors with embedded ties to the manufacturer received notification, they were able to effectively adapt to the loss of business in ways that the arm's-length ties could not. The manufacturer also enabled the productive resources of the contractor to be recovered by increasing the chances that it would make a successful transition to new exchange partners (Uzzi 1997a). The arm's-length ties by contrast adapted by going through a disruptive period of layoffs and financial distress or were forced to shut down by the abrupt departure of the manufacturer (Uzzi 1997b). Similar results have been observed under conditions where incentives for opportunism do not produce malfeasance (Larson 1992; Portes and Sensenbrenner 1993; Granovetter 1994; Lazerson 1995; Powell et al. 1996).

The main implication is that organizations that employ the logic of embeddedness can generate strategic opportunities for sticking with a partner rather than incurring the costs of switching. A key difference is that the unit of analysis in the embeddedness approach is the interfirm relationship as it has developed from its inception. This unit of analysis shifts the focus of inquiry from the qualities of the transaction to the qualities of the relationship.

Another difference is how structuration influences economic action. In the embeddedness approach, relationship density and small ego networks create these outcomes. These structural conditions are important because they serve as sociological analogues to the transaction cost variables of high asset specificity and small numbers bargaining situations. In the next section I outline the arguments by which relationship density and network size affect sticking.

Relationship Density

Relationship density refers to the intensity of exchange between two exchange partners. Like asset-specificity, it is often operationalized as the proportion of total business that is dedicated to a network partner (Burt and Carlton 1989; Baker 1990; Romo and Schwartz 1995; Uzzi 1996a). The embeddedness approach holds that the intensity of exchange at time t is positively associated with stability at time $t+1$. This happens for several reasons. First, trust develops as a function of interaction. The more exchange partners interact, the more each exchange partner samples the other's behavior, thereby building trust and lowering the economic and psychological costs of monitoring and haggling in the ongoing relation (Coleman 1988).[7] Second, Homans (1950) found that the intensity of voluntary exchange between actors increases their level of mutual liking and empathy (see Simon 1952 for similar findings based on a mathematical model). In a similar vein, Granovetter (1985) reasoned that intensive exchanges "generate standards of expected behavior that not only obviate the need for but are superior to pure authority relations in discouraging malfeasance...[and arise in part from] the desire of individuals to derive pleasure from the social interaction that accompanies their daily work, a pleasure that would be considerably blunted by spot-market procedures requiring entirely new and strange work partners each day" (Granovetter 1985: 489). These social forces motivate ongoing interactions because actors are more likely to attempt to settle differences by voice rather than exit and to want to preserve the relationship for its own sake. Consistent with this argument, Larson (1992) and Helper (1990) showed that intensive interfirm relationships promoted the use of voice rather than exit mechanisms that enabled firms to jointly resolve transactional problems through collaboration rather than through "hostage taking" or vertical integration. Uzzi (1996a) found that concentrated exchanges encouraged cooperation because each exchange partner experienced more opportunities to reciprocate and extend non-standard resources voluntarily than they would in short-term arm's-length ties. Taken as a whole, these arguments suggest that the greater the level of exchange intensity, the greater the probability that the organizations will stick rather than switch.

Thus, the root difference between the embeddedness approach and transaction costs economics seems to lie in the assumed responses of human behavior to structural conditions. Whereas the embeddedness approach holds that the intensity of exchange is likely to motivate empathy and an interest in searching for cooperative positive sum outcomes, the transaction costs approach predicts the opposite consequence. Intensive exchange (and its companion, asset-specificity) spurs opportunistic behavior that would make continuation in the relationship riskier than exit or vertical integration. Furthermore, the embeddedness approach does not dismiss the reality that actors can be selfish, but instead views opportunism not as a constant, but as a variable in exchange relationships.[8]

Network Size

The embeddedness approach argues that a limited number of network partners promotes structuration and sticking for several reasons. First, as the network grows in size, the number of substitutable firms in the network also grows which increases the likelihood of using exit to solve problems or to take advantage of new opportunities (Hirschman 1970). Second, large networks limit interaction between exchange partners because an actor's time and resources are spread thinly over many contacts. This reduces the opportunity to establish joint-problem solving routines that can be drawn on to solve problems within the borders of the relationship and decreases the ability of exchange partners to form a shared identity or values that enrich the relationship with value beyond immediate economic returns (Granovetter 1993). Consistent with this argument, Uzzi (1997a) found that organizations with large networks committed more self-interested acts and overlooked more opportunities to act altruistically because opportunism was more easily justified and the benefits of altruism were more difficult to imagine for anonymous trading partners than for partners who were known well. Third, research has shown that large networks produce incentives for opportunism (Helper 1990; Smitka 1991; Dyer 1997). As a firm's network grows in size, it is better able to play the other actors in its network against each other for the purpose of bargaining down price (Baker 1990; Burt 1992: 30). Consistent with this logic, Helper (1991: 820) found that GM's large supplier network was used to whipsaw its suppliers on price.

> US automakers also face a legacy of mistrust, resulting from their years of "cutting the legs out from under…our suppliers," as one Ford executive put it. A supplier

executive, after citing several instances in which his firm had made investments in R&D only to see another firm awarded the contract using his firm's design, described one of the auto companies in this way: "They're nasty, abusive, and ugly... they make uneconomic demands, like 'follow us around the globe, and build plants near ours. *We need good suppliers like you—but if you can't do it, we'll find somebody else.*" (Italics added)

These arguments suggest an inverse relationship between network size and sticking in an exchange relationship.

In summary, the above outline of transaction costs economic arguments and embeddedness arguments suggest that these two approaches to the "stick or switch" question offer diverging explanations. On the one hand, transaction cost economics begins with the assumption that human motives and interests are hard-wired, whereas the embeddedness approach views interests and motives as variable and emergent features of social structure. These differences lead to separate predictions regarding two structural conditions: the level of exchange between partners and the number of trading partners. Transaction costs economics argues that a high level of exchange between transactors leads to asset-specificity, which should produce incentives for opportunism in market relationships because the market provides an incompatible governance structure. Consequently, as the intensity of exchange increases, market relationships should be more likely to dissolve. Conversely, the embeddedness approach argues that intensity of exchange promotes collective rationality and motives for the joint pursuit of Pareto-improved outcomes that bind the relationship more tightly. Similarly, the transaction cost economic approach holds that small numbers bargaining situations create incentives for opportunism by discrediting the threat of exit. On the contrary, the embeddedness approach argues that a small network size signals commitment and increases the likelihood of joint problem-solving, which in turn creates new value in the relationship and increases the probability of stability.

Data and Methods

The data analyzed come from several sources and contain information on the network, organization, and market characteristics of all unionized apparel firms in the Greater New York apparel economy from 1985 to 1995. The data on firms and their networks were collected by the International Ladies Garment Workers Union, now called UNITE (Union of needle trades and industrial and textile employees). UNITE has organized about 85 percent of all the garment firms in the US. These data are considered high quality. To insure reliability, the union has taken several steps. First, the union audits the financial statements of each company to verify their reported transactions with other firms that are also audited. Second, the union physically inspects shops to verify location changes and reported organizational failures. Third, the union locates and organizes most sweatshops in the New York area—helping to reduce sampling bias.

The data record the level of sales, in dollars, between each manufacturer and each contractor and the length of time the two firms have been trading partners. From these data, I derive for each firm a measure of network size and intensity of exchange. Organizational characteristics included in this date base are the age and annual sales volume of each organization and whether it is generalist or specialist. From the New York State Department of Labor, I merged data on the entry and exit rates of firms in this sector. Data on market growth and uncertainty came from the *Merchandising and Operating Results of Retail Stores* apparel industry trade periodical.

The analysis uses a sample of the full data set that focuses on the Better Dress sector of the industry, a midscale market niche that (retails: $80–$180) comprises off-the-rack dresses, skirts, and jackets, typically sells in department stores and chains, and tends to be moderately priced, of good quality, and fashion-sensitive. I focused on Better Dress because the data for this sector were the most complete. Interfirm ties in the Better Dress sector revolve around manufacturers, "jobbers," and contractors. Manufacturers normally design and market a garment, but manufacture only sample designs and collections. The actual production is done by contracting out production to a network of legally independent producers called contractors who grade, cut, and sew the garment together from the jobber's design. The economic exchange relationships examined in this study are between jobbers and contractors.

Thus, these data offer several advantages for the study of structuration. First, the data contain information on the characteristics of "sending" and "receiving" firms—permitting the unit of analysis to be the relationship. Second, these interfirm relationships reflect typical open-market ties; no restrictions, legal or otherwise, prohibit competitive in-house production or limit the number of ties a firm may possess—thus minimizing the confounds that can occur in highly regulated contexts. Third, this conservative setting closely approximates the idealized, perfectly competitive market. There are few barriers to entry, low start-up and search costs, high rates of entry and exit, many substitutable shops, and a low-level of market concentration (New York State Department of Labor Statistics 1988–95; McLean and Padgett 1997).

Measures

Dependent variable. The dependent variable is a binary variable that is coded to 0 if a firm sticks with an exchange partner and coded to 1 if it switches out of that relationship. Sticking implies that a firm reconstitutes a tie with a firm that it has worked with before (when it has ample opportunity to dissolve the relationship and form a new tie). In the context of this study, a tie refers to a production "job" with a finite period of production (e.g., 120 days) and a discrete finished product (e.g., number of garments produced) that define the boundaries of the exchange relationship.

In the apparel industry, the vast majority of jobs between firms follow the fashion seasons of Fall, Winter, Spring, and Summer. For example, a manufacturer may engage a contractor to produce a Fall or Spring collection that spans a continuous set of production days per year. This suggests that the best way to code a stick is if a firm reconstitutes a tie at least once each year. This represents the modal practice of a manufacturer using the same contractor to produce their Spring collection each year. In a few exceptional cases, a firm may transact for a spell with another firm and then "skip" a year before reconstituting their tie. Since fewer than five percent of the cases fit the "skip" pattern and there is no clear theoretical ground for defining it as a stick or a switch, I coded these cases both ways and examined the pattern of results. No differences in results occurred, so I coded it as a stick.

Independent variables. The underlying constructs of relationship density and asset-specificity are operationalized using a continuous variable of the percentage of a firm's total sales that are dedicated to an exchange partner ($RELPROP_{mc}$). The underlying constructs of network size and small numbers bargaining are operationalized using a continuous measure of the number of exchange partners used by the firm ($XPARTNRS_{mc}$). The interaction effect of number of exchange partners and proportion of exchange is operationalized as ($RELXPART_{mc}$). For each variable, the subscript $_m$ denotes that the variable represents a manufacturer's value and the subscript $_c$ denotes that the variable represents a contractor's value. The subscript $_{mc}$ denotes the relative proportion of work that a manufacturer sends to a contractor and the subscript $_{cm}$ denotes the relative proportion of work that a contractor sends to a manufacturer.

Control variables. Several variables were added to the equation to control for organizational and market characteristics that might affect the probability of sticking or switching. RELYRS is a continuous variable that measures the number of years the relationship was maintained between a manufacturers and contractor. Levinthal and Fichman (1988) and Baker, Faulkner, and Fisher (1998) have argued that time in a relationship may be correlated to the propensity to repeat contract in linear or non-linear ways. Since there is no strong theoretical argument for one specification over another, I used the log of RELYRS (LOGRELYR) and RELYRS squared (RELYRS^2) to capture non-monotonic effects. Two organizational attributes, size and age, have been identified as important causes of a range of organizational activities and place in context the effects of unit attributes and social structure on stability (Nelson and Winter 1982; Hannan and Freeman 1989). MKTUNCER measures the level of uncertainty in the retail demand market for better dress clothing and is operationalized using the standard industry measure of the percentage difference between the original price of clothing and its final selling price. Larger markdowns indicate that organizations lacked the information needed to accurately forecast their products' demand. These data are from the Merchandising and Operating Results of Retail Stores (MORS). LOGSALES is measured as the log of the firm's annual sales. ORGAGE is a measure of the firm's age in years. LAGENTRY is the log of the number of births of new organizations in the prior calendar year. LAGEXIT is the log of the number of firms that disbanded in the prior calendar year. MKTGWTH measures the percentage change in sales of the retail market from the previous period as reported in the MORS. Growing markets reflect lower competitive pressures on firms and access to more resources (Gort 1963). I coded each left-truncated tie with an indicator variable, LEFTRUNC to control for left-truncation. Ties existing prior to 1985, the opening of the observation window, are left-truncated if both firms were born before 1985, since this implies that a relationship existed before it was observed in the dataset. Ties in existence in 1995, the close of the observation window, are right-censored. A subset analysis that removed the left-truncated observations from the analysis produced no substantive differences from those reported with the indicator variable for left censoring. PRE1990 is an indicator variable set to one if the relationship formed prior to 1990, a time of heavy retailer consolidation in the apparel industry, and zero otherwise. It is added to control for period effects not controlled for by the other variables. Cases of breakup that coincided to the death of either the manufacturer or contractor were excluded from the analysis since they correlated perfectly with the dependent variables.

Statistical Model

I use a random effects panel probit model with a control for unobserved heterogeneity (Butler and Moffitt 1982). Unobserved heterogeneity is a condition that may create spurious state dependence and needs to be controlled for in populations where time in a state is a potential predictor of the probability of transition from that state (Petersen and Koput 1991). The model has the following form for panel data: i represents the independent units, $i=1, 2, 3,\ldots n$, measured at times $t=1, 2,\ldots T_i$.

$Y_{it} = x_{it}\beta + v_i + \epsilon_{it}$

$Y_{it} = 1$ if $Y^*_{it} > 0$ and 0 otherwise

Where Y_{it} = the probability that firm i and j switch out of their exchange relationship at time t; $v_i \sim N(0, \sigma^2_v)$, $\epsilon_{it} \sim N(0, \sigma^2_\epsilon)$ and v_i and ϵ_{it} are independent and independent of x_i.

Results

Tables 3.1a to 3.1c display the results of the random effects panel probit models in a nested format to reveal the net effects of the control and independent variables. Models 1–3 display the results of just the control variables. Models 4–6 show the effects of combinations of independent variables in the absence of control variables. Models 7 and 8 display the results of combinations of the independent variables in the presence of controls. Finally, models 9 and 10 show the results for the full models.

Models 1–3 suggest that duration dependence, market structure, and unit actor features have an effect, but that these effects are partially netted out by relationship variables. LOGRELYR and RELYR and RELYRS² reveal that time in a relationship affect switching (Levinthal and Fichman

Table 3.1a Random Effects Panel Probit Estimates of the Probability of Switching (1) versus Sticking (0) with an Exchange Partner: Better Dress Apparel Manufacturers and Contractors, 1985–1994

	Models		
	1	2	3
LOGRELYR		.164	
		(.115)	
RELYRS			.172
			(.094)
RELYRS^2			-.021*
			(.009)
MKTUNCER	.146**	.143*	.141*
	(.053)	(.056)	(.055)
LAGEXIT	.001**	.001**	.002**
	(.000)	(.001)	(.001)
LAGENTRY	.000	.000	.000
	(.000)	(.000)	(.000)
MKTGRWH	.057**	.065**	.0565**
	(.013)	(.015)	(.015)
ORGAGE$_M$	.008	.006	.0126
	(.020)	(.023)	(.023)
ORGAGE$_C$	.031	.030	.034
	(.016)	(.018)	(.018)
LOGSALES$_M$	-.110**	-.119**	.122**
	(.019)	(.022)	(.022)
LOGSALES$_C$	-.053**	-.057**	-.058**
	(.019)	(.021)	(.020)
GENRLIST	-.021	-.025*	-.020
	(.087)	(.096)	(.093)
PRE1989	.140*	.171**	.1221
	(.063)	(.071)	(.069)
LEFTRUNC	-.610**	-.715	-.641**
	(.067)	(.104)	(.094)
CONSTANT	-7.71*	-7.82*	-7.48*
	(3.13)	(3.29)	(3.24)
# of cases	7369	7369	7369
Chi^2	174.56	44.42	182.99
Rho	0.393	.478	0.459
Pseudo Rho^2	0.0198	0.020	0.020

*: $p<0.05$; **: $p<0.01$. All tests two-sided. Subscripts explained in text.

1988) and suggest that the quadratic specification offers a marginally better fit using the pseudo R^2 criterion. MKTUNCER lowers the probability of switching as expected (Podolny 1994), but this effect disappears once relationship variables are introduced into the model. This suggests that the effect of market uncertainty is reduced when other variables related directly to the relationship are controlled for statistically. In line with Kranton's (1996) argument that abundance lowers the need for cooperation among traders, MKTGRWTH increases the probability of switching. LAGENTRY had no statistical effect, while LAGEXITS has the expected effect of increasing the probability of breaking up standing relationships (Kranton 1996). The effect of FIRM_AGE suggests that older firms are more likely to dissolve their ties but the statistical significance of this effect varies widely by model, which alludes to the need for a cautious interpretation of this variable. Consistent with Podolny (1994) and Uzzi (1997a), LOGSALES has a positive effect on the likelihood of sticking.

Models 4–6 as well as models 7–10 demonstrate a consistent set of patterns regarding the effects of the main relationship variables on the probability of sticking or switching. Consonant with the embeddedness approach, the effects of bilateral exchange and number of trading partners are positive and negative respectively whether they are entered with or without controls. These results indicate that an increase in the level of bilateral exchange (RELPROP) decreases the probability of switching exchange partners across all models. As noted above, this result fails to support transaction cost economic arguments. According to transaction costs economics, intensity of resource exchange increases the level of asset-specificity which is supposed to promote opportunism and create high powered incentives to break off the relationship or formalize it through vertical integration (Joskow 1996). Future analysis should further examine these issues and the scope conditions under which embedded ties result in stability as opposed to instability or intercorporate absorption.

The results for number of exchange partners (XPARTNRS) are also consistent with the embeddedness approach. Stable findings across all models indicate that the smaller the network, the greater the likelihood of sticking. In contrast, transaction cost economics arguments hold that small networks should produce incentives to act opportunistically—thus building up pressure to rupture the relationship. Future research should continue to examine these important differences and the conditions under which small numbers bargaining begets opportunism or lays the foundation for embeddedness.

Table 3.1b Random Effects Panel Probit Estimates of the Probability of Switching (1) versus Sticking (0) with an Exchange Partner: Better Dress Apparel Manufacturers and Contractors, 1985–1994

	Models		
	4	5	6
RELPROP$_{MC}$	-1.59**		-1.32**
	(.087)		(.121)
RELPROP$_{CM}$	-1.10**		-.888**
	(.054)		(.097)
XPARTNRS$_{MC}$		.000	.000
		(.001)	(.001)
XPARTNRS$_{CM}$		.147**	.060**
		(.008)	(.010)
RELXPART$_{MC}$			-.023**
			(.005)
RELXPART$_{CM}$			.000
			(.020)
CONSTANT	0.347**	-1.07**	-0.007
	(0.31)	(0.52)	(0.07)
# of cases	7809	7818	7809
Chi^2	50.74	247.72	39.52
Rho	0.187	.400	0.168
Pseudo Rho^2	0.163	0.033	0.172

*: $p<0.05$; **: $p<0.01$. All tests two-sided. Subscripts explained in text.

Finally, the interaction effect of RELPROP and XPARTNRS (RELXPART) provides the most stringent test of the effects of bilateralbilateral exchange and number of network partners on relationship switching. The interaction term, RELXPART$_m$ is negative and significant. This suggests that the effect of a small network on the probability of sticking is not dependent on the level of bilateral exchange. Rather, the effect of a small network is positive at any level of bilateral exchange. In contrast to this pattern of results, the transaction cost economic model suggests that small numbers bargaining should lead to the dissolution of the relationship, especially in the presence of high levels of asset specificity (Williamson 1985). Finally, the interaction term for contractors (RELXPART$_c$) was not statistically significant, which also rebuts transaction cost economic predictions. Taken together, the results for RELPROP, XPARTNRS, and RELXPART align with predictions from the embeddedness approach, even in the presence of key controls and in an

Table 3.1c Random Effects Panel Probit Estimates of the Probability of Switching (1) versus Sticking (0) with an Exchange Partner: Better Dress Apparel Manufacturers and Contractors, 1985–1994

	Models			
	7	8	9	10
Independent Variables				
RELPROP$_{MC}$	-1.46**		-1.22**	-1.20**
	(.131)		(.146)	(.146)
RELPROP$_{CM}$	-1.23**		-1.24**	-1.24**
	(.084)		(.126)	(.126)
XPARTNRS$_{MC}$		.009**	.010**	.010**
		(.001)	(.001)	(.001)
XPARTNRS$_{CM}$		.125**	.050	.052**
		(.008)	(.011)	(.011)
RELXPART$_{MC}$			-.012*	-.013*
			(.006)	(.006)
RELXPART$_{CM}$			.038	.0350
			(.021)	(.021)
Control Variables				
LOGRELYR			.133	
			(0.081)	
RELYRS	.226**	-.158*		.223**
	(.075)	(.068)		(.076)
RELYRS^2	-.030**	.004		-.030**
	(.008)	(.006)		(.008)
MKTUNCER	.059	.110*	.057	.0564
	(.052)	(.045)	(.051)	(.052)
LAGEXIT	.001	.001*	.001**	.0008
	(.001)	(.000)	(.001)	(.001)
LAGENTRY	0.00	0.00	0.00	-0.00
	(.000)	(.000)	(.000)	(.000)
MKTGRWH	.023	.034**	.030*	.0215
	(.013)	(.011)	(.014)	(.013)
ORGAGE$_M$	-.001	.035*	.015	.0206
	(.018)	(.016)	(.018)	(.018)
ORGAGE$_C$	.013	.056**	.035*	.0386*
	(.015)	(.013)	(.015)	(.015)
LOGSALES$_M$	-.060**	-.169**	-.155**	-.156**
	(.020)	(.024)	(.028)	(.029)
LOGSALES$_C$	-.140**	-.135**	-.169**	-.170**
	(.022)	(.017)	(.025)	(.024)

*: p<0.05; **: p<0.01. All tests two-sided. Subscripts explained in text.

Continued on next page

Table 3.1c (*Continued*)

	Models			
	7	8	9	10
GENRLIST	-.053	.016	-.018	-.019
	(.076)	(.064)	(.075)	(.075)
PRE1989	.0470	.014	.051	.0070
	(.063)	(.055)	(.062)	(.063)
LEFTRUNC	-.217**	-.327**	-.254**	-.196**
	(.075)	(.069)	(.075)	(.074)
CONSTANT	-1.23	-3.94	-0.138	0.019
	(3.06)	(2.70)	(3.06)	(3.05)
# of cases	7369	7369	7369	7369
Chi^2	12.61	0.21	8.95	8.00
Rho	0.181	0.032	0.156	0.152
Pseudo Rho^2	0.1802	0.059	0.190	0.191

*: $p<0.05$; **: $p<0.01$. All tests two-sided. Subscripts explained in text.

industry that is unlikely to be biased in favor of the embeddedness thesis. The implications of these findings are that social structure plays a unique role in the structuration of business ties and in the boundary of markets and networks.

Conclusion

Recently two questions have become important to the study of organization and economic development. The first concerns the factors that increase or decrease the structuration of economic ties. The second question concerns the extension of the markets and hierarchies boundary question (i.e., the make or buy decision) to the level of markets and networks (i.e., the stick or switch decision). This study examined the factors that affect the propensity of organizations to stick with exchange partners when transactions are finite and discrete in the context of manufacturer-contractor relations in the New York apparel industry. Two theoretical frameworks were used to analyze the dynamics of stick and switch decisions: transaction cost economics and the embeddedness approach. Consistent with the embeddedness approach, increasing levels of bilateral exchange and a limited number of exchange partners increased the propensity to stick with an exchange partner. These results are interesting because the transaction costs economics framework suggests that high levels of bilateral exchange and/or a limited number of exchange partners should increase the propensity to switch—since these factors increase asset specificity and create small numbers bargaining situations respectively. Moreover, support for the embeddedness approach suggests that actors' motives and interests are not hard-wired but are variable and predictably emerge from social structure. Future work in economic sociology and the embeddedness approach that examines how social structure influences rationality and motivates the search for Pareto-improvements and the use of reciprocity in critical exchange relationships seems fruitful, particularly in regard to the question of the boundaries of markets and networks.

Acknowledgement

I thank Jia You Sheu, Ruey-ling Tzeng, Tony Tam, and Kuo-Shien Su, for their valuable comments. The financial assistance of Academic Sinica is gratefully acknowledged.

Notes

1. Interest in structuration is widespread in the social sciences: the right to make or break ties is a first principle of law (Macneil 1978) channels is a subfield of marketing (Iacobucci and Hopkins 1992); client—auditor attachments is a sub-discipline of accounting (Levinthal and Fichman 1988); and in management (Harrison 1994) and public policy stable interpersonal and intercorporate ties are considered essential to economic development.

2. Asset specificity supposedly takes on importance only "in conjunction with bounded rationality/opportunism and in the presence of uncertainty" (Williamson 1985: 56). While this qualification is consequential, it applies to isolated cases only. First, bounded rationality and uncertainty are ubiquitous in real-world transacting (Simon 1991). Second, Williamson (1996: 51) has noted that "…all forms of organization are subject to the hazards of opportunism." Thus, their existence is assumed in my description of the effect of asset-specificity on dissolution.

3. Four types of specific assets have been identified. Site-specific assets are immobile once placed at a site and affect transport and inventory costs. Physical assets are specific to a design and lose value in other applications. Dedicated assets are investments by a supplier in the good of a buyer for the sole prospect of selling a product to a buyer. Human assets are intangible and include tacit know-how and learning-by-doing. In the apparel industry, four types of specific assets can develop, although site specific investments in technology or people are unlikely to be immobile once placed at a site. I do not attempt to distinguish between types of specific assets but simply note that one or all may develop in line with the theory's predictions (see Lazerson's [1995] discussion of asset-specificity in the apparel industry).

4. See Walker and Weber (1987), Lazerson (1995), Pisano (1990), Coase (1991), Smitka (1991), Freeland (1996), and Masten (1996) for empirical analyses of make or buy decisions that examine the role of asset-specificity.

5. Williamson (1985: 50) uses a 2x2 to classify exchange theories on two dimensions: Actor's Motivation (self-interest vs. cooperative) and Actor's Rationality (Bounded vs. Pure). Embeddedness does not fit neatly into this scheme because actor's motivations and interests are not purely selfish and boundedly rational (e.g., TCE), nor purely selfish and purely rational (e.g., agency and game theory), nor purely cooperative and boundedly rational (e.g., team theory). Rather they are emergent properties of the social structure within which actors are embedded. Embeddedness would add a new row for rationality (expert rationality) and a new column for motives (emergent rationality) to Williamson's typology. Thus, Williamson's typology appears best suited for ontological categorization of economic rather than sociological theories of exchange (Uzzi 1997a).

6. These causal mechanisms are buttressed by ample social science research which shows that close personal ties or identification with a distinctive group heightens empathy, which increases altruistic behavior—an outcome which is itself sustained by social and psychological processes that are set in motion by embedded ties (Batson 1990).

7. Economic based accounts observe that some level of trust is important for the functioning of the economic system (Arrow 1974). These accounts leave out an explanation of the origins of trust or assert that it follows from some generalized norm of business conduct that exists because it rationally benefits everyone in the system. These arguments are difficult to reconcile with the standard assumptions of free-riding and opportunism however and leave unanswered the key question of discerning when trust is operative, latent, or eclipsed by avarice.

8. On this point, see Ghoshal and Moran's (1996) critique of transaction costs economics. While their sophisticated argument is not quickly summarized, a main conclusion is, "...even though one contextual variable (i.e., asset specificity) may systematically influence an individual's perceived valance of (or scope for) opportunistic behavior and another variable (i.e., sanctions) may moderate the individual's expectancy from this behavior, context is believed not to have any effect on the individual's attitude toward opportunism that is independent from its effect on opportunistic behavior" (Ghoshal and Moran 1996: 19–20). Ronald Coase the creator of transaction costs economics, makes a similar critique. He cites as evidence the paradigmatic example of A. O. Smith, GM's supplier of asset-specific auto frames. "It is difficult to believe that this business relationship could have continued for over fifty years if either General Motors or A. O. Smith had acted opportunistically...It would appear either that General Motors did not do so or that A. O. Smith was a slow learner" (Coase 1991: 70–72).

Chapter 4

The Transformation of Family Firms in Taiwan under Initial Public Offerings

Yunshi Liu and Kuang S. Yeh

In his seminal book, *The Visible Hand*, Chandler (1977) proposed that "as the multiunit business enterprise grew in size and diversity and as its managers became more professional, the management of the enterprise became separated from its ownership" (p. 9). Since Berle and Means (1932) raised the issue of separation of ownership and control 60 years ago, corporate governance remains one of the most exciting research topics in various disciplines, including law, economics, and organization theory (Blair 1995). With the increasing importance of business sectors in developing countries, study of the evolution of governance structure should be one of the most important research topics in institutional development.

Virtually all of Taiwan's private businesses were established after World War Two when the Nationalist government took over Taiwan's sovereignty from Japan. A great number of these businesses are still under the original founders' control. However, as time passes, many of these founders are gradually relinquishing control to their successors. Many of these firms are in fact in the process of transformation from traditional small family-managed systems to modern large professionally-operated business systems in which the demands for capital and organizational expertise are serious issues that must be dealt with. Although firms can become more professional no matter whether they remain private or not, the regulatory and institutional environment in Taiwan makes it difficult for unlisted private firms to raise capital and recruit qualified professionals. As a company goes public, it can greatly increase its funding capability through public capital markets. In order for a private firm to become a public company, however, it has to fulfill strict regulatory requirements that require the company to follow certain managerial professional standards. Thus, the standard which companies must ultimately achieve in order to benefit from initial public offerings (IPOs) allows them to concurrently solve both capital and management problems.

Through interview with representatives from 20 public companies, five private companies, one accounting firm, and three underwriters, Yeh et al. (1996) have found that the IPO incentive has been an institutionalizational force for transforming management practices in Taiwan's business community. After IPO, a firm can rapidly raise needed expanding capital and increase its size.[1] That is, the IPO is a process that increases the legitimacy, and thus survival chances, of companies (Meyer and Rowan 1977). This process includes the rational and non-rational issues of diversification of capital-funding sources, improving the company's image, and increasing the owner's "face," or prestige. Moreover, all three of the institutional processes described by DiMaggio and Powell (1983), namely coercive, mimetic, and normative are involved in the IPO process. Firms preparing for IPOs experience coercive government influence, mimetic influences from companies that have carried out IPOs successfully, and normative influences from professionals such as underwriters. Therefore, for Taiwanese companies, the IPO can be a very important event or opportunity for organizational changes or developmental processes. This research thus continues the work of Yeh et al. (1996) and Yeh (1997) by looking at the effect of the IPO process on Taiwan's businesses, specifically inquiring as to whether family members decrease their board participation, paving the way for the separation of ownership and management. Further, because regulatory requirements and constraints are much more strict for public companies than for private firms, and because listed public companies are subjected to all kinds of scrutiny from various investors, in this paper we also examine whether the transformation process continues after companies have become public institutions. To our knowledge, no other research on Taiwan has dealt with the issues with which we are here concerned.

It is difficult to define and categorize what "family-owned business" means exactly (Litz 1995). Here we define a family-owned business as a firm whose major executives are members of one or several families, and most likely are related to the firm's founder(s). The families are also major shareholders of the company. In other words, a family-owned business is *owned and controlled* by a family or a few families. Hereafter in this paper, we use the above definition, unless otherwise specified. For the sake of efficacy, we simply use the phrase *family firm* to mean family-owned and controlled firms. By this definition, most Taiwanese companies are family firms, regardless of their size, public or private, although it is possible that a family might own less than 50 per cent of a public company's stock and the company still be considered a family firm. Based on an examination by Peng (1989), of 46.3 per cent of the top 200 manufacturing companies, the chairman of the board and president are either father and son or these positions are held by the same person whose family is most likely the largest non-institutional shareholder. In the top 50 companies, the ratio of companies with the chairmanship of the board and presidency held by father and son (or the same person) is even bigger, at 63.4 per cent. Yeh and Tsao (1996) investigated succession processes for top management of the top 25 firms in 1972, and found that by 1992, 23 out of 25 firms had either completed or were in the process of completing the succession by transferring the management control from father to son. It is thus clear how entrenched family-owned companies are in Taiwan.

As Taiwan's economy is moving from entrepreneurial capitalism, where most firms are owned and managed by entrepreneurs, to managerial capitalism, where most firms are managed by professional managers, it is important and interesting to know whether corporate governance structures move from traditional family-owned to modern professionally managed styles. Will the IPO process allow the interests of companies to become independent of families, promote the appointment of talented professionals into important management positions, and decrease the role of the family, thus rationalizing the companies' management? In other words, will the separation of ownership and management become more institutionalized in Taiwan's business community? This question is the crux of this paper.

To answer the question raised above, this research attempts to gain an understanding of the nature and composition of the companies' boards. In this paper, we first classify the board types based on directors' relationships, and then try to discover if the distribution of the board types has changed through the IPO processes. We then use the proportion of family members or close friends on the board as an indicator of the changing processes. We attempt to explore whether companies tend to become less family-controlled through the IPO processes, specifically addressing the question of whether or not the proportion of traditional types of boards and family members/friends tends to decrease after companies go through IPO processes.

Below, a brief description of the institutional environment of IPOs and boards of directors in Taiwan is followed by a literature review, descriptions of relationships, board classification and data collection. An analysis of the evolutionary change of board composition is then presented, followed by a discussion of our findings and conclusions.

Institutions of the IPO and the Board in Taiwan

Institutions of the IPO

The Taiwan Security Exchange (TSE), which includes the Taiwan Stock Market, was established in 1961. The Market officially began operations the following year when only 16 companies had carried out IPOs at the time. Before 1985, the Market was not very active, with only about 100 companies listed. The Taipei Composite Index (Taiex) had been below 1,000 points for a long period, and the trading value was only about US$100 million. On average, no more than 10 companies went public each year. There used to be a saying in the business community that "a good company will not go public, only those bad companies who need to suck money from the capital market will go public." Many firms interviewed by us stated that one major reason for them to keep private in the old days was the following way of thinking: "Why do we want to share our profits with other people?"

Beginning in 1986, however, fluctuations in the stock market grew in range due to Taiwan's rapid economic growth and to the maturity of Taiwan's capital market. The Taiex rose tenfold, from 839.73 to over the 10,000 in 1989 alone. The Taiex plunged to 3,000 points the following year, however. Since then, the Market has been steadily fluctuating between 3,000 and 10,000 points each year from 1991 to the present. With the maturity of the capital market, the belief that "a good company will not go public" has been gradually reversed. Now, the general public believes that only good and qualified companies are capable of going public. Interviews in Yeh et al. (1996) indicate that one major reason for companies to go public is "to enhance corporate image" (p. 22). After a company successfully carries out IPO, the pressure for maintaining corporate performance and image is much greater than the pressure on a private firm. Due to this change of concepts and beliefs, there has been a sharp increase of IPO firms since 1985. Calculating statistics from various issues of two official series, *Taiwan Stock Exchange Materials* and *Taiwan Securities and Futures Management,* about 30 firms on average have gone through IPOs each year since 1985. As of the end of 1996, the trading volume on the Taiex has expanded to about 4 billion U.S. dollars, and 385 Taiwanese companies were listed on the Market. It is estimated that there are still about 300 companies that are presently "under guidance" in preparation for being listed on the market. Of these companies, it is estimated that one-half to two-thirds will be approved to go public.

Compared to the USA, Hong Kong, and Singapore, Taiwan has relatively strict procedures and regulations for companies going public[2] (Tung 1996). To get approval for an IPO, companies must meet the requirements of the Securities Exchange Commission (SEC). According to the regulations, companies that plan to go public have an obligation to reveal their financial information first. The companies must then choose an accounting firm and security underwriter(s) to guide them for a 2-year-minimum term of IPO preparation. When a company is ready, the company will then file an IPO application, which includes auditing and evaluation reports from the accounting firm and underwriter(s). After 1–2 months of documentary review and on-the-spot auditing carried out by the TSE, the report produced by the TSE investigators must be submitted to and get approval from (in that order) TSE's IPO department, review committee, and board of directors. After the company completes the review process, it must submit the IPO agreement to the SEC, and begin the public offering. This entire process lasts approximately two and a half years. Going through all necessary requirements, firms have to show tenacious patience to prepare and adjust to many operational routines, such as an internal control system and auditing procedures. Many of those adjustments are necessary because traditional family-owned firms are used to mixing the family property with that of the business. When the application goes to TSE's review committee, executives from the applicant firms have to stand for "oral examinations." Questions regarding the firm's future business plans, relationships between directors and executives, investment status, and related issues are raised in the oral examinations. According to Yang (1996), the review committee is especially concerned about the possibility of directors using company's resources to advance personal interest. On the other hand, some firm owners also like to use IPOs as a justification or opportunity for pressuring employees to make the company more competitive, since employees might have to change their work habits to get IPO approval (Yeh et al. 1996). Thus, it is clear that the IPO can be an institutionalization vehicle for corporations to engage in organizational change.

Institutions of the Boards of Public Companies

Regulations are fairly strict in terms of the position and stock holdings of the directors of public companies. These regulations stipulate that the board members of companies must also be shareholders, often very large shareholders, and that they must maintain their positions as shareholders during their terms as directors. According to government regulations, total shares owned by the entire members of the board have to be larger than 15 per cent for companies having less than NT$300 million capital, larger than 10 per cent for companies having capital between NT$300 million and NT$1 billion, larger than 7.5 per cent for companies having capital between NT$1 billion and 2 billion, and larger than 5 per cent for companies having capital larger than NT$ 2 billion. At the end of 1996, there were 385 public companies and 86.5 per cent of these firms' board holdings were more than or equal to 10 per cent. One has to be reminded that most of these directors are non-institutional investors. Thus, directors' share holdings are quite large. In essence, it appears that discouragement of the separation of ownership and management is the spirit of the stock holding regulations. Therefore, it is difficult to demonstrate whether or not IPOs can cause firms' ownership to be separated from management.

In *Investor Capitalism*, Useem (1996) argues that institutional investors such as fund managers can now exercise tremendous power on board structures in the United States. The situation is very different in Taiwan. The total holding of institutional investors only accounts for about 4 per cent of total stock market capitalization, and typical trading volume is only around 8 per cent to 10 per cent of the total trading volume.[3] In other words, most stock holdings and trading are held and exercised in the hands of individual investors in Taiwan. Firms and their boards, therefore, are more likely to be under family or individual control in such situations. Through complicated arrangements, such as cross share-holding, the controlling family can effectively command many resources from the company and other related businesses.

To protect minority shareholders' interests, public firms are required to have independent auditors who are to perform tasks similar to that of an auditing committee in a U.S. public company's board of directors. Auditors have to be shareholders of the company and cannot exercise voting power on the board. Auditors, however, represent shareholders in supervising corporate financial operations. They have the right to investigate any financially related corporate matters. However, many auditors are relatives of directors, and it is very unlikely that auditors perform their required functions independently. However, the common practice in Taiwan is for auditors to be equated with directors; therefore, in this paper we do the same.

A board needs to have at least 3 directors and 1 auditor who are elected by the shareholders in a general meeting. As indicated earlier, directors have to be stockowners and they are required to be re-elected every three years. The size of boards varies from 4 (required minimum of 3 directors and 1 auditor) to more than 20 directors. Most of the companies have about 6 to 10 directors. Usually, the controlling family uses complicated tactics to control every seat of the board often by proxy. When the controlling family invites institutional investors to invest in the family business, some seats of the board might be yielded to institutional investors. Sometimes, the controlling family does not have enough votes and loses some seats to individual investors. Occasionally, the controlling family might even lose control of their firm. This process may be construed as being a form of merge and acquisition (M/A) Taiwanese style. M/A are not strategic competitions between firms, but more likely to be competitions between individuals or families.

Literature Review

There is much academic research that investigates Taiwanese businesses (Gereffi and Pan 1994; Hamilton and Biggart 1988). This is especially true following the increased vitality visible in Taiwanese businesses and Taiwan's growing political and economic influence, which has sparked great interest among scholars. Literature on board structure and composition in Taiwan, however, is very limited. In the following, we focus on family businesses and boards in general. Since the IPO is an institutional process, this research employs perspectives from institutionalism to study the evolution of governance structures. Literature on institutionalism, therefore, is also reviewed.

Family Businesses

Family businesses are the predominant form of enterprise around the world (Gersick et al. 1997). In overseas Chinese businesses, the family form is also the most important and common form of organization, even among large public corporations (Redding 1993). Taiwan is not an exception. One would not be able to understand the actual operations of Taiwanese businesses without a discussion of family businesses. As is mentioned in the introduction, most Taiwanese companies are family businesses by the definition employed in this paper, regardless of their size and public or private status. Family businesses have advantages such as very fast decision making and action taking. However, some less positive characteristics of Taiwan's family businesses are apparent: protection and favoritism among relatives, business succession based on kinship ties, a family-style way of conducting business, autocratic management, a confused organizational structure, and a non-systematic distribution of labor and specialization (Hwang 1988; Wong 1985; Negandhi 1973).

The above characteristics of family businesses prevent them from beginning the process of instituting modern corporate management practices (Redding 1993; Hwang 1988). When the overall corporate interests conflict with that of the family, the interests of the company are often forsaken to the interests of the family. In fact, directors and executives transfer firms' resources for their private uses and scandals such as insider trading are quite common in Taiwan. This is one major reason why the TSE's review committee is very much concerned about the relationships between directors and executives. They are afraid that minor stockholders' interest might be sacrificed by major stockholders' via inside trading and embezzlement. Presumably, by going through strict regulatory requirements, executives at public companies will act on behalf of the general shareholders and not only family shareholders. By passing many requirements set up by the SEC during IPO processes, firms are expected to strengthen, systematize, and modernize their business organization and management structure (Yeh et al. 1996).

Most studies of family business in Taiwan focus on fiscal issues and the proportion of shares that families actually control (e.g., Wu 1996; Shih 1994; Hwang 1993). Few have investigated the relational structures among board members and executives. These relational structures, however, are the keys to understanding the nature of Taiwanese businesses, since relationship (*guanxi*) is a dominant determinant in many important business decisions. Although it is fair to state that virtually all of the major businesses in Taiwan are family controlled, it is not always clear from the complex shareholding structure how these families control these businesses. The issue becomes even more intriguing since the controlling family might include close friends in its governing bodies.[4] The relationships between close friends can be categorized as quasi-family type (Chen 1994). The families also often utilize investment companies or other institutions (e.g., non-profit institutions such as hospitals controlled by the family) to hold stakes in companies or to avoid paying tax. It is, therefore, probably not enough to examine board composition in order to understand the complex nature of family-owned businesses in Taiwan. Studying governance structure, however, is one of the first steps to probe this maze.

Board

Since the board of directors represents the governance structure of a company, one cannot overstate the importance of board study. Pettigrew (1992) has commented that the study of boards is among the most under-researched of management topics, but should rank near the top of any management scholars' lists of priority areas for the 1990s. In the past few years, research on boards has gradually gained attention from scholars. Several studies have focused on board composition and how it is related to corporate behavior and performance (e.g., Westphal and Zajac 1997, 1995; Daily and Dalton 1994; Stearns and Mizruchi 1993). Board compositions in these studies are broadly defined by board directors' demographic attributes. Therefore, much of the literature studies the board members' characteristics and how these attributes are connected to corporate performance or successions.

It is a well-known fact that *guanxi* is a key concept in understanding Taiwanese and Chinese social behavior. Thus, it is probably more important to examine how board members are related to each other, instead of using demographic attributes commonly used in current literature. In Chinese society, *guanxi* is a complicated concept. It indicates how and to what extent two persons can trust each other. When two persons have close *guanxi* it means they can put more trust in each other. One important factor in determining how close the *guanxi* between individuals is, is to consider how close their kinship relations are. Thus, one of the tasks of this paper is to decipher how relations among board members of public firms evolve in Taiwan.

Molz (1985) has shown that as an economy shifts from entrepreneurial capitalism to managerial capitalism, managers and outside directors[5] tend to dominate boards. The rising funding capacity of institutional investors makes individual investors (capitalists) rarely able to own large shares of an old public company. Ownership of most companies belongs to large institutions. Useem (1996) even argues that institutional investors are controlling firms' boards in the United States. In such a situation, separation of ownership and management are very natural and unavoidable, and professional managers prevail over ordinary owners. Although Taiwan is a very different context, this idea is the basis for this inquiry—that is, whether board compositions tend to include more professional managers who are non-family members or outside directors when firms go public. Does this separation process continue even after IPO? There is no doubt that Taiwan's economy still belongs to the entrepreneurial capitalist system, since most of the firms, including very large public companies, are still controlled and managed by entrepreneurs or their descendants. With the aging of first generation entrepreneurs and the maturing of young managerial professionals, however, board compositions are beginning to include more professional managers or outside directors, although at what speed and on how large a scale this process is occurring is unclear. On the other hand, it is possible to speculate that families try hard to keep their positions and interests in their firms, thus, leaving board compositions unchanged. In addition, as stated earlier, regulations on directors' stockholding also make directors tend to be holding family members.

Institutionalism

Why is there such startling homogeneity of organizational forms and practices? This is the fundamental question that the institutionalist approach addresses (DiMaggio and Powell 1983). Although much of the literature uses neoclassical economic theory to describe and predict organizational forms and behaviors (Williamson 1975), institutionalism argues that non-economic explanations are dominant forces that determine organizational behavior. Organizations have to gain legitimacy in order to increase survival chances (Meyer and Rowan 1977). Going public has had such a legitimating effect in Taiwan since the general public's conception has shifted from a belief that "only bad companies will go public" to "only good and qualified companies are capable of going public." However, this process of legitimacy can have the effect of separating a firm's ownership and management. This institutional process is actually different from what DiMaggio and Powell suggest. Here we have homogeneous organizations transformed from traditional family owned and controlled into separation of ownership and controlled. As mentioned earlier, Yeh et al. (1996) find that in addition to economic rationality, institutional reasons—such as legitimacy, image, and face—are also central to firms' decisions to go public. Once a decision is made to go public, a firm has to endure a minimum two-and-a-half years of IPO preparations. One would assume that these preparatory processes would push firms to become more institutionalized, under the guidance of underwriters and accounting firms. Auditing and reviewing during the IPO by the regulatory body would also be thought to force firms to become more professional. Thus, all three mechanisms of the process of institutionalization identified by DiMaggio and Powell (1983), namely mimetic, coercive, and normative, are employed in the IPO process. Thus, here we are attempting to determine whether or not there is a pattern of separation of ownership and management that appears, when firms prepare for IPOs and after firms successfully carry out IPOs.

The institutionalization process continues even after a firm successfully carries out an IPO. Compared to private companies, public companies are more likely to mimic each other, since other public companies' practices are much easier to reveal. Public companies also get much more attention from regulatory agents and investors. The number of stakeholders and interest parties in a public company is larger than that of a private firm, in general. On the other hand, the increasing popularity of MBA programs, management training courses, and the spread of related management norms enhance the image of "non-family-controlled" as a "good and modern" practice.

As an economy moves from entrepreneurial capitalism to managerial capitalism, entrepreneurs and their family members gradually relinquish their managerial control to professionally trained managers due to increasing diversity and size of firms (Chandler 1977). Being in a better position to raise capital, a public company is also more likely to increase its diversity and size by adopting an expansion strategy. Thus, a public company has to confront both economic and institutional pressures to become less family controlled. In fact, although most of the large firms in Taiwan are still family owned and controlled, they depend heavily on professional managers to handle many important operations. Among managers, usually only the CEO and possibly a few high level executive positions are held by family members. Following this trend, one would suspect that more and more professional managers (including institutional investors) who are not family members would gain seats on boards.

According to Yang (1996) and to our interviews with several TSE review committee members, the IPO review process in Taiwan actually takes this "non-family-business image" very seriously in granting the IPO approval. Although there is no regulation prohibiting every member of a board from belonging to the same family, the TSE review committee is very concerned about the possibility of board directors making business decisions based on their own private interests (e.g., family interest), instead of the general (or minor) shareholders' interests. This is a very different kind of agency problem from that studied in the economic literature (Fama 1980). Typical agency problems deal with the possible conflicts of interest between owners (shareholders) and managers. In Taiwan, the "agency problems" are more likely to be conflicts of interest between controlling families, who control and manage firms, and small shareholders, who are passive investors. If a firm is wholly family owned and managed, there is no such "agency" issue. But when a firm goes public, this kind of "agency problem" is a serious issue with which the TSE wants to deal. In fact, that is one of the major reasons why IPO approval is so strict in Taiwan. Thus, in order to get IPO approval, firms will try to make their boards look more "public" (i.e., less family owned), at least on the surface.

However, as DiMaggio and Powell (1983) point out, these firms exist in an organizational field that constrains their behavior. Although the IPO process might make firms less family controlled, it is highly likely that firms will resist this tendency, owing to other institutional forces. According to Granovetter's (1985) classical argument, people are embedded in their ongoing relations. Similarly, organizations are embedded in their ongoing relations, which cannot be easily dismantled. A good example is Japan's prewar *zaibatsu*, which evolved into postwar *keiretsu* (Gerlach, 1992b). Taiwan's firm owners are no exception in this regard. They are embedded in *guanxi*. Thus, once a firm becomes a public company, the firm might change the course of "de-family-business" to return to a more firmly family controlled board. On the other hand, it might continue the process of separation of ownership and control due to pressures from general investors, other related stakeholders, and other related institutional forces. Which direction will prevail is an empirical question.

Classification, Hypothesis, and Data Collection

Classification of Board Types

Based on in-depth interviews with five public companies and from data observation of corporations' prospectuses, we classify boards into three types: family (f-type), professional (p-type), and hybrid (h-type). If more than half of the directors come from the same family or are friends/partners, a board will be classified as f-type. If more than half of the directors are professional managers or institutional investors that are not related to the major share-owning family, a board will be classified as p-type. Boards that cannot be classified as family or as professional will be classified as h-type. One major reason that a board becomes h-type is because individual investors purchase enough shares (or votes) to become directors. As long as there are enough directorial positions held by individual investors, it is possible to have an h-type board. As a matter of fact, many family members are professionally competent and respected. Many second-generation members have shining MBA degrees from the United States, and have gone through well-planned business career paths. However, these members are counted as family-type directors, not professional directors. One has to remember that there is no value judgment involved in this classification of boards according to type. F-type is simply more commonly seen in entrepreneurial capitalism, while p-type is more likely to emerge under managerial capitalism.

Understanding the distribution of board types can give us an overall picture of a business society. This might not be an issue in a well-developed managerial economy. For an economy in transition like Taiwan, however, one can use this distribution as an indicator to measure how business society evolves. If more than half of the directors are from the same category, meaning from the same family or from the same professional background, it indicates that this board can be fully controlled by that category of persons. A higher proportion of f-type boards indicates that family-owned firms dominate the business community. On the other hand, an increasing proportion of p-type boards indicates families are relinquishing their controls. Since board compositions are easily accessed public information, a firm's image is closely related to its board type. Although a p-type board could be still firmly controlled by a family, this type of composition at least indicates an openness of the firm to a non-family-business image, which might be a first step in the direction of separation of ownership and control.

The other way to measure the degree of a board's departure from the family controlled model is by using the proportion of family-members and close friends on the board as an indicator.[6] The index, FX, is developed to measure the degree of family control, based on the relationships between directors. FX is calculated based on the basis of proportion of family members and close friends on the board. A friend is defined as a person who is a founding partner of the firm or is a close friend of the controlling family. A higher FX indicates a higher degree of family control.

Hypotheses

Based on much of the earlier discussion, we present two competing hypotheses in this paper. Hypothesis A states that as a firm goes public, the institutional process of IPO forces the firm to become less-family-owned for economic, image, political, or other reasons. This "de-family" process is said to continue even after the firm successfully carries out an IPO. In terms of board composition, a firm's board evolves from a stronger family controlled board into a weaker family controlled board. Thus, treating all the public companies as a population, Hypothesis A expects that as firms go through the IPO processes, the proportion of f-type boards decreases, while the proportion of p-type boards increases. Regarding FX, it is expected that FX is smaller for public companies when compared with pre-IPO companies. This "de-family" tendency is believed to continue even after the company has successfully carried out an IPO due to pressures of public image.

Hypothesis B, the reverse of Hypothesis A, states that the control family maintains its control of the board, be the firm private or public.

To test these two hypotheses, board compositions from three time-points, pre-IPO, post-IPO, and current, are analyzed and compared sequentially. Here we define pre-IPO as the time immediately prior to the IPO, post-IPO as the time when the first re-election of a board has been completed right after the IPO, and current as the end of 1996.

Data Collection

Data for those companies that went public in the early years of the Taiwan Stock Market are extremely difficult to collect. Our study sample, therefore, includes only those companies that had IPOs after 1985 and that re-elected their board members at least once after IPO. By the end of 1996, there were 259 companies that had IPOs after 1985. Forty-six of these 259 companies have not re-elected their directors after the IPO. In addition, we have attempted to collect three time-point-data sets for the rest of the 213 companies, with these three time-points being pre-IPO, post-IPO, and current. The board member lists at each time-point are collected from company prospectuses and the *Taiwan Economic Journal Database* (Taiwan *Jingji Xinbao*). We then identify the relationships of directors of each board, using the companies' prospectuses and several other sources (e.g., back issues of *Wealth Magazine* (*Zai Xyun*) and personal information). These relationships have then been cross-checked through telephone interviews with each company's spokesperson. If there was any difficulty in identifying the relationship between directors, the company was not included in the study. As a result, we have determined that 159 public companies have re-elected their boards at least once since IPO, and 96 have re-elected their boards at least twice since IPO. The 159-company sample will be used to compare the board compositions of two time-points, pre-IPO and post-IPO, and the 96-company sample will be employed to compare the board compositions of three time-points, pre-IPO, post-IPO, and current.

Analysis

Data Description

Among the 159 companies in the study sample, 144 companies were listed after 1988, and more than half of these companies (89) were listed after 1991. In other words, more than half of the sample companies were listed less than five years by the end of 1996, which is a very short period to study the tendency of changing processes of board compositions. However, this is the best available data for collection at this point. These companies, on average, have been founded for about 18 years, which implies that most of the companies' founding entrepreneurs are very likely still in charge of business. This probably also explains why most of these firms are still family-controlled.

Mean board size of the 159 sample companies has monotonically decreased from 10.6, pre-IPO, to 9.6, post-IPO. For the 96 sample companies, mean board size has decreased from 10.6, pre-IPO, to 9.3, post-IPO, and to 8.8, currently. It is interesting to note that the average size of boards has decreased from pre-IPO to the current time. Based on our interviews with several companies' directors, the main reason for the decrease in size was to prevent hostile investors from becoming directors when the companies' stocks became publicly traded. As the size of the board decreases, hostile investors need more shares to be elected as directors. This is one of many methods that a family can use to continue controlling the company it "owns," even if it is designated as a "public" company. In fact, directors (most are controlling family members) we interviewed express that they prefer to have control over all seats of the board, not just simply the majority. Controlling families do like to have institutional representatives to sit on the board for networking and information purposes. In general, these representatives are pre-negotiated and pre-arranged. Directors that are not pre-arranged but elected through shareholders' general meetings are not welcomed by controlling families. If all directors are either family members or arranged institutional investors, the board then serves as a rubber stamp. This is exactly the kind of boards that many family firms would like to have.

Trend of Separation of Ownership and Control

The study sample does not include a control group, which includes firms that have not gone public. Theoretically, it is possible that these unlisted firms have also undergone a process of separation of ownership and control without having undergone an IPO. Thus, it is possible that the IPO is a result of this process, not a cause of the separation process. In reality, this rival hypothesis is highly unlikely. We see no theoretical reason to believe that unlisted firms tend to make their boards less-family-controlled, unless some external forces are imposed upon them. Unlisted firm board information is not public information; thus, it is difficult to relate board compositions to corporate images. Unless the unlisted corporation has a strong incentive to separate ownership and control, there is no reason for these privately held firms' boards to include non-family members, who are professional managers employed by the company. However, we must ask why would a firm wants to separate ownership and management and remain in private? Since an IPO requires at least two to three years to prepare *after* a firm decides to go public, many adjustments are made during this preparatory stage. One important business operating principle of unlisted companies' is "tax oriented," which enables such businesses to pay as little tax as possible and which, of course, allows the controlling families to become as rich as possible. Manipulating accounting reports are common practices in these firms. In contrast, public companies' business operating principle is "finance oriented," where standard accounting principles are employed and legally required taxes are paid. If a firm decides to go public, the first area it has to change is its financial control system. As a result, the controlling family cannot freely use firm resources or money anymore.

Thus, unless a firm decides to go public, few are willing to tolerate these strict regulations. In addition, unlike in the United States, regulations request that all firms reveal their financial information after they grow to a certain size although these firms can choose to remain private. In other words, a firm can stay unlisted but has to reveal its financial information when it grows beyond a certain size (when capital is larger or equal to NT$200 million). Many of these unlisted firms are government-owned companies. For most non-government owned companies, there is no reason for them to reveal their financial information and remain unlisted (i.e. choose to trade or distribute stocks in private not in the open market). Under such regulations, virtually all firms will go public after growing beyond a certain size. If a firm wants to stay unlisted and does not want to reveal its financial information after growing beyond a certain size, it has to split into several smaller firms. Therefore, it is virtually impossible to compose a meaningful statistical control group that is composed of unlisted firms, since all of these firms have to be much smaller than public firms are.

Although we cannot construct a control group, we have devised an alternative regression model to test the possibility of "separation process without having undergone an IPO." Using FX as a dependent variable, we employ the time that a company began IPO as a predictor, and other control variables, including firm size, performance, age, industry, and board size. Should there be a separation trend, then the time that a company started the IPO should be negatively related with dependent variables. In other words, for companies that go public later, their degree of family control (FX) should be lower at the time of IPO.

The time variable is measured from the year the company began IPO, with 1985 assigned the value zero and later years assigned the value equal to "number of years since 1985." For example, the time variable is assigned a value of 10 for a company that underwent IPO in 1995. Five control variables are company size, performance, age, industry type, and board size. Company size is measured on capital. The larger the size of a company, the greater the chance managers will tend to be non-family members. Company performance is measured in terms of return on sales. The better a company's performance, the greater the chance managers will be non-family members, as non-family managers tend to act in the interests of the company, not of the controlling family. Age is measured in number of years since the company was founded. The greater a company's age, the more likely that the firm has a higher FX, as most companies which started at an earlier date were entrepreneurial family businesses. Later founded companies are more likely to have founding capital from institutional investors (e.g., venture capital companies); hence, they are more likely to have institutional representatives serve as directors. Dummy variables were assigned to industry types, and board size is measured by the number of directors.

Table 4.1 shows the results of the multiple regression analysis. Results from the table implies that when a company is unlisted, the degree of family control of the board is negatively related to the company's capitalization level and size of the board. The larger the level of capitalization or the

Table 4.1 Time Impact on the Degree of Family Control of the Board

Variables	Coefficients
Predictor: Time Factor	-.007529
Firm Attributes	
Capital	-.002375*
Return on Sales	.002050
Age	.007838**
Industry	
Petrochemical	-.023515
Textiles	-.018362
Foods	.138245
Steel	.092055
Electronics	-.090160
Machinery	.001724
Construction	.082360
Finance	-.205939*
Board Size	-.024076**
Constant	.439505**
F	4.70397**
Adjusted R^2	.23357
N	159

*: $p<0.05$; **: $p<0.01$.

larger the size of the board, the less family-controlling the board is. Age is significantly positively related to FX, which is consistent with what we predicated in the last paragraph. Most important of all, time is not a significant factor. This means that if a company remains private-held, then there is no time-trend for increasing the probability of the board becoming less family controlled. Thus, if there is a tendency towards separation of management and ownership in public firms, it is more likely due to IPO events and being a public firm, not due to the trend of the separation of ownership and control across all firms.

Board Type Distributions

Table 4.2 shows the distribution of board types based on the classification defined earlier. As shown in the table, the number of f-type boards has declined from 100 (63 per cent), pre-IPO to 89 (56 per cent), post-IPO. Although f-type boards have decreased, the change is not very large, at only 7 per cent. As a result, f-type is a dominant type, both pre and post-IPO. Accompanying the decline of these f-type boards, p-type boards have increased from 30 (19 per cent), pre-IPO to 37 (23 per cent), post-IPO, while h-type boards have increased from 29 (18 per cent) to 33 (20 per cent). Thus it is not clear how strong the institutional IPO forces are. The direction of change, however, tends to the separation of ownership and control, albeit it is clear that most firms remain firmly under family control.

Table 4.2 Type of Board Pre-IPO and Post-IPO

Type of Board	Pre-IPO No.(%)	Post-IPO No.(%)
f-type	100 (62.89)	89 (55.97)
h-type	29 (18.24)	33 (20.75)
p-type	30 (18.87)	37 (23.27)
Total	159 (100.00)	159 (100.00)

Since some companies have only re-elected their directors once, we cannot analyze how the distribution of these companies' board type changes after the post-IPO's first board election. We therefore analyze only those companies that have at least two board re-elections post-IPO. Ninety-six companies are included in this analysis. Table 4.3 indicates that as a company goes public, the process of transforming its board to be less-family-controlled is not limited to the IPO event, but is a continuing process. The number of f-type boards has monotonically decreased from 62 (65 per cent), pre-IPO to 56 (58 per cent), post-IPO, and further decreased to 49 (51 per cent) currently. Concurrently, the number of p-type boards has increased from 18 (19 per cent), pre-IPO to 23 (24 per cent), post-IPO, and continued to increase to 24 (25 per cent). H-type boards have also increased from 16 to 17, then, from 17 to 23. It should be noted that the board changing process is more oriented toward h-type, instead of p-type after IPO. In other words, although the f-type boards are continuing to decrease, it is interesting to note how the decreasing numbers distribute to the other two major types (i.e. p-type and h-type). It is found that p-type grows by a higher percentage than h-type does, when comparing pre-IPO and post-IPO, with p-type increasing about 28 per cent (18 to 23), and h-type increasing only about 6 per cent (16 to 17). However, h-type dominated p-type when comparing post-IPO and the present. H-type increased 35 per cent (17 to 23), while p-type increased only 4 per cent (23 to 24). It is possible that the IPO event pushes a company to have a board which is family-controlled to a lesser degree, while this process slows down after companies gain approval for listing. Since the stock is publicly traded, it is also likely that some non-family related individual investors control enough votes to be elected as directors, changing the board to h-type. More than half of the boards (49 out of 96), however, remain f-type at the current time-point. Thus, there is no doubt that family owned business is the dominant type among Taiwan's businesses, whether privately or publicly held.

Table 4.3 Type of Board: Pre-IPO, Post-IPO, and Current

Type of Board	Pre-IPO No. (%)	Post-IPO No. (%)	Current No. (%)
f-type	62 (64.58)	56 (58.33)	49 (51.04)
h-type	16 (16.67)	17 (17.71)	23 (23.96)
p-type	18 (18.75)	23 (23.96)	24 (25.00)
Total	96(100.00)	96(100.00)	96(100.00)

The results shown in Tables 4.2 and 4.3 indicate that the number of f-type boards does decrease, indicating a tendency toward separation of ownership and control. This transformation process does not stop even after firms successfully carry out IPOs. However, the changing scale is not very large: one can definitely argue that most firms are still firmly under family control even after IPO. This reflects how strongly families in Taiwan control their firms.

We also compare firms' boards based on FX index defined earlier. It is found that FX decreases after firms' IPOs, as shown in Table 4.4. Of the 159 firms we analyze, 43 of them actually have higher FXs, in contrast to the 48 lower FXs, when pre-IPO and post-IPO are compared. Mean FXs are 41.59 per cent and 38.94 per cent, pre-IPO and post-IPO, respectively. The result is consistent with the "separation process hypothesis," albeit the strength of this process is a different issue.[7]

Table 4.4 Proportion of Non-Professional Directors: Pre-IPO and Post-IPO (N=159)

Indicators	Pre-IPO (%)	Post-IPO (%)	Number of Boards Increasing or Decreasing
FX	41.59	38.94	+: 43
(S. D.)	(0.28)	(0.28)	−: 48
			ties: 68

Table 4.5 shows results by comparing three time-points (pre-IPO vs. post-IPO and post-IPO vs. current) using 96 available sample companies. Interestingly, it is found that there is virtually no change between pre-IPO and post-IPO here (in fact, FX increases very slightly). This result is not consistent with what we found when 159 firms were analyzed as indicated in the preceding paragraph. Since the sample size in Table 4.5 is smaller than what we used in Table 4.4, we tend to support what we found in Table 4.4. Nevertheless, it is clear that the "separation process hypothesis" is very weak, even if we concur that it is happening.

It is our finding that a much higher number of firms have decreased their FXs after IPOs (44 decreasing vs. 16 increasing). The results found here are quite interesting, as they indicate that FXs decrease at a much higher rate *after* firms successfully carried out IPO.

Combining our results from this section and the previous section, we have found that a firm has a slight tendency to increase non-family members into its board composition right after it has carried out IPO. Nevertheless, individual investors are also more likely to be included in the board after the firm has been listing for a period of time. It is possible that individual investors can assume ownership and control of a public company after accumulating a certain number of shares. In such a case, the firm could be owned and managed by a new family and remain a public company. Up to this point, it is safe to assert that neither the IPO event nor being a public company have much impact on the separation of ownership and control.

Table 4.5 Proportion of Non-Professional Directors: Pre-IPO, Post-IPO and Current (N=96)

Indicators	Pre-IPO (%)	Post-IPO (%)	Current (%)	Number of Boards Increasing or Decreasing
FX	42.26	42.65	38.47	+: 36, 16
(S. D.)	(0.30)	(0.30)	(0.29)	−: 35, 44
				ties: 25, 36

*: Numbers in the first column are comparisons between Pre-IPO and Post-IPO; numbers in the second column are comparisons between Post-IPO and Current.

Summary and Discussion

As Taiwan's economy moves from entrepreneurial capitalism to managerial capitalism, one would expect that ownership and control would become more separated in the process. However, family business is still the dominant form in virtually all businesses, whether listed or unlisted, large or small companies. Whether these family-owned businesses will become more public (less-family-controlled) has important social implications. This paper attempts to determine if IPO events can force families to relinquish their control by investigating the evolution of board compositions. Two issues are raised here. One is the degree of family involvement, and the other is the degree of separation of ownership and control. It is possible that a family still owns the majority of stocks but relinquishes the firms' control to professionals. It is also possible that a family no longer owns and controls a firm, but the firm is owned and controlled by a group of professional managers.[8] Due to complicated legal requirements and data constraints, this paper does not make a clear distinction between these two types of transformation processes.

It is very difficult to understand the nature of the family business since it is difficult to delve deeply into family-controlled companies. It is virtually impossible to expect a family to respond to inquiries in regard to how it arranges investment vehicles and proxies. The paper thus takes public companies' board compositions as a starting point to explore the possible structural change of boards. Based on the relationships between board members, 159 public companies' boards are classified into three major types, namely, family-controlled, professional, and hybrid. This paper also uses an index, FX, to measure a board's degree of family-controlling. In the paper we explore the possibility that the IPO process is an important institutional event. Here we examine whether the IPO typically forces companies' boards to become less-family-controlled, and if the process continues even after firms successfully carry out IPOs.

Results shown in this paper are inconclusive. The separation process of ownership and control seems to exist after firms go public, as the proportion of traditional relations have shown a decreasing trend, albeit not very strong. However, most boards are still very much in family control, as indicated by the dominance of f-type boards after IPO. Thus, the transformation process of a family business into a more public business is very slow and not very significant up to this point. The finding is interesting and has important implications. We suspect that two opposite forces are working here. One is the global force behind the legally guided IPO process, which tries to separate ownership and management in the same way as has occurred in advanced economies. The other force is a local institutional constraint that inhibits owners' willingness to transform. The trend of globalization is a convergent force that moves firms toward professionalization; however, the ongoing relations embedded in the local context create a divergent force that keeps firms sticking with their local practices and staying away from the global trend of professionalization. Apparently, the goal of IPO is to make firms converge, but institutional life might keep firms operating as usual.

Due to data constraints, several research issues have to be addressed here. First, the sample companies' listing history is too short to carry out a methodologically sound analysis of the changing process of board compositions. Specifically, it is virtually impossible to disentangle the impact caused by the IPO event and the force imposed by other institutional environments. For example, it is highly likely that a firm's controlling family may typically sell too many stocks after IPO, and lose its control of the board. It is also likely that Taiwanese firms are going through an institutional transition process that makes family businesses difficult to maintain their legitimacy. Nevertheless, the multiple regression results shown earlier indicate that even if there are other institutional factors, these factors are effective only *after* firms became public companies. Second, the decision process for a family-controlled firm to release some board seats might be much more complicated than we suggest in this paper. When and why does a professional manager replace a family-tied director? It is possible that a p-type board is actually more strongly family-controlled than a f-type board is, under a complicated arrangement. For example, many people who serve as "nominal" people are "hired" by actual owners. On paper, these people are directors; in reality, these people might simply be rubber stampers. Third, the institutional process is a continuous process and many companies adjust their board structures right before the IPO. In other words, the impact of the IPO could be greater before the IPO event than after the IPO itself. Due to data constraints, we are not able to assess the pre-IPO impact here. Nevertheless, this paper shows some stimulating results.

It is fair to assert that most of the boards in Taiwan's firms only have nominal functions. The chairman of the board usually is the single most powerful person in the company, and many of them also serve as general managers. On the other hand, a general manager that is not a director of the company may simply implement the chairman's policy. In fact, it is not unusual that companies' general managers are not directors. As one can see, the function of the board in Taiwan is not very strong and is not independent enough, and is hardly able to represent or protect general investors' interest. According to Taiwan's regulations, a director has to own a certain amount of stocks. Therefore, the separation of ownership and control is not encouraged by the regulative regime. If a firm truly wants to hire professional directors, it has to give some stocks to these directors. In addition, about 40 per cent of corporate auditors, who are supposed to represent stockholders by independently monitoring corporations' financial matters, are relatives of chairmen. Therefore, it is very clear that corporate governance is still very much under the largest shareholders' control. Due to this lack of independence, frequent scandals involving many companies' chairmen have occurred in the past couple years. Scandals typically are caused by the transference of corporate assets to the controlling shareholder, faking corporate financial statements and manipulating stock prices. The restructuring of the board now emerges as one of the most important issues in Taiwan's business regulations. The SEC is now considering requiring each public company to include an outsider director on its board. Many other reforming proposals such as the strengthening of auditors and the corporate accountants' legal responsibility are also currently being debated. How these reforms will evolve is very unclear at this point.

It is very important to understand how companies evolve when the economy moves from entrepreneurial capitalism to managerial capitalism. Although literature on this topic is quite rich, little of it is concerned with newly industrializing countries. Since the board is the most significant and prominent structure that a corporation bears, one cannot over emphasize the significance of studying the change process of board composition. Yeh (1997) and this paper are the first studies dealing with such issues in Taiwan. Although our findings here are quite provocative, though a longer and more detailed study is, of course, needed. We hope that our endeavor has opened a new avenue to study the governance structure in developing economies.

Acknowledgement

This research is partially supported by grants from National Science Council (NSC 86-2416-H-110-022, 88-2416-H-110-016). We thank Ruey-Ling Tzeng and two anonymous referees for their helpful suggestions. Please direct correspondence to Kuang S. Yeh, e-mail: ksyeh@mail.nsysu.edu.tw.

Notes

1. On the other hand, failure of a public firm is a much more serious problem than failure of a private firm in general, since ordinary investors typically put pressure on the government to recover their loss. In addition, unlike in the United States, individual investors have more than 90 per cent of the stock market transaction volume in Taiwan's stock market. The description in this section is modified from Yeh (1997).
2. Taiwan's SEC is taking steps to loosen the regulations for companies going public.
3. It is based on estimates from the 1997 Taiwan Economic Journal Database, which contains historical and current data on every listed Taiwanese company's stock and directors' information.
4. For example, some directors might be elected by proxy votes controlled by the family.
5. By the term, "outside director," here we mean directors that are not executives of the corporation and not family members of the holding family.
6. Thanks to an anonymous referee of this volume for this suggestion.
7. We have not conducted a statistical test in this regard. The 159 number of firms included in this study is close to the population we study. Thus, the result is a description of reality, and no statistical test is needed.
8. This situation is analygous to management buy out in the States, but here the Taiwanese company remains public.

Chapter 5

Corporate Responses to the Issue of Sexual Harassment in the Workplace in Taiwan—Lessons from the United States

Cing-Kae Chiao

Introduction

As more and more local women have entered the labor market in recent years, various issues concerning gender equality in employment have received attention from the public. Among them, sexual harassment in the workplace has been widely publicized. Media coverage of high profile sexual harassment cases in the 1990s raised international awareness to the seriousness of the problem. The worldwide influx of women into the labor market as well as public offices placed greater emphasis on this problem, which has led national governments world-wide to adopt measures to address the issue. Legislation specifically related to sexual harassment has been enacted or is pending in several countries. In Taiwan, a series of these incidents at work sites and on campuses were exposed by the press in the early 1990s, and a number of studies and surveys confirmed that a substantial portion of working women, between 15 and 43 per cent, had experienced or noticed this kind of unwelcome or unwanted conduct in their workplace. Since Taiwan does not have a statute specifically prohibiting sexual harassment in the workplace and the existing provisions in the Civil Code, the Criminal Code, the Statute for Maintaining Public Order and Stabilization, and even some labor statutes, are not suitable to cope with this new problem, the government has finally decided, under pressure from local women's rights groups, to take legislative initiative to correct this situation. It has added a new provision in its proposed Gender Equality in Employment Bill to give the concept of sexual harassment a clearer definition and to legally require employers to adopt necessary preventive measures and training programs to eliminate the problem. Other bills offered by local organizations also contain similar provisions. It is clear that if these bills become formal legislation in the near future, which is quite possible because all major political parties have put them on the priority list of their legislative agendas, local business firms will have to assume an important role in dealing with this new issue in the workplace. A close examination of the provisions contained in these bills reveals that they are strongly influenced by American legal interpretations of sexual harassment. For instance, most of them not only literally copy the definition of sexual harassment from the famous Guidelines promulgated by the Equal Employment Opportunity Commission (EEOC) in 1980, they also stress the importance of employers' responsibility for preventing this conduct from occurring and for providing remedies for the victims. In addition, they all suggest the establishment of an EEOC-type independent specialized agency to oversee and enforce this new law. Furthermore, these bills encourage business firms to set up formal or informal complaint mechanisms and to adopt preventive and corrective measures to settle the disputes internally. Finally, most of the bills also urge employers to cooperate with labor unions or representatives of their employees to promote awareness through information campaigns and training programs designed to strengthen employees' understanding of this issue. Given the similarity between the proposed legislation and American law, an examination of the experiences of American business firms in dealing with this issue (after the passage of Title VII of the Civil Rights Act of 1964) can certainly provide their counterparts in Taiwan with important lessons.

The purpose of this paper is to provide a general account of the problem of sexual harassment in the workplace in Taiwan in recent years and to analyze local business firms' reactions to this emerging issue. The factors that Taiwan must account for in dealing with this issue are outlined. External factors comprise the international awareness arising from common recognition of the issue from press coverage of high profile cases and the resulting legal precedents or policy decisions, which in turn influence the awareness of Taiwan's public and political leadership. Internal factors manifest themselves as pressure from interest groups and friction due to cultural and institutional incongruities resulting from efforts to address the problem. This paper discusses the constraints that shape the interpretation of sexual harassment as it occurs in various countries. While an internationalized concept of sexual harassment may exist and foreign practices or court decisions may influence the interpretations of sexual harassment in many countries, most ultimately adopt their own interpretations and approaches to this problem. The paper attempts to use the practices in the United States as a model to see whether corporate strategies towards the issue there can be "transplanted" to this country. Aside from introductory and concluding remarks, the main contents of the paper are divided into five sections. Section (II) provides an overview of the international recognition of sexual harassment as a serious problem and the difference in approaches, shaped in part by institutional and cultural factors, taken by various national governments in addressing it. Section (III) uses a number of local surveys and studies to illustrate the prevalence of sexual harassment problems in Taiwan in general and in the workplace in particular. It also points out that the current legal regime governing workplace conduct and other related statutes are not suitable to effectively handle this new issue. It then details the provisions dealing with sexual harassment in the four proposed Gender Equality in Employment Bills to illustrate the new legislative developments in this field. Section (IV) examines local business firms' attitudes towards sexual harassment in the workplace. It first uses the findings of a large-scale research program commissioned by Executive Yuan of the Council of Labor Affairs (CLA)[1] to demonstrate employer's general reactions to this workplace problem. It then uses another survey sponsored by the CLA to analyze local business firms' degree of acceptance of the sexual harassment provisions contained in the new bills. Although the findings of these two surveys are not conclusive due to under-representativeness of their samples, they still provide some useful information about local corporate reactions to this issue. Section (V) describes the prevalence of sexual harassment in the workplace and legal responses to these problems in the United States. In addition to several major fair employment statutes and administrative regulations, a number of significant court decisions are also discussed. In Section (VI), the paper examines how companies in the United States have attempted to cope with sexual harassment issues in the workplace and evaluates the general merits and shortcomings of the American system. It also tries to analyze the possibility of "transplanting" several American practices to Taiwan.

The Global Phenomenon of Sexual Harassment at Work

The issue of sexual harassment has had global implications in recent years. Many countries have passed legislation or handed down important court decisions on sexual harassment, which reflect their own unique interpretations and approaches to the problem. Institutional and cultural factors have a profound effect in determining the outcome of national approaches to resolving sexual harassment issues.

Around the world, there has been a high incidence of sexual harassment in the workplace. In Germany, in a 1997 study of 2000 women coming from all sectors, 93% of the respondents claimed that they themselves or persons known to them had experienced some form of sexual harassment (European Industrial Relations Review 1998). In France, in a related study conducted by the secretary of state for women's and consumers' rights, 21% of the 1300 women surveyed reported that they have had a personal experience of sexual harassment, and 14% of the women said that the incidents resulted in dismissal or resignations. In the United Kingdom, the number of sexual harassment claims received by the Equal Opportunities Commission increased from 317 in 1990 to 735 in 1995 (European Industrial Relations Review 1998). While many factors can be used to explain the high incidence—increased participation of women in the labor market and public office, growing awareness due to increased media coverage—the high incidence also demonstrates awareness of the problem among populations in several countries.

Influences from other countries such as U.S. legal precedents may play an influential role in shaping legal and policy decisions made in other countries; however, the approaches taken by those countries remain "remarkably different." Many jurisdictions are adopting the approach taken by the United States courts; namely, that sexual harassment should be clearly identified as a form of sexual discrimination and, as such, a barrier to women's integration in the labor market (Aeberhard-Hodges 1996). However, certain countries, for instance, Austria, Belgium, Spain, France, and Germany, all have specific legislation regarding sexual harassment (Commission of the European Communities 1996). In other countries, such as Canada, Finland, Luxembourg and the United Kingdom, sexual harassment falls under general equality and or under sex discrimination legislation similar to the U.S. (European Industrial Relations Review 1998). In some countries, such as Denmark and Italy, sexual harassment in the workplace is regulated by sectoral or national collective agreements between social partners. The social partners for their respective industries create guidelines and procedures. Institutional constraints invariably shape effectiveness in dealing with sexual harassment, especially in legal and administrative matters (Aeberhard-Hodges 1996). For instance, the procedural aspect of handling sexual harassment varies from country to country.

Although international recognition of sexual harassment exists, each country invariably resorts to its own initiatives and attempts at creating an internationalized standard for the prevention of sexual harassment in the workplace have so far proven difficult. In July 1996 and March 1997, the European Commission issued a two-part consultation document to European Union social partners in regards to collective action for preventing sexual harassment in the workplace. The results of this consultation showed that the social partners were divided. Employee groups represented by the European Trade Union Confederation (ETUC) favors an EU-wide binding instrument that will require member states to pass legislation preventing sexual harassment in the workplace. On the other hand, the Union of Industrial and Employers' Confederation of Europe (UNICE), which advocates employers' positions, opposes such a measure, citing existing national measures as well as stressing that the assessment of behavior is influenced by cultural differences and thus should be left up to the member states themselves to determine (European Industrial Relations Review 1997). The debate between the social partners underscores the difficulties in enforcing an internationalized standard upon distinct nationalities due to cultural differences or institutional barriers.

The different ways in which countries adopt measures of dealing with sexual harassment in the workplace show that while this issue is globally relevant, various factors, such as a pre-existing legal framework or national initiatives and institutions such as labor or employer unions, ultimately result in unique adaptations.

Sexual Harassment in the Workplace in Taiwan

Prior to the 1990s, sexual harassment cases have been muted due to Taiwan's conservative, patriarchal society and the lack of awareness among the public. Although some local feminists in Taiwan raised the issue of sexual harassment in the workplace in the 1980s (Chao 1984; Ku 1984; Yu

1984a, 1984b), their opinions did not receive wide-spread attention due, in part, to the fact that most people were uninformed on this subject and regarded such conduct and behavior as personal flirtations between members of the opposite sex. A few relevant surveys were released but they did not specifically focus on incidents that had occurred in the workplace (Hsieh 1984; Luo 1990; Taipei City Women Rescue Foundation 1990) and they treated these incidents only as a kind of public nuisance (Hwang 1994). As in many countries, the whole issue only began to unfold, rather unexpectedly, at the beginning of this decade (International Labor Office 1992). The rise of local interest groups and increasing public awareness of the issue have begun to place increasing pressure on government and firms.

General Background

Given that Taiwan is a male-dominated society, it is not surprising that various forms of sexual aggression against women are among the most serious social problems in Taiwan and have received extensive discussions from local scholars (Luo 1995; Hwang 1995). However, the problem of sexual harassment in the workplace is a new phenomenon and had not attracted attention until the early 1990s when several high profile cases were covered by the local media. In October 1991, a group of flight attendants from China Airlines accused an airline-employed physician of unprofessional conduct during medical examinations. This incident took place at an extremely opportune moment because during that time, allegations that U.S. Supreme Court Justice-nominee Clarence Thomas had sexually harassed his subordinate Ms. Anita Hill when he was Chairman of the EEOC were widely reported by the local press and the term "sexual harassment," which in Chinese language literally means sexual annoyance, had become a very popular parlance. Numerous women's rights groups rallied to their support and the whole event attracted tremendous publicity, although the accused physician was subsequently cleared (S.-C. Wang 1993). During the same month, the Modern Women Foundation[2] released the results of a pair of surveys on sexual harassment. In the first report, a total of 1,253 female high school and vocational school students in Taipei were surveyed through questionnaires about their experiences with, feelings and reactions towards, knowledge about, and willingness to receive assistance concerning sexual harassment. Among them, almost one-half admitted that they had received unwanted physical touching, and 13.4 per cent of them claimed that they had experienced some type of serious sexual harassment, such as touching of breasts, genitals or even forced sexual intercourse (Modern Women Foundation 1992a). In the second report, 923 working people of both sexes between the age of 16 to 50 were surveyed using the same method with nearly identical questions from the first survey. Among them, 36.1 per cent of working women claimed that they had experienced some form of sexual harassment in their workplace (Modern Women Foundation 1992b).

In 1992, after a series of sexual harassment incidents occurred on university campuses, female student organizations started to build up intermural networks for mutual support (Hsieh 1995). In October of the same year, a comprehensive study on university students' attitudes towards sexual harassment commissioned by the Ministry of Education was released. It indicated that among 2,174 students questioned, almost one-half of them had experienced unpleasant sexual encounters. For those who had experienced these before entering universities, 23 per cent of these incidents had occurred in schools while 35 per cent of them happened on buses (Chen 1994). In March 1993, local news media exposed that an intoxicated female secretary of a local businessman was sexually assaulted by another businessman and a secret service agent after a business dinner. This incident aroused wide-spread indignation and a new bill entitled "The Prevention of Sexual Violence Against Women" was proposed by several female legislators from the opposition Democratic Progressive Party (DPP) and a number of local women's rights groups. Subsequently, a series of public hearings on this bill were held and the issue of sexual harassment dominated these discussions. In the same year, a large-scale survey and research program sponsored by the CLA to investigate the occurrence of sexual harassment in the workplace in Taiwan was released (Lu and Fu 1993). Since this survey was the first to focus specifically on incidents of sexual harassment in the workplace, and since the government indicated that the findings would be used as a basis to determine whether or not to add a new provision about prohibiting sexual harassment in the workplace to the official Gender Equality in Employment Bill (which was first drafted in 1992), the presentation of the findings of this report received wide-spread attention. Although the report did not reveal the exact percentage of surveyed employees who had experienced sexual harassment, it did provide some useful information about local employers' perceptions of sexual harassment in the workplace (to be discussed in the following section). In the same year, another small-scale survey conducted by Dr. Tsan-Yin Luo of World News College of Journalism also discovered that among 493 working women surveyed in Taipei, one per cent claimed that they had been sexually assaulted (Luo 1993, 1995).

In March 1994, a female student from National Normal University accused one of her professors of sexual harassment and rape. The issue again received extensive coverage from the local press. Since some local women's rights groups were not satisfied with the handling of the case by the Ministry of Education and the university itself, they held a series of public hearings on the issue of sexual harassment on campus and a number of telephone hot-lines were set up to receive related complaints from college students. In addition, a new "The Prevention of Crimes of Sexual Violence Bill" was also proposed by a female legislator affiliated with the ruling KMT Party in the Legislative Yuan. On May 22, a large-scale parade was staged by a number of women's rights groups in Taipei to protest sexual harassment against women and to show their displeasure with government inaction on this social problem. It was attended by thousands of women and men and was hailed as the first demonstration organized by women's groups and advocating a single feminist issue held without support from political interest organizations. Although the theme of that demonstration was the issue of sexual harassment in general, its repercussions were far-reaching. Sexual harassment, whether on campus or in the workplace, was no longer treated as a private or personal matter but instead had become a social issue in the public domain. In that year, a survey sponsored by the Department of Labor Affairs of Taiwan Province to examine workers' living conditions in Taiwan Province also showed that over 15 per cent of female workers had experienced or noticed incidents of sexual harassment in their workplace (Department of Labor Affairs of Taiwan Province Government 1994).

From 1995 to the present, several surveys published in Taiwan have also demonstrated that once local people became more familiarized with this issue, their knowledge about the prevalence of this problem increased dramatically. For instance, according to a survey sponsored by the Bureau of Public Health (Executive Yuan) and released in February 1995, over 43 per cent of medical personnel claimed to have experienced some form of sexual harassment during medical treatments, either by doctors, colleagues or even patients (Bureau of Public Health, Executive Yuan 1995). In March 1995, a report published by the Formosa Cultural and Educational Foundation also pointed out that of the 937 women over the age of 20 polled by telephone interviews, over 30 per cent of the working women expressed that they had experienced similar encounters (Formosa Cultural and Educational Foundation 1995; Chang 1995). In addition, a report issued by the Twenty First Century Foundation in the same year also showed that almost twenty per cent of women surveyed listed sexual harassment as the social issue that most concerned them (The Twenty First Century Foundation 1995; Chang 1995). In the same year, a survey about sexual harassment on campus conducted by the Jen-Ben Educational Foundation, a public-interest advocacy group devoted to the reform of the educational system in Taiwan, also discovered that among 1,978 students from middle and high schools to universities, over 5.1 per cent reported that they had been sexually assaulted by teachers or personnel at schools; 51.3 per cent of these reported incidents had taken place when they were attending elementary schools (Hsieh 1995; Jen-Ben Educational Foundation 1995; Luo 1995). In September of 1996, a survey done by the Taipei City Working People's Association also showed that of the 947 white-collar employees (both male and female) questioned, over 25 per cent of them indicated that incidents of sexual harassment in the workplace occurred frequently or occasionally (Taipei City Working People's Association 1996).

Based on the results of the foregoing surveys, it is estimated that a substantial proportion of working women, between 15 and 43 per cent, in Taiwan, have experienced some kind of sexual harassment in their workplace (Hwang 1995). Generally speaking, this ratio cannot be regarded as unusually high as compared to that in other industrialized countries (Chiao 1996b; Lipper 1992; International Labor Office 1992; U.S. Merit Systems Protection Board 1981, 1988, 1995). However, since most local working women are still not assertive in matters concerning gender equality in general, and also because they tend to be conservative in dealing with these kinds of sexual offenses in particular (Lu and Fu 1993), it is believed that the actual numbers of women suffering from sexual harassment in their workplace are likely much higher (Hwang 1995; Luo 1995). Moreover, the above-mentioned surveys also did not provide any information about the percentage of working men experiencing sexual harassment in the workplace. As the power structure in Taiwanese workplaces is still dominated by men, this phenomenon suggests that sexual harassment is essentially an issue of imbalance of power between both sexes in society and in the labor market. The incidents of men being sexually harassed by women are, for example, very rare. Finally, cases of same sex, sexual orientation-related harassment were also not reported by those surveys. This is probably due to the fact that Taiwan is still a conservative society and the study of this issue is only at an embryonic stage. However, sexual harassment has been recognized as a serious concern, and this has prompted activity from several women's groups as well as increased public awareness, all of which pressure the government and firms to adopt policies that address the problems associated with sexual harassment in the workplace. Taiwan's internal pressure to adopt some form of protection against sexual harassment has increased due to growing awareness coming from the periodically released surveys on sexual harassment conducted by prominent women's rights groups. Several recent court decisions regarding sexual harassment have had the effect of placing greater pressure on employers to prevent sexual harassment in the workplace by holding them liable for such occurrences (Chiao 1999).

Current Legal Regime Governing Sexual Harassment in the Workplace

Even now, Taiwan still does not have a law specifically addressing sexual harassment in the workplace. Therefore, it has to rely on a variety of related provisions scattered through out other statutes, such as the Civil Code, the Criminal Code, the Statute for Maintenance of Public Order and Social Stability, or even the labor statutes to deal with this new form of workplace conflict. Take the Civil Code as an example. Since some types of sexual harassment can cause harm to the reputation of the victims, they can claim that their individual rights were damaged and require the court to eliminate that infringement, pursuant to Article 18 of the Civil Code of 1929 (as amended in 1982). However, the remedies provided by the Code are extremely limited. According to Paragraph 2 of the same Article, plaintiffs may only receive compensation for violations of rights specifically stipulated in the law. Currently, the Code lists exclusively those rights concerning life, body, name, reputation, freedom, status, and capabilities as those rights qualified to receive this special protection. Under such circumstances, even if a plaintiff can win the case through protracted civil procedures (normally lasting four to five years), the plaintiff's chance of getting compensation is quite slim due to the fact that the meanings of those listed rights are vague and abstract at best. Moreover, judges are typically reluctant to recognize sexual harassment as a cause of action under current legal standards because of the very heavy burden of proof imposed on the plaintiffs by the law. Furthermore, expensive legal fees can also serve as a deterrent for the potential plaintiff who is typically in a weaker economic position. Therefore, the Civil Code is certainly not a useful means of redressing this kind of work site conflict (International Labour Office 1992; Chiao 1995; H.-L. Wang 1993; S.-C. Wang 1993; H.-C. Yu 1993; M.-N. Yu 1984a, 1984b).

There are also a number of provisions in the current Criminal Code that are relevant to several forms of sexual behavior and therefore can in some cases be used as legal sanctions against perpetrators of sexual harassment in the workplace. For instance, some serious forms of sexual misconduct in the workplace—such as rape, attempted rape or other types of sexual assault—constitute a level of sexual aggression that is prohibited by Chapter 16 of the Criminal Code of 1935 (as amended in 1992), which deals with a variety of crimes relating to obscenity. In addition, some types of sexual harassment involving physical contact or touching are clearly in violation of those provisions concerning assault and battery, false imprisonment, confinement or restraint of personal freedom (Chapter 26). Furthermore, some misconduct, especially that of a verbal nature, can also presumably be interpreted as reaching the level of defamation or libel against a victim (Chapter 27). Finally, if a "quid pro quo"-type of sexual harassment or assault is committed, then Article 228 of the Code, which addresses the crime of an individual sexually assaulting a subordinate through the abuse of his authority, is a particularly relevant provision. However, using the criminal statutes to solve sexual harassment problems also has some inherent drawbacks as the civil statutes and their effectiveness in dealing with this workplace issue is quite doubtful (International Labour Office 1992). For instance, the burden of proof for a criminal offense, which is much stricter than that of civil cases, is always the most insurmountable obstacle a plaintiff has to overcome. Since civil remedies are normally denied except in extreme circumstances, simply punishing an offender for his misconduct sometimes cannot make a victim whole. Furthermore, a long, and costly criminal trial is also nightmarish for a plaintiff. Therefore, resorting to the Criminal Code is also not a practical tool to resolve conflicts arising out of sexual harassment in the workplace (Chiao 1994; H.-L. Wang 1993; H.-C. Yu 1993; M.-N. Yu 1984a, 1984b).

In addition to the Criminal Code, Article 83 of the Statute for Maintenance of Public Order and Social Stability of 1991, formerly a police law, has often been mentioned by local scholars as an alternative means of handling controversies over sexual harassment in the workplace (H.-L. Wang 1993; Yu 1984b). That provision prohibits several types of indecent conduct in public places, such as peeping, exposing oneself, and forcefully teasing or accosting members of the opposite sex. However, as this provision only deals with a very limited range of misconduct, it is inadequate to cover the whole spectrum of sexual harassment in the workplace. Besides, it only imposes an administrative fine on an offender and cannot provide the victim with any other compensatory remedy. Furthermore, using a police statute to govern behavior in the private sphere is inconsistent with the purposes of that law because it is designed mainly to handle conduct in public spaces. Therefore, that statute is also not a suitable mechanism for settling these kinds of disputes.

Theoretically, several "general protection" provisions in the Labor Standards Law of 1984 could provide employees with some protection in cases of sexual harassment. For instance, Article 11 of the law prohibits employers from terminating labor contracts without prior notice. However, the article is not applicable to sexual harassment because this kind of incident does not fall into any of the five categories of events that require special protection. Paragraph 2 of Article 14 of the law allows employees to terminate labor contracts without prior notice to their employers in cases when the employer, or the employer's relatives or agents, commit violence or other serious misconduct against them and requires employers to pay severance payment. Clearly this particular article can only serve as a last legal resort for employees who are forced to quit due to sexual harassment in their workplace. Fortunately, there is a new labor statute—the Employment Service Law of 1992—which has one article that can at least offer employees some form of legal remedy if they become the victim of sexual harassment in the workplace. According to Article 5 of that law, employers are prohibited from discriminating against applicants or employees because of the following factors: race, status, language, thought, religion, party affiliation, place of ancestry, sex, appearance, figure, disabilities, and labor union membership. Paragraph 2 of Section 5 of the Implementing Regulations of the law also stipulates that municipal and county governments may set up commissions on employment discrimination to determine whether a discriminatory act has been committed by the employer. Until now, these commissions have been established in eight municipalities and counties in Taiwan (Council of Labor Affairs 1996). Among these commissions, the most active is the one set up in Taipei in 1995. It has settled a number of employment discrimination disputes, one of which directly dealt with sexual harassment in the workplace. The ruling of this case has been widely covered by the local press and acclaimed by women's rights groups. Currently, these commissions are functioning on a trial-and-error basis and their merits and shortcomings have not yet been thoroughly assessed. One of the drawbacks of this law is that the sanction it can impose on the employer is rather light. For instance, in the sexual harassment case mentioned above, the commission could only suggest that the Bureau of Labor Affairs of Taipei City impose an administrative fine of NT$30,000 (equivalent to US$1,111)[3] on the employer. For a wealthy employer, this penalty is merely a slap on the wrist and therefore fails to serve as an effective deterrent.

Several Reform Proposals

In order to cope with the increasingly serious problems of sexual harassment in the workplace, the government and several women's rights groups have decided to make the prevention and elimination of these types of misconduct from the workplace an integral part of their efforts to enact a new Gender Equality in Employment Law. In the following pages, all relevant provisions in the four proposed bills will be summarized.

CLA. The bill prepared by the defines sexual harassment in the workplace as when "in the workplace or in the process of performing a labor contract, an individual, for the purpose of satisfying his (or her) own sexual desires, uses any physical conduct, explicit or implicit language, picture, film or other methods to accost another individual against her (or his) will, resulting in the infringement upon or interference with her (or his) personality, dignity, personal liberty, or work" (Para. III, Article 11). The bill also prohibits employers or supervisors from using the acceptance of sexual harassment by employees or applicants as a condition to decide upon the establishment or continuity of a labor contract, or to influence their conditions of employment (Para. IV). The bill further requires employers to work with labor unions or representatives of their employees to design necessary measures to stop sexual harassment and to display these measures publicly (Para I). Employers are also required to hold educational programs on this matter and to adopt appropriate disciplinary measures against those who commit sexual harassment (Para II). Finally, if Para. IV is violated, the bill imposes a fine of NT$50,000 to NT$300,000 on offending employers or supervisors (Article 22).

Taiwan Congressional Office. In the bill drafted by the Taiwan Congressional Office,[4] Article 16 stipulates that "no one shall use language, conduct or other methods of a sexual nature to cause annoyance to employees or applicants; to influence the evaluation of their work performances that can have a potential impact on employment; or actually cause a harm to their occupational safety." Article 17 of the bill also provides that "no employers shall use their authority to condition benefits or detriments of the job on employees' or applicants' responses to requests, made explicitly or implicitly, for sexual favors." For those employers or business firms violating these two provisions, a fine of NT$20,000 to NT$100,000 will be imposed and for those recidivist offenders, a double fine will be imposed. (Article 32).

Awakening Foundation. In the bill offered by the Foundation of Women with New Knowledge (Awakening Foundation)[5], an active women's rights group composed of professional working women, an entire chapter is devoted to the issue of sexual harassment in the workplace. It has four articles, each of which deals with an important topic. Article 20 of the bill stipulates that "employers, business entities and supervisors shall not, explicitly or implicitly, ask for sexual favors from employees or applicants, or use other language or conduct of a sexual nature as an exchange for the establishment, continuity or alteration of a labor contract." Article 21 of the bill provides that "employers and business entities shall prohibit anyone from asking for sexual favors or using language or conduct of a sexual nature in the workplace to cause an intimidating, hostile or offending work environment for employees; to infringe upon or interfere with their personality, dignity or personal liberty; or to affect their job performance. When employers and business entities knew or should have known of these instances of sexual harassment, they shall adopt prompt and effective corrective measures." Article 22 of the bill declares that "employers and business entities shall work with labor unions or representatives of their employees to design necessary measures to stop sexual harassment; to establish complaint procedures and disciplinary regulations; and to display them publicly in the workplace. Employers and business entities shall hold educational programs on this matter periodically." Article 23 of the bill provides that "the Central Competent Authority shall promulgate guidelines for identifying sexual harassment; measures for combating sexual harassment; and procedures for handling this matter and require employers and business entities to comply with, and to display them publicly in the workplace. Each level of the competent authorities shall also hold necessary educational and awareness programs to combat sexual harassment periodically." In case of violating Articles 20–21, employers and business entities are held liable for the loss incurred by the employees or applicants (Article 24). If employers and business entities are in violation of Article 22 of the bill, a fine of NT$10,000 to NT$50,000 will be imposed and can be assessed on multiple occasions for those recidivist offenders (Article 28).

Modern Women Foundation. The bill prepared by the Modern Women Foundation for dealing with sexual harassment in the workplace is probably the weakest among the proposed reform measures discussed. It merely copies the definition of sexual harassment in the workplace literally from that in the bill offered by the CLA. As for the major types of sexual harassment, it also omits the most serious one about prohibiting employers or supervisors from using their authority to extort sexual favors from their employees or applicants. The only meaningful provision in this bill is one which severely penalizes employers for not holding the necessary educational programs or for not adopting appropriate disciplinary measures (Article 22).

Corporate Responses to the Issue of Sexual Harassment in the Workplace in Taiwan

Of the surveys mentioned above, only a few deal specifically with the reactions of the local business community towards various issues concerning sexual harassment in the workplace. In the following pages, two major surveys commissioned by the CLA will be examined to analyze employer responses to this issue. Since employers' commitment plays a pivotal role in the successful implementation of measures to prevent and stop sexual harassment in the workplace, their views on several crucial aspects of the issue merit special attention.

It should be pointed out, however, that although these findings can provide the government with some useful information about local business firms' attitudes towards the issue of sexual harassment in the workplace if it decides to enact a new law in the near future, both of the surveys had similar problems of being under-representative because of the low rate of reply from local employers. For instance, in the 1993 survey, researchers randomly sent out 868 letters to local private enterprises to solicit their answers, but only 99 of them bothered to reply and from that, only 85 were valid samples. The responses of the government departments to the same survey were much more enthusiastic—250 letters were sent, 147 of them replied and 112 were valid samples. The total valid response rate was 17.62 per cent (Lu and Fu 1993). The response rate of the 1996 survey was slightly higher. In that survey, researchers sent out 500 letters to the biggest local companies and 122 of them replied, with a response rate of 24.4 per cent (China Institute of Industrial Relations 1996). Since over 95 per cent of business firms in Taiwan are medium or small size enterprises, the findings of this survey would also not precisely reflect the opinions of the entire business community.

The 1993 Survey

Generally speaking, corporate reactions to the issue of sexual harassment in the workplace are mixed. According to the findings of the above-mentioned research commissioned by the CLA in 1993 (Lu and Fu 1993), most of employers agreed that all of the twenty types of particular conduct listed in the questionnaires constituted sexual harassment and that the degree of acceptance of these types of conduct was consistent with the seriousness of the behavior. For instance, over 90 per cent of them agreed that sexual assault, sexual coercion, sexual bribery or other types of unwanted physical touching should be regarded as sexual harassment. Between 70 to 80 per cent of them agreed that unsolicited sexual advances or propositions and the display or posting of obscene or pornographic materials could be treated as sexual harassment. And between 50 to 60 per cent of them agreed that habitually making lewd jokes, commenting on figures or physical characteristics, talking about personal sex life or history, and expressing sexist comments could be defined as sexual harassment.

However, a substantial portion of them still regarded these incidents as personal matters between female and male employees. For instance, over one-third of surveyed employers thought many so-called sexual harassment incidents were only flirtations between the opposite sexes (35.6 per cent), did not regard them as serious matters (37.3 per cent), or attributed them to the fact that some women were simply too sensitive or jumpy to take a joke (37.3 per cent). Besides, they tended to have some deep-rooted sexual stereotyping perceptions about women that led a large majority of them to believe that beautiful or attractive women were much more likely to become the target of sexual harassment (74.3 per cent) and that working women would sometimes deliberately accost their superiors for the purpose of gaining certain privileges (53.4 per cent). Furthermore, a vast majority of them even adopted a blame-the-victim stance towards those women who claimed to have been sexually harassed. For instance, over three-fourths of employers questioned replied that decent and self-respecting women normally would not become the target of sexual harassment (77.7 per cent). If a woman did become a target, most employers agreed that her conduct or attire must have been questionable (61.6 per cent).

As for the actual complaints about incidents of workplace sexual harassment received by employers, most of them belonged to the categories of habitually making lewd jokes (29.6 per cent), comments regarding figures or physical characteristics (25.5 per cent), sexist comments (13.8 per cent), and unwanted sexual attention (10.7 per cent). Only a very small portion of the conduct complained of had reached the level of sexual assault, sexual coercion and sexual bribery (0.5 to1.5 per cent). When employers received these complaints of sexual harassment, they normally adopted one of the following methods to handle these grievances: (1) comforting the victim (35.6 per cent); (2) admonishing or disciplining the alleged harasser (27.8 per cent); (3) suggesting that the victim take measures to stop or resist the harassing conduct by herself (25.6 per cent); (4) reassigning the alleged harasser to a new post (16.7 per cent); (5) reporting the incidents to a higher superior (16.7 per cent); (6) ignoring these complaints (12.2 per cent); or (7) reassigning the victim to a new post (10 per cent).[6]

Among those employers surveyed, a little less than one-third suggested that in order to combat sexual harassment in the workplace more effectively, the government should enact a new Gender Equality in Employment Law, provide a clear definition of sexual harassment in it for them to follow, clarify the nature of the penalties, and emphasize employers' responsibilities (29.6 per cent). They also proposed to hold awareness campaigns to promote the concept of gender equality (28.9 per cent) and to strengthen public understanding that sexual harassment is an inappropriate conduct or behavior (18.3 per cent). A small portion of them also asked for the government to promulgate guidelines to help local business firms handle sexual harassment (6.3 per cent). Other proposals included: strengthen sex education (4.9 per cent); impose heavier employer liability (4.2 per cent); penalize harasser with criminal sanctions (2.8 per cent); use current legal provisions and let victims file their own cases to the courts to seek redress directly (2.1 per cent); and the establishment by the government of an independent specialized agency to deal with this matter (0.7 per cent).

As for specific measures which employers themselves should adopt in their workplace, almost one-half of them replied that training and seminar programs should be held to let employees know that sexual harassment is an inappropriate behavior and to provide instruction on how to handle it individually (49 per cent). Over 20 per cent of them also agreed to establish internal complaint mechanisms for the victims to report their cases (22.9 per cent). The third priority on their list was the promulgation of a policy statement on sexual harassment which would clearly declare that these kinds of conduct or behavior are prohibited (15.3 per cent). Other preventive or corrective methods offered by employers also included: punishing and warning the perpetrators (5.1 per cent); holding training sessions and group discussion programs for supervisors or managerial personnel to let them know how to handle this matter (1.9 per cent); allowing representatives of employees to organize a special group to handle this issue (1.9 per cent); punishing or warning those supervisors or managerial personnel who had inappropriately handled these cases (0.6 per cent); and submitting sexual harassment cases to neutral organizations for arbitration (0.6 per cent).

The 1996 Survey

The CLA also sponsored another research program in 1996 to evaluate corporation's and labor unions' responses to the enactment of the proposed Gender Equality in Employment Bill. Among the variety of questions asked, a few of them were directly related to the issue of sexual harassment in the workplace. According to the findings of this survey, which was released in June 1996, the local business firms' reactions towards this issue seemed to be very encouraging (China Institute of Industrial Relations 1996). For instance, over 60 per cent of them agreed to set up special work rules to prohibit sexual harassment in their workplace (64.2 per cent). Among those employers willing to establish these rules, most of them acknowledged that they needed help designing a suitable manual on sexual harassment for their employees (72 per cent) and 65 per cent of them expressed the need for assistance in designing necessary training programs. The survey did not ask employers whether incidents of sexual harassment had actually occurred in their workplace or if they had already established any internal mechanism to deal with this problem, but nearly 20 per cent of labor unions questioned in the same survey reported that these kinds of incidents had happened in the companies with which they were affiliated (19.7 per cent) and that only a few of these business entities had established any procedure to handle this kind of labor dispute (6.7 per cent). Among those business firms who did not promulgate any work rules to prohibit sexual harassment in their workplace, most of them regarded these incidents as if they had never or only occasionally happened, and therefore believed that there was no urgent need to do anything. Some of these companies had decided to adopt a "hands-off" approach because they viewed this issue as a personal matter and thought it was better if matters like these were left for the employees themselves to solve. A few of them also indicated that the whole issue was so complicated that no norms in the workplace could be all-inclusive enough to cover all aspects of it.

A number of other related findings contained in this survey can also be used to gauge local business firms' attitudes towards the issue of sexual harassment in their workplace. First, it was discovered that currently only a small portion of companies have established any internal procedures to resolve grievances and settle disputes about employment discrimination in their workplace (16.7 per cent) and that, among firms with no such procedures, their intentions to establish these mechanisms in the future are low (21.7 per cent). This finding clearly indicates that using internal procedures to cope with disputes and grievances related to employment discrimination in general and sexual harassment in particular within the enterprises themselves is still not a common practice in Taiwan. Second, the survey found out that although most of employers prefer to use the procedures in the current Settlement of Labor Disputes Law of 1987 to solve disputes over gender issues in the workplace (47 per cent), a substantial number of them also pointed out that they would support the creation of a new independent agency to resolve these disputes (34.2 per cent) or would submit these disputes to the above-mentioned Commission on Employment Discrimination for settlement (14 per cent). Only a very small portion of them preferred to use litigation in judicial courts to settle these types of disputes (4.4 per cent). This finding clearly indicates that a large number of local employers have gradually concluded that disputes over sex discrimination in employment can be better handled through informal and non-judicial procedures. Third, for those employers supporting the idea of establishing a specialized agency, a majority of them suggested that this proposed institute should be affiliated with the CLA (52.4 per cent) and one-third of them expressed their opinion that the status of this agency should be upgraded to a cabinet-level position (31 per cent). Less than 17 per cent of them wanted it to become a sub-unit of the county government (16.7 per cent). Finally, regarding the composition of this specialized agency, over 90 per cent of employers agreed that representatives from employer associations, employee organizations and government officials should have equal membership and they overwhelmingly supported the proposal that women comprise at least half of the membership of this agency (95.8 per cent).

Sexual Harassment in the Workplace in the United States

In the past thirty years, through the operation and regulation of various fair employment opportunity statutes, the interpretations of numerous related judicial decisions, the protection offered by a vast majority of collective bargaining agreements, and the numerous preventive and remedial measures adopted by employers, the United States has developed an integrated legal system to deal with the problem of sexual harassment in the workplace. In fact, according to a survey of twenty-three industrialized nations published by the International Labor Organization (ILO) in 1992, the United States was rated as having the soundest system for preventing and combating this problem (International Labor Office 1992). Thus, if Taiwan really tries to set up a similar system under the proposed Gender Equality in Employment Bill, it should pay a close attention to the development of the system in that country and to the experiences it has accumulated.

Prevalence and Seriousness of the Problem

Sexual harassment has been a serious problem in the American workplace. According to a famous survey of working women released by the *Redbook Magazine* in 1976, among 9,000 respondents over 88 per cent claimed that they had experienced some type of sexual harassment at work (MacKinnon 1979; Pollack 1990). Subsequently, a series of small-scale surveys released between 1980 to 1989 also revealed that between 36 to 53 per cent of female workers claimed that they were the victims of sexual harassment (Gutek 1992). Since a large number of these incidents were not reported through formal complaint channels, it is estimated that the actual numbers of such incidents were much higher (Note 1991; Pollack 1990).

Employees who have experienced harassment may develop a variety of psychological and physical syndromes and their job performance tends to deteriorate noticeably. Oftentimes they are discharged or forced to resign as a result of these events. In this way, the adverse impact of sexual harassment extends to their economic interests and well-being (Chiao 1995; Schoenheider 1986; Lipper 1992). For companies and employers, sexual harassment not only contributes to a variety of personnel difficulties, such as divided loyalty, low morale, reduced productivity, and absenteeism among employees, but also can increase the risk of turn-over (Bravo and Cassedy 1992; Kandel 1988; Larson 1992). The publicity of a sexual harassment scandal can also irreparably damage the corporate image. Worst of all, it has become a nightmare for employers in terms of monetary expenditures. For instance, a survey of 160 *Fortune*-500 corporations in 1988 discovered that, on average, a corporation loses around $6.7 million dollars each year due to these incidents—not including legal fees (Chiao 1993). By 1993, this amount had increased to $8 million (Chiao 1997a). A well-publicized sexual harassment lawsuit can also cost employers a tremendous amount of money. For instance, in 1994 Baker & McKenzie, a famous law firm, was ordered by a jury to pay $7.1 million U.S. dollars to a victim of sexual harassment as punitive damages for one of its senior partners' transgressions (later reduced to one-half by a lenient judge) (Chiao 1994).

In the public sector, especially in the federal government, where personnel statutes and policies are supposed to offer employees better protection against sexual harassment, the situation is no better. For instance, according to the often-quoted findings of three large-scale surveys conducted in 1980, 1987 and 1994 by the U.S. Merit Systems Protection Board, between 42 to 44 per cent of female employees and between 15 to 19 per cent of male employees claimed that they had encountered some type of unwanted sexual attention in the past two years (U.S. Merit Systems Protection Board 1981, 1988, 1995). As for federal government expenditures on sexual harassment, they have steadily increased from $180 million U.S. dollars (1978–1980) to $260 million U.S. dollars (1984–1986), and then to $327 million U.S. dollars (1992–1994) (Chiao 1997a).

Recently, the most serious incidents of sexual harassment in the public sector have taken place in the military. In 1991, the "Tailhook Scandal," in which a group of navy and marine pilots sexually abused and assaulted twenty-six female colleagues, was first exposed by the American Broadcasting Service (ABC). It became such a national issue that not only were the alleged offenders were court-martialed, the Secretary of Navy and a number of high-ranking naval generals were also forced to resign as a result of the scandal (Chiao 1994). In the same year, after the Persian Gulf War, a number of woman soldiers alleged that they had been sexually molested and assaulted during Operation Desert Storm. Subsequent congressional investigations revealed that at least one-third of woman soldiers on active duty in the military had experienced similarly unpleasant incidents (Chiao 1994). In December 1996, the press again reported a series of allegations of sexual harassment and assaults at a U.S. Army training camp in Aberdeen Proving Ground, Maryland, where a large number of veteran drilling sergeants were accused of sexually attacking and intimidating their female subordinates. In a disturbing twist of events, a sergeant master in charge of investigating and overseeing the issue of sexual harassment in the Army was implicated in a separate sexual harassment charge by a former subordinate and was suspended from his duty (Chiao 1997a). The entire scandal is still unfolding, and the integration of the sexes in the military has once again become a hotly debated political topic.

In recent years, sexual harassment in the federal government has reached such an unprecedented level that even some of the most powerful office-holders in the three branches of the government are embroiled in these scandals. In addition to the above-mentioned Anita Hill v. Clarence Thomas saga, Senator Robert Packwood (R-Oregon), chairman of the influential Senate Finance Committee, was forced to resign in September 1995 after a group consisting of seventeen female secretaries from his own staff accused him of sexual harassment and assault (Chiao 1997a). Even President Clinton has been embroiled in a long-drawn-out legal battle in light of the sexual harassment allegations coming from Paula Jones.

Finally, another useful indicator to gauge the prevalence of sexual harassment in the American workplace is the number of formal complaints received by the EEOC each year. After the Senate confirmation hearings on Clarence Thomas's nomination to the U.S. Supreme Court in 1991, sexual harassment cases filed with that independent federal agency increased dramatically. In 1992, it received about 10,000 complaints of sexual harassment, almost seventy per cent more than the previous year. The number of cases reached nearly 12,000 in 1993 and, in 1994, the number rose even higher, to 14,000. In 1995 and 1996, the numbers reached to 15,000 and slightly less than 15,000 respectively (Chiao 1997a). Burdened with such a heavy caseload, it is no wonder that this specialized agency has been unable to perform its statutory functions effectively in recent years (to be discussed later).

Current American Legal Regime Governing Sexual Harassment in the Workplace

Currently, the most important federal statute governing sexual harassment in the workplace is Title VII of the Civil Rights Act of 1964. Under this law, it is unlawful for an employer to discriminate against any individual with respect to his (or her) compensation, terms, conditions, or privileges of employment because of this individual's "race, color, religion, sex, or national origin" (emphasis added). Because the term "sex" was added by a congressman from Virginia at the eleventh hour during the congressional debate of this landmark legislation to sabotage its passage, Congress did not elaborate on the meaning and the scope of this prohibition (Estrich 1991; Mathews 1991). Due to the ambiguous legislative history of the prohibition of sex discrimination in Title VII, courts initially had trouble interpreting sexual harassment as a form of sex-based discrimination prohibited by this Title (Abrams 1989; Korn 1993; Lindermann and Kadue 1992). However, from 1976 on, the courts have gradually recognized sexual harassment as an actionable form of sex discrimination under Title VII and this principle received a strong endorsement from the U.S. Supreme Court in 1986 (to be discussed later). The 1964 statute also establishes an independent EEOC to enforce this federal fair employment opportunity law. After two substantial amendments in 1968 and 1972 respectively, this law now applies to the government at all levels and to all employers in the private sector with fifteen or more employees engaging in an industry affecting commerce. Normally, the Commission settles disputes over sexual harassment through informal procedures, such as conference, conciliation and persuasion. But it can also file suits in federal district courts on behalf of the complainants or it can allow them to sue in person after receiving a "right-to-sue" letter from the Commission (Chiao 1996b).

The Commission has played an important role in shaping workplace sexual harassment law in the United States. In 1980, it promulgated the famous *Guidelines on Discrimination Because of Sex* (EEOC Guidelines). According to these guidelines, sexual harassment is defined as unwelcome sexual advances, requests for sexual favors, and other verbal or physical conduct of a sexual nature when (1) submission to such conduct is made either explicitly or implicitly a term or condition of an individual employment, (2) submission to or rejection of such conduct by an individual is used as the basis for employment decisions affecting said individual, or (3) such conduct has "the purpose or effect of unreasonably interfering with an individual's work performance or of creating an intimidating, hostile, or offensive working environment." These guidelines recognize four forms of sexual harassment: quid pro quo harassment, hostile (or abusive) work environment harassment, sexual favoritism (indirect or "reverse" quid pro quo sexual harassment), and harassment by non-employees (Chiao 1993; Hwang 1995). The guidelines also clarify employer liability in these cases. An employer is responsible for the acts of its supervisors, regardless of whether the employer knew or should have known that the harassment occurred. The employer is liable for the conduct of a co-worker or non-employee only if the employer knew, or should have known, about the conduct and failed to take immediate corrective action. Finally, the guidelines also emphasize prevention as the best tool for the elimination of sexual harassment. They urge an employer to take all necessary steps to prevent these incidents from occurring through raising the subject, expressing disapproval, imposing sanctions, educating employees, and sensitizing all concerned. Generally, these guidelines are only of an interpretative nature and are not binding in the courts. Nevertheless, most federal courts regard these guidelines as a body of experience and informed judgment to which the courts may properly resort for guidance. Accordingly, the guidelines have had a profound impact on the development of sexual harassment law in the United States (Chiao 1997a). Subsequently, the EEOC also issued a *Policy Guidance on Current Issues of Sexual Harassment* in March 1990. The *Guidance* clarifies several controversial aspects of sexual harassment law, based on a growing body of legal precedent. It redefines the meaning of hostile work sexual harassment and reassesses employer liability in these disputes. Although this document is only for internal use by local staff of the agency, its importance is no less significant than the guidelines discussed above (Chiao 1997a).

Although Title VII of the Civil Rights Act 1964 has become the most important fair employment opportunity statute in dealing with sexual harassment in the workplace, the remedies it can provide are quite limited. Plaintiffs can only demand equitable relief, such as injunctions, back pay, interest on back pay, reinstatement, and reasonable attorney fees. The courts have typically decided that monetary damages, both compensatory and punitive, are not practicable in such cases. Therefore, for those plaintiffs not suffering any tangible economic loss in sexual harassment, their incentive to file these lawsuits is very low (Baxter, Jr. and Hermle 1989; Note 1995). In 1991, Congress passed the Civil Rights Act of 1991 to overturn several controversial U.S. Supreme Court rulings on employment discrimination issues in the term from 1988 to 1990 (Appruzzese 1992; Carrillo 1992–93; Chiao 1996b; Hartstein and Wilde 1994; Petrocelli and Repa 1995). The new law made substantial amendments to Title VII of the Civil Rights Act of 1964, providing monetary damages for the winning plaintiffs in intentional discrimination cases (with a cap from US$50,000 to $300,000, depending on the size of employers' business) and allowing a jury trial when compensatory or punitive damages are sought. It also provided for an award of fees for experts whose testimony has become more and more relevant in these disputes. The new law also encouraged disputants to use alternate dispute resolutions (ADRs), including settlement negotiations, conciliation, facilitation, mediation, fact-finding, mini-trials, and arbitration to settle their sexual harassment claims informally (Appruzzese 1992). Finally, the Act reiterated the principle of extra-territoriality by declaring that this Act, along with other relevant federal fair employment opportunity statutes, can apply to American firms overseas for the purpose of providing necessary legal protection for those American employees working outside the U.S. territories (Chiao 1996b).

Important Court Decisions

In the past three decades, it is estimated that the federal courts have decided over three hundred and seventy workplace sexual harassment cases (Chiao 1997a). In the following pages, a number of major decisions will be described chronologically in order to illustrate judicial attitudes towards this important social issue (Chiao 1993, 1994, 1995, 1996a, 1997a, 1997b).

From 1974 to 1976. Most of the federal courts generally did not recognize sexual harassment as actionable under Title VII. Some courts held that sexual harassment only involved a personal urge or personal proclivity on the part of the harasser and therefore that it was not sex discrimination under Title VII. Such rulings can be found in *Barnes v. Train*, *Corne v. Bausch and Lomb, Inc.*[8], and *Tomkins v. Public Service Electric & Gas Co.*[9] Some courts also denied such claims under Title VII for fear of unleashing an unmanageable increase in caseloads. The ruling in *Miller v. Bank of America*[10] is a good example of this (Bureau of National Affairs 1988).

From 1976 to 1979. The courts gradually started to recognize sexual harassment as actionable sex discrimination under Title VII. For instance, in *William v. Saxbe*[11], the federal district court for the first time ruled that quid pro quo harassment, that is, conditioning tangible employment benefits on sexual favors, is an illegal act of sex discrimination prohibited by Title VII. In deciding *Barnes v. Costle*[12], a case which involved an African-American woman who refused her supervisor's sexual advances and was subsequently discharged, the Court of Appeals also ruled that Title VII was violated. However, there were still many district courts which did not treat sexual harassment as a form of sex discrimination or did not recognize that employers should be held liable for these incidents (Bureau of National Affairs 1988; Chiao 1997a).

From 1980 to 1986. After the famous EEOC Guidelines were promulgated, the Courts of Appeals gradually started to recognize hostile work environment harassment as a violation of Title VII. For instance, in Bundy v. Jackson[13], a circuit court for the first time ruled that hostile environment sexual harassment was actionable under Title VII. Afterwards, in the famous *Henson v. City of Dundee*[14] case, an appellate court stated that a victim need not prove tangible job detriment in order to state a claim under Title VII. Instead, the victim need only prove that the conduct is sufficiently pervasive to alter the conditions of employment and create an abusive work environment. Furthermore, the Henson court also established the following five-prong test to apply to hostile work environment sexual harassment claims: (a) that the employee is a member of a protected class; (b) that the employee is subjected to unwelcome sexual harassment; (c) that the harassment is based on sex; (d) that the harassment affects a term, condition, or privilege of employment; and (e) the existence of respondent superior liability, i.e., that the employer knew or should have known about the harassment and failed to take prompt remedial action. Subsequently, other courts have also relied on these five elements in evaluating hostile work environment claims (Burns 1994–95; Chiao 1993; Korn 1993; Pollack 1990).

In 1986. The U.S. Supreme Court made its first decision on sexual harassment in the workplace in *Meritor Savings Bank FSB v. Vinson*[15]. In this landmark case, the Court relied heavily on the EEOC Guidelines and held that hostile work environment sexual harassment, like quid pro quo sexual harassment, violated Title VII. It held that this type of harassment existed when the conduct had the intent or effect of unreasonably interfering with an individual's work performance or of creating an intimidating, hostile, or offensive working environment. However, for sexual harassment to be actionable, it must be sufficiently severe or pervasive to alter the conditions of employment and to create an abusive working environment. The Court also used "welcomeness" instead of "voluntariness" as the gravamen of any sexual harassment claim and regarded the plaintiff's own attire and speech as relevant to such a finding (Note 1992). It also held that, in this case, the employer's policies and procedures for the prevention of sexual harassment policy were inadequate to shield the employer from liability because they required the plaintiff to file her complaint to her supervisor, in this case, the harasser himself. Finally, it ruled that the employer was not automatically liable for conduct of its supervisory personnel that created hostile environment sexual harassment and that the principle of agency law should apply to determine employer liability (Burns 1994–95; Carrillo 1992–93).

From 1986 to 1993. The federal courts handed down a series of cases to clarify the aftermath of *Meritor*, two areas of which split the lower courts' opinions substantially: the elements necessary to assert a hostile work environment sexual harassment claim, and employer liability for supervisory employees' conduct in such a case. In the first area of difference, the Sixth Circuit Court of Appeals required in *Rabidue v. Osceola Refining Co.*[16] that to prove the existence of a hostile work environment, a plaintiff must show that her (or his) psychological well-being was seriously affected. Conversely, the Ninth Circuit Court of Appeals in *Ellison v. Brady*[17] rejected this psychological well-being requirement and adopted an innovative "reasonable woman" standard to evaluate the pervasiveness of the harassing conduct (Chiao 1993; Note 1994). In addition, the appellate courts also expressed divergent opinions, six different standards in twelve circuits, on the issue of employer liability in cases where supervisory employees created a hostile work environment (Chiao 1997a). Finally, in the famous *Robinson v. Jacksonville Shipyards*[18] case, a federal district court even designed a comprehensive sexual harassment policy for a losing defendant to adopt (Chiao 1997a; Connell 1991).

In 1993. The Supreme Court ruled in *Harris v. Forklift Systems, Inc.*[19], its second decision on sexual harassment in the workplace, that a hostile work environment claim does not require that the victim suffer serious psychological injury. Furthermore, it also ruled that this type of sexual harassment must be both objectively perceived to be hostile by the finder of fact and subjectively perceived to be hostile by the victim. Therefore, the Court resolved the split of opinions among the appellate courts by clarifying the definition of sexual harassment (Burns 1994–95; Chiao 1996b, 1997b; Note 1994; Hartstein and Wilde 1994). The Court did not, however, solve the issue of employer liability in this case and the lower circuit courts are still struggling to find an answer (Chiao 1997b).

From 1993 to the present. After *Harris* has made it easier for the victim to make a sexual harassment claim, a number of lower court decisions have been concentrated on whether employers have adopted adequate preventive and corrective measures to determine the degree their liability. For instance, in *Baskerville v. Culligan International*[20], employer liability was absolved by the Seventh Circuit Court of Appeals because the company had taken prompt and effective actions to stop the claimed sexual harassment. However, in *Fuller v. City of Oakland, California*[21], the employer was held liable by the Ninth Circuit Court of Appeals for not implementing necessary remedial measures. In *Chalmers v. Quaker Oats Co.*[22], the Seventh Circuit Court of Appeals even allowed the employer to adopt stricter preventive measures than the federal laws required (Chiao 1997a). All of these decisions clearly illustrate the importance of prophylactic measures adopted by the employers to prevent sexual harassment in their workplace after the Supreme Court in *Meritor* and *Harris* decisions made it easier for victims to raise this claim in the courts. In 1998, the U.S. Supreme Court passed down three more decisions. In *Oncale v. Sundowner Offshore Services Inc.*[23], the claim of same sex sexual harassment was allowed in accordance with Title VII of the Civil Rights Act of 1964. In the next two cases, *Faragher v. City of Boca Raton*[24] and *Burlington Industries v. Ellerth*[25], the Court gave a clearer definition of employer liability for supervisory harassment in the workplace, thus placing the employer in a position of greater responsibility to implement preventive and corrective measures against sexual harassment.

The Applicability of American Corporate Practices to Taiwan

In the following pages of this section, various preventive and corrective measures adopted by American business firms to deal with sexual harassment problems in the workplace will be discussed. Then the merits and shortcomings of the American system in general will be briefly analyzed. Finally, this section will discuss how employers in Taiwan can learn from their American counterparts in effectively preventing sexual harassment in the workplace.

Corporate Responses to Sexual Harassment in American Workplace

Business firms in the United States react very seriously to the issue of sexual harassment in their workplace. According to the information available, all *Fortune*–500 corporations have already set up a variety of mechanisms to prevent these problems from occurring or to minimize their legal liability when these disputes go to the EEOC or the courts (Baxter, Jr. and Hermle 1989; Bryson 1990; Chiao 1997a; Commerce Clearing House 1991; Federal Personnel Management Institute, Inc. 1989; National Association of Manufacturers 1987; Note 1991; Oh 1992; Sepler 1990;

Simmons 1993; Wagner 1992). The following is a summary of common practices they have adopted to respond to and prevent sexual harassment.

Developing and implementing a comprehensive and well-publicized policy statement to prohibit sexual harassment in the workplace. Many employers have implemented such policies, since an employer may offer proof of a well-established harassment policy as a defense against sexual harassment claims by employees. Likewise, courts may view an employer's failure to set up a comprehensive sexual harassment policy as condoning misconduct among employees. Therefore, companies in the United States now have a very strong incentive to develop an effective harassment deterrence policy. Typically, the key elements of a policy include: an unequivocal statement proclaiming that sexual harassment will not be tolerated in the company; a clear definition of sexual harassment and a list of examples of actionable conduct; a brief description of the internal procedures for bringing complaints and a list of the individual(s) designated to receive and address such complaints; a promise that the company will maintain a complainant's confidentiality to the fullest extent possible; a guarantee that the employee will not be punished for voicing a complaint; and a statement of the corrective action the company will take in the case of sexually harassing conduct, if substantiated, up to and including disciplinary discharges. In order insure that all employees (supervisory and non-supervisory) are aware of this important policy, the company usually communicates and disseminates it as widely as possible, by posting it on notice boards, including it in personnel manuals and training materials or even on E-mail and by asking employees to submit a written acknowledgement of receipt.

Adopting an internal complaint procedure. There are two types of complaint procedures, formal and informal, and the company can utilize one or both of them according to its own needs. Normally, if there is a collective bargaining agreement in existence with grievance procedures that are capable of handling this kind of issue, then a formal mechanism is not necessary. However, it is recognized that these procedures must be able to: (a) provide the victims with ample opportunity to state their grievances; (b) guarantee procedural due process for both parties involved in the incidents; (c) demonstrate effectiveness in settling these disputes in a prompt and timely fashion; (d) have appropriate mechanisms for appeals and reviews; (e) have stipulations to assure confidentiality; and (f) provide protection against retaliatory action (Wagner 1992). Generally speaking, informal procedures can provide a number of flexible approaches for settling these conflicts. The company usually designates one or more Equal Employment Officers (EEOs) (a majority of them are female personnel, depending on the case itself) to offer consultative services to the employee and to solve the problem as quickly as possible. The company sometimes encourages its employees to use this procedure before filing a formal complaint. Because most of the victims in these cases generally only want the perpetrators to stop their offensive conduct, methods such as conference, conciliation or mediation can often achieve results that are satisfactory to both parties.

Conducting a prompt, objective, thorough, and confidential investigation on all sexual harassment claims. When the company receives a complaint from an employee, it usually starts a preliminary investigation (Bryson 1990; Oh 1992; Simmons 1993). Through this process, the complainant is interviewed by EEO personnel and all related information is collected. Her (or his) preferred response from the company is ascertained and she (or he) is also assured that no retaliatory measures will be taken against her (or him). If the preliminary investigation proves that sexual harassment did occur, then a formal investigation procedure will be triggered. Normally, a neutral third party will be appointed to conduct this investigation. During this process, a series of interviews will be conducted. Different questions will be asked in accordance with the status of the interviewees (complainants, harassers, supervisors, and witnesses). Procedural fairness and the protection of privacy are normally strictly observed during the investigation. Confidentiality is also maintained to the greatest extent possible in order to encourage employees to use complaint procedures and to protect the employer from defamation lawsuits by the alleged harasser (Kennedy 1994). If the accusation cannot stand after the investigation, the company normally will inform the parties involved and reiterate its commitment to the prohibition of sexual harassment in the workplace. If the accusation cannot be substantiated by the investigation, the employer can still take other measures to ensure that questionable, if not harassing, conduct will not occur (Baxter, Jr. and Hermle 1989).

Taking appropriate corrective action. If an investigation reveals that harassment did occur, then the company will take a variety of corrective actions. Normally, the company will adopt progressive disciplinary measures against the harasser in correspondence to the severity of the misconduct. In addition, these actions also are designed, insofar as is possible, to end the harassment and prevent future occurrences. The company generally will impose one or more of the following punishments: an oral reprimand, a written warning, transfer to another department or post, demotion, and delay in receiving promotion or raise in salary. In some extreme and serious cases, the offender will be discharged to protect the interests of the company and other employees. In addition, after corrective action is taken, the company will adopt follow-up measures to monitor the situation to ensure that harassment does not recur and that the victim is not retaliated against. Finally, some companies will compensate her or him for lost job benefits (back pay) or opportunities (posts or promotion). In some cases, free counseling or other medical and psychological assistance are offered. After the company has adopted corrective measures, it will typically reiterate its commitment to the eradication of sexual harassment in the workplace to all employees. However, in order to avoid a defamation suit by the alleged or discharged harasser, the company is usually quite cautious to avoid exposing his (or her) identity (Kennedy 1994).

Adopting additional preventive measures. In addition to the above-mentioned action, some companies also execute a variety of supplementary measures to improve their practices. For instance, some of them conduct exit interviews to determine whether the departing employee was forced to resign due to harassment. If this is discovered to be true, then the employee will be persuaded to stay until the whole matter is resolved. Under such circumstances, the employer not only can discover an unexposed incident, but also can avoid future wrongful discharge claims (Wagner 1992). Some companies have also set up special telephone hot-lines or mailboxes to encourage their employees to blow the whistle. Although anonymous tips are generally not processed, they can certainly serve as an early warning system (Oh 1992). Some employers also vigilantly inspect their workplace to find out whether employees have displayed offending materials or engaged in inappropriate sexual horseplay (Wagner 1992). In the meantime, some employers treat gossip and rumors of their employees attentively and actively pursue an investigation if the same person has been repeatedly mentioned (Wagner 1992).

Strengthening awareness among employees and providing necessary educational programs for them. Because employees at different levels of a company play different roles in these incidents, these programs always are tailored to their special needs. For instance, since managerial and supervisory employees are in a pivotal position to handle this issue in the workplace, their training programs normally are concentrated on the contents of relevant statutes, administrative regulations, company policy, and employer liability; the operation of internal complaint procedures, investigation processes, and other administrative or judicial relief; and the methods and skills to prevent and stop these incidents from occurring. Some companies also offer group discussions, critiques of video programs and role-playing to ensure that these personnel are equipped to handle their responsibilities (Wagner 1992). For non-supervisory employees, training programs are mainly focused on the norms of person-to-person relationships and not on related legal problems or personnel administration. During these training sessions, in addition to emphasizing the companies' stance on sexual harassment, they also encourage employees to participate actively in the development of the company's harassment policy, complaint procedures, investigation processes, and other corrective programs (Wagner 1992). For those personnel in charge of investigation, their training programs consist mainly of the techniques of asking the right questions, handling hesitant or uncooperative witnesses, discovering evidence, determining the credibility of the interviewees, using informal means to mediate the disputes, and preparing findings and recommendations for the employers. Occasionally, they may have to work with in-house or outside legal counsel to process their investigation, therefore, a certain amount of training on sexual harassment law is also useful (Bryson 1990; Oh 1992; Wagner 1992).

A Critical Evaluation of the American System

Generally speaking, the American system has the following merits in dealing with sexual harassment in the workplace. First, in the past three decades, it has developed an integrated legal system to handle this issue that can provide the victim with adequate legal protection. In addition to Title VII of the Civil Rights Act of 1964 and the Civil Rights Act of 1991, victims of these workplace incidents can also resort to various state fair employment opportunity statutes to seek redress. In addition, a variety of remedies provided by common law, such as torts and contracts, can also be used to supplement statutory protection offered by anti-discrimination laws. Furthermore, several public-interest state labor statutes, such as the workers' compensation statutes and the unemployment insurance statutes, can also be invoked to offer the complainant supplementary remedies (Lindermann and Kadue 1992). Collective bargaining agreements also play an important role in combating sexual harassment at work. Currently, almost ninety five per cent of these agreements contain anti-discrimination and anti-sexual harassment provisions. Labor unions are under contractual and statutory obligations to fairly represent their members in processing these kinds of grievances and labor arbitration has been widely used to handle these disputes. Second, in addition to utilizing various internal complaint procedures in the companies, grievance procedures in collective bargaining agreements, administrative processes of the fair employment opportunity agencies and judicial processes of the courts, victims of these incidents can also rely on other informal channels for assistance. For instance, numerous human and women's rights groups, such as the American Civil Liberties Union (ACLU), the National Organization for Women (NOW), 9 to 5, National Association of Working Women, the National Women's Law Center, the Women's Legal Defense Fund (WLDF) and the Women's Alliance for Job Equity, etc. can offer necessary information or even legal services (Baxter, Jr. and Hermle 1989; Petrocelli and Repa 1995; Wagner 1992). Finally, the courts at every level in the United States have also played a constructive role in promoting the awareness of this issue. In addition to using the EEOC Guidelines to render various useful interpretations to clarify the issues of "run-of-the-mill" sexual harassment, they have also handed down a number of innovative rulings that can be used as guidance for employers to handle such disputes as same sex harassment, office romance, sexual favoritism, or even e-mail harassment in their workplace (Abrams 1989; Bureau of National Affairs 1988; Chiao 1997a; Larson 1992).

However, the shortcomings of the American system have also been gradually exposed in the past thirty years. First, because Title VII of the Civil Rights Act of 1964 does not apply to enterprises with less than fifteen employees, those employed in the small-scale companies become the most vulnerable in terms of receiving legal protection from sexual harassment in the workplace. Although the Equal Employment Opportunities Act of 1972 enlarged the scope of coverage from business firms with twenty five employees to fifteen, further reforms to remove this limitation on coverage have not materialized. Therefore, the United States is the only industrialized country that still has a major fair employment opportunity statute with limited application (Chiao 1996b). Second, the EEOC's capacity to settle disputes arising out of sexual harassment has been hampered in recent years by a reduced budget, inadequate manpower, and heavy caseload. It is estimated that over seventy per cent of its budget is earmarked for personnel expenditures and after a substantial budget cut in the Federal Government, its ability to handle employment discrimination cases has been impeded considerably. On average, it takes over 270 days to process a complaint and the number of unsettled cases has reached over 70,000 per year (Chiao 1996b). As mentioned earlier, the number of sexual harassment complaints surpassed 15,000 cases per year in 1995 and 1996 respectively. It is extremely doubtful that under the present circumstances, the Commission can perform its statutory mission to the satisfaction of all the parties concerned. Finally, after the passage of the Civil Rights Act of 1991, the incentive for the victims of sexual harassment to file their suits in the courts has increased tremendously (Appruzzese 1992; Carrillo 1992–93; Chiao 1997a). Basically, the United States is a very litigious society. It is reported by the American Bar Association (ABA) that the total costs of all litigation have reached over US$300 billion annually. It is impossible to estimate the exact costs of sexual harassment litigation to the whole society, but an article in *Fortune* magazine in August 1993 reported that an average company spends approximately US$200,000 handling each valid complaint. Likewise, a labor lawyer also predicted in the same article that sexual harassment litigation will cost over one billion U.S. dollars for companies in damages and attorneys' fees in the next five years (Chiao 1997a).

Lessons of the American Practices for Business Firms in Taiwan

Transplantation of the entire American framework for dealing with sexual harassment is improbable for Taiwan, due to distinct cultural and institutional differences. Furthermore, as demonstrated by the experiences of other countries, which all recognized the seriousness of sexual harassment problems, each country has its own legal interpretations along with distinct institutional approaches for addressing the problems as they arise. However, since Taiwan has been heavily influenced by the United States in the course of its economic and political development, American's practices in preventing sexual harassment can provide a useful framework for Taiwan to emulate.

Employees in Taiwan are in a particularly vulnerable position when they suffer sexual harassment in the workplace. The current legal regime cannot provide them with adequate protection. Most local employers are indifferent to this issue and labor unions are too weak to represent their members' interests in this respect. The only feasible way to proceed is for the government to enact a new fair employment opportunity statute to proclaim sexual harassment in the workplace an illegal conduct and to provide the victims with suitable remedies. The four Gender Equality in Employment Bills discussed above all offer the similar proposals in this regard. All of them impose legal obligations on employers to adopt preventive and corrective measures to stop and eliminate sexual harassment in their workplace. If they become law in the near future, local employers will bear the brunt of responsibility and will necessarily assume an important role in this endeavor. Fortunately, business firms here can easily draw on the experiences of their counterparts in the United States because all reform measures proposed here closely follow the American practices.

Differences in cultural backgrounds and legal systems, however, may make a whole-sale "transplantation" of American sexual harassment law to Taiwan impracticable (Chiao 1996b). Taiwan is still basically a Confucian society and group harmony is strongly valued. As a result, advocacy of any individual rights, such as exposing sexual scandals in the workplace, is a rare phenomenon. Generally, victims of sexual harassment are prone to be isolated and find it very difficult to receive support from either inside or outside their organizations. In addition, the legal system in Taiwan is modeled after the German and Japanese systems and rights in the workplace, such as freedom from sexual harassment or other unpleasant sexual encounters, are still regarded as personal matters belonging to the private sphere and public authorities are reluctant to intervene.

Nevertheless, the following corporate practices in the United States still can provide local business firms with some valuable lessons:

First, since employees in Taiwan generally are not assertive when faced with sexual harassment in the workplace (Lu and Fu 1993; Luo 1993), local business firms should hold relevant awareness campaigns and training programs to promote understanding among their employees. Three of the four proposed bills require the employer to affirmatively implement these measures. Actually, the CLA has already held a series of these programs for employers, union officers and representatives of employees with the assistance of several local women's organizations and the results are generally encouraging. Most of the training materials used in these programs are the Chinese version adapted from American sources. Therefore, the influence from the United States in this respect is the most direct.

Second, the promulgation of a sexual harassment policy and the establishment of an internal mechanism to handle this issue by the employer is also required under the proposed bills. Currently, only a small fraction of local business firms have implemented such a system (China Institute of Industrial Relations 1996). Since the American experience has shown that this policy and related complaint procedures are the most effective measures to prevent sexual harassment, local businesses should adopt them as soon as possible. According to the above-mentioned 1996 survey, most of the local employers questioned indicated that they are willing to set up this mechanism but they need guidance from the government (China Institute of Industrial Relations 1996). Actually, a brochure on how to set up this mechanism in the enterprise, which is closely following American practices, was prepared by a local women's organization under the auspices of the CLA in 1994 and has received positive responses from the local business community (Chiao 1997a).

Third, practices in the United States demonstrate that various public interest groups can play an important role in helping employers to develop an integrated system to combat sexual harassment. In Taiwan, local interest groups, especially women's organizations, have also gradually started to promote the awareness of sexual harassment at workplace. Nevertheless, their functions are limited to handling or exposing individual complaints. The American experience of combining the resources in public interest groups with those in the business community to deal with this new workplace issue can certainly offer a good example for business firms in Taiwan to emulate (Chiao 1997a).

Fourth, American practices also illustrate that cooperation between employers and labor unions can make the task of dealing with the problems of sexual harassment much easier, as collective bargaining agreements have become important instruments in handling this type of labor conflict. Conversely, labor unions in Taiwan are quite ignorant to their mission in tackling this issue. For instance, according to the 1996 survey discussed above, less than 73.2 per cent of those unions replied agreed that work rules against sexual harassment should be promulgated by the employer (China Institute of Industrial Relations 1996). Since the proposed bills require local employers to cooperate with labor unions or representatives of their employees to cope with this issue, local business firms have to turn to their American counterparts and learn from their experiences in this respect (Chiao 1997a).

Finally, the definitions of sexual harassment in the four proposed bills pay too much attention to the "sexuality" of the offending conduct and omit other types of harassing behavior, such as sexist language or some particularly hostile action of no overt sexual nature. They also do not include incidents of sexual harassment by non-employees and sexual favoritism (indirect or "reverse" quid pro quo sexual harassment). Same sex harassment or harassment against persons with special sexual preference and orientation are also not mentioned. As the working environment in Taiwan has become more and more diverse and complicated in recent years, local business firms may have to look to the American practices in this area to cope with these new forms of discrimination (Chiao 1997a).

Conclusion

Sexual harassment in the workplace has reached epidemic proportions in Taiwan in recent years, coinciding with a worldwide trend. It presents a number of economic, social, and personal problems for employees, families, and business firms. Surveys reveal that a substantial number of working women have experienced unwanted or unwelcome sexual encounters during their careers. The proportion is even higher for women employed in traditionally male-dominated job markets. Both employees and employers are adversely affected by these incidents. The government has moved one step closer to enacting a new gender equality in employment law to eradicate these incidents by imposing legal responsibilities on employers to prevent and stop sexual harassment from taking place in their workplace. The experience of the United States shows that employers are in the best position to play an active role in this endeavor. Since the reform proposals in this country are closely modeled after the American system, corporate practices in preventing and correcting this form of sex discrimination in the workplace from that country certainly can provide business firms in Taiwan with valuable lessons. Although it is impossible to make a whole-sale transplant of American practices to this country, several practical courses of action still can be adopted by local business firms to prevent sexual harassment from occurring in their workplace, to solve them to the satisfaction of the parties concerned, or to minimize their legal liability when these disputes lead to litigation in the courts.

Notes

1. Council of Labor Affairs (CLA), formerly a sub-unit in the Ministry of Interior Affairs of the Executive Yuan (Cabinet), was upgraded to a cabinet-level status in 1987. The Government plans to further expand its roles and functions with the enacting of the proposed Organizational Law of the Executive Yuan in the near future.

2. Modern Women Foundation was founded in 1987 by Ms. Pang, Wei-Kan, an active member of the Legislative Yuan (Parliament) affiliated with the ruling KMT Party.

3. This sum is calculated according to the official foreign exchange rate of 28 NTS to 1 US$ as of May 1997.
4. Taiwan Congress Office is a sub-group affiliated with the opposition DDP Party in the Legislative Yuan. The Bill was proposed by Mr. Lee, Gin-Yon in 1994.
5. Foundation of Women with New Knowledge (Awakening Foundation) was founded in 1982 by a group of professional women. It has played a very active role in the promotion of gender equality in various aspects in Taiwan. The Foundation drafted the first Gender Equality in Employment Law in 1990 and the current bill is its fifth draft.
6. Since employers may choose to adopt more than one method to cope with these grievances, the aggregate percentage of their responses may exceed 100 per cent in this survey.
7. 13 FEP Cases 123 (D. D. C. 1978).
8. 390 F. Supp. 161 (D. Ariz. 1975), *vacted*, 562 F. 2d 55 (9th Cir. 1977).
9. 422 F. Supp. 553 (D. N. J. 1976), *re'vd*, 568 F. 2d 1044 (3rd Cir. 1977).
10. 418 F. Supp. 233 (N. D. Cal. 1976), *re'vd*, 600 F. 2d 211 (9th Cir. 1979).
11. 413 F. Supp. 654 (D. D. C. 1976), *rev'd in part and vacated in part*, 190 App. D. C. 343 (1978).
12. 561 F. 2d (D. C. Cir. 1977).
13. 641 F. 2d 934 (D. C. Cir. 1981).
14. 682 F. 2d 897 (11th Cir. 1982).
15. 477 U.S. 57 (1986).
16. 805 F. 2d 611 (6th Cir. 1986).
17. 924 F. 2d 872 (9th Cir. 1991).
18. 760 F. Supp. 1486 (M. D. Fla. 1991).
19. 114 S. Ct. 367 (1993).
20. 50 F. 3d 428 (7th Cir. 1995).
21. 47 F. 3d 1522 (9th Cir. 1995).
22. 61 F. 3d 1340 (7th Cir. 1995).
23. 118 S. Ct. 998 (1998).
24. 118 S. Ct. 2275 (1998).
25. 118 S. Ct. 2257 (1998).

Chapter 6

The Political Economy of State-owned Enterprises in Foreign Investment: The Case of Taiwan

Hsing-Chou Sung

In the literature on state-owned enterprises (SOE) and multinational corporations (MNC), the multinational state-owned enterprise (MSOE) is seldom mentioned and discussed by scholars. Due to its dual status as both SOE and MNC, classifying the MSOE and identifying its role in the world economy has often puzzled researchers. Although the idea that MSOEs use state capital to invest overseas in order to gain more capital and then transfer this capital back to the home country is logically comprehensible, MSOEs are not solely profit maximizing corporations. Indeed, the business management of these corporations is often concerned with other factors, including political factors, as well. The question of how MSOEs balance their economic goals and non-economic goals in an international context is not only important for the corporations themselves, but is also crucial for scholars seeking a better understanding of the MSOEs operations.

There is currently extensive discussion and debate underway on the role of SOEs in the Republic of China (ROC) on Taiwan. This debate stems not only from the impact of worldwide privatization on the economy, but also from the national goal of elevating economic competitiveness and, particularly, of eliminating inefficiency in SOEs. The case of Taiwan's

SOEs foreign investment, however, has been seldom discussed and explored in the context of this debate. If the SOEs are less competitive and less efficient than private enterprises, then why have the SOEs adopted the strategy of foreign investment? Is it possible for SOEs to profit from this investment? If so, on what basis? Or does the outward movement of SOEs stem from considerations other than economic? This paper will address these questions regarding SOEs in Taiwan and will attempt to present some preliminary answers.

The following discussion is divided into five parts. First of all, in order to understand why (or under what conditions) an SOE becomes a multinational corporation, it is necessary to review the theoretical literature on SOE foreign direct investments (FDI). This brief survey will provide us with a scale on which to measure and evaluate whether the FDI of Taiwan's SOEs meets the necessary conditions to be considered MSOEs. The second part of this paper will describe and analyze the current FDI situation of Taiwan's SOEs. With this discussion, we can indicate whether there are other explanations for SOE FDI not dealt with in the literature. In third section, the discussion first situates the role of both the state and SOEs in Taiwan's economic development from an historical perspective. Since the 1980s, the state in Taiwan has encountered challenges to its legitimacy, both domestically and internationally. In order to maintain its legitimacy, the state has adapted itself to the challenges and adopted several strategies. Next, this section presents an explanatory model characterizing the direct and indirect factors that could possibly bring Taiwan's SOEs to initiate FDI. The fourth part of this paper then affords a detailed explanation of the aforementioned factors that result in the state utilizing SOEs to achieve the goals of its southward strategy. The fifth section summarizes and offers conclusions to the findings of the previous four sections.

The FDI of SOEs: A Theoretical Review

Generally, SOEs are less efficient than private companies, mainly because they are controlled by the state, which wants SOEs to serve various conflicting objectives or goals, such as job creation, greater public welfare, trade balance, urban planning, stimulating the economy, etc. Thus, the viewpoint that SOEs cannot possibly be well managed is understandable. Further, experts suggest that in order for SOEs' management to be improved, certain conditions must be satisfied. First, SOEs' objectives must be defined by assessing and compensating the costs of all non-economic goals imposed by the state. Second, there must be control without interference, i.e., the control must be organized (for example, the appointment of an SOE manager should not be on the basis of purely political criteria). Third, the managers of SOEs must be accountable for results. Fourth, managers should be given greater autonomy and managerial efficiency and incentives should be developed (Shirley 1983).

If inefficiency is a common problem for SOEs, then the question is: how can SOEs become multinational in the context of international economic competition. In fact, some experts argue, SOEs will tend to follow the same patterns as their private counterparts in becoming multinational corporations: when they become large companies and when their size is accompanied by a relaxation of constraints imposed by the state. Once this has happened, managers of SOEs will have more autonomy and will pursue profits by investing abroad purely on economic considerations. Like private multinationals, SOEs engage in foreign direct investment for two reasons: (1) to expand markets by selling abroad; and (2) to acquire foreign resources (for example, raw materials, production efficiency, and knowledge).

First of all, market expansion investment can be attributed to a company's monopolistic advantage. The advantages may be in capital, technology, managerial expertise, economies of scale, product design, brand recognition, and patent. An investing corporation may strengthen its monopolistic position by producing the same products outside of the home country if it wants to sell these products there. Of course, saving transportation costs is one of the most important factors to be considered. When the cost of transportation is added to production costs, some products become impractical to ship over great distances. Therefore, when companies move abroad to produce basically the same products that they produce at home, their direct investments are known as horizontal expansions (Matsuura 1991: 44).

Secondly, resource-seeking investment has several purposes. As products and their marketing become more complicated, there is a greater need to combine resources that are located in more than one country. This control of the different stages (as a product moves from raw materials through production to its final distribution) is so-called vertical integration. Advantages of vertical integration may accrue to a firm through either market-oriented or supply-oriented investment in other countries. In addition to vertical integration, companies increasingly produce different components or different portions of their production line in different parts of the world to take advantage of varying costs of labor, capital, and raw materials. This process is known as rationalized production. In addition, gaining access to production factors (such as capital market or technological knowledge) is another motivation for foreign direct investment (Daniels and Radebaugh 1995: 297–300). In short, SOEs are most likely to commit resources to FDI if they are successful domestically and they are less constrained by the state.

The above explanation of SOEs' motivation for FDI is based on the multinational model operating in the world market. It emphasizes the autonomy of the SOE in its decision-making and a lack of interference from the state. There is another model explaining how SOEs become multinational corporations by means of the state's assistance. In this model, three principal arguments are specified. First, the SOEs receive, in the form of subsidies for research and development, massive aid from their own government. Moreover, they invariably benefit from orders placed by the government. Thus, SOEs can offer foreign countries high-technology products (namely, sell their best products abroad) at a price which does not take into account the initial investment (that is, the real costs). Second, since profitability is not the sole criterion for evaluation of performance, subsidies accorded by the state to cover operating losses enable the SOEs to sell their products on foreign markets at a loss. In other words, the state can always compensate SOEs' deficits. Lastly, the state can also help through economic and diplomatic pressures or bilateral agreements with other countries. For example, governments wanting to help foreign countries in the process of industrialization might have a tendency to favor their SOEs rather than their private firms. In such cases, the SOE will enjoy protection, which is usually inaccessible to private corporations (Anastassopoulos et al. 1987: x–xi, 80–81, 90).

In fact, all governments, including those advocating a free market economy like the United States, intervene massively to distort the free play of market forces, and the consequences of such interventions are not limited to their national territory. The set-up abroad of SOEs is only a variant of this kind of action. For instance, since SOEs have received considerable funding in research and development, the state would assign them the mission of protecting the country's technological independence by FDI. In addition, one objective of state intervention is to support an entire ailing economic sector such as the shipbuilding industry. Accordingly, the state, wanting to bail out the ailing SOEs, would have the tendency to encourage the corporations to invest abroad. Furthermore, all states try to protect their enterprises, either state-owned or private, by practices aimed at limiting international competition. When these enterprises have achieved the growth stage, they can sell their production not only in the domestic market, but also in foreign countries. And the companies, including SOEs, may decide to invest in production facilities in those foreign countries in order to earn profits there (Anastassopoulos et al. 1987: 84–89).

Nevertheless, the state ownership of an SOE still represents an almost insurmountable obstacle in the company's development as a multinational, because it is subject to the requirements of national policies. In terms of industrial and technological policy, SOEs are usually the chosen instruments to fulfill the national goals. Since the objective of an industrial policy is to find a national solution in all sectors where problems arise, the state can influence SOEs, which often use advanced technologies, to choose a technology conceived in their own country over a foreign one. Of course, the choice depends on the quality and the price of this domestic technology. If an SOE is forced to buy domestic equipment that is less efficient and/or more expensive than the best available on the market, it is evident that at the international level it will be handicapped in relation to its foreign competitors. The consequences of these policies can be serious. The SOE may be deprived of its foreign assets or handicapped in its domestic market by activities that prove to be burdensome. Here, it should be noted that the above case could occur in developed countries but seldom in developing ones. Yet, even when SOEs have the possibility of expanding abroad and when the government is not opposed to this on principle, they still have many obstacles to overcome, namely, the financial, social, and foreign policies of the government. The following will discuss each of these obstacles to SOE international expansion.

Investing abroad requires substantial financial resources. In this respect, SOEs are at a considerable disadvantage in relation to private multinationals. Because the shareholder of an SOE is by definition the state, the only way an SOE can increase its capital is by obtaining specific budgetary grants. However, these grants are seldom easily available since in most countries the state budget is in deficit and governments are interested in cutting public spending. Even if these grants are approved by the controlling authority, the financial sanction (depending on the treasury, for example) is difficult to obtain. Furthermore, there is acute competition among different SOEs for government financial support. Under these circumstances, the government is often forced to assign the greater part of its resources to few of these SOEs. Inevitably, there is not much left for the most efficient companies, which are precisely those aiming at multinationalization (Anastassopoulos et al. 1987: 69).

Certainly, the SOE can resort to borrowing (including selling bonds) in its home country or to accessing foreign capital. But, in return, for government non-interference in their management, the government requires that SOEs be self-financing. If borrowing leads to serious financial imbalance or problems, eventually SOEs have to appeal to the government for help and, thus, lose their autonomy (Anastassopoulos et al. 1987: 70–71). Consequently, it seems that this borrowing strategy may not be workable.

As for social policy, the governments have three principal objectives: the improvement of employee satisfaction, the development of employment opportunities, and a better geographical distribution of jobs. The government seeks to reach the first goal through high wages. In both developed and developing countries, SOEs offer much higher salaries than other organizations (at least higher than the average nation-wide salaries). Also, a greater number of fringe benefits are provided for SOE employees. While generous social policies leave SOE workers satisfied, the costs incurred do not favor SOEs' competitiveness on an international level. In fact, the employees of SOEs, who are used to good treatment and consider their allowances as a right, may not appreciate the government's generosity and work hard in return (Anastassopoulos et al. 1987: 72–74). Thus, higher personnel costs limit SOEs' capacities to expand internationally.

Since SOEs cannot easily lay off their personnel, their employees represent a long-term immobilization for them. Therefore, the protection of employment is an almost insurmountable obstacle for the multinationalization of SOEs. The government faces a dilemma of choosing between employment and efficiency/effectiveness. Moreover, SOEs find it very difficult to close down factories and lay off employees at a time when they are creating jobs overseas through multi-national expansion. In other words, SOEs have to tolerate overstaffing to a certain extent. They also have to deal with grievances from trade unions without enjoying the alternatives of laying off personnel or closing down plants. At the same time, the local authority of a host country may demand an SOE to serve the goal of regional development by expanding job employment (Anastassopoulos et al. 1987: 74–75). Under these circumstances, SOEs encounter considerable constraints when they aim at multinationalization.

Once an SOE sets up subsidiaries in a foreign country, the home government will tend to use these firms as instruments for its own foreign policy. That is to say, the SOE is subject to all kinds of pressure (orders) from its government which at times cannot but put aside to pursue its own interests. This exemplifies the connection between political and economic considerations. More often, a pure investment for economic profit is politicized by the government. In addition, government interference does not allow SOEs to invest in countries they favor, but limits investment to a list of "priority" countries in accordance with the foreign policy of the home government. Usually, governments negotiate projects involving their respective SOEs. Once agreements are achieved between two countries, the government will impose them on SOEs. In these cases, the autonomy of SOEs is obviously limited (Anastassopoulos et al. 1987: 75–76).

In brief, after discussing the cases of SOEs' FDI, we can conclude that only when SOEs enjoy the monopolistic advantages of being publicly owned and gain much of the autonomy of private companies can they become more successful multinationals.

The FDI of Taiwan's State-owned Enterprises: The Current Situation

According to "the Cooperative Project of SOE Overseas Investment" formulated by the Ministry of Economic Affairs (MOEA), the main purposes of SOEs' FDI include: (1) to control overseas natural resources and the needed raw materials; (2) to assure the commodity market-share and access to distributive and sales markets; (3) to acquire key productive technologies and the experiences of operative management; (4) to develop international economic and technological cooperation; and (5) to help the structural adjustment of domestic industry and to promote the upgrading of production level (The Abstract of MOEA 1996: 1). That is to say, the SOE can invest abroad as long as it (1) follows one of the five purposes; (2) submits proposal(s); and (3) gets approval by the standard procedure of project reviews.

There have been only three cases recorded for SOE foreign investment before 1991 (Table 6.1). The earliest happened at the end of 1979, when Taiwan Fertilizer Corporation co-invested with the Saudi Arabian government to establish a fertilizer company in the Jubail industrial park for producing urea. This company still operates its business today, but has had

Table 6.1 State-owned Enterprise (SOE) Foreign Investment before 1990

SOE	Declared Object of Investment	Content of Investment Rights	Sum of Investment/ Shares of Ownership	Starting Year
Taiwan Fertilizer Corporation	Jubail Fertilizer Company (Saudi Arabia)	Production of urea	NT$1550 million/50%	End of 1979
Taipower	Denison Coal Company (Canada)	Exploitation of coal mining	C$10 million/10%	1981
China Petroleum Corporation	Huffington Company (U.S.)	Exploitation of natural gas (Indonesia)	US$600 million/ 100%(investment); 16.67% (rights of natural gas)	1990

Source: Ministry of Economic Affairs (1996).

no annual dividends as of yet. This investment seems to be a case of diplomatic considerations. It was rumored at the time that Saudi Arabia planned to cut off its diplomatic ties with Taiwan, although Saudi Arabia only normalized its foreign relations with the People's Republic of China (PRC) in 1990 (Chung-Hua Institution for Economic research 1991: 74). According to the 1996 annual budget report of Taiwan Fertilizer Corporation, it has invested NT$2,900 million and is expected to get investment returns in 2008 (Taiwan Fertilizer Corporation 1995: 19–20).

The second foreign investment was done by Taipower in 1981, when Taipower, worrying about the arrival of a second energy crisis, took preventive measures and co-invested with the Canadian Denison Coal Company to exploit the Coalspur mining field. Because of the high costs of coal mining, exacerbated by the decreasing coal price in the market, this project still has not begun yet. It was not until 1990 that the China Petroleum Corporation started Taiwan's third SOE foreign investment. It put in a tender and purchased 100 per cent stock share of the American Huffington Company (US$600 million), thus giving it 16.67 per cent ownership rights in an Indonesian oil field (Chung-Hua Institution for Economic research 1991: 74).

Following this project, the outward movement of SOEs stopped for three years and has been renewed only since 1994.[1] Based on data (1994–1997) provided by the MOEA, there have been 6 investments in Vietnam and the total sum is NT$5,442.184 million (Table 6.2A); 4 cases in

Table 6.2 State-owned Enterprise (SOE) Investment in Various Countries

SOE	Declared Object	Sum of Investment (Thousand NTS)	Share of Capital	Starting Year
A. Investment in Vietnam				
Taiwan Sugar Corporation	Sugar Production	285,120	40%	1994
Taiwan Sugar Corporation	Pig Farm	348,000	100%	1996
China Petroleum Corporation	Oil Refinery	4,476,645	30%	1995
China Petroleum Corporation	Chemical-Solvent Plant	129,479	40%	1995
China Petroleum Corporation	Liquefied Natural Gas Reservoir	102,290	35%	1995
Taiwan Fertilizer Corporation	Fertilizer Production	100,650	35%	1996
B. Investment in Indonesia				
China Petroleum Corporation	Lubricant Mixtur Plant	165,000	30%	1996
China Petroleum Corporation	Asphalt Plant	107,008	40%	1996
China Petroleum Corporation	Oil Naphtha Splitting Plant (such as ethylene)	1,831,414	30%	1996
China Petroleum Corporation	LNG Ship-Building Facility	391,685	40%	1996
C. Investment in Australia				
Taiwan Sugar Corporation	Cow Farm in Queensland	72,770	45%	1996
Taiwan Sugar Corporation	Sugar/Syrup Plant: Relocating a Processing Plant from Taiwan to Australia	605,800	40%	1994
Taipower	Mining, Marketing and Agriculture (associated with Bengalla Ltd.)	6	10%	1996
Taiwan Salt Corporation	Salt Lake Macleod Company	127,484	49%	1995
D. Investment in the Philippines				
Taiwan Sugar Corporation	Pig Farm	80,000	40%	1997
E. Investment in Qatar				
China Petroleum Corporation	Fuel Additive Plant	1,484,000	12.5%	1995

Source: Ministry of Economic Affairs (1996).

Indonesia, total sum NT$2,495.107 million (Table 6.2B); 4 investments in Australia, total sum NT$806.060 million (Table 6.2C); one case in the Philippines for only NT$80 million (Table 6.2D); and one investment in Qatar for NT$1,484 million (Table 6.2E). The total sum of investments between 1994 and 1997 was NT$10,307.351 million. The highest sum of investments was in Vietnam, followed by Indonesia, Qatar, Australia, and the Philippines, in that order.

Arranged in chronological sequence, there were two cases and investment funds equal to NT$890.920 million in 1994; five cases and NT$6,319.898 million in 1995; eight cases and NT$3,016.533 million in 1996; and one case of only NT$80 million in 1997. The chronological ranking, according to total sum of investment, is 1995, 1996, 1994 and 1997.

There are five SOEs involved in FDI. They are: Taiwan Sugar Corporation, five cases, NT$1,391.690 million investment; China Petroleum Corporation, eight investments for a total of NT$8,687.521 million; Taiwan Fertilizer Corporation, one case for a sum of NT$100.650 million; Taipower, one investment of NT$6,000; and Taiwan Salt Corporation, one case for NT$127.484 million. Of these, The China Petroleum Corporation, eight investments for a total of NT$8,687.521 million; Taiwan Fertilizer Corporation, one case for a sum of NT$100.650 million; Taipower, one investment of NT$6,000; and Taiwan Salt Corporation, one case for NT$127.484 million. Of these, The China Petroleum Corporation invests the most, followed by Taiwan Sugar Corporation, Taiwan Fertilizer Corporation, Taiwan Salt Corporation, and Taipower.

Strangely, Taipower invested only NT$6,000 (less than US$300) in 1996. One might wonder why Taipower made such an investment, which was actually more of a disbursement than an investment. While some of the investments made by China Petroleum Corporation could fulfill the MOEA's first goal (to control overseas natural resources and necessary raw materials), the rest of the investments seem to fit ambiguously either the second or the fifth purposes mentioned above.

Unfortunately, due to MOEA's unwillingness to disclose the SOEs' foreign investments in detail, the aforementioned analysis is somewhat superficial. One way of gaining access to more information is to look at the Central Government's annual budget reports. The following discussion will be based on the three consecutive annual budget reports from 1996 to 1998 (from July 1st, 1995 to June 30th, 1998). Before proceeding, however, one thing should be noted. The actual figures for number of projects, amount of investments, and SOEs involving FDI could be different from the sources mentioned above or even sometimes contradictory to them. In light of the fact that there is no better way of justifying these figures available, the discussion will follow the figures indicated in the annual budget reports. According to the Budget Reports, there are only four SOEs engaging in foreign investments. They are Taiwan Sugar Corporation, China Petroleum Corporation, Taiwan Fertilizer Corporation, and Taiwan Salt Corporation.

Taiwan Sugar Corporation (TSC) has planned several investment projects. The first one is Joint Venture in Northern Vietnam (cf. Table 6.2A). The construction of this sugar factory started in July 1994 and its sugar production began in January 1997. The total sum of this investment is NT$1.782 billion (NT$712.8 million in cash and NT$1.0692 billion from a long-term loan), and the cash investment of TSC's share is 40 per cent, that is, NT$285.120 million. The purpose of this project is to coordinate government policy that encourages domestic manufactories' foreign investment. The private investors, including Yimai, Fumai and Ginchu Biscuit Company, thus have the opportunity to cooperate with an SOE and extend their businesses overseas. For TSC itself, the sugar production costs, due to the shortage of the labor force in rural areas and rising wages, are relatively high in Taiwan at this point. This foreign investment would increase the sale profits in Vietnam and ensure sugar resources in the future. On the other hand, the Vietnamese would benefit from this project as well, including technological transfers, the inflow of foreign capital, the increase of employment rate, and the promotion of economic growth (Taiwan Sugar Corporation 1995: 42–47, 1996: 50–55).

TSC's second foreign project is the relocation of a by-product-processing factory from Pingtung to Australia (cf. Table 6.2C). Because of inefficient management and heavy profit losses, this processing factory in Pingtung has fallen into decay and will be closed down within five years under the pressure of local government. At the same time, the Australian law that forbids the burning of bagasse for environmental protection has encouraged the Australian government to establish a sugar/syrup factory in Queensland to handle the vast volume of bagasse. Thus the TSC, once having achieved the agreement with the Australians to co-invest in the sugar/syrup plant, could relocate the extant equipment from Pingtung to Queensland and take advantage of the modern techniques and personnel in Queensland to run this newly reestablished factory. The project was scheduled to be developed between July 1994 and January 1997 (the expected date of formal production). The total sum of this investment for TSC's share (40 per cent) is NT$3.029 billion (NT$469 million in 1994; NT$1.652 billion in 1995, NT$908 million in 1996). This project helps not only solve the problem of Pingtung's processing factory, but also to expand its sales and distributive markets in Pacific Asia (Taiwan Sugar Corporation 1995: 48–58, 1996: 56–66).

The third and fourth of TSC's projects are the investments in pig farms in Vietnam and in the Philippines (cf. Table 6.2A and Table 6.2D). While the former is a sole TSC investment and the sum of the total investment is NT$348 million, including NT$253 million (the capital) and NT$95 million (the purchase of a good breed of pigs), the latter is co-invested by TSC and a Philippines local company (the PTSC) and TSC's share of the total investment is 40 per cent (NT$80 million). The investment for the Vietnamese project is from July 1996 to June 1999, whereas the Philippines' project is from July 1996 to July 1998. Indeed, these two projects would help both countries provide some of their pork supply. In addition, the purpose of these two projects is nothing more than coordinating with the ROC government's policy which directs and encourages domestic enterprises (public and/or private) to invest in Southeast Asia (Taiwan Sugar Corporation 1996: 39–50, 72–81, 1997: 37–55, 70–79).

The fifth project, another agricultural-related investment, is to invest in a cow farm in Australia in order to supply the increasing beef demand in Taiwan (cf. Table 6.2C). The project began in July 1996 and will be finished in December 1998. The total sum of investment is NT$323.421 million (Taiwan Sugar Corporation 1996: 82–90, 1997: 80–88). TSC's sixth and the last project is the relocation of a sugar refinery plant from Taiwan to Vietnam (cf. Table 6.2A). This project, started in July 1997 and ending in December 1999, will help the Vietnamese acquire skills for sugar production. The targeted market would be Vietnam itself and the total sum of this investment will be NT$400 million (US$14.5 million) (Taiwan Sugar Corporation 1997: 58–64). In short, according to the annual budget reports, TSC will spend NT$4,465.541 million for six projects in Australia (two projects), the Philippines (one project) and Vietnam (three projects) from 1994 to 1999.

China Petroleum Corporation (CPC) focuses its FDI in three countries, Qatar, Vietnam, and Indonesia. Owing to domestic shortages of the major ingredients of unleaded gasoline (MTBE and methanol, or methyl alcohol), CPC decided to invest in a fuel additive plant in Qatar for source supply (cf.

Table 6.2E). It would share 21.3 per cent of the total investment of NT$6,969.5 million, that is, NT$1,484 million (China Petroleum Corporation 1995: 33–34, 1996: 37, 1997: 35). The CPC has three investments in Vietnam (cf. Table 6.2A). The first is a co-investment of an oil refinery cooperating with the Vietnamese Petroleum Corporation (state-owned), the Luck Golden Star (a Korean company), and the Malaysian Petroleum Corporation (state-owned). The target market will be Vietnam and Southeast Asia. CPC's share will be 3.6 per cent (NT$1,385.212 million or US$50.679 million) of the total (US$1,408 million) (China Petroleum Corporation 1995: 34, 1996: 37, 1997: 35). The second investment is to build a chemical-solvent plant utilizing local crude oils. This also is set up as a joint venture for three years with the PV-RC and the Chingfeng business groups. The share is 40 per cent (NT$129.479 million) of the total (NT$323.698 million). The third investment is to build a liquefied natural gas reservoir that is expected to be completed in three-years. The partners in this joint venture are CONDITAB, the Chingfeng business groups, and the CPC, which owns a 35 per cent share of the investment (NT$102.290 million) (China Petroleum Corporation 1995: 34, 1996: 37–38). Both the second and the third projects, however, disappeared from "the 1998 Annual Budget Report" without any reason being given. There is no way of tracing these consequences and determining whether they were terminated or canceled.

The CPC's investments in Indonesia include four projects: (1) a lubricant mixture plant; (2) an asphalt plant; (3) a relocation of a naphtha splitting-off plant (such as ethylene) from Taiwan to Indonesia; and (4) a LNG ship construction (China Petroleum Corporation 1996: 38–40, 1997: 35–37) (cf. Table 6.2B). The lubricant mixture plant has been planned to be located at Ujung Pandang and will produce 50 thousand kiloliters a year of the lubricant mixture. Since the Indonesian law regulates that the oil-related industry is allowed to be run only by the Pertamina (an Indonesian state-owned petroleum enterprise), the success of this joint venture will enhance CPC's opportunity to enter into the Indonesian market. And the capital invested by CPC will be NT$165 million (30 per cent share of the total). The purpose of constructing an asphalt plant in Balikpapan is to supply the asphalt for the Indonesian market by refining the vacuum residues from crude oils and to yield 400 thousand tons of asphalt a year. The total investment is NT$267.520 million and CPC's share is 40 per cent (NT$107.008 million). This project was made possible partly because the CPC followed the government's economic policy to extend its international business, and partly because the Pertamina planned to expand its refinery factory in Balikpapan. The decision to relocate a naphtha splitting-off plant[2] from Taiwan was made because the plant was to be shut down. If this whole plant including all of the facilities and equipment moves to Indonesia, it can not only continue to provide the petrochemical products as usual but also open up the overseas market. This third project will cost CPC NT$1,817 million (18.24 per cent of the total NT$9,962 million). The last CPC projected investment in Indonesia is to build a LNG (liquefied natural gas) ship. Because CPC signed a contract with the Indonesians in 1984 that CPC would purchase a certain amount of LNG from Indonesia for the next twenty years, it is necessary for CPC to have a ship for loading and delivering the LNG to Taiwan. Thus, conveniently, the CPC will cooperate with Indonesian and foreign shipbuilding companies to construct a ship with loading capacity of 137 thousand kiloliter.[3] The total sum of the investment is NT$9,792.12 million and CPC would share 40 per cent (NT$391.685 million).

In addition to the investment in Jubail Fertilizer Company in 1970 (cf. Table 6.1),[4] Taiwan Fertilizer Corporation (TFC) added one foreign investment project in 1996. The Vietnam Fertilizer Co-investment Corporation was organized by five companies including one Japanese, three Vietnamese, and TFC. And TFC will offer the necessary techniques to produce and supply multiple fertilizers for the local market. The total investment will be US$34.86 million, and TFC shares 10.5 per cent, which is US$3.66 million (Taiwan Fertilizer Corporation 1996: 17–18, 1997: 17–18).

The fourth SOE involving FDI is Taiwan Salt Corporation. Since Taiwan Salt Corporation invested NT$87.318 million in the Salt Lake Macleod Company of Australia in 1995, the price Macleod has sold salt to Taiwan Salt Corporation for is the same as its production cost (cf. Table 6.2C).[5]

In addition, two other SOEs need to be mentioned here. The China Steel Corporation, according to its 1996 Budget Report, invested NT$32.26 million in Paraguay in an alloy of iron factory before 1995 (date not available) (China Steel Corporation 1995: 26). As for Taipower Company, there are plans for undertaking two mining explorations, although they have not yet begun. One is for the exploration of uranium in Sage, Arizona, U.S.A. The other is for the exploration of coal in Bengalla, Australia (Taipower Company 1997: 120–121). Because these projects have not yet begun, they can not be counted as investment projects.

In summary, based on the Central Government's annual budget reports, we can conclude that all those foreign investment projects were evaluated and decided upon separately. They are sparsely located in different countries and very little capital was used. In fact, these investments show no consistency. In other words, there is no trend indicating that Taiwan's SOEs are becoming multinational corporations.

Nevertheless, the MOEA has indicated many times that SOEs going abroad would be an appropriate strategy. Probably, what state officials have in mind is not to revamp SOEs to become multinational corporations, but rather to find a temporary expedient for solving SOEs' operational difficulties in Taiwan, where the appeals for environmental protection and the pressures/claims for privatization have been highly politicized. Of course, state officials understand that it is not easy for an SOE to become a successful multinational corporation. Official documents state that for the future success of overseas investment, SOEs have to improve and adjust their structural deficiencies; develop and expand businesses in international markets, either singly or jointly with domestic/foreign firms; upgrade industrial technologies; improve management efficiency; and help realize economic growth (The Abstract of MOEA 1996: 3). But the question is, how can all this be achieved? Until recently, these recommendations were mere formalities by the state bureaucracy. That is, SOE FDI practices were not expected to be consistent with the above requirements.

According to the annual budget of SOEs, the total overseas investments, including ten projects, will be over NT$3,054 million in 1997, while there were seven whole foreign projects costing NT$7,286 million in 1996 (*The Liberty Times* April 28, 1996: 14). However, the legislators of the Democratic Progressive Party, in reviewing and examining the 1997 SOE budgets, charged that the lists of capital expenditures were a mess, that blind investments appeared in all places, that the return rates of investments showed negative growth, and that the planned projects were all behind schedule and the rate of progress lagged behind by 20 per cent (*The Commercial Times* June 7, 1996: 2). For instance, the investing projects of fixed assets would cost NT$158.7 billion, comprising 13.9 per cent of all projects (NT$11,400.2 billion). The sum of cumulative total investments by 1997 was as high as NT$720.7 billion (*The Commercial Times* June 7, 1996: 2). Even though these charges may be exaggerated, particularly as they come from the opposition party, there is no way of falsifying them. And it seems that the MOEA has not rebutted and denied the charges.

After the controversy over SOE proper investments, the newly appointed minister of MOEA, Wang Chih-kang, made an announcement on October 7, 1996 that all overseas investments by SOEs would stop immediately. The priority of SOE investment would focus in the future on the domestic market, not only for the preparation and coordination of the Asia-Pacific Regional Operations Center, but for the promotion of the ten-new-industries policy. Those projects already having been invested in foreign countries will continue until they are completed (*The United Daily News* October 8, 1996: 4). As for SOE foreign investment in the future, the MOEA will adopt a strict standard to review the SOEs' proposals (*The Liberty Times*, November 30, 1996: 13). Thus, SOEs' mission and assignment of foreign investments in Southeast Asia comes to an end at the moment.

The FDI of Taiwan's SOEs: An Explanatory Model

From an historical perspective, the state plays an important role in economic development (that of leading the country's developmental direction). Alexander Gerschenkron has argued that the state generally plays a much stronger role in late-developing societies, because economic competition already existed and industry had become highly complex, massive, and expensive. The catch-up nature of industrialization in the late developers required rapid and massive accumulations of capital for infrastructure and new industries, which was simply beyond the capabilities of private entrepreneurs in poorer economies. More broadly, state ideological commitment and industrial strategy appeared necessary to push backward economies toward industrialization (Gerschenkron 1962: 5–30).[6]

Albert Hirschman has attributed the important role of the state in Third World countries to "organizational scarcity" in those societies. Because of organizational weakness in the private sector, the state must play the role of both extracting and combining "hidden, scattered or badly utilized" resources (Hirschman 1958: 5). Furthermore, Douglas McKinnon emphasizes that an inefficient "fragmentation" of a Third World economy induces state intervention in economic development (McKinnon 1972).

Peter Evans identifies four different roles played by the state in development: the demiurge (creating enterprises by itself); the custodian (protecting some enterprises, and regulating and preventing other enterprises from entering); the midwife (acting as a promoter via procurements, subsidies, and protection); and the husbandry (assisting to locate firms to advance their technology) (Evans 1995: 77–81; Comisso 1996). If a state can play these four different roles well, then it has achieved "embedded autonomy," which "provides the underlying structural basis for successful state involvement in industrial transformation" (Evans 1995: 12). This generalization seems to fit the case of Taiwan, where the state has played an important and successful role in economic development.

In fact, many analysts have argued that the state in Taiwan has assumed the role of stimulating economic growth and transformation, and that Taiwan's development has been a result of state policy which moved from a strategy of import-substitution industrialization during 1950s toward a strategy of export-oriented industrialization (EOI) since the 1960s (Amsden 1985: 78–106; Gold 1986; Pang 1992; Wade 1990; Aberbach et al. 1994). Further, SOEs have been the instrument of choice for government in its efforts to develop many sectors, including fuels, chemicals, mining, metals, fertilizer, and food-processing. In other words, SOEs have had a major role in the economy throughout the period of EOI (or outward-looking growth).

The centrality of SOEs in Taiwan's economy owes much to the doctrines of Dr. Sun Yat-sen, which emphasized a mixed economy, or a socialist-capitalist economic system that focused on public expenditures and public-owned industries. Following these doctrines, the KMT government has restricted wealth accumulation through land ownership, financial dealings, urban real estate, military office, and legislative office, and has thereby helped to channel investment into productive activities. As a result, the state has insured that it has ample power resources to dominate the economy and to take an active role in industrialization.

Significantly, Taiwan has had one of the biggest SOE sectors in the world since the early 1950s onward, excluding the communist bloc and Sub-Saharan Africa (Wade 1990: 176). Individual SOEs are typically among the largest corporations in their sectors. For example, in 1980, the six biggest industrial SOEs had sales equal to the fifty biggest private industrial concerns. Furthermore, SOEs are concentrated in upstream, capital-intensive, and oligopolized sectors, thus giving the KMT government indirect influence over downstream sectors through acts such as adjusting raw material prices throughout the economy (Wade 1990: 178–179).

Nevertheless, one should not be misled into believing that only those firms for which 50 per cent or more of equity is owned by the state are legally public enterprises. There are actually many other firms that are highly influenced by parts of the state without being included in the public enterprise sector, such as China Airlines and several larger banks. Also, the government may take a minority share in an important firm and make up the balance through the KMT party's holding company (Central Investments Holding Company). Moreover, there are many special status "private" firms linked to the KMT party, the military, government agencies, or senior individuals of these organizations. Thus, public and semipublic enterprises have a large place in the social structure of investment in Taiwan.

In spite of two oil shocks to the world economy in the 1970s, economic growth in Taiwan continued in 1980s. This stable economy mainly resulted from the government's efforts. On the one hand, the technology transfers and the industrial structure were promoted and upgraded, thus deepening the infrastructural transformation, especially in capital-intensive and high-technology industries. On the other hand, the government loosened and liberalized many regulations on foreign capital to attract more capital inflows and investment in Taiwan. However, the KMT government faced several challenges to its legitimacy from both the internal and external milieu.

Figure 6.1 depicts the sources of challenges to Taiwan's state legitimacy. At first, China, just as in the past, insisted on the one-China principle and used a two-pronged tactic in dealing with Taiwan. The larger challenge is that there still exists the possibility that China may employ a military maneuver against Taiwan. The smaller challenge is that leaders from both sides (Taiwan and China) can have peaceful talks and negotiations, and that the rapprochement between Taiwan and China may be settled once and for all. Secondly, the ROC government has encountered a diplomatic predicament internationally and has found itself having difficulties earning more formal/diplomatic recognition. Thirdly, the world economy and politics have changed rapidly since the 1980s. One impact of these changes is globalization. Politically, the third wave of democratization[7] (since 1974), originated in southern Europe (Portugal and Spain) and has expanded to Asia and Latin America. Economically, along with rapid technological innovations and the globalization of production and trade, there emerges a worldwide consensus that government should reduce its role in the economy (deregulation and privatization), and that each country should abandon protectionism for greater openness to the outside world (reduced barriers to trade and openness to foreign capital). In other words, economic liberalization is the key to economic stability and growth. Both democratization and liberalization have had much impact on Taiwan's

Embeddedness and Economy 187

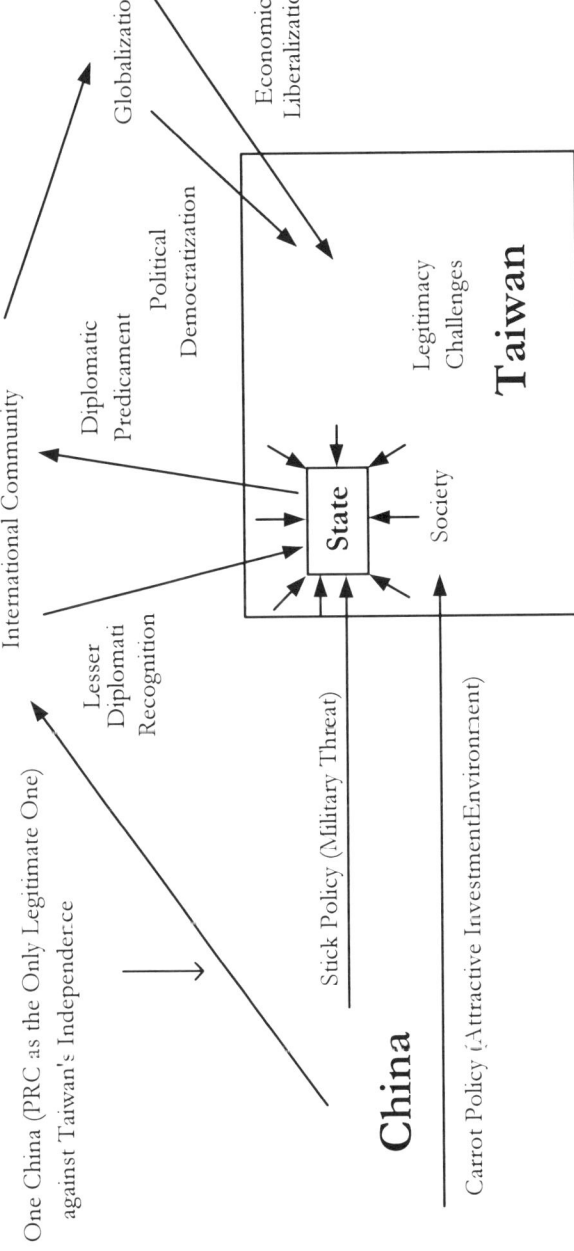

Figure 6.1 The Source of Challenges to State Legitimacy

188 State-owned Enterprises

Figure 6.2 The State's Alternative Strategy for Maintaining its Regitimacy

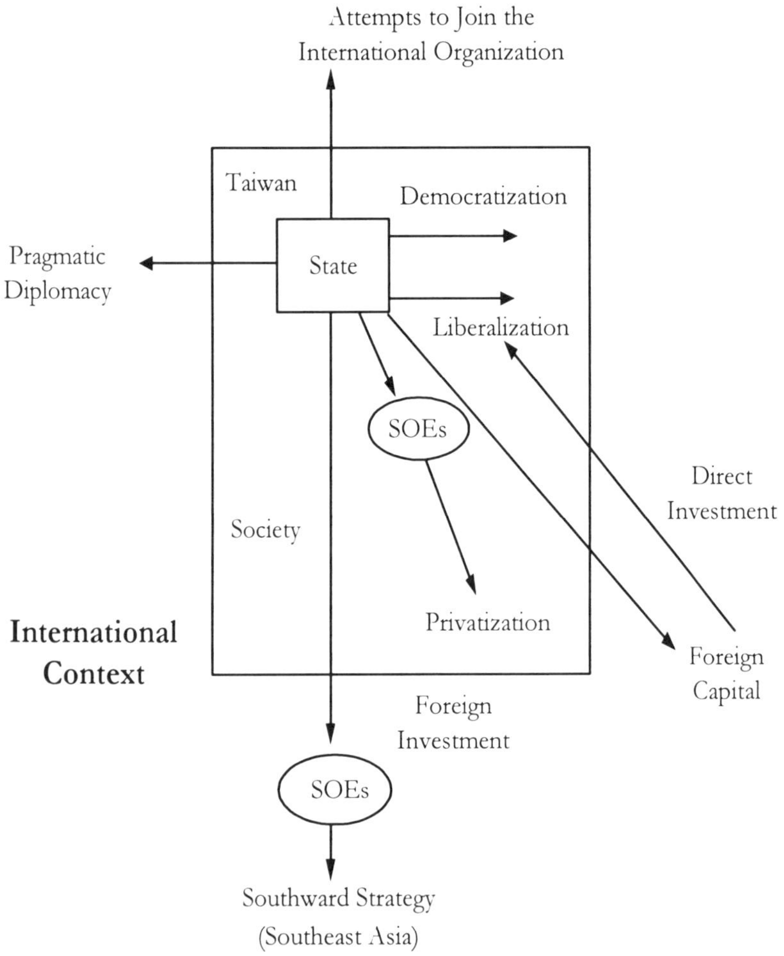

```
                    Attempts to Join the
                    International Organization
                              ↑
        ┌─────────────────────┼─────────────────────┐
        │  Taiwan             │    Democratization  │
        │              ┌──────┴──┐        →         │
Pragmatic │  ←──────────│  State  │                  │
Diplomacy │             └─────────┘      Liberalization│
        │                  │  ↘         →            │
        │                ┌─┴─┐                       │
        │               (SOEs)                        │
        │                                    Direct   │
        │                                  Investment │
        │  Society          ↓                        │
        │                                             │
        │              Privatization                  │
International│                              Foreign    │
Context   │                                 Capital   │
        └──────────────────┬──────────────────────────┘
                       Foreign
                      Investment
                         ↓
                      (SOEs)
                         ↓
                   Southward Strategy
                    (Southeast Asia)
```

development. Finally, the state in Taiwan has confronted challenges from domestic forces. These pressures have come from the demands made and input offered by the people. Taiwanese claims included not only political and economic reforms but also social and political movements.

In return, the KMT government has tried to maintain its legitimacy by choosing several strategies. Figure 6.2 exhibits these strategies. Internationally, the KMT government attempts to break through the diplomatic predicament by showing its willingness to be a member of international community and by devoting much effort to becoming the legal member of international organizations. At the same time, the ROC government modifies its diplomatic strategy from flexible diplomacy to pragmatic diplomacy. To maintain economic stability by luring foreign capital to invest in the domestic market is the KMT government's other means of justifying its legitimacy. In addition, political democratization (rescission of martial law, acceleration of constitutional amendments, full-scale openness in all kinds of elections, etc.) and economic liberalization (the reduced role of government in the market, the unbound regulation of economic activities, etc.) have been exerted cautiously by the KMT government.

Thus, only when we understand the background of what is shown in Figures 6.1 and 6.2 can we talk about the role of SOEs in FDI in Figure 6.2. Even though the privatization of Taiwan's SOEs in the domestic market is not the major concern of this paper, a few words on that matter are essential. Because SOEs are neither efficient nor profit oriented, their pubic images are of bureaucratic firms that are distant from their customers. Economists have been highly critical of the public enterprises sector and have urged privatization.[8] Although the government has frequently repeated its intention to sell public enterprises to the private sector, only a few small industries (fishing, textiles, and chemicals) have been divested since the 1953 land reform, when several public enterprises (cement, paper and pulp, agricultural and forestry, industrial and mining corporations) were divested.[9] It is obvious, then, that the ROC government has paid little more than lip service to the idea of divestment. It was not until 1989, that then premier of Executive Yuan, Lee Huan, announced that the government was going to accelerate and promote the privatization of public enterprises in order to follow global trends. The Legislative Yuan amended the 1953 "The Ordinances of Transferring Ownership of Public Enterprises to the Private Sector" (OTOPEPS) and passed three readings in June 1991 (Chen et al. 1991: 20).

In fact, state officials in Taiwan have shown great reluctance to privatize SOEs by turning them into public corporations, thus making their shares available to the public through local equity markets. But even when the SOEs are privatized (such as when public corporations are created), they do not actually move beyond state control. As mentioned above, it is misleading to believe that any corporation of which the state owns less than 50 per cent of the total shares is not a legal SOE. A privatized public corporation simply obscures the lines of authority, resulting in a lack of clarity as to whose responsibility it is. In this case, it becomes easier for the state to manipulate all the activities of this privatized public corporation. The China Steel Corporation is a good example of such a company. In other words, the privatization of SOEs could be a guise to ward off accusations of too much state control, while in fact the state still takes charge of everything behind the scenes.

As for the FDI of SOEs, Figure 6.3 provides an explanatory model. Based on what we have discussed in Figure 6.1 and Figure 6.2, this model presents a framework of several inter-related variables. For an understanding of the reasons for Taiwan SOEs' FDI in recent years, it is necessary to look retrospectively at the relationships among these variables. The following will give a detailed explanation of the interrelationships among the variables in Figure 6.3.

The Political Economy of SOEs' FDI: An Explanation

Intuitively, FDI involves both the world market (economic reasons) and international relations (political considerations). However, an analysis focusing only on external factors may not manifest the whole picture of SOEs' FDI decisions. Recently, international theories have focused on domestic sources of foreign economic policy and on the relationship between changes in (domestic) preferences and policy outcomes (Simmons 1994; Garrett and Lange 1995; Gourevitch 1996). Based on the model in Figure 6.3, this section will first discuss Taiwan's foreign relations, then discuss the relationship among Taiwan's democratization, its foreign economic policy, and the "Mainland fever" of investment by private business groups. It will then show that the interactions among these factors have direct/indirect causal effects on SOEs' FDI.

From Flexible Diplomacy to Pragmatic Diplomacy

Since 1949, the KMT government has held a "One China policy," which sees Taiwan as an inalienable province of China. During the leadership of Chiang Kai-shek, however, everything the government did in Taiwan was directed towards preparing to retake Mainland China. The KMT government's principle of One China policy was that, prior to

Figure 6.3 The FDI of Taiwan's SOEs: An Explanatory Model

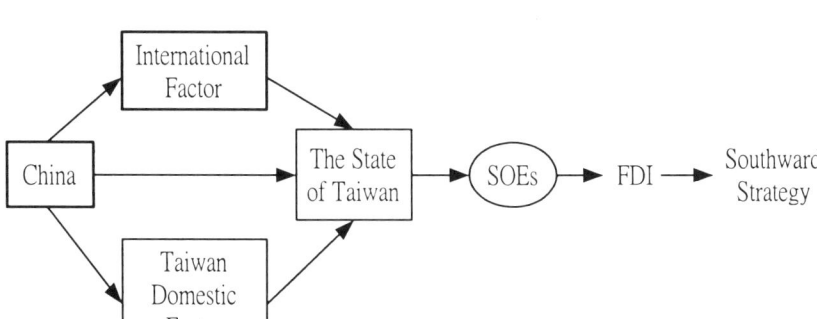

unification: "As two parties claim to run the legitimate government of all China, foreign countries can only have full diplomatic relations with one; the other is a bandit regime" (Gold 1986: 142, fn 27).

In the early 1970s, with the rapid change in the international situation such as the stalemate of the Vietnam War, the border conflict between the Soviet Union and the People's Republic of China (PRC), the detente between the East and the West, and the beginning of strategic arms limitation talks between the U.S. and the Soviet Union), the United States wanted to free itself from the mire of the Vietnam War. The U.S. sought the PRC's help in doing so, in exchange for giving up support of Taiwan's position in the United Nations. As a result, Taiwan was expelled from the UN as a formal member and replaced by the PRC in 1971. At that time, Taiwan held diplomatic recognition by 54 countries. This figure, however, fell to 39 in 1972, when President Nixon officially visited Mainland China (Peng 1990: 133–134).

When Chiang Ching-Kuo, the elder son of Chiang Kai-shek, became the premier of Executive Yuan in 1972, he reoriented ROC's foreign policy toward so-called "flexible diplomacy." In fact, "flexible diplomacy has occasionally meant head-to-head competition with Peking [Beijing] for diplomatic relations with Third World states, but it has also emphasized the value of substantive contacts, primarily economic, which no longer are used primarily as wedges in the question for more direct relations" (Evans 1990:

180–181; Paquette 1996: 37). In other words, the KMT government on Taiwan adopted three strategies (no contact, no talk, and no compromise) against the PRC, while it took an aggressive stance in participating in international organizations, especially the non-governmental organizations. When both the ROC and the PRC have had the opportunity to send their representatives to the same international meetings, the KMT government has decided not to turn away or withdraw from the meetings. For example, the KMT government accepted the title of "Chinese Taipei" and took part in the 1984 Olympic games in Los Angeles. The ROC also adopted the strategy of "protesting without leaving" on the occasions of the annual meetings of the Asian Development Bank (ADB) in 1986 and 1987. In short, the embodiment of flexible diplomacy includes: (1) strengthening miscellaneous cooperation with those countries with which ROC has diplomatic relations; (2) enhancing substantial relations with those countries with which Taiwan has no formal ties, for the purpose of establishing diplomatic relations as the final goal; (3) seeking support from Third World countries; and (4) participating actively in international organizations, conferences and activities (Lee, 1996: 3).

Moreover, in order to develop a flexible diplomacy, Chiang Ching-Kuo made an effort by increasing economic aid to small-size nations in exchange for their political support and diplomatic recognition. Internationally, Chiang Ching-Kuo upheld President Reagan's Caribbean Basin Initiative and the Brady Plan to relieve the foreign debt crises of Latin American countries. Domestically, he abandoned martial law, deregulated the foreign exchange control, allowed private businesses to invest abroad, opened foreign trade with most Socialist countries, and permitted Taiwan's mainlanders to visit their relatives in Mainland China.

Although flexible diplomacy to some extent improved ROC's foreign relations, the number of countries with which ROC had diplomatic ties decreased year by year: 37 in 1973; 31 in 1974, 26 in 1975, 23 in 1977, 21 in 1978. There were only 22 countries with diplomatic relations with Taiwan when Chiang Ching-Kuo died in January 1988 (Peng 1990: 134).

Afterwards, Lee Teng-hui succeeded Chiang Ching-Kuo as the president of ROC. In terms of foreign policy, Lee announced that he would follow Chiang's flexible diplomacy. In July 1988, Lee addressed in the KMT's Thirteenth Congress, declaring that the ROC should "strive with greater determination, pragmatism, flexibility, and vision in order to develop a foreign policy based primarily on substantive relations"(Wu 1995: 31). Three months earlier, the President of the Central Bank, Chang Chi-

Cheng, represented the ROC at the annual meeting of the ADB. At the same time, Chang declared that the government would establish the International Economic Cooperation and Development Fund (IECDF) with an appropriation of US$1.1 billion.[10] Although this policy initiative signifies that the ROC has transformed from a recipient of foreign aid to a donor of financial assistance to developing countries, it clearly serves as a political motive to pursue the diplomatic support from those countries receiving the financial assistance, regardless of whether they recognize the PRC or not. For instance, the ROC had advanced loans totaling about US$1.12 billion at the end of 1989, in a bid to influence the Philippine National Assembly to pass the Taiwan Mutual Relations Act (Wu 1995: 26).[11]

In spite of the PRC's incessant reproach of Taiwan's flexible diplomacy and its "two China policy," Lee Teng-hui made an informal visit to Singapore in March 1989. The Singapore media called Lee, "the president coming from Taiwan." Lee Teng-hui, in a press conference after his return, responded to this designation by saying that he was, "not satisfied but [it was] acceptable." Later, a United Daily News telephone survey indicated that 86 per cent of respondents supported Lee Teng-hui's foreign policy. In the same year, ROC normalized relations with Grenada, Bahamas, Liberia, and Belize. Thus, the number of countries which had normalized ties with the ROC increased from 22 in 1988 to 26 in 1989. In 1990, two more countries, Nicaragua and Lesotho, established diplomatic relations with the ROC. The figure changed to 30 in 1993 (Hsiao 1995).

Under the leadership of Lee Teng-hui, the ROC actually adopted a more pragmatic strategy, the so-called pragmatic diplomacy. Basically, the pragmatic diplomacy is "flexible, non-ideological, and multi-directional" (Paquette 1996: 29). Taiwan has achieved relative economic success during the past forty years and became the world's thirteenth largest trading nation in 1991. Moreover, Taiwan's accumulated foreign exchange reserve fund grew from US$22.6 billion in 1985 to US$100.316 billion by May 1995 (Wu 1995: 23). With rapid economic growth and industrialization, Taiwan has wielded this economic power in foreign affairs. Indeed, the so-called "silver bullet policy," including trade, investment, and economic aid, has been Taiwan's primary strategy in attempting to achieve political aims since the 1970s.

Due to popular support for Lee's visit to Singapore in 1989, the mode of "unofficial visit by the head of state" was employed again in 1994. This time it was in the name of a "diplomatic vacation." First of all, the premier of the Executive Yuan, Lian Chan, spent a week visiting both Malaysia and Singapore in early January. Next, Lee Teng-hui traveled to the Philippines, Indonesia, and Thailand in early February. In fact, the minister of MOEA, Chiang Ping-Kun, advocated the Southward policy as early as August 1993. The purpose of this policy was to "cool Taiwan businesses' fever of investment in [the] mainland while...strengthen[ing] its economic and trade ties with its southeastern neighbors"(Abuza 1996: 115). Therefore, Lee's traveling vacation in Southeast Asia can be seen as giving the highest blessing to the "Southward Strategy."

Specifically, the major argument against a westward (Mainland oriented) strategy is that "too much trade with, and investment in China is risky due to the latter's potentially unstable domestic policy and tough position on Taiwan's international status." Secondly, "trade with, and investment in China may make Taiwan's economy too dependent on China's market." Thirdly, "heavy manufacturing investment in China may lead to deindustrialization in Taiwan—the so-called 'hollowing out'" (Chen 1996: 458–459). On the other hand, the primary reason for a southward policy is based on the comparative economic advantages. Southeast Asian countries have cheap and abundant labor, vast land, large markets, and adequate engineering and technological capacity in selected industries. Taiwanese companies can treat these conditions as an edge in their business expansion. In addition, the KMT government perceives less risk in developing economic ties with these countries. Most ASEAN countries have bilateral government agreements with Taiwan to guarantee its investment. For example, an agreement of assured investment was signed by Malaysia and Taiwan in 1992 (*The United Daily News* January 10, 1994: 4). Second, Southeast Asian countries such as Indonesia, the Philippines, and Vietnam are potentially large markets for Taiwanese firms, which have a long history of investing in the region, and are familiar with this area's environment. Besides, some ASEAN countries introduced several incentives to attract foreign companies. For instance, Indonesia and the Philippines allow foreign firms to invest and own 100 per cent equity ownership in specific industries. The Philippine government offered Taiwanese some of its textile and garment export quotas to the United States (Chen 1996: 459).

Owing to the unreliability of private investments (lack of protection, regulatory and political uncertainties) in Mainland China, the KMT government clearly wanted to redirect Taiwanese foreign trade and investments. In March 19, 1994, the Legislative Yuan passed the "Operation Outline for Strengthening Economic and Trading Relations

with Southeast Asia," which included four objectives (Abuza 1996: 115):
1. Expand two-way economic, trade, and investment relations with Southeast Asia.
2. Help Taiwan businesses invest in Southeast Asia in order to decrease trade dependence on Mainland China.
3. Increase good will toward the ROC by helping to develop Southeast Asian economies and increase prosperity.
4. Participate in the activities of Southeast Asian international economic organizations.

Interestingly, according to MOEA, the statistics show that the total sum of Taiwanese investment in Southeast Asia was more than US$1 billion between 1986 and 1990. The sum of investment in Indonesia by June 1992 was equal to US$3,980 million, while the investment in Thailand was US$4.3 billion (*The China Times* February 7, 1994: 3). However, the investment in the region declined rapidly between 1991 and 1993. For example, the investment in Indonesia was US$1 billion in 1991 and the sum decreased to US$560 million in 1992. During the first half year of 1993, the total investment in Indonesia was only US$24 million. The reasons for decreasing investments in Southeast Asia, according to the MOEA, could be attributed to the skyrocketing wages in Malaysia, rapid change of environment (including inflation) in Indonesia, and social instability and insufficiency of electric power in the Philippines. Under these circumstances, Taiwanese firms moved their capital to Mainland China accordingly (*The China Times* February 7, 1994: 3). While the KMT government encouraged the Taiwanese to turn to Southeast Asia lest they run too much risk in China, the deteriorating conditions in the Southeast Asian region did not offer the Taiwanese a better opportunity. It seemed that the southward strategy was mainly driven by the political aspiration to achieve the goals of pragmatic diplomacy.

In March 26, 1994, one group, led by the minister of MOEA, Chiang Ping-Kun, visited Vietnam to deal with SOEs' investment over there. At the end of March 1994, another group, lead by the director of business management committee of KMT-owned enterprises, Liu Tai-Ying, visited Indonesia to make arrangements with investment projects. In the beginning of April 1994, another group, led by the undersecretary of MOEA, Lee Shu-Chiu, also visited Indonesia to deal with investment project by SOEs. Obviously, KMT-owned and controlled firms, as well as SOEs, rather than the private sector, which has tended to prefer investing in the Mainland, have dominated the southward strategy. If these projects (including two in

Malaysia) had all been agreed to and signed between the two sides, the total investment would have been over US$2 billion. The involvement of SOEs in these investments included China Petroleum Corporation, Taiwan Sugar Corporation, China Petrochemical Corporation, Taiwan Salt Corporation, China Steel Corporation, Taipower, Taiwan Fertilizer Corporation, and Chinese Engineering Corporation. As for KMT-owned enterprises, they had already invested US$200 million in Vietnam and planned to spend another US$500 million in Southeast Asian countries (*The Liberty Times* March 28, 1994: 13).

In June 1994, "the MOEA issued 'The Detailed Plan of the Guidelines for Enhancing Economic and Trade Relations with Southeast Asia,' which authorized the establishment of three separate task forces to deal with Taiwan investment in Indonesia, the Philippines, and Vietnam. Moreover, the MOEA authorized three means to enhance economic ties with Southeast Asian countries: (1) provide relending/low interest loans to small and medium-sized enterprises; (2) develop industrial parks and zones, which will specifically facilitate FDI by Taiwan firms; and (3) provide technical assistance—both technical support and personnel training" (Abuza 1996: 115–116). It seemed that the southward strategy led by SOEs and KMT-owned enterprises was operating at full speed.

Democratization and the Pragmatic Diplomacy

Before proceeding with the discussion, it should be noted that the linkage between democratization and pragmatic diplomacy may not improve or directly result in improvements in Taiwan's SOE FDI. The linkage, however, provides the domestic background for the ROC government's adoption of pragmatic diplomacy. Although it may seem irrelevant to SOE FDI, understanding this linkage is essential to identifying the domestic sources of Taiwan's foreign policy. Only when we understand not only the foreign, but also the domestic factors which reoriented the ROC government's foreign policy can we make a clear connection between SOE FDI and the pragmatic policy. The following discussion, therefore, will explore the relationship between democratization and the pragmatic policy in Taiwan.

In terms of democratization in Taiwan, there is a consensus that five interactive structural forces resulted in the transition from an authoritarian regime to a democratic one: (1) the withering of the first-generation mainlanders, thus weakening the Chinese identity and unification awareness, and the emerging of the Taiwan-oriented awareness against the unquestioned acceptance of reunification; (2) the rise of political opposition groups calling for democracy; (3) the increasing pressures on the ruling KMT elites for accelerating the political reforms; (4) the pluralization of civil society in confrontation with the authoritarian state's domination; and (5) the impact of the world-wide democratic wave and the pressure of the international democratic community (especially the United States) (Wong 1997: 178).

Undeniably, the formation of an opposition party, the Democratic Progressive Party (DPP), in 1986 was the most important driving impetus for Taiwan's democratization, despite the fact that both Chiang Ching-Kuo and Lee Teng-hui pushed toward democratization. As a result, "Taiwan has managed to remove or alter many of the authoritarian structures of the past, including lifting marital law, broadening freedoms of press and expression, legalizing opposition political parties, releasing political prisoners and reducing the use of the judicial system to stifle dissent, and last, but not least, introducing for the first time in forty years full elections for the National assembly in 1991, the Legislative Yuan in 1992, the governor of the Taiwan Province in 1994, and the direct election of the President of the ROC in 1996" (Wong 1997: 179). On the other hand, the DPP gained popularity and political strength in the elections since 1989.[12] Another party, the New Party, organized in 1993 by a group of KMT elites who accused the KMT leadership of betraying the party's ideals, also captured about 13 per cent to 15 per cent of the popular vote in the subsequent elections. Thus, the development of multi-party politics and the weakening of the KMT's domination in elections promote the democratization of Taiwan.

Along with the democratization, the taboos on criticism of unification policy and the "One China" policy have been relieved. The consciousness of popular sovereignty has been on the rise as well. Partly because the DPP advocates Taiwan independence and 98 per cent of DPP's supporters are ethnic Taiwanese, and partly because the ROC has become more isolated in the international community, people in Taiwan are increasingly supporting the DPP. This support stems from their eagerness for international recognition that Taiwan is a member of the international community whose autonomy should not be intervened in by foreign forces. Taiwan's Independence movement has been more or less reserved to challenging of official ideology that Taiwan is only a province of China. However, the controversial discrepancy between the ROC's *de facto* sovereignty over Taiwan and its claim of *de jure* sovereignty over the whole China has incurred serious skepticism among the people in Taiwan. In spite of debates on Taiwan's future and the variety of possible national identities (for example, Chinese nationalism, status quoism, Taiwan prioritism, Taiwanese nationalism, and confused identity), the Taiwan-oriented awareness has increasingly been held by most of the people in Taiwan. For instance, opinion polls conducted by the Twenty-First Survey Fund showed that:

> The supporters of an independent Taiwan (include "make Taiwan independent as soon as possible" and "preserve the status quo and then move towards an independent Taiwan") have been on the rise, from 14 per cent in 1993 to 16.1 per cent in 1995, while the supporters of unification ("unify with mainland China as soon as possible" and "preserve the status quo and then move towards unification") have been declining, from 34.7 per cent to 22.2 per cent. Meanwhile, the supporters of "preserve the status quo forever" and "preserve the status quo and decide Taiwan's future later" also rose from 10.1 per cent to 17.2 per cent and 22 per cent to 34.1 per cent, respectively. (Wong 1997: 184)

In addition, if we exclude those opinions that support reunification with China, then the total percentage supporting the status quo and independence reached 67.4 per cent in 1995, while the figure was 46.1 per cent in 1993.

Under the circumstances of democratization, the KMT regime cannot choose but to adopt the DPP's political ideas, policies, and propositions in order to keep its ruling position. At the same time, the KMT government has to demonstrate that Taiwan is a sovereign state independent from foreign control or pressure. China policy (military defense on the one hand, rapprochement with China on the other) and foreign affairs are the two major domains in which the KMT government strives for settlement. In other words, a two-fold strategy (toward China and toward the international community) was launched at the same time.

In October 1990, President Lee Teng-hui set up the National Unification Council (NUC) to delineate Taiwan's new China policy of urging the PRC not only to normalize cross-straits relations but also to recognize Taiwan as a political entity. In the same month, the Mainland Affairs Council (MAC) was formally created under the supervision of the Executive Yuan. According to the National Unification Guidelines issued in February 1991 by NUC, the short-term goal of the China policy would be mutual recognition and equal treatment between Taiwan and Mainland China. Later (in May 1991), President Lee officially abolished the

"Temporary Provisions during the Period of Mobilization against the Communist Insurgency." At the same time, Lee also announced that ROC would neither treat the Communist Chinese Party as a "bandit" organization nor perceive of the PRC as an "illegitimate" government. Afterwards, the MAC in September 1992 issued the report on "Issues and Prospects of Direct Transportation Links across the Taiwan Straits." The report indicated that the ROC would like to open air and sea transportation directly between Taiwan and China, on the condition that the CCP renounces the threat of force against Taiwan and recognizes the ROC as an equal political entity.

Indeed, calling for ameliorating the relationship between Taiwan and China does not mean that this is just a wishful thinking. The PRC has repeatedly proposed the opening of direct transportation to the ROC since 1979. However, it is doubtful that the PRC would acknowledge Taiwan as a political entity and not just a province. The authority in Taiwan understands that this demand for equal treatment is impossible from China's perspective. Given this circumstance, the KMT government seeks to establish a self-help system (i.e., the military security system) in case of emergency or crisis across the straits and, therefore, the buildup of the military self-defense system has been underway. For example, in September 1992 both the American and the French governments agreed to sell 150 F-16 fighter planes and 60 Mirage 2000-5 fighters to Taiwan. And the defense budget has amounted to around 25 per cent of the total government budget between 1991 to 1995 (Wong 1997: 188).

In addition to seeking equal recognition from the PRC and strengthening its defense capability, the ROC has launched its so-called "pragmatic diplomacy" mentioned above, in order to break its current international isolation. The rationale for this policy is that, "if it can obtain diplomatic recognition from the international community, it would be difficult for Beijing to negate the political existence of Taipei. Moreover, no matter how small the chance to gain international recognition, the very action of pragmatic diplomacy itself should help internationalize the question of Taiwan" (Wong 1997: 189). In June 1993, President Lee endorsed the models of Germany and Korea in explaining that the ROC's changed position was not inconsistent with the China policy. At the same time, the KMT government openly expressed its willingness to reenter the United Nations (UN). Although this idea was first proposed by the DPP in 1988, the pressure to break Taiwan's isolation encouraged the government to accept this proposal and mobilize seven Latin American states to move for a resolution in UN granting Taiwan new membership. Despite the foreseeable defeat of this proposal in the UN, Taiwan continues to promote it.

Within the framework of pragmatic diplomacy, the aforementioned "vacation diplomacy" is another strategy for opening up international recognition. In addition to the visits in Southeast Asian countries, Lee Teng-hui extended his international visits to Latin America and Africa, including Nicaragua, Costa Rica, South Africa and Swaziland in May 1994. In April 1995, Lee took another trip to Middle East, visiting the United Arab Emirates and Jordan. Two months later, Lee Teng-hui even visited the United States. The PRC's furious reaction to this series of diplomatic visits was expected. On many occasions, the spokesmen of PRC government accused Lee of intending to seek Taiwan independence and threatened Taiwan with the use of force to crack down Taiwan's separatism. Military exercises (the so-called the "test" of M-9 and M-11 ballistic missiles off the Taiwan coast) near Taiwan were maneuvered between July 1995 and March 1996. In response, President Lee reiterated that the ROC would continue to pursue the two-fold policy of equal recognition and pragmatic diplomacy. Lee's message clearly indicates that before unification, Taiwan and Mainland China should be equal, and that both have the same sovereign status and rights to participate in the international community.

Economic Policy and the China Factor

The success of Taiwan's economic development in the past fifty years is mainly due to the adoption of an export-oriented strategy since 1960. In effect, the surplus of exports and foreign exchange reserves have been increasing rapidly since 1970. However, due to American pressure between 1985 and 1990, the Taiwan dollar appreciated by almost 40 per cent. For instance, the exchange rate between the New Taiwan dollar and U.S. dollar was 39.9 to 1 in 1985, then the rate changed rapidly to 28.6 to 1 in 1987. The direct impact of the NT dollar's appreciation is that production costs have increased, thus causing private business groups, especially small and medium-sized enterprises (SMEs) considerable loss of orders for goods from foreign countries. The United States also forced the ROC government to adopt a series of import liberalization measures, which opened the domestic market not only to American products but also to cheap goods from foreign countries. In addition, there was a sharp shortage of labor supply in domestic markets, followed by rising labor wages.

Furthermore, growing environmental consciousness added additional costs to production. With all these disadvantages in costs, private business groups, particularly SMEs, took an optional strategy of exit, that is, investment in foreign countries (Kuo 1994: 13–14; Tu 1994: 108).

On the one hand, the development in Southeast Asian countries has attracted many Taiwanese businessmen. For instance, Thailand passed the Investment Promotion Act in 1977, giving foreign companies favorable edges in investment. The Malaysian government passed the Law on Investment Promotion in 1986, providing foreign corporations preferential conditions and incentives for investment. The Indonesian government issued the Priority Scale List in 1977 in order to improve the administrative procedures of investment application and has introduced a series of economic liberalization measures since 1985. In the Philippines, the revised Foreign Investment Act of 1986 and the proclamation of the Comprehensive Investment Act in 1987 were designed to encourage inflows of foreign capital. On the other hand, the ROC government liberalized the foreign exchange and financial policies, rendering help to the private business community. In June 1987, the Legislative Yuan passed the revised measures of the Ordinances of Foreign Exchange, which allowed Taiwanese to personally hold foreign currency without having to save in the bank and permitted each individual to remit US$5 million to foreign countries each year. These measures loosened the government's financial control and provided a good opportunity and convenience for foreign investment. As a result, the instances and amounts of Taiwanese investment in Southeast Asia have increased abruptly since 1986 (Tu 1994: 109).

In fact, during 1959–1980, the bulk of Taiwan's total overseas investment was concentrated in Southeast Asia, especially Malaysia and Thailand (Chen 1996: 454). The reasons could be that many overseas Chinese live in that region, that this area is in close proximity to Taiwan, and that the labor costs for production are low. Since the Taiwanese are familiar with this region and strong incentives are provided both by Southeast Asian countries and the ROC government, a large amount of capital moves to Southeast Asia. For example, the approved investments in Southeast Asia were 44 cases, and the total sum was US$61 million in 1986. The total sum increased to US$410 million in 1987. Between 1988 and 1991, the total investments approved were 2,308 cases and the sum was US$11.7 billion. On average there were, 462 investments, US$2.9 billion each year. Comparatively, Taiwanese investments in Mainland China were only

US$3.2 billion during the same period (1988–1991) (Tu 1994: 109–110).

However, investments in Southeast Asia sharply declined in 1992 (the cases and the total sum both decreased by about 40 per cent), whereas investments in China increased (the number of cases increased by 2.7 times and the sum increased by three times). In comparison, investments in Southeast Asia were NT$2 billion, whereas the sum in China was 5.5 billion. Until 1993, the gap between these two areas enlarged. The investments were worth US$1.1 billion in Southeast Asia, while the amounts of money invested in China were US$6.1 billion (Tu 1994: 111).

As a matter of fact, the PRC has tried to support economic linkage with Taiwan since 1979. For example, the Standing Committee of the National People's Congress in 1979 proposed "three exchanges" (trade, transport, and postal) and "four flows" (economic, cultural, scientific, and sports) in the hopes of eventual reunification. Since 1979, a series of practical measures designed to facilitate the development of economic ties with the ROC have been implemented. The State Council issued the Special Preferential Measures for Taiwanese Investment in Economic Zones in 1982. In response, the ROC announced the relaxation of restrictions on indirect exports to PRC in 1984, and allowed 29 agricultural and industrial raw materials from Mainland China imported into Taiwan in August 1987 and extended to 90 items in 1989. The CCP then announced 22 measures of the Regulation on Urging Taiwanese Investment in July 1988. Moreover, in 1990, the PRC gave Taiwan's business community favorable treatment in terms of tax reduction, investment areas and the means of investment. In return, the ROC government permitted the Taiwanese banks to establish branches in Hong Kong in 1991 and the PRC opened its service sector and domestic markets to foreigners in 1992 (Tu 1994: 113–114). Taking count of all these factors, plus the cultural and linguistic similarities between Taiwan and China, we should not be surprised that the Taiwanese total investments in China rose to US$6.1 billion in 1993.

Due to China's cheap labor, abundant natural resources, and the easing-up of restrictions on foreign capital, Taiwanese businesspeople have taken advantage of the opportunity to "go west." This phenomenon is often referred to as "Mainland fever." In addition to increasing investment in China, exports to China via Hong Kong have grown exponentially. For example, trade with China grew from 3.54 per cent of Taiwan's total trade in 1981 to 12.27 per cent in 1995, while Taiwan's trade with the United States dropped from 36.1 per cent to 21.91 per cent over the same period (Leng 1996: 121). As for the percentage of Taiwan's total exports, export to

China increased from 7.19 per cent in 1981 to 21.49 per cent in 1995 (Leng 1996: 120). Although the ROC government tries to impose bureaucratic obstacles on cross-Strait economic relations, Taiwan's dependence on Mainland China's market has been growing.

Initially, the ROC government regarded the economic relations with China as "tantamount to aiding the enemy and high treason" (Wang 1992: 54). However, the government has found it difficult to formulate economic policy toward the PRC, because neither complete prohibition nor full liberalization would be the optimal choice. In fact, the government has to take both economic and politico-military security considerations into account. On the one hand, "too great a dependence on exports to the PRC could impede efforts to reorient Taiwan's economy toward more high-technology product areas, by removing the incentive for firms to abandon marginal product areas." On the other hand, "too great a dependence on exports to the PRC will produce vulnerability to manipulation by the PRC for political purposes" (Boutin 1997: 81–82).

The ROC has endeavored to satisfy both sets of security requirements simultaneously. In addition to the relaxation of restrictions on indirect exports to the PRC, the ROC government established the Kaohsiung the Asia-Pacific Regional Operations Center (APROC) in 1995. The project envisions developing operations centers in financial services, telecommunications, air transportation, shipping, manufacturing, and media. The goal is to make the island both a base for domestic enterprises and a gateway for Western nations that are targeting Asian markets, especially those in Southeast Asia and Mainland China (*Free China Review* 1996: 2–3). Also, this project was intended to make Kaohsiung a cargo transshipment center that would eventually handle shipments in the Asia-Pacific region. There are three stages, according to the ROC government plan, to achieving the goals of APROC: (1) the establishment of an offshore shipping center; (2) the establishment of storage and processing zones; and (3) the establishment of an economic operation special zone.[13]

Taiwan's Shipping Association and China's Shipping Exchange Association met in Hong Kong on January 22, 1997, and signed the "minutes of talks," a preliminary agreement on the establishment of an offshore shipping (or "point-to-point direct transportation" in Chinese) center. This despite the facts that the APROC cannot reduce transportation costs for SMEs and that China still insists on a direct cross-Strait link. By April 1997, Taiwan had approved five Mainland shipping companies for use of the offshore shipping center, whereas China had approved six

Taiwanese shipping companies to engage in shipping between Kaohsiung and Mainland ports. On April 19, 1997, the first Mainland Chinese ship (*Shengda*) arrived in Kaohsiung. Five days later, the first Taiwanese ship (*Lishun*) arrived in Xiamen (Kung 1997: 51, 63–64).

Another of the government's endeavors is to encourage Taiwanese companies to shift their exports to other areas, mainly to the United States and Southeast Asia. Because the U.S. has been a well-established market for Taiwanese exporters, the ROC government has made many concessions in opening up sectors of its economy for American enterprises, thus securing continued access to the U.S. market. In addition, through pragmatic diplomacy, ROC government officials visited Southeast Asian countries to discuss cooperation and promote closer economic ties, thereby paving the way for increased exports from Taiwan.

As for politico-military security concerns, there are no effective control mechanisms to prohibit the export of high-technology products to the PRC. In order to maintain a lead over the PRC in terms of core export activities and ensure the continued competitiveness of Taiwan's exports, the ROC government strives to promote local technological development. The goal of this approach is to stay "a few jumps ahead in technology" and continue to "produce goods and services beyond the reach of her opponent" (Boutin 1997: 85).

In terms of investment in PRC, the ROC government incipiently prohibited all investment (direct or indirect) in China. However, this strictness encounters an inevitable dilemma. On the one hand, realizing that China as a hinterland is important to Taiwan's economic growth and prosperity, the ROC government informally sanctioned investment in China in 1991. On the other hand, the trend of growing Taiwanese investment in China still worries the ROC government, since this increasing flow of capital could be used by the PRC as an instrument of political leverage against Taiwan's security. Therefore, the ROC government announced the "Regulations Governing Investments and Technical Cooperation with Mainland China" in 1993, which established the requirements for indirect investment in China.[14] The purpose of this regulation is both to restrict the investment in China and minimize the security risks. In fact, the investment restriction imposed on Taiwanese businesspeople involves both the size of individual projects and the nature of the project. "Approval is granted to investment projects only if they meet the following criteria: (1) they do not compete with the ROC's domestic industries in the international market; (2) they are labor-intensive;

(3) they use raw materials produced in the PRC; and (4) the business involved would not be competitive if the projects remained in Taiwan"(Boutin 1997: 88–89). At the same time (1993), the ROC government launched the "southward" policy, encouraging local businesses to invest in Southeast Asia as an alternative to the PRC.

Although the ROC government issued the "Regulation Governing Business Activities in Mainland China" in 1994 to revise and simplify the investment screening process, the PRC did not respond positively in turn, especially when President Lee visited the United States in 1995. During Lee's trip to the U.S., for example, "a number of Taiwanese firm's operations were subject to apparently politically-motivated harassment when they were 'besieged' by inspectors, police, and auditors 'looking to find something wrong'" (Boutin 1997: 80). After the PRC's test of ballistic missiles, Lee Teng-hui won the presidential election in March 1996. On August 15, 1996, Lee appealed for restraint in investment in the PRC, proposing that Taiwan companies limit themselves to 20–30 per cent of their total foreign investment and retain 20 per cent of their investment in Taiwan (Boutin 1997: 90). On another occasion, September 14, 1996, when Lee made a speech at the National Meeting of Managers, he warned that the PRC had adopted the means of "using the people to force government yielding, and using the business to siege the politics." President Lee, then, asked the business community to follow the principle of "No haste, be patient." In the following year, the MOEA announced further restrictions on investment in the PRC: individual investment projects can be no more than US$5 million; Taiwanese firms are not allowed to invest in energy projects, property development, and transport facilities in Mainland China. As a result, Taiwanese investment in the PRC has decreased dramatically since then.

In short, the complicated interplay of domestic politics, foreign policy and economic policy in Taiwan derives from the China factor, thus pushing the ROC government to seek an alternative foreign investment policy, the southward policy. The goal of the southward strategy is to establish economic ties with Southeast Asian countries. SOEs' FDI is seen as the instrument for fulfilling this policy.

Conclusion

In terms of capital, projects and the region, the FDI of Taiwan's SOEs appears to be insignificant. However, the question is: above all, what is the political implication of those foreign investments? Obviously, those decisions are not judged solely by comparative advantages and/or assistance of state subsidies. In other words, the cases of FDI do not demonstrate that Taiwan's SOEs have become multinational corporations. Therefore, the literature of multinational state-owned enterprises does not provide an explanation for Taiwan's SOEs in FDI. As a matter of fact, the impetus for SOEs' foreign investment actually stemmed from the ROC government's southward strategy, which links democratization, pragmatic diplomacy, and economic security policy. The alternative of the southward strategy is mainly a reaction to the threat of an emerging great power, that is, China. Because of Taiwan's international isolation, de facto separation between Taiwan and the Mainland, and the unsolved "One China" issue, the ROC cannot extricate itself from the predicament by ignoring China. The shadow of Mainland China always disturbs Taiwan's domestic politics and foreign and economic policy. This ambivalence toward China excludes many optimal options for the ROC decision-makers.

Ironically, the relative decline in state autonomy led the ROC government to treat SOEs as a forerunner in FDI. In order to accomplish the southward economic policy, the KMT government utilizes the SOEs as the symbolic assurance of reducing investment risks and of profit-making protection, thereof encouraging private business enterprises to invest in Southeast Asia. If the state was still strong in terms of capability, it would not be necessary to exert such great effort in persuading business groups to shift their trade and investment from China to Southeast Asia. However, as it is, the state has to instruct the SOEs to invest southward first, and then induce the private sector to follow the step.

Indeed, from an historical perspective, SOEs in Taiwan have made a great contribution to Taiwan's economic development and industrialization. When SOEs have finished their missions at different phases, they should accommodate the changes in the internal/external milieu and make adjustments to their structure and management, including organizational types, operation processes, personnel transfers, technological innovations, and upgrade of the level of industry. Because of their monopolistic nature, however, SOEs always re-adjust themselves passively unless faced with an inevitable challenge and/or pressure.

Now that political transition from an authoritarian regime to a democratic one has been undertaken, the tight control by KMT government no longer exists.[15] The liberalization and democratization have resulted in the relative decline of state domination and autonomy. Under this circumstance, SOEs now face a dilemma between two strong and pulling forces. One force comes from the society—to privatize themselves as soon as possible. The other force comes from the state—to accomplish assignments as quickly as possible. Under the pressure of these two forces, therefore, SOEs have become less and less autonomous. In terms of foreign investment, this study shows, the decisions of SOEs are much influenced by the KMT government's diplomatic policy. How they can adjustment and struggle for autonomy, and whether they can do so, are the two critical questions that remain to be answered.

Notes

1. There is no legitimate reason for this stoppage. It could be that the long-term profits of outward investment were worth little, that the expected revenues could not be earned in a short of time, or that the domestic markets were more attractive. As for the revitalization of foreign investment, it can be attributed to political considerations that will be discussed below.

2. There are five naphtha splitting-off plants in Taiwan, and the sixth one is currently under construction (Chu 1995). The second plant, which will be relocated to Indonesia, was built between 1970 and 1975.

3. However, the question is why it takes so long (not until 1996, twelve years later) to make such decisions when the contract was signed in 1984.

4. It should be mentioned that the contract was signed in 1970, whereas the construction of the company was started at the end of 1979. It was completed and has been operating since 1984. The government has 50 per cent ownership (the other half belongs to the Saudi Arabian company) and allowed Taiwan Fertilizer Corporation to purchase it in 1996 (Taiwan Fertilizer Corporation 1995: 19–20).

5. The amount of money shown in Table 6.2C (NT$127.484 million) seems to be exaggerated by MOEA, because the budget reports of Taiwan Salt Corporation from 1996 to 1998 show that the investment was only NT$87.318 million (Taiwan Salt Corporation 1995: 96–97, 1996: 100–101, 1997: 94–95).

6. Chu (1995) also supports Gerschenkron's (1962) arguments in her study of Taiwan's Petrochemical Industry.

7. According to Huntington (1991: 15), "A wave of democratization is a group of transitions from nondemocratic to democratic regimes that occur within a specified period of time and that significantly outnumber transitions in the opposite direction during period of time. A wave also usually involves liberalization or partial democratization in political systems that do not become fully democratic."

8. According to Sun Chen, one of the most famous economists in Taiwan, "pubic

enterprises used 30 to 35 per cent of cumulative capital formation in the period 1965–79 and produced only 12 per cent of Net Domestic Product, while privates used 45 to 50 per cent of cumulative capital formation to produce as much as 75 per cent of NDP." Therefore, he "concludes straightforwardly that the productivity of capital would be increased by comprehensive denationalization" (Wade 1990: 181, fn24).

9. They were divested in the late 1960s. In 1983 a loss-making public smelter was sold to private capital (Wade 1990: 181).

10. In fact, the IECDF was established in October 1988.

11. Chen (1996: 463) also noted that, "Taiwan signed an official agreement with the Philippines to provide a low-interest loan of US$60 million through the IECDF to improve the physical infrastructure in Subic Bay; the first installment of US$23 million has already been committed to building the Taiwan industrial park."

12. DPP obviously has stabilized its popularity in Taiwan's politics and gained steady support from the electorate: "in the 1989 Legislative Yuan supplementary elections, it captured 29.9 per cent of the popular vote; in the 1991 National Assembly full elections, 23.6 per cent; in the 1992 Legislative Yuan full election, 31.4 per cent; in the 1993 Mayors and County Magistrates elections, 41.2 per cent; in the 1994 Mayors of Taipei and Kaohsiung and Governor of Taiwan elections, 32 per cent; in the 1995 Legislative Yuan elections, 33.2 per cent, and in the 1996 National Assembly elections, 29.9 per cent" (Wong 1997: 179).

13. For the evaluation of APROC, see Kung (1997).

14. These requirements include: "investment conducted through a branch of a Taiwan firm located in a third country, investment in another firm located in a third country, investment through a firm in a territory outside China, or investment through indirect remittance" (Boutin 1997: 88).

15. For discussion of Taiwan's political transition, for example, see Kau (1996).

Part Two:
Embeddedness and the Co-evolution of Markets

Chapter 7

Business Globalization and Local Embeddedness: The Case of Foreign Investment in Taiwan

Rueyling Tzeng

Increasing cross-border activities, such as the movement of people, capital, goods and services, has made globalization a key topic among social scientists. Although globalization did not become a catchword until the late 1980s, the process of globalization can be traced to the dawn of history and its scope spans economic, political and cultural arenas of social life (Waters 1995). In spite of this pervasiveness of globalization, there is no consistent definition of the concept (Cook and Kirkpatrick 1997) and it is "not a finished theory...rather a set of concerns"(Amin and Thrift 1994: 1). Two of the most important concerns related to globalization are the power of the nation state and the related issue of the dialectics between global and local levels that unfolds in the globalization process. While some scholars worry about a loss of state power and local diversity due to globalization, others argue that the role of the state in the global economy will be re-strengthened and local diversity will be maintained in the process of global integration.

These two concerns about business globalization are most effectively captured by the notion of embeddedness, as reintroduced by Granovetter in his highly acclaimed 1985 article, "Economic Action and Social Structure: The Problem of Embeddedness." When reframed in terms of embeddedness, globalization becomes a question of whether or not the increase in multinational corporations' cross-border economic activities will make firms more like atomized actors that can freely invest and divest according to their wills. In other words, does globalization make multinational corporations behave independently, irrespective of the larger institutions in which they are embedded? This research answers this question with a decisive "no." This paper will use the case of foreign investment in Taiwan to argue that the operations of multinational corporations are constrained by the institutions in which they are embedded—in home and host countries, as well as in the global environment. That is, the global economic system is not something "out there" that imposes constraints; rather, it is the result of interaction among a group of related actors such as nation-states, multinational corporations, and transnational or global economic organizations.

The issue of the role of the state in facing the rise of multinational corporations has received tremendous discussion in academic literature. The issue of the dialectics between global and local relations, on the other hand, has been largely ignored. In the past, due to the dominant role in the world economy of the world's leading powers, westernization has been perceived as a global force sweeping over the local in developing (non-Western) countries. While the localization of subsidiaries was addressed at a time when multinational corporations were predominantly organized by a vertically integrated structure of mass production, these studies' emphases on the central control of the home company did not leave much room for analysis of localization. In this literature, subsidiaries were generally considered to be economic enclaves within host countries, characterized by little interaction with the local. The relation was one in which the host country's cheap labor was used for assembly of parts that were imported, only to be re-exported back to the home country as finished goods.

Recently, a new organizational structure of flexible production and vertical disintegration (Piroe and Sabel 1984) has emerged. This change has revitalized discussion of the relationship between the global and the local levels for subsidiaries of multinational corporations. For example, the network structure of Japanese multinational corporations has signaled the importance of localization (local sourcing and R&D) for the global economy (Morris 1991). On the other hand, the growth of the service industry, which emphasizes local markets rather than, or in addition to, cheap labor, makes localization more important. These phenomena have lead to questions of the extent to which localization is actually possible and whether a new mixture of global and local elements will thus emerge.

From an economic perspective, the most important single indicator of localization is the degree of local sourcing (Dicken et al. 1994). Other economic factors include Research and Development undertaken, capital obtained, sales contributed, value added, equipment purchased and products made in the local host country. In addition, I argue that localization of a subsidiary also reflects on its compliance with local regulations and its adaptation to local management customs and marketing strategies. Moreover, the emergence of localization is a result of the dialectics between global and local interactions in the globalizing economy. Some aspects of localization will maintain some global elements, and vice versa.

There are three significant reasons for choosing Taiwan as a case study for globalization. First, Taiwan has assumed not only a vital place in the global production structures of corporations from the U.S. and Japan, but also has been a battleground of intense competition in the global economy between these two countries for the past three decades (Bello and Rosenfeld 1990). Nevertheless, not until 1980 did Taiwan start campaigning for economic internationalization and liberalization. Its long history of involvement in the global economy, as well as recently active pursuit of a free market in accordance with global demand, makes Taiwan a perfect case to study globalization. Second, since the present study of globalization emphasizes the dimension of localization, this paper can provide a local perspective. Third, the successful economic development of Taiwan as a deviant case of dependent development has been largely attributed to the role played by the Taiwanese state. The study of the Taiwanese state's regulation of multinational corporations can facilitate the present discussion of the state's role in the globalizing economy.

In the following sections, I will first discuss the debates surrounding the effects of the globalization of multinationals on the nation-state. Particularly, I will emphasize their neglect of local influences on the subsidiaries of multinational corporations and recent trends in foreign direct investment (FDI). Next, I will discuss foreign investment in Taiwan and the approach of the Taiwanese state towards it. Following that, I will discuss localization of foreign firms in Taiwan, using survey data from the Taiwanese government, supplemented by interviewing data, to analyze localization of present foreign investment in Taiwan. Finally, I will draw conclusions about all these issues and discuss how they relate.

State, Local and Emerging FDI in the Service Industry

The increase in foreign investment from developed countries to developing countries has created an international division of labor in which the roles assumed by these two types of countries are different. Fröbel, Heinrichs and Kreye (1980) maintain that the 1960s were a watershed period for the transformation of the international division of labor. Prior to the 1960s, the world economy could be characterized as a classic international division of labor, consisting of two parts: a few developed countries that produced capital goods and consumer goods, and the majority developing countries that produced mineral and agricultural raw materials. However, since the 1960s, an international market has developed and developed countries are increasingly invested in developing countries. The new international division of labor (NIDL) thus arose to exploit the reserve supplies of labor in developing countries on a worldwide scale, with production in developing countries primarily undertaken for foreign markets in developed countries. Fröbel et al. also recognize that the NIDL has brought crises to developed countries such as stagnating or declining investment and rising unemployment, among other problems.

The globalization of production (GOP) theory (Bluestone and Harrison 1982; Gordon 1995 [1988]), an extension of NIDL, argues for the increasingly centralized control and coordination of multinational corporations in addition to the emergence of the global manufacturing system. Both NIDL and GOP contend that multinational corporations enhance their leverage over national governments and domestic unions by moving their production to developing countries in order to seek out cheap labor. A third theory, the dependency theory (Evans 1979), contends that multinational corporations ally with a weak state and local capital in the host country in order to exploit the economic profits of developing countries. In this view, the state in developing countries cannot protect the local economy from the intrusion of multinational corporations. All of the above three theories label multinational corporations as greedy, seeking profits at the expense of economic development in both home and host countries and inhibiting the power of nation-states. The notion of "dependent development," on the other hand, draws on the experiences of Asian countries' economic expansion in the 1970s to contend that foreign investment can play a significant positive role in the economic development of host countries. This modified version of the dependency theory argues that a strong or developmental state in the host country can direct the multinational corporations to facilitate the expansion of the local economy (Gold 1981, 1986; Evans 1989). Nevertheless, although multinational corporations and the state in the host country can play contradictory roles, the majority of discussion of state weakness has been confined to discussion of the home country as powerless.

Since the 1980s, partly due to the assistance of new technology and new organizational forms, the world economy has become more globalized and deregulation is on the rise. New systems governing the global, or transnational, economy, have formed (such as North American Free Trade Agreement [NAFTA], European Union [EU], Asian Pacific Economic Cooperation Forum [APEC] and World Trade Organization [WTO]) to promote liberal and open markets. For example, two agreements from the Uruguay GATT meeting, now succeeded by the WTO, severely limit the sovereign rights of all states to regulate foreign investment. The agreement on trade related investment measures (TRIMS) forbids local content requirements, domestic sales requirements, trade balancing requirements, nor remittance and exchange restrictions. And the agreement on trade related intellectual property rights (TRIPS) strengthens the international property rights of ultima foreign investors (while neglecting the contribution of the host countries where the products are developed).

Reich (1992) argues that unbridled nationalism can have disturbing consequences for the market. He points out that there is no longer any legitimate reason for a nation to protect, subsidize, or otherwise support its corporations above others. States, should thus regulate their economies to meet the demands of deregulation in the global market. It is this paradox of "regulation for deregulation" that does not eliminate, but rather enhances the controversy over the role played by the state in the global economy (Hoogvelt 1997). I therefore agree with Sassen's argument (1996) that the role of state is not declining in the globalizing economy, but has actually been reconfigured to be more involved in the emerging transnational governance system. Nevertheless, scholars should keep in mind that there are some states (especially in the peripheries) that are excluded from playing a role in the transnational governance system and that there are some doubts as to whether the reconfigured state (especially in developing countries) can remain as strong as before in the globalizing economy.

Debates on the relative strength of the state have been expressed in discussion of the disappearing nationality of multinational corporations. Along with his argument regarding the diminishing role of the state in the global economy, Reich (1992) has also noted that the very idea of "American" products made by "American" firms is becoming obsolete. As the world has entered an era in which economic activities cross national boundaries, products usually consist of components manufactured and assembled in a variety of countries. Gereffi (1995: 101) argues that corporations are becoming increasingly disconnected from their home nations as they scour the globe for profitable opportunities. In a similar argument, Ohmae (1990) contends that nationality will disappear in the globally linked economy. In general, proponents of the theory of disappearing nationality of multinational corporations take the stance that multinational corporations are not rooted in any particular setting and can freely move their activities from one place to another.

In contrast, Porter (1990) argues that the globalization of competition makes the nation more important. He not only emphasizes the importance of national competitiveness, but also firm identity. He claims that a firm can only have one true home base for each distinct business or segment. If it attempts to maintain several, it will sacrifice the dynamism that arises from true integration with a nation. According to this view, an enterprise's nationality is important because it shapes the norms of business management by which the essential competitive advantages of enterprises are created and sustained. Similarly, Whitley (1996) insists upon the importance of the national business system in which a firm is embedded, although he contends that internationalization of economic activities and the national business system can be complementary.

Several studies categorize firm behavior by nationality. In a comparison of American and European firms, Lawrence G. Franko (1976) finds that American technology economizes on labor while European technology economizes on raw materials. Kojima (1978) portrays four behavioral differences between American and Japan multinational corporations: (1) Japanese foreign investment is mainly concentrated in disadvantaged and labor-intensive industries such as textiles, clothing and assembly, while American investment is concentrated in relatively advantaged industries which are innovative and monopolistic; (2) small- and medium-sized Japanese firms tend to engage in foreign investment through manufacturing, while American enterprises involved in foreign investment are generally large; (3) Japanese firms prefer join venture as their form of foreign investment, while American firms prefer sole ownership; and (4) export is the main purpose of Japanese foreign investment, while American multinational corporations seek to open up the local market. Although neither Franko nor Kojima explain why firm behaviors differ according to their nationality of origin, Wilkins (1991 [1986]) explains the differences between American and European multinational companies from their home perspective. Nevertheless, the roles played by host countries in shaping behavior patterns of multinational corporations are not taken into consideration in these studies. Similarly, the argument of the GOP theory, according to which multinational corporations increase centralized control to achieve coordination of their decentralized production, also neglects the local influences of host countries.

In contrast, Harrison (1994) argues that since the 1970s, large organizations have taken the form of "lean and mean" core firms connected by networks of other firms. According to this model, multinational corporations are not able to centralize control of spatially extensive production networks. Gereffi (1989) also argues for the emergence of decentralized control of multinational corporations over geographically dispersed manufacturing systems. Following this logic, it is clear that the new network structure of multinational corporations has increased the possibility of localization. While Harrison's and Gereffi's research is promising, work that brings out the centrality of localization is still rare and needs to be further developed.

Both the NIDL and GOP theories argue for the importance for the home country of finding cheap labor in developing countries. These theories neglect, however, that developing countries can serve as a major market for goods produced locally or imported by foreign firms from developed countries. In fact, this market function provided by developing countries accounts for two-thirds of the investment from developed countries in developing countries (Kaplinsky 1993). In spite of this fact, consumption capacity of developing countries has been neglected. A new network structure of multinational corporations should include not only local production but local consumption. Moreover, it should be recognized that the local force may have more influence on local marketing than does local production, since the former involves the whole population of the host country while the latter involves only the small locally employed labor force.

Foreign multinational firms' focus on cheap labor and neglect of market forces stem partly from the fact that manufacturing was the main economic force in the past industrial society. More recently, thanks to the support of modern technology, labor costs constitute only 15–20 per cent of total production costs in most industries (Gold 1982) and are as low as only 5–10 per cent for electronic items (Markides and Berg 1988). Moreover, with the emergence of a post-industrial society (Bell 1973), the importance of the service sector is also increasing. The share of overseas investment in financial and trade services from the U.S. has increased dramatically since the early 1970s. Foreign direct investment (FDI) from the U.S. into developing countries has also become increasingly selective, in particular ignoring many of the traditional manufacturing industries (Gordon 1995 [1988]). The fastest growth of FDI in the 1980s actually occurred in the service sector, especially in trade and finance; 50–55 per cent of all FDI in 1992 was in the tertiary (service) sector (Dunning 1995: 135). Dunning (1993) contends that the service sector will certainly increase in the 1990s for three reasons: (1) a rising proportion of services in consumer spending, (2) the increasing service intensity of manufactured goods (particularly in the core technology sectors), and (3) the liberalization of cross-border markets, coupled with the technological advances in telecommunication facilities. Obviously, FDI in the service industry is market-oriented.

Foreign Investment in Taiwan and Taiwan's State

Over 95 per cent of Taiwanese businesses are small- and medium-sized firms. They are mainly export oriented and are the main actors in Taiwan's economic development. The deviant case of dependent development in Taiwan (as in other East Asian NICs) lies in its heavy reliance on foreign aid and foreign trade in contrast to the economic development of Latin American NICs, which results from those countries' extensive involvement with multinationals and transnational banks (Gereffi 1989). In other words, compared to foreign investment, foreign aid and foreign trade have made greater contributions to Taiwan's economic development. This finding accords with Haggard and Cheng (1987) argument that foreign firms in Taiwan do not play a crucial role except in a few industries such as electronics.

Barrett and Whyte (1982) find that although Taiwan depended heavily on foreign investment in the 1950s and 1960s, the country nevertheless created an economic "miracle" in growth of equity in the 1970s. This deviant case of Taiwan's economic development has been greatly attributed to a strong state (Amsden 1985; Deyo 1987; Gold 1981, 1986, 1988). Further, according to Gold (1981, 1986, 1988), the triple alliance model which hindered economic development in Brazil has been absent in Taiwan (Evans 1979). For example, the establishment of export-processing zones in Taiwan has isolated foreign firms and made triple alliances impossible (Haggard and Cheng 1987). Nevertheless, Taiwan remained a paradise for foreign investors up until the mid-1980s (Bello and Rosenfeld 1990), when land became expensive and hard to obtain, labor became more active, and environmental activism increased.

Foreign firms invest mainly in the leading industries in Taiwan, including the electric and electronic machinery, chemicals, nonelectric machinery and metals sectors. Foreign investment in these four manufacturing industries accounted for 80 per cent of total foreign paid-up capital in 1987. In general, foreign investment in Taiwan has been concentrated heavily in the manufacturing sector, which accounted for 78 per cent of all approvals and 88 per cent of paid-up capital by 1987 (Schive and Tu 1991: 148).

The economic impact of foreign firms in Taiwan from 1980 to 1993 can be illustrated in five areas, as illustrated in Table 7.1. During this period, on average, foreign firms contributed about 12 per cent of business income tax revenue and employed about 3–4 per cent of the total labor force. The gross domestic product and gross domestic capital formation accounted for by foreign firms increased from 6.95 per cent to 18.99 per cent and from 7.55 per cent to 13.45 per cent, respectively. As compared with the approximately 2 per cent of the gross domestic capital formation contributed by foreign firms in Taiwan before 1980 (Haggard and Cheng 1987), the importance of foreign capital is increasing. The proportion of Taiwanese exports accounted for by foreign firms has decreased from 21.21 per cent to 16.46 per cent, giving some evidence of the increasing importance of the local market to foreign firms. In general, foreign firms have made higher contributions to Taiwan's exports than they have to its gross domestic product, gross domestic capital formation and employment. One of the important contributions of foreign firms to Taiwan's economy, which is not available in public records, is the technology they bring with them.

The inflows of FDI into Taiwan have had a great bearing on political and economic conditions domestically as well as internationally (Schive and Tu 1991).[1] FDI in Taiwan faltered in 1972, 1975, 1979 and 1982. In 1972, it faltered due to the loss of Taiwan's seat in the United Nation; in 1979,

	Exports by Foreign Firms as Percentage of Total Exports	Shares of Gross Domestic Product from Overseas Chinese and Foreign Investment*	Foreign Investment as a Share of Gross Domestic Capital Formation	Shares of Total Employment Hired by Foreign Firms	Shares of Corporate Income Tax From Foreign Firms
1980	21.21	6.95	7.55	4.03	13.11
1981	20.83	6.37	7.20	3.82	9.73
1982	20.88	5.92	7.95	3.81	7.94
1983	14.43	7.13	4.03	2.83	9.97
1984	19.53	9.09	9.29	3.55	14.70
1985	13.09	6.00	8.81	2.49	11.19
1986	14.24	7.50	9.24	2.79	11.19
1987	15.56	8.29	7.10	2.96	14.03
1988	16.30	11.35	7.27	2.97	12.44
1989	15.42	12.61	6.87	3.03	7.69
1990	22.89	13.96	3.14	3.51	13.26
1991	17.89	7.80	16.84	4.02	14.30
1992	16.55	8.50	11.05	4.04	13.63
1993	16.46	18.99	13.45	3.41	12.99

*: The percentages in this column are inflated because the contributions from overseas Chinese are included.

Sources: Abstracted and recalculated from *Report on the Operations of the Overseas Chinese and Foreign Investment and Their Contributions to Our National Economic Development*, published annually by the Investment Commission, Ministry of Economic Affairs, Taiwan, Annual Reports from 1970-1993.

Table 7.1 Contributions of Foreign Investment to Taiwan's Economy (in %)

because of the break in formal diplomatic relations between Taiwan and the U.S.; and in 1975 and 1982, FDI slowed as a result of worldwide decreases in economic growth rates. However, the inflow of foreign capital to Taiwan has been increasing greatly since 1980, primarily due to the country's policy of economic liberalization. The sharp increase of FDI between 1987 and 1989 reflects several fundamental changes in the Taiwanese economy, including: (1) the substantial and stable appreciation of the new Taiwanese dollar; (2) the liberalization of controls on movement of capital; (3) the reduction of tariffs and other import controls; and (4) the unprecedented expansion of the domestic market, especially in the services sector (Schive and Tu 1991).

The Taiwanese government has established policies to encourage and regulate foreign investors to aid Taiwan's economic development. Between 1950 and 1959, Taiwan's economic policy focused on import substitution. American foreign AID (Aid to Industrial Development) was the major source of foreign capital in Taiwan during that period. When AID started to be phased out at the end of 1950s and ended totally in 1965, it was gradually superseded by investment from American firms. The Statute for Investment by Foreign Nationals was set up in 1954, which encouraged foreign investment with restrictions. While setting up high tariffs and limits on importing goods during this period, the Taiwanese government also allowed foreign firms to take advantage of the investment encouragement act as a means of circumventing trade barriers and safeguarding the Taiwanese market. Therefore, foreign investment was mainly concentrated on the import substitution sector, supplying goods needed by the local market. In 1960, restrictions on profit remittance by foreign firms was lifted, as was the requirement for local parties to hold shares in foreign firms. As a result, foreign investment surged.

Between 1960 and 1969, the Taiwanese government switched to an export-oriented economic policy. Unlike the previous stage, the purpose of foreign investment in this period was to export goods to the market abroad by taking the advantage of cheap local labor. The Government established the Kaohsiung Export Processing Zones (EPZ) in 1965, which might account for another surge of foreign investment as shown in Table 7.2. Later, the Nantz and Taichung EPZs were opened in 1969. Investors in the zones were expected to take full advantage of cheap labor and a tax exemption on imported parts, but were required to export all of the products manufactured. As a result, FDI rose quickly and rather continuously during this period (Schive and Tu 1991). Taiwan became the

Table 7.2 Private Foreign Investment in Approvals by Area

Period	Total		U. S. A.		Japan		Europe		Others	
	Case	Amount	Case	Amount	Case	Amount	Case	Amount	Case	Amount
Total (1952-95)	5,215	19,376,710	1,112	5,836,393 (30.12%)	2,435	5,859,548 (13.97%)	553	2,706,548 (13.97%)	1,115	4,974,399 (25.67%)
1952	---	---	---	---	---	---	---	---	---	---
1955	2	4,423	2	4,423	---	---	---	---	---	---
1960	8	14,338	5	14,029	3	309	---	---	---	---
1965	36	35,140	17	31,104	14	2,081	1	43	4	1,912
1966	52	20,904	15	17,711	35	2,447	2	746	---	---
1968	122	53,445	20	34,555	96	14,855	2	1,762	4	2,273
1969	111	81,938	30	27,862	75	17,379	4	36,311	2	386
1970	71	109,165	16	67,816	51	28,530	4	11,694	---	---
1971	44	125,148	17	43,736	17	12,400	4	66,135	6	1,125
1972	52	100,190	17	37,307	26	7,728	4	6,842	5	2,877
1973	150	193,688	29	66,876	92	44,599	14	33,874	15	48,313
1974	83	108,736	21	38,760	50	38,901	3	14,761	9	48,339
1975	41	70,940	13	41,857	22	23,234	2	4,193	4	16,314
1976	45	102,032	8	22,236	26	30,760	2	32,796	9	1,656
1977	50	95,186	17	27,833	20	24,145	3	28,001	10	16,240
1978	66	136,719	18	69,765	43	50,336	1	4,468	4	15,207
1979	73	181,483	19	80,375	39	50,462	2	19,766	13	12,150
1980	71	243,380	15	110,093	35	86,081	11	14,428	10	30,880
1981	73	356,294	25	203,213	27	64,623	8	12,636	13	32,778
1982	82	320,286	33	79,606	24	152,164	11	46,570	14	75,822
1983	100	375,382	35	93,294	33	196,770	8	20,745	24	41,946
1984	101	518,971	41	231,175	28	113,978	13	90,973	19	64,573
1985	107	660,702	42	332,760	32	145,236	12	100,010	21	82,845
1986	206	705,574	56	138,428	88	253,596	23	134,837	39	82,697
1987	363	1,223,069	74	414,061	207	399,240	37	214,322	45	178,713
1988	438	1,061,161	60	134,726	212	431,867	64	96,574	102	195,446
1989	477	2,241,026	54	343,003	233	640,552	58	314,438	132	397,994
1990	376	2,081,657	61	540,366	179	826,801	49	282,681	87	943,033
1991	324	1,558,957	61	587,662	138	526,183	42	161,421	83	431,809
1992	338	1,149,228	71	183,820	117	417,777	44	164,963	106	283,691
1993	261	1,089,975	51	207,970	88	272,512	39	209,974	84	382,668
1994	332	1,523,927	52	293,710	115	391,001	40	243,590	125	399,519
1995	370	2,756,786	67	1,275,623	157	569,414	39	334,887	107	595,626

Source: Taiwan Statistical Data Book (1996: 244).

assembly factory of multinational corporations, exporting finished goods to worldwide markets. In general, this was the era in which developed countries began to increase their investments in developing countries for the purpose of manufacturing and exporting finished goods. Nevertheless, foreign firms did not neglect the importance of the local market in Taiwan during this period (Duan 1992). The volume of the local sales of foreign firms in Taiwan accounted for 40 per cent of their total sales. In the chemistry and machinery industries, the percentage was even over 68 per cent, and in the electronic industry, the top exporting industry in Taiwan, the percentage was 28 per cent.

During 1970 and 1979, although the government switched its economic policy back to import substitution, this applied only to selected industries such as petro-chemicals and cars and an export-oriented economy was still dominant in Taiwan. Under export-oriented policies, the government consistently provided fiscal, financial and other incentives, such as protective tariffs and import bans, to protect domestic production. Foreign investment in Taiwan was restricted during this period.

Beginning in the mid-1970s, foreign firms in Taiwan switched from an export orientation to a local-market orientation. Schive (1978) proposed three factors to explain this change. First, the worldwide economic stagnancy that occurred between 1973 and 1974 directed foreign firms in Taiwan to look towards the local market instead of focusing on the outside market through exporting. Second, labor costs in Taiwan dramatically increased and could no longer attract foreign firms that were export oriented. The average wage increase in manufacturing was 27 per cent between 1973 and 1975, while previously it had been only 10 per cent over ten years. Third, the Taiwanese government adopted a more selective policy regarding foreign investments.

Since 1980, the ill effects of Taiwan's export-oriented policies have been strongly criticized by developed countries and liberal economists as inviting protectionism abroad, distorting domestic resources, discouraging technology renovation, impeding economic efficiency and hurting domestic consumers. The Taiwanese government has thus adopted an economic policy of internationalization and liberalization in order to upgrade its industrial structure from labor-intensive to capital- and technology-intensive industries. In 1980, the Hsinchu Science-based Industrial Park was set up to attract foreign investment by fostering the development of high-technology industries.

Since the mid-1980s, the Taiwanese government has revised several policies in favor of foreign investment. By 1986, when Taiwan was on its way to becoming a post-industrial society (the GNP from the service sector was increasing while the GNP from manufacturing was decreasing) (Lee 1994), the Statute for Investment by Foreign Nationals subsumed the service industry into the foreign investment scope. At the same time, export ratio and local content requirements, the investor's greatest concerns, began to diminish. Under current statutes, the export ratio requirement only applies to the seafood cultivation industry, seeds and seed-growing, and handicrafts, due to the saturated domestic market. Local content requirements cover some textile, machinery, electronic and electrical industries, as well as automobile industries, in which the quality and quantity of local supplies are adequate, thereby linking domestic industries and foreign direct investments. Nevertheless, local content requirements in select industries were rarely implemented successfully.

The opening of the service industry, which is often local market oriented, to foreign investment and the lifting of export requirements have helped foreign firms in Taiwan to become local market oriented. Moreover, the economic power of the Taiwanese market lies in considerable Taiwanese foreign reserves, which rank among the top few largest amounts in the world,[2] and in the high per capita national income (US$11,315 in 1995). In addition, foreign firms can use their experience from Taiwan's market to launch products into Mainland China's market. Consequently, the percentage of export sales in relation to total sales for foreign firms was 50 per cent in the 1980s (dropping from 60 per cent in the 1970s), and is expected to decrease further in the future.

In 1987, restrictions that required the remittance of invested capital one year after the commencement of an investment project were lifted, thereby enhancing capital mobility. In May 1989, the Statute for Investment by Foreign Nationals was revised to adopt a so-called "negative list legislation" to replace the existing case-by-case screening procedures for foreign investment. That is, any foreign investment was allowed, except in industries prohibited or restricted by the Statutes. Industries that threatened public security or public policy, or that were monopolistic or created high levels of pollution, were prohibited. Public utilities, insurance and banking industries, and news and publishing industries were restricted from foreign investments.

In November of 1997, the Statute for Investment by Foreign Nationals was further revised to facilitate the policies of economic liberalization and internationalization, to meet the requirement for joining the WTO in the future, and to achieve the goal of making Taiwan an Asian Pacific operating center. To that end, the restriction that required the remittance of interests and profits for one year after the commencement of an investment project was lifted. Further, eight of the prohibited investment industries on the negative list were changed to restricted categories, which had the effect of enlarging the scope of foreign investment.

The liberalization measures discussed above had the result of relaxing foreign direct investment restrictions and gradually opening the domestic market to foreign investors. The openness of the domestic market in Taiwan to foreign goods and investments was considered to be a necessity for introducing competition into domestic industries and to heading off rising protectionism in the U.S. In an under-developed economy, it is not likely that the government would be willing to open all investment opportunities to foreign investors because the domestic economy would not yet be mature enough to accept such competition. Yet, the Taiwanese government has shifted from a developmental government to a catalyst[3] government since the mid-1980s. The change has been from encouraging foreign investments with some restrictions in order to prevent the country from becoming a victim of globalization to encouraging foreign investments with little restrictions in order to be included in the global open market.

The change of Taiwanese state policy on foreign investment since the 1980s might be viewed as a transformation of a strong state to a weak state which will yield to multinational corporations and the WTO. Or, it might be considered to be a sign of maintaining a strong state and attempting to actively join the global governance system. Nevertheless, the change cannot simply be attributed to the behavior of a strong or weak state; rather it is influenced by the global situation as well. A strong Taiwanese state was possible before the 1980s first, because the U.S. wanted to guard Taiwan against communism (Koo 1987), and later, because both the U.S. and Japan took advantage of cheap and passive labor in Taiwan to include Taiwan as a receptor of their matured manufacturing in the product life cycle (Cumings 1984). In recent years, however, in the face of rising domestic labor costs, as well as economic protectionism from Western countries (including the institution of a quota system to limit goods from developing countries such as Taiwan), the Taiwanese state has had to loosen its market regulation in order to attract foreign investments and join the WTO. The Taiwanese state could have maintained its strong role as other developing countries have and been excluded by or excluded itself from the global economy. However, the Taiwanese economy based on worldwide subcontracting and its export orientation does not allow this choice. Moreover, joining global economic organizations and associations is an important symbol for a Taiwanese government that is struggling to achieve political recognition in the world (which has been strongly opposed by Mainland China). The political significance of this recognition may be more important to Taiwan than the economic benefit.

The Taiwanese case seems to suggest that the role of state, be it strong or weak, is reconfigured by the global situation, and is thus a result of the various competing forces which shape the governance system of the global economy. Understanding the surrounding environment that makes a state strong or weak is more meaningful than discussing the strength of the state itself. On the other hand, while nation-states ostensibly have their power limited by visible borders, they can extend their sovereign power in the globalizing world beyond those borders by establishing a new global or transnational economic organization.

Localization and Nationality of Multinationals

Since the mid-1980s, Taiwan's economic policy has been dramatically liberalized. This change, and especially its manifestation in the opening of the service industry to foreign investors in 1987, raises questions about how the dialectic between the global and the local in subsidiaries of foreign firms in Taiwan has changed. Very little research has examined this important issue. As reviewed above, previous research has emphasized the impact of the home nationality and neglected the local elements in the localization of subsidiaries. The questions that arise, however, are whether or not the globalizing economy will reduce the importance of multinationals' home nationalities and what role local elements will come to play in the globalizing economy. This section will first summarize previous studies and then analyze the latest available data (the 1993 Survey on the Operations of the Overseas Chinese and Foreign Investment conducted by Investment Commission, Ministry of Economic Affairs, Taiwan, supplemented by several interviews in the service industries in Taiwan) to answer these questions.

The United States and Japan have been the two biggest investors in Taiwan (Table 7.2). Each account for 30 per cent of the total approved FDI in Taiwan from 1952–1995, while FDI from Europe only accounts for 14 per cent. However, European investors have been catching up with the other two since the mid-1980s. On average, Japan has had the highest number of approved investment cases but the smallest investment amount per case. Although Dutch settlers first began colonizing Taiwan and integrating it into the world's economic system in the seventeen century, Holland was not able to retain any of its influences after it was chased out by Chinese from the Mainland. In contrast, Japan colonized Taiwan from 1895 to 1945 and has continued business relationships with the Taiwanese since then. After World War II, the United States gave Taiwan AID to safeguard it against communism, and American firms later superseded their government's influence on economic development in Taiwan via investment.

According to previous research, localization of foreign firms in Taiwan is differentiated by the nationality of the home companies.[4] Japanese investment is small in terms of the amount involved in each case, and tends to be correlated with a preference for joint ventures with local enterprises. During the fifty years of Taiwan's colonization by Japan, the Japanese not only learned a great deal about Taiwan's economy, language, and culture, but also built up cordial relationships with numerous Taiwanese businessmen. This unique relationship, based largely on personal contacts, helped reduce the risks of small investors and the necessity for large investments. The reason why the Japanese adopted a strategy of joint venture was also to seek out the local market (Liu et al. 1993). Finally, Japanese firms in Taiwan employ many more expatriates from the home country than its counterparts do (Tzeng 1995). In contrast, American and European firms have tended to maintain sole ownership (except American firms during the 1950s, when they needed to rely on local government to seek out the local market) and send far fewer expatriates from home. In other words, Japanese firms seem to practice "managerial control" over their subsidiaries in Taiwan by sending more expatriates, while Western firms appear to practice "financial control" via sole ownership.

According to Gupu (1992), American firms in Taiwan are involved in a higher export rate than are Japanese firms in Taiwan. While this assertion contradicts Kojima's (1978) argument, Gupu nevertheless explains the difference in terms of the organizational structure between the home and overseas units. American multinational firms are more integrated; subsidiaries often produce parts or assemble finished goods for the home country, and trade between the two is very frequent. The American policy of the value added tariff, which only taxes the added value of the imports produced by the overseas American firms, also helps the American subsidiaries take advantage of cheap labor. While this scenario is consistent with reality, another possibility is described by the product life cycle theory. According to this theory, the products of multinational corporations are initially innovated for the needs of developed countries, and when products are produced in developing countries, it is only because of the cheap labor. Only when the living standard of the developing countries rises can local residents afford to buy products made by foreign firms. Since the standard of living is more similar between Taiwan and Japan than between Taiwan and the U.S., Japanese goods are more acceptable to the Taiwanese than are those produced by American firms. This logic can also partly explain why Japanese firms in Taiwan have higher local sales than do American firms.

Japanese firms in Taiwan have much higher rates of parts and median materials purchased locally (either from other Japanese firms or from local firms) than do American firms (Gupu 1992; Chen and Wang 1994). There are many explanations for this phenomenon. For one, as mentioned above, unlike the large vertically integrated American firms, Japanese firms are often small, their overseas units and home companies are not well-integrated, and trade between the two sides is infrequent. Second, rather than arising from individual firms, foreign investment from Japan tends to arise from a group of related firms, including producers interested in the local market and its suppliers. This might explain why there are so many Japanese firms in Taiwan and why their local purchasing rates are high. Third, the small size of Japanese firms and their strategy of building local partnership also increase their willingness to purchase materials and parts from local firms; Taiwanese firms are more similar to Japanese firms in their technology scale than to American firms.

In summary, previous studies seem to come to the conclusion that Japanese firms in Taiwan are more localized than Western firms in terms of incorporating local capital, targeting the local market, and purchasing intermedium materials from local firms, but less localized in terms of adapting to local management. Indeed, these three dimensions of localization seem to influence each other. The higher the local ownership is in a subsidiary, the higher the proportion of local sales and median materials locally purchased. In other words, it is essential to recognize that the three dimensions may all exist simultaneously, or that one of these dimensions may bring on any of the others. Nevertheless, localization in previous research is explained mainly from the home perspective.

Although there have been national differences in localization among multinational corporations, time effects are also an important factor. While both Japanese and American firms in Taiwan are export-oriented, over time the proportions of their exported goods decline and they become more oriented towards the domestic market (Liu et al. 1990). American firms have increased local sales between 1975 and 1989 (Chen and Wang 1994), in part because the Taiwanese have increased their standard of living and can afford to buy American goods produced locally. In addition, as time has passed, American firms in Taiwan have, to a certain extent, produced goods to fit local needs. Because Taiwanese firms have improved their technology and American firms have established relations with local firms, it has become easier for American firms to find local suppliers.

Therefore, a more recent study of national differences in localization among foreign firms is needed, especially when few studies have been conducted in this respect since the opening of the service industry to foreign investors in 1987. The following will bring these differences to light using the 1993 Survey on the Operations of the Overseas Chinese and Foreign Investment conducted by Investment Commission, Ministry of Economic Affairs, Taiwan to analyze the localization of foreign investment. Due to the limitation of available data, the dimensions of localization examined in this paper include capital obtained, sales allocated, and materials, parts and equipment purchased in the local country.[5]

There were 1,939 foreign firms in the survey. However, this research excluded foreign firms owned by overseas Chinese whose investment is not economically significant but has political connotations (Gold 1981; Liu 1992), investors in the primary sector, construction and other fields, firms located in the export-processing zones,[6] and firms from developing countries. As a result, there were 1,256 foreign firms in Taiwan in 1993 involved in 12 manufacturing industries (electronic and electric appliances, chemicals, machinery equipment and instruments, basic metals and metal products, non-metallic minerals, plastic and rubber products, food and beverage processing, textile, garment and footwear, leather and fur products, pulp paper and products, and lumber and bamboo products) and in four services (trade, banking and insurance, transportation and other miscellaneous services) (Table 7.3). Among these 1,256 firms, 66.45 per cent (835) were from Japan, 21.18 per cent (266) were from the United States, and 12.34 per cent (155) were from Europe (UK, Germany, France, Netherlands and Switzerland).

The top five concentrated industries for Japanese firms in Taiwan were trade,[7] basic metals and metal products, services,[8] electronic and electric

	Japan		U.S.		Europe	
	Rank	Percentage	Rank	Percentage	Rank	Percentage
1. Trade	1	23.83	2	18.05	1	27.10
2. Services	3	13.53	1	29.70	2	13.55
3. Banking & Insurance	12	0.84	5	7.14	2	13.55
4. Electronics & Electric Appliances	4	2.34	3	13.91	5	6.45
5. Chemicals	6	9.46	4	12.41	2	13.55
6. Machinery Equipment & Instruments	5	10.30	7	4.51	5	6.45
7. Basic Metals & Metal Products	2	14.61	6	5.26	5	6.45
8. Other*		11.02		9.02		12.90
		(N=835)		(N=266)		(N=155)

*: Other = 100-(1+2+3+4+5+6+7).

Table 7.3 Distribution of Foreign Firms in Taiwan by Industry in 1993

appliances, and machinery equipment and instrument. For American firms, the top five industries were services, trade, electronic and electric appliances, chemicals, and banking and insurance. For European firms, the top five were trade, service, chemicals, banking and insurance, and electronic and electric appliances. Obviously, service and trade industries have replaced manufacturing as the most concentrated investment industries for foreign firms in Taiwan. This can in part be attributed to Taiwan's opening of the service industry to foreign investment since 1987, while it also coincides with the new FDI trend. Trade and services account for 37 per cent of Japanese firms in Taiwan, 47.8 per cent of American firms and 40.7 per cent of European firms.

The highest concentration of manufacturing investment by foreign firms from the three areas are in basic metals and metal products for Japan, electronic and electric instruments for American firms, and chemicals for European firms. This reflects the fact that foreign investment from the triad is not only located in the local key industries, but also reflects the industrial characteristics of the home country: the United States has been leading the world in electronics production and European countries have been the principle source of chemicals. Foreign investment, therefore, is often an extension of the domestic economic structure of the home country.

One striking finding in the service industries among foreign investment in Taiwan is that banking and insurance, combined, are the second most concentrated industries for European firms in Taiwan and fifth most concentrated for American firms, but only the twelfth for Japanese firms. (Government data lumps banking and insurance together; thus the two areas cannot be studied separately.) In the case of the banking industry, foreign banks are often important in providing finance for other foreign firms from the same home country. While banking has accounted for the highest Japanese foreign investment in most countries, the lack of a Japanese banking presence in Taiwan can be attributed to diplomatic reasons. Both the Japanese and Taiwanese governments prohibit Japanese banks from setting up overseas units in Taiwan because of the establishment of diplomatic relations between Japan and the People's Republic of China. The Dai-Ichi Kangyo Bank had been the only Japanese bank in Taiwan, only because it was in Taiwan during Japanese colonization and did not divest when colonization ended. Recently, both the Taiwanese and Japanese governments have adopted more liberal policies, and there are more and more Japanese banks applying for permission to open offices in

Taiwan. This situation of political stalemate between Japan and Taiwan might also be applied to the lack of Japanese insurance companies in Taiwan.

In contrast to the Japanese case, the Taiwanese government first granted U.S. banks permission to set up offices in Taiwan and did not allow European banks to enter until 1980. As the restrictions on foreign banks in Taiwan have been loosening, Western banks have shifted their service emphases in Taiwan from wholesale (international banking and company loans) to retail (consumer banking and investing banking). That is, foreign banks can better penetrate the Taiwanese market by expanding their customer bases from a limited number of business firms to the far greater number of available individual customers.

Because the majority (86 per cent of 1,256) of foreign firms in Taiwan from the three areas have mainly concentrated in the seven industries listed in the tables, foreign firm investment in other industries is not included in the following analysis (Table 7.4) to reduce the bias that would result from collapsing a large number of disparate categories. The industry variable is dichotomized into service (including trade, services, and banking and insurance) and manufacturing (electronic and electric appliance, chemicals, machinery equipment, and basic metals and metal products). The proportion of foreign firms engaged in the service industry was 51 per cent in 1993. The average percentage of local ownership per firm was 33 per cent; 75.13 per cent for local sales (which demonstrates the importance of the local market to foreign firms in Taiwan), 71.01 per cent for materials and parts locally acquired, and only 23 per cent for equipment locally purchased.

In contrast to Japanese firms, European and American multinational corporations have quite similar influences on the localization of their subsidiaries in Taiwan. Japanese firms in Taiwan tend to have higher local ownership, and to purchase more local parts and materials (although there is no data indicating if they are from local Taiwanese firms or local foreign firms). However, there is no national difference in percentage of local sales for each foreign firm, as shown in the previous study, nor is there national difference in percentage of equipment locally purchased. The influence of the nationality of multinational corporations toward its subsidiaries in Taiwan seems to be declining.

On the other hand, sector, the type of industry that a subsidiary is engaged in, influences all four dimensions of localization. Foreign firms located in the service industry tend to have a smaller percentage of local

Variable	1	2	3	4	5	6	7	8	Mean	S.D
1		-0.73***	-0.52***	-0.15***	-0.14***	-0.04	0.20***	0.06	0.65	0.48
2	1086		-0.20***	0.10***	0.08*	0.05	-0.10**	-0.03	0.22	0.42
3	1086	1086		0.09**	0.11***	0.01	-0.17***	-0.06	0.12	0.33
4	1086	1086	1086		0.18***	0.17***	-0.32***	-0.28***	0.51	0.50
5	1086	1086	1086	1086		-0.14***	-0.02	0.09	66.90	34.59
6	1012	1012	1012	1012	1012		-0.20***	-0.20***	75.13	35.16
7	836	836	836	836	836	808		0.22***	71.01	44.95
8	437	437	437	437	437	425	437		23.03	24.14

*: p≤0.05; **: p ≤ 0.01; ***: p ≤ 0.001

1: Japanese firms
2: American firms
3: European firms
4: Service firms
5: Percentage of foreign shares
6: Percentage of local sales
7: Percentage of materials and parts locally purchased
8: Percentage of equipment locally purchased

Table 7.4 Zero-order Correlation between Variables

ownership and a smaller degree of materials, parts, and equipment locally purchased, but have more local sales. As the service industry primarily attends to manufacturing and consumers, it naturally focuses on the local market. For this reason (a desire to protect its local market) the Taiwanese government did not open the service industry to foreign firms until 1987 when Taiwan became a post-industrial society and its service industry had sufficiently developed. An emphasis on brand names in the service industry might explain why foreign service firms have fewer locally purchased median materials.

As for the four dimensions of localization, they are somewhat related, but not in precisely the same ways as indicated by previous research. First of all, the higher the percentage of local shares held by a foreign firm in Taiwan, the higher the percentage of its products are sold locally. This finding is consistent with previous research. However, the former factor has no relationship with materials, parts and equipment locally purchased. Further, the percentage of materials and parts locally purchased and the percentage of equipment locally purchased are positively associated with each other, but the percentage of local sales is negatively associated with these latter two variables. That is, the higher the percentage of local sales that a foreign firm in Taiwan has committed to, the higher percentage of materials, parts and equipment that this firm will import from abroad. This may be because foreign firms oriented toward the local market will have an edge over local firms by importing median materials. All of the above findings suggest that localization is a quite dynamic process in Taiwan. Some dimensions of localization might either bring in another local dimension or contain global elements; this later point has been overlooked by previous research.

Foreign investment in Taiwan is not an enclave completely isolated from the local, rather, it reveals a mutual penetration of the global and the local. Nevertheless, export oriented foreign firms, which are usually in manufacturing, have less sensitivity to the local culture because purchasing materials from the local is primarily a matter of economic transaction and because their local employees are mainly under the local manager's supervision. In contrast, foreign firms focusing on local sales, especially those firms located in the services, have to be more sensitive toward the local culture in order to open up the local markets. This necessity has been repeatedly highlighted in several interviews about foreign firms in Taiwan. For example, Domino Pizza's president once said in a TV interview that when it first started business in Taiwan, they first had to teach Taiwanese what a pizza was and they then had to innovate new flavors to meet Taiwanese appetites. Although McDonald's has a sweeping influence in Taiwan, American tourists in Taiwan feel that hamburgers taste somehow different from those made in the U.S. Moreover, McDonald's in Taiwan is usually used as a social place where youngsters gather, rather than only an eat-and-go place. Further, a manager in one foreign drug company states that at home their salesmen used to provide professional services to their customers, such as providing updated medical research reports to doctors. But in Taiwan they have to adapt to the local custom and run errands for doctors in order to establish good customer relations.

In addition to adapting to the local culture, the foreign firms provide diversity and threaten local firms. For example, a manager at Pepsi points out that their major competitor in Taiwan is not Coca Cola, but local companies that produce all kinds of tea based soft drinks. Another case in point is the introduction of Western grocery stores (such as the Dutch Makro and the French Carrefour). Although they have dominated many small local mom-and-pop shops, the traditional Chinese markets where people can get really fresh vegetables, fruits, and meats have continued to thrive. The co-existence of both kinds of markets and drinks suggests that globalization might threaten the existence of the local culture but can also beget diversity.

To summarize, both survey data and interview cases seem to suggest that the dialectic between global and local elements unfolding in the subsidiaries of multinationals creates a global-local nexus. In this nexus, both global and local elements can zoom in or out or transform into a new pattern. Unlike in earlier times (and previous studies), it is always the global force (especially that originating in the home country), which has the upper hand over the local force.

Conclusion and Discussion

The globalization of business firms is not a new phenomenon. Debates over the power of the nation state and the localization of subsidiaries have been revitalized in recent years due to the dramatic increase in the growth of the multinational corporation and its new organizational form. This research has analyzed this argument by choosing foreign investment in Taiwan as a case study.

The dominance of developed home countries has fostered the concept of the powerless host state in analysis of FDI in developing countries. On the contrary, Taiwan, as a host country, has maintained a strong state, not only to prevent exploitation by foreign investment, but also to direct foreign investment for its own benefits. The Taiwanese government established regulations to censor and approve its outward investment, and also to encourage foreign investment to meet the domestic needs of industrial restructuring. The strong state of Taiwan was viable in the context where the U.S. was fighting against Communist expansion and developed countries were seeking cheap labor. As Taiwan has lost its advantage in providing cheap labor, Taiwan is moving toward a liberalized economic policy to actively join the globalizing economy through loosening its regulations toward foreign investment. A nation state's power is not given, but activated according to the surrounding conditions. The government of the United States is another example: while it once had a quite liberal attitude (no regulations) toward both inward and outward investment, it has adopted a policy of encouraging foreign investment from Japan and Taiwan in the face of problems of over-importing and de-industrialization. Thus, the U.S. government seems to have changed from a weak to a strong state in its policy towards foreign investment.

The changing role played by the state in confronting multinational corporations provided evidence to confirm Sassen's (1996) argument that the role of state is not declining in the globalizing economy but rather, is being reconfigured to be involved in the emerging transnational governance system. Nevertheless, the governance system of the global economy is not an imposing system that is "out there." Rather, it is the result of the competing forces of states, multinational corporations, transnational economic organizations, etc.

The localization of foreign investment in Taiwan is primarily manifest in local sales and materials and parts locally purchased, and less so in local shares and equipment locally purchased. These four dimensions of localization are associated in various ways which reveal either deep localization or the global contents in localization. In terms of the home influence on localization, the influence of the nationality of foreign corporations is not as dominant as the type of industry in which a subsidiary is engaged. Study of foreign firms in the service industry in Taiwan reveals many possibilities for a dialectic between the local and the global levels that is unfolding in the process of business globalization. While these firms may at times threaten local firms, they also have to adapt to the local culture to compete with local firms. The coexistence of both firms represents the variety of choices available.

Firms often encounter difficulties in a particular country that are caused by the embedded environments. Although multinational corporations can choose to move investment from one country to another, transfer is very costly. Moreover, no matter where they invest, multinational corporations are embedded in and constructed by the social and political environments of the home, host and global situations. Markets are not based exclusively on economic exchanges, but are shaped by culture, norms, tastes and regulations. Future research should pay more attention to multinationals in the service sectors, where markets are particularly strong driving forces.

Acknowledgement

I would like to thank the Institute of European and American Studies and the National Science Council (NSC 84-2411-H-001-011), Taiwan, for their financial support of this research.

Notes

1. The actual ebb and flow of FDI in Taiwan described below are not quite consistent with the data shown in Table 7.2 because it only shows the approved cases. Although the Taiwanese government does release statistics on government-approved foreign investment every year, it does not make statistics on the actual amounts of foreign investment in Taiwan available to the public.
2. The amount of Taiwanese foreign reserves had been comparable with Japanese as the largest two in the world through the early 1990s. But lately, Mainland China has caught up, and Taiwanese foreign reserves have fallen below the top two places in the world.
3. The idea of catalyst was inspired by a talk given by Linda Weiss in the Sun Yat-Sen Institute for Social Sciences and Philosophy, Academia Sinica on April 2, 1997.
4. The previous research has rarely discussed European investment in Taiwan due to its small amount.
5. The number of years that a foreign firm has been established in Taiwan is an important variable that affects localization. Since it is unavailable in the data, I, in the following analyses, could not control its influence away from that of the firm's nationality.
6. Foreign firms located in the export-processing zones have quite different characteristics from their counterparts outside and their numbers are just a few.
7. Trade includes sales, department store and import-export trading.
8. Service includes repair, professional service (law, accounting, engineering etc.), individual service, entertainment, renting, copying, public utility etc.

Chapter 8

Foreign Companies and the Transformation Processes in Poland: The Role of Western Financial and Human Capital

Hedwig Rudolph

Introduction

The implosion of the socialist regimes in Central Eastern Europe (CEE) at the end of 1980s confronted the countries of this region (some of which were recreated in this same process) with immense problems. It was clear from the start that the transition to democracy and a market economy that these countries undertook during this period would not be easy. This paper focuses on the economic aspects of the transformations, although the two areas are interrelated: implementing successful economic reform programmes was often a crucial condition for gaining sufficient political support from the population for transition. Not surprisingly, there were different views as to the optimal path that the nation should take. Moreover, conflicting interests concerning the mode of transformation were articulated both inside and outside the former socialist countries. The two opposing positions, shock therapy, on the one hand, and gradualism, on the other, had different implications for the roles of domestic versus external/international players.

In addition to this paradigmatic battleground, an additional arena was opened up in the CEE: competition among western[1] countries for the transfer of their particularly national institutional frameworks. For the western countries involved, successful transfer of their institutional frameworks could be expected to pave the way for their economic goals and, at times, the transfer of institutions was tied to bilateral financial support programmes. On the supranational level, too, a broad spectrum of public programmes targeted at CEE countries was initiated by western industrialised countries in order to create or modernise the institutional and infrastructural basis for private investment in the east. It is an open question whether, and to what extent, the criteria and priorities of these programmes corresponded with ideas for national transformation within CEE countries.

A fourth factor shaping the transformation processes in the CEE countries was the struggle by (mainly large) western companies to enhance their globalisation strategies and gain stronger positions in international competition by taking advantage of the collapse of the Council for Mutual Economic Assistance (CMEA) (ILO 1995). When the Iron Curtain fell, this fundamental change in the global divide inevitably had major implications for the world market, overshadowing existing competitive positions. Increased mobility of goods, services, capital and people from east to west and west to east (or, at least, the potential for such an increase) challenged the established structure of the international division of labour. This factor acted as an incentive for western companies to reappraise their global strategies.

To summarise, the processes of economic transformation, and the speed at which they were undertaken in the various CEE countries, can be interpreted as reflecting the complex articulation of four factors: (1) the countries' own reform programmes; (2) policies of individual western countries to defend or improve their positions vis-à-vis the rearrangement of global centres and peripheries; (3) the political efforts of the western bloc (mainly EU and OECD); and finally, (4) the strategies of western companies in taking advantage of the emerging new structure of the international division of markets and profits.

This paper focuses on one aspect of the process by which the transformation from planned to market economies in the former socialist countries was produced: the transfer of financial and human capital from west to east. The enormous financial resources needed for the modernisation of infrastructure, institutional bases, and production facilities could not be expected to come from the eastern countries' sources.

Equally, the human capital bases of these economies was deficient because the workforce had been trained and was qualified for the planned economies in place prior to the collapse. Human capital constitutes an important component of national production regimes. It incorporates expert knowledge (the so-called hard skills), as well as so-called extra-functional abilities, modes of behaviour, and cultural values (soft skills). Fundamental changes in the production regime require an adjustment of human capital, a demand which cannot be met in the short run by the local educational system, but rather, has to be imported.[2] The delegation of western managers and experts is essential in order to accelerate the implementation of a capitalist regime. Thus, this study investigates the processes and results of the introduction of modern business practices and access to world markets in the CEE countries. We argue that the type, volume, and persistence of flows of financial capital and highly skilled people from west to east reflect the path of the transformations and are indicators of the mode of integration of the respective country into the global economy.

We have selected Poland for our case for two principle reasons: (1) As a country bordering the European Union (EU) and a part of the Visegrad group (comprising, in addition, Hungary and the Czech and the Slovak Republics), Poland was one of the first countries to initiate politico-economic transformation. (2) Moreover, with a population of about 40 million, Poland offers the biggest market in the CEE and is particularly attractive for western capital searching for additional customers and consumers (Quaisser 1996: XII).

We have decided to focus on two sectors, the food industry and the information and telecommunications industry (comprising computer-facilities and telephone services). This choice was guided by two arguments: (1) the changes in both industries are among the central indicators of the pace of economic and social modernisation. Moreover, information and telecommunications are instruments to this end (that is, it enables more general development). (2) A considerable share of private budgets (in Poland 30 per cent) is spent on food, and information and telecommunications account for a high percentage of business expenses.

The paper is organised as follows: We begin with a brief description of the Polish government's transformation concept, followed by an outline of the structure and volume of western public and private capital transfers. This background information will provide the context for our analysis of the interrelation between market and personnel strategies of large western companies in Poland, of which the majority are engaged in joint ventures.[3]

Poland's Political Priorities for a Market Economy

There was no blueprint for an ideal solution to the transition from planned to market economy at hand in the late 1980s. The transformation of industrialised countries from one economic regulatory regime to another had never been on the agenda before. Thus, when eastern governments turned to western experts for advice (as most of them did), those experts had no real experience with challenges of this magnitude. The reforming countries thus became the battleground for conflicting western economic paradigms. The advocates of liberal market theory proposed a *big bang* (shock therapy) solution: a radical and rapid deregulation of practically all sectors of economic activity. Their argument was that only by rigorously cutting ties to the past (and stopping the inflation rate) would the new system have a chance to develop successfully (Sachs 1996).

In contrast to this position, the representatives of the neo-institutionalist school insisted on the idea of the social embeddedness of the economy. They argued for a more gradual transition process, a recognition of path dependencies and the relevance of institutions (Stark 1992). It was the focus on institutional settings that highlighted the existence of a spectrum of "capitalisms" among western industrialised countries characterised by different modes of regulation/coordination (Soskice 1994).

The Polish path to democracy and a market economy was not without failures and drawbacks, mostly unexpected ones. Decades of membership in the CMEA, which was dominated by the interests of the Soviet Union, had left their mark in the form of structural imbalances of the Polish economy: an explicit prioritisation of heavy industries, on one hand, and the notorious undersupply of consumer goods, on the other. In an attempt to rectify the situation, the Polish government initiated a crash programme (the so-called Balcerowicz plan) in early 1990 which focused on the goals of macro-economic stability, private ownership, and a general Liberalization of the economy (that is, a reduction of state regulation as well as function). This policy was to favour foreign trade with western industrialised countries and to attract foreign direct investment (FDI).

While successive Polish governments reappraised this transformation programme several times because of its unintended negative effects, the prioritisation of Liberalization was never seriously challenged (Juchler 1995). The year 1992 marked a positive turning point for the Polish economy: because most economic indicators at the time showed an upward trend, mass privatisation was begun and important legal regulations facilitating FDI were introduced. Since that time, Poland has become one of the most successful reform countries in the CEE, as evidenced by strong economic growth rates, progressing mass privatisation, a falling inflation rate, rising income levels, and shrinking (official) unemployment figures (Kleer 1996).

The transformations in Poland are also reflected by changes in international migratory flows. Soon after the Liberalization of Polish migration policy in 1988, the share of highly skilled people decreased among the emigrants, while increasing among immigrants to the country. Recently, the number of skilled immigrants exceeds that of skilled emigrants, a phenomenon Jazwinska and Okólski (1996a) label "inverse brain drain." Official statistics indicate that workers coming from western countries to Poland are mainly managers and experts.

One focus of our study is on the role of these foreign managers and experts in Poland's transformation process (Hillmann and Rudolph 1996). In contrast to the myriad of political statements and academic output concerning the potential or actual "mass migration" from the east, little evidence is available concerning the migration of people with higher levels of qualifications. The few empirical studies at hand (Futo et al. 1994; Holtbrügge 1994a, 1994b; Redei 1995; Redor 1994) are predominantly oriented towards business practice, although they do indicate the importance of highly skilled personnel from abroad for the implementation of the market strategies of foreign investors.

This study of the role of foreign managers and experts in Poland's transformation process supports the central positions of recent scientific debates concerning the international mobility of highly skilled manpower (Miles 1990; Salt 1992; Castles and Miller 1993). The paper argues that fundamental changes in social structures and institutions make the adaptation of human capital mandatory. In some areas or periods, however, changes may be too fundamental to be adequately met by mobilising indigenous resources. Consequently, the import of "experts" is intended to transfer, in addition to new standards of technical skills (in a broad sense), matching norms, values and habits.

Western Public Support Programmes: Intentions and Implications

The implosion of CMEA was perceived as a threat to global political and economic stability by western countries and international organisations. It was evident that the affected eastern European countries would need foreign assistance for their impending transformations. Various international and bilateral programmes were established early on, with the aim of channelling support in the form of humanitarian aid, consultation frameworks, loans and debt relief.[5] No master plan for co-ordinating the multitude of programmes was agreed upon, however, because the various national governments and international organisations involved had different views on how best to handle the situation. These differences of perspective were and are strongly related to the potential problems that the respective donors would expect in the event of negative developments in the east and, conversely, to the potential gains to be had from positive developments. This rationale is evident from Table 8.1, which shows that Germany alone, Poland's biggest neighbour, contributed 36.6 per cent of western aid to the countries of the CEE and the former Soviet Union during the first three years of the transformation process. In the years 1994–1996, Poland received the largest share of German funds for CEE countries.[6]

Poland has also managed to keep a strong position in the PHARE programme (Poland and Hungary Action for Restructuring the Economy), which was later opened for all other CEE countries and has since then become the major EU support framework for the CEE. Between 1990 and 1994, about a quarter of all PHARE commitments were targeted at Poland (OECD 1995: 71). Financial and technical aid was provided in a wide spectrum of project areas, ranging from political and administrative institution building to the modernisation of infrastructure and privatisation, as well as support for small and medium sized companies. In principle, the programme is demand-driven, which means that the recipient countries apply for financing of and expert support for specific transformation issues. Over time, a shift in the programmes from more basic to more specific projects cannot be overlooked. PHARE contributed to a certain "standardisation" of transformation policies among CEE countries by providing a particular spectrum of categories for priority financing which changed in the successive programmes. Since 1994, when the European Commission published its White Paper elaborating the criteria for access to

Embeddedness and Economy

Commitments	CEE (Jan. 1, 1990 – Dec. 30, 1992)			CIS (Jun. 18, 1993)			CEE + CIS Total	
Donors	Aid and Commitments	Allocation in Loans		Aid and Commitments	Allocation in Loans		Aid and Commitments	Percentage of Total
Germany	8,304.56	5,492.94	(66.14%)	39,779.39	28,037.10	(70.48%)	48,083.95	36.60
France	1,809.43	1,588.15	(87.77%)	1,995.90	1,920.02	(96.20%)	3,805.33	2.90
UK	740.90	651.48	(87.93%)	1,050.83	829.57	(78.94%)	1,791.73	1.36
Total EU countries	14,412.04	9,776.47	(67.84%)	49,996.14	37,769.23	(75.54%)	64,408.18	49.10
EU budget	3,026.15	562.50	(18.59%)	3,576.50	1,750.00	(48.93%)	6,602.65	5.03
EBRD	5,083.14	5,036.10	(99.07%)	85.05	51.70	(60.79%)	5,168.19	3.93
Japan	2,532.06	1,975.80	(78.31%)	3,890.03	3,397.13	(87.33%)	6,422.09	4.89
U.S.	5,546.28	1,964.53	(35.42%)	8,448.92	6,118.98	(72.42%)	13,995.20	10.65
G-24 total	37,786.80	23,640.52	(62.56%)	—	—		—	—
IMF	7,071.97	7,071.97	(100.00%)	853.00	853.00	(100.00%)	7,924.97	6.03
World Bank	6,298.16	6,298.16	(100.00%)	588.28	563.43	(100.00%)	6,886.44	5.24
Total	52,800.07	38,606.75	(73.12%)	78,591.64	57,896.71	(73.67%)	131,391.71	100.00

CEE = Central Eastern Europe
CIS = Commonwealth of Independent States
EBRD = European Bank for Reconstruction and Development
EU = European Union
IMF = International Monetary Fund
UK = The United Kingdom
— = Not Available

Source: Winterberg (1994: 13).

Table 8.1 Financial Aid for the Transformation: Selected Donors (in Millions ECU)

the EU, that document has indeed structured national priorities in the CEE countries.

Foreign Direct Investments in the Context of Transformation Processes

As do the other reform countries, Poland associates a range of positive outcomes with the activities of foreign companies, particularly the multinationals (MNC). These expectations include: creation of jobs in the private sector; upgrading workers' skills; stimulating efficiency and competitiveness; transferring advanced western production technology and processes; introducing modern business practices; and improving access to world markets. How realistic are these hopes in view of the global strategies of MNCs? There is substantial empirical evidence to demonstrate that there is a recent trend common among large western companies towards increasing flexibility (Hirsch-Kreinsen 1996; Hagedorn 1993). CEE countries are attractive locations for western companies insofar as their investment decisions are based on the criteria of access to new markets. Low wage costs, contrary to widely held beliefs, are far less relevant (OECD 1995: 54). This growth strategy may be implemented with the goal of becoming pioneers in the market or of following quickly in the path of competitors (Szanyi 1994).

Obviously, the CEE region offers several important advantages as a location for western companies: geographical proximity and historical links to Western Europe, skilled labour force, relatively low wage level and large domestic markets (UN 1992).[7] The degree of integration of these post-socialist countries in international economic activities can be characterised by several indicators: foreign trade statistics, employment figures in foreign-owned firms/joint ventures, and inflows of FDI. Taking all three of these factors into consideration, the attractiveness of CEE countries for western capital is rather unequally distributed: The Czech Republic, Hungary and Poland were and are the most attractive countries by far (see Chart 8.1). Further, since 1994, the inflow of FDI seems to be positively correlated with the growth rates of Gross National Product (Stankovsky 1996). Increasing regional disparities are clearly evident: while the share of FDI of CEE countries is rising, the opposite holds true for the countries of the south, such as Bulgaria and Albania, as well as for the Baltics (Meier 1996).

Although the growth of western FDI in CEE seems impressive, the

Chart 8.1 Foreign Direct Investment in Central Eastern Europe, 1989–1995 (in Millions US$)

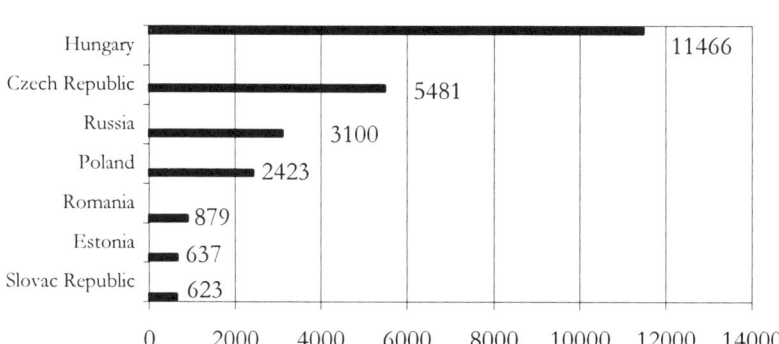

Source: European Bank for Reconstruction and Development (1997).

amount, compared to the gross inward investments of OECD countries, remains marginal.[8] The relatively low figures reflect the continued existence of substantial deficits in the infrastructure of many post-socialist countries that act as disincentives for potential investors (Stankovsky 1996). This argument is supported by the fact that Hungary has already managed for several years to attract about half of western FDI, thanks to its superior institutional setting and favourable political climate (Gabrisch 1995). Thus, the problem seems to be one of the chicken and the egg: FDI is needed in order to foster economic development, but it is exactly the inferior conditions that present obstacles to large flows of foreign capital. Overall, the internationalisation of economic activities is regarded as having mostly positive impact on the restructuring of the reformer countries. However, a central argument in the 1995 OECD report must be kept in mind:

> More than the net inflows of capital represented by FDI, it is the way in which value-adding activities are structured and integrated within TNC's global production networks that is likely to have the most durable effects on national patterns of industrial specialisation and hence economic growth and employment in the long-term. (p.69)

This means that, over and above indirect imitation of western practices, transnational companies may act as crucial mediators in bringing about modernisation and longterm structural transformation in these countries.

In Poland, FDI had a rather slow start. Only 2,700 investment permits were issued during the years 1989 and 1990 and the investors were mainly Polish remigrants (Wellisz et al. 1993). A major positive impact came with the abolition of investment licensing and the right to transfer profits abroad in 1991 and 1992. This resulted in a growth of western business activities from 2,700 to 8,400 (mostly joint ventures) between the end of 1991 and the end of 1993. The volume of FDI increased: from $280 million to $1,580 million[9] in the same period (Kubielas 1994).

Yet, the volume of FDI in Poland was lower and the capital flows showed weaker dynamics than was hoped for (and, in fact, lower than that which was experienced by neighbouring countries). What is worse, there are indications that only a quarter of even the very big investments in the country represented the highest level of available technology; in many cases second—or even third-rate technologies are reported to have been transferred (Kalinowski 1996: 259). Moreover, a number of foreign companies delayed substantial investments in the country. "Small and even declining average size of statutory capital suggests that most investors tend to follow a so-called 'foothold strategy' that is characterised by a cautious commitment and a wait-and-see attitude" (Cieslik 1996: 33). Similarly, the high public foreign debt was viewed as a risk factor (Winterberg 1994: 35f.). This problem was resolved by an international agreement on public debt reduction in 1994, covering more than 40 per cent of Poland's debt load (Clement et al. 1995: 24). In 1994, in light of the unsatisfactory development of FDI, the Polish State Agency for Foreign Investment (PAIZ) was created with the support of the EU as a semi-public institution. The agency was to attract foreign funds by providing information and support to potential foreign investors and to channel the funds in accordance with the priorities defined by the government. Unfortunately, no account of the activities of PAIZ is available that would indicate the extent to which this institution lived up to its crucial mandate.

Sectoral Perspectives on the Transformations

How well did the food sector and the information and telecommunications sector, the two branches at the centre of our study, develop? The attractiveness of the Polish food sector for FDI derives from several factors: (1) a large Polish market and the even larger neighbouring markets in the former Soviet Union; (2) a relatively well qualified and low wage labour force; (3) inexpensive raw material; and (4) protection from foreign competition. The technological level of this sector was quite low before the country began its transformation. Western standards of technology had been implemented only in the production of standardised mass goods (e.g., sugar, butter) and in partly processed food stuff for export (bacon in tins, concentrated apple juice). Foreign capital was targeted to this sector beginning in the 1980s. In fact, food was the most important industry for Polonia firms, small private enterprises that were legally allowed during the late socialist period for the investment of Polish people living abroad.

Regarding internal private demand for food, a tremendous drop was registered after 1989 (see also *Ost Wirtschafts Report* 1996a: 24f.). This decrease mainly affected basic products, which had been heavily subsidised under the socialist regime. The demand for western products came mostly from the 10 per cent of the population that could afford them. Recently, however, overall demand for non-basic food is increasing. Foreign companies dominate this market segment.

The transformation and modernisation of the food industry in Poland, which accounts for 21 per cent of national production (Quaisser 1996: 63), has made good progress to date. In some segments, such as breweries and the production of sweets, poultry and vegetable oils, the privatisation process is quite advanced. FDI in the food sector has shown a steady and quick increase since 1992 and reached $1.32 million in 1995, 20 per cent of all FDI in Poland. There have been various forms of foreign economic engagement in Poland, including setting up new companies, buying privatised firms, and establishing joint ventures. By late 1995, about 60 large foreign companies were doing business in the Polish food sector, of which 16 were from Germany, 14 from the U.S., and 15 from the Netherlands, France, Austria and the UK. In accordance with their major marketing strategies of upgrading quality and diversification, these foreign investors have implemented the highest standards of western technology. As imports to Poland are considered to be expensive and troublesome due to bureaucratic procedures, many western companies, particularly in the food sector, have adopted the strategy of increasing the local content of their products and of their production technology (Ost Wirtschafts Report 1996b: 223). Thanks to privatisation and restructuring, increases in food production have been considerable in the last several years. The share of state companies in food production was only 30 per cent in 1995, whereas it had been 75 per cent a decade before.

As for the information and telecommunications industries, this sector was poorly developed in Poland at the end of the 1980s, both in its capacity and in the level of technology. Previously, it had not been possible to upgrade the generally low level of technology through western imports, due to political restrictions imposed on the socialist countries as an instrument of the Cold War. Moreover, supply commitments vis-à-vis the Soviet Union had absolute priority for Poland's industry; the next priorities were the state administration and the army, while private demand was artificially compressed. There were no opportunities for private activities or FDI in the information and telecommunications sector in Poland prior to privatisation in the 1990s.

Thus, the information and telecommunications sector in particular had to be restructured and built from scratch in the early 1990s because of the huge lag in its infrastructure and its outdated domestic production technology. The Communications Act of 1990 did not affect the state-owned company TP S.A.'s *de facto* monopoly of the "upper levels" of the telephone network (international and long-distance calls). However, some competition ("planned diversity") was introduced into the other segments. Altogether, more than 100 operators' licenses have been issued for (parts of) the national market, the most important going to Noctia. Investment permits were allocated in 1992 and 1993 for three big joint ventures with western companies for producing telecommunications equipment. The aim was to gain access not only to foreign capital but also to the latest standards of technology and know-how. With overall investments amounting to US$330 million, the production facilities for telecommunications in Poland were successfully modernised. At the same time, licences for two stationary systems (one based on analogue, one on digital technology) were granted to private investors. A joint venture between US, French and Polish companies has established a mobile telephone network covering the whole country (Ost Wirtschafts Report 1996b: 233). Although the White Paper of the European Commission of 1994 had asked for alignment with requirements of the EU's internal market, the 1995 law was not co-ordinated with EU legislation. Yet, a number of foreign companies have already established offices in Poland so as to be ready when the chance opens up. The Polish authorities have announced a tender for minority shares in the state telephone company (TP S.A.) for the "near future." As of yet, however, no activity has begun.

The computer industry in Poland—a sector which is almost the antithesis of the telecommunications industry as far as regulations are concerned—was in a similarly precarious situation around 1990.

Unrestricted imports of modern western or Far Eastern equipment combined with the shrinkage of the ex-Soviet market caused a sudden collapse of the branch in Poland. A large number of firms have been set up since 1990—often outlets of western, Japanese or Korean companies. However, most of these firms have restricted their activities to sales and services. By the end of 1995, as many as 3,000 computer firms were operating in Poland, among them two giants: Optimus and ComputerLand Poland. FDI in the computer sub-sector in Poland has been relatively low, although intellectual imports from the west are substantial (organisation, management, software).

By now it is clear that foreign investors have a significant impact on the regional structure of Poland's economy. Information and telecommunications companies are heavily concentrated in Warsaw, the country's capital, which indisputably has become a major "growth pole" of the Polish economy since 1989. This development reflects the desire of the joint ventures to be close to the sector's most important customers, to the supply of skilled and innovative workers, and also to the sites of the political power play (deregulation). In contrast, the food industry is now much more regionally dispersed than it was during socialist times. Instead of restructuring traditional areas of industrial activities, joint ventures in this branch have established locations in the less developed central and eastern districts of the country, illustrating the market orientation of the sector, but also the attendance to production costs.

Obviously, the economic transformations in Poland, as reflected in the development of food and information/telecommunications joint ventures, gave impetus to the emergence of new growth poles, and, to some extent, initiated the reshaping of the geography of Polish industry (Okólski 1996b).

The Role of Western Managers and Experts in the Joint Ventures

It was clear from the outset of this project that we could not create a representative sample for the empirical part of the project. The topic of our research was a moving target, so to speak, and the extreme dynamic of new openings and closings and changes in mode of cooperation and location made such standardization impossible.[10]

Although we had intended to select medium- and large-sized companies as our target group, we had to relax the criteria in order to increase the sample size. We finally managed to access 50 companies of foreign ownership or with foreign capital input which met our criteria: in operation for at least six months and with more than five employees, one of whom (at least) was an expatriate.[11] Slightly more than half of the companies represent the food industry, the rest of them are from the information and telecommunications sector. During the second half of 1995, interviews were conducted in these companies on the basis of a semi-standardised questionnaire; in almost all of the companies not only the general manager but also an expatriate were interviewed.

A number of details characterise the companies forming the sample: only a small number of the foreign companies in our food-sector sample and none in the telecommunications sector had been in business in Poland before 1990. Most of the outlets were established in the period between 1991 and 1994. The large Polish market was reported to be the main argument underlying these companies' strategic decisions to enter the market. There were secondary arguments, too, such as the high educational standard of the work force and the proximity to the even larger Russian market.

In foods, a typical and by far dominating profile was production, whereas in information and telecommunications, combinations of sales and services were predominant. The distribution by branch was strongly diversified in the food industry, in contrast to the information and telecommunications sector; this reflects the differences in the structure of the two sectors in Poland. In the food industry confectionery firms prevailed, followed by meat products, concentrates and nonalcoholic beverages. The telecommunications sector was represented by wire telephone equipment, office communication equipment, mobile phones and cable television, on the one hand, and computer assembling, distribution and servicing firms (including software dealers), on the other.

Regarding company size, as indicated by number of employees, almost all of the food companies fell into the category of over 150 workers. A large majority of the information/telecommunications companies, on the other hand, had 50 workers or fewer. In all cases except two, the foreign partner was a large company (i.e., employing more than 1,000 workers).

Considerable problems arose concerning the value of sales per year, an alternative indicator of a company's size. A number of firms declined to provide relevant data, some others had only recently started business so that their turn-over was still oscillating, whereas a few others gave information highly unlikely to be reliable relative to their employment statistics. The rest of the data seems to support the impression that the spectrum of sales levels is lower and much less differentiated in the information and telecommunications sector than in the food industry.

While foreign investors in the food sector obviously sought opportunities in larger firms than was the case in the information and telecommunications sector, practically all investors saw the role of the Poland-based firm as central, or at least important, relative to their outlets in other CEE countries. However, compared to western branches of the company, the role of the Polish firm was considered to be much less pronounced, even marginal.

Although companies in the food industry represent only slightly more than 50 per cent of our sample, the number of foreign managers and experts that they employed was double that of the information and telecommunications sector. This reflects higher overall employment figures in the food sector. Firms employing two to three foreign managers predominate in both industries. It was this group of people that was the focus of our empirical research.

As mentioned above, our analysis of the role of western managers and experts in the transformation processes of CEE is guided by an interest in contributing to an understanding of how globalisation is produced. Implementing the expansion policy of a company in a new country is a complex task, implying a substantial amount of responsibility. The tasks involved demand a spectrum of qualifications and professional experience in view of the numerous challenges. As Paauwe and Dewe formulate, geographic subsidiary managers have to play at least three roles: "bicultural interpreter, national defender and advocate, and frontline implementer of corporate strategy" (Paauwe and Dewe 1995: 97). The latter role in particular includes difficult aspects. The managers' activities "must be sensitive enough to respect the limits of the diverse local constituencies, pragmatic enough to achieve the expected corporate outcome, and creative enough to balance the diverse internal and external demands and constraints" (Bartlett and Ghoshal 1992: 788). These tasks are even more demanding in countries that are struggling with the transition from planned to market economy. We argue that, in this context, the relevance of western managers and experts must be analysed not only in terms of their contribution to successful foreign investment (coordination and control functions) but also to the promotion of the transformation process in the host country.

Our analytical perspective is institution oriented, which means that we regard the institutional settings as highly important for the success of transformation policies. By "institutions" we mean the spectrum of shared norms, rules, standards, criteria, etc. held in place by custom as well as by explicit or tacit agreement. These institutions coordinate socio-economic interactions in specific ways by providing incentives for the adoption of some modes of activity or behaviour and disincentives for others. As is evident, the success of regulation via institutions depends on a shared understanding or interpretation of the institutional signals. It is exactly this crucial condition which cannot be taken for granted if the institutional setting is imported from a different social, economic and/or political context, as is the case in practically all former socialist countries. This is where the human factor enters the equation. Special expertise is needed in order to identify to what extent the implanted institutions conform to the socio-economic context and to decide how to bridge the obvious or potential gaps. Mismatches might be handled by changing the institutions and/or the people that are expected to act in the institutional setting. The second alternative is the much more cumbersome option because, in the case of a radical change of regime, it amounts to a re-socialisation of people, which means they first have to unlearn before they can start to learn the new rules of the game. These are the processes currently under way in the former socialist countries.

We based our research on the following four hypotheses:
1. The international mobility of the highly skilled is institutionalised. This means that it mainly follows the logic of specific institutions; personal motivations are of secondary relevance only.
2. The policies of western companies concerning the delegation of managerial staff to foreign outlets differ according to industry sector.
3. Western companies are taking advantage of international mobility processes in order to extend and/or deepen segmentation on their internal labour markets as a means of hierarchical coordination and control.
4. The volume and persistence of delegation of western managers/experts to the CEE (and *vice versa*) can be taken as indicators for the extent to which and the ways in which these countries are integrated in the world market.

The companies under review have different types of personnel policy. In almost all cases a foreigner held the highest management position, chief executive officer (CEO), at least at the time of our investigation. Most of these managers were recruited via headhunters because of a scarcity of internal pools of the western companies. Placing an expatriate as CEO was often declared to be "essential" by our interview partners as a kind of guarantee for the preservation of corporate interests. These interests gained importance in view of the strategic position of the Polish outlet for CEE countries, an argument that was repeatedly underlined. In addition, three out of four expatriates belonged to upper management (other than the CEO position), the level at which crucial decisions are made. In contrast to the CEO position, candidates for upper- and medium-level management that could not or should not be filled locally were mostly selected via internal labour markets.

The CEOs were normally the first to come to Poland: they investigated conditions and sites and began the recruitment of personnel. Managerial positions demanding primarily technical qualifications were rarely taken by expatriates, except when a new generation of technology had to be introduced. This reflects the fact that technical skills are rather little affected by system-specific context. Managerial positions staffed by foreigners were mostly those that had not existed under the socialist regime, or that had had a completely different orientation, such as accounting, finance, marketing and sales. These functions were very important for the access to and development of markets, given that almost half of the companies had opted for "quality" as their competitive edge in the Polish market. Our results parallel the findings of Borg and Harzing (1995), who identify two main aims underlying the transfer of expatriates: coordination and substitution of missing local skills.

Some sector-specific differences could be observed. In the food sector, finance and marketing were also often staffed with foreign experts, and almost exclusively via internal labour markets. Conversely, in the information and telecommunications sector, expatriates were concentrated in sales functions.[12] Making a career by "hopping" from company to company seemed to be rather common in this sector, which means that internal labour markets were less important. The vast majority of representatives of western companies pointed to the lack of adequately skilled local staff as an explanation for the transfer of foreign managers. However, in some companies these transfers formed a normal part of the career development programme for managers.

The positions held by foreign managers were often better paying than similar posts in the "mother" country, the differences varying between 20 and 40 per cent. Still, there was no automatic pay increase connected with a transfer to a CEE country. The main challenges associated with a management job in Poland seemed to be the more demanding tasks and the greater discretionary power than most of the managers and experts had experienced before. The functional upgrading was said to be on average higher than in the case of a delegation to a western country. However, accepting a transfer to Poland did not guarantee a promotion on return, nor did it definitely improve one's career prospects.

Much to our surprise the expatriates in our sample turned out to be a rather homogenous group. The most common home countries for expatriates were the UK, the US, France, the Netherlands and Germany (in that order), a distribution that did not correspond to the ranking of source countries for FDI. In addition, the average age of the expatriates was between 30 and 39, with only very few under 30 years of age. This reflects the fact that the specific demands of the transformation economies necessitated the transfer of senior managers, because those qualifications were particularly scarce on the local labour markets. Almost all of these western expatriates had higher-level educational certificates, mainly in economics or technical fields. However, all interviewees stressed that professional experience had been more relevant for their recruitment than formal qualifications.[13] This is in line with other studies reporting technical competence and knowledge of company systems as the most important selection criteria (Barham and Devine 1990). Finally, the expatriates were predominantly male, with only a few token women (mostly in human resources management). The gender asymmetry was so pronounced that it could not have been accidental. The low representation of women among expatriates is repeatedly stated in the literature (Adler 1993; Harris 1995). The reasons given for their scarcity (estimated at about three to five per cent) are a combination of organisational and socio-cultural factors. More specifically, informal organisational systems excluding women, assumptions about host-country cultural prejudices against women and dual-career problems are supposed to interact, forming substantial barriers (Adler 1993; Harris 1995). All expatriates denied the existence of biased recruitment procedures in their companies and all (both men and women) argued strongly against the need for affirmative action for women's career advancement. This, in spite of the fact that equal opportunity programmes have had a long (albeit ambivalent) tradition in CEE countries.

At two to three people, as mentioned above, the average number of expatriates (in the strict sense) was rather low in all companies. In official terms an expatriate is a foreign passport-holder whose employment contract includes an expatriation package including supplements for higher living costs and "hardship," health insurance contributions, flights home, etc. About one-third of the foreign managers and experts in our sample were members of the *Polonia*, that is, they were Poles who, or whose parents, had emigrated either during war-time or during the 1970s or 1980s.[14] They had been socialised in a western context (mostly the UK or the US) *and* had Polish cultural and social capital, a combination that promised a significant advantage, especially during the first years of the transformation process. Members of the *Polonia* were overrepresented among the so-called hybrid employees, who may have similar contracts to the expatriates, but without the extra benefits. Getting the expatriate package obviously depended on the candidate's bargaining power. Members of the *Polonia* were expected to have a high personal motivation to take a management position in their "home country," an assumption that had a negative impact on the salaries they could command.

Our study shows that the foreign owned companies and joint ventures structured the labour market for highly skilled personnel into three segments. These segments are rather isolated, have different career paths and show marked differences concerning income and other working conditions. The three segments are comprised of: (1) non-Polish managers and experts with expatriate status; (2) non-Polish managers and experts without expatriate status (hybrids, quite often remigrants); and (3) Polish managers/experts. The result is not only a differentiation but also a hierarchical ordering. Polish junior managers are not yet fully participating in international mobility, at least not toward the west. The two main arguments given by the upper management for this differential treatment allude to the companies' greater need for this local junior staff in Poland (in view of plans for business expansion there) and to the staff's function as a seedbed for managers who will be transferred to other, less developed reform countries of the east.

Foreign managers and experts were expected to combine a job that was professionally demanding with the role of trainer and model for appropriate decisions and behaviour vis-à-vis Polish managerial colleagues and staff. The socialisation and coinciding substitution process was organised in about half of the companies via on-the-job training and in the other half via special training courses; some companies used both methods. On-the-job training was organised either through the transfer of a potential future Polish manager to another foreign outlet or through coaching by a foreign expert (generally the person to be replaced) (also Hillmann and Rudolph 1997). The second mode, the organisation of long-term training programmes in the form of conferences, trainee meetings or problem-oriented courses in Poland or abroad, was practised mainly by larger companies. The instructors were mostly experienced professionals from headquarters, consultants working in Poland, or foreign managers of Polish outlets. It is no coincidence that the different ways to qualify local personnel had two traits in common: the significance of "personal relationships" and stays abroad. These traits reflect the fact that the transfer of hard and soft skills is what is at issue. The latter can hardly be acquired by reading books or listening to lectures; they are transmitted via observation in specific contexts, by imitation and interpretation. Presumably, this process is particularly critical in functional areas (such as sales) that existed under socialism but demand different and more complex qualifications in a market-oriented regime. What is needed is not only learning of the new skills and habits, but first of all unlearning of the old. During the interviews, the western managers repeatedly emphasised that they regarded it as one of their major tasks to establish "western thinking" in the heads of their Polish successors. Some called themselves "development assistants," indicating that they assumed a role beyond the corporate level.

Not all of the expatriates in our sample were well prepared for this challenge. Most of them had accomplished a number of career steps already, but some of the expatriates transferred to Poland would hardly have been entrusted with a similar position in a western country. Moreover, and surprisingly enough, almost one out of two expatriates could not rely on any former professional experience abroad. This implies the risk that, feeling insecure, they might not be able to interpret actions by their Polish counterparts correctly or quickly enough, and would offer sub-optimal learning arrangements. It must be kept in mind that the "good progress" of the substitution process reported in our interviews represents the perspective of the foreign management. It will remain to be tested in practice whether and to what extent this holds true.

By 1995, a considerable number of the companies in our sample were already at an advanced stage in replacing expatriates at middle-management levels with local personnel. This was not only due to cost considerations, but also indicates their belief that both hard and soft skills had been successfully transferred to junior local managers. Moreover, the universities and business schools in Poland had produced classes of newly graduated experts and/or had upgraded experts to fill the lower ranks.

Summary and Conclusions

Our empirical investigation of 50 large foreign companies and joint ventures in Poland in the food and information and telecommunications industries allows at least tentative answers to the questions formulated above.

1. The investments of foreign companies in Poland are both indicators and instruments of the country's integration into the international division of labour. Thanks to its geographical location and large market, there is only a low risk of Poland becoming marginalized in these rearrangements. However, it is not very likely that all regions of the country will take advantage of the new developments, as the locational patterns of FDI indicate.
2. The internal labour markets of foreign (often multinational) companies function as an important institutional framework for the international mobility of managers and experts between east and west. The personnel policies of western companies differ according to industry sector. Only to the extent that professional experience in foreign countries is a positive factor in management careers is there an interface between institutional norms and individual motivations.
3. The main and essential task of expatriate managers is the transfer of functional and extra-functional skills that are not (yet) available in adequate quantity and/or quality on the local labour market. The quite rapid substitution process—except for the highest management level—indicates that considerations of corporate control are only of secondary importance for the transfer of foreign personnel.
4. Professional competence is said to be the crucial criterion in the companies' selection processes concerning expatriates. However, the rather homogenous structure of our sample indicates that personal characteristics like age, gender and ethnicity are acting as "filters"; in this respect our findings support Tzeng's results (1995). This homogeneity among the expatriates may reflect the (implicit or explicit) assumption of the headquarters that "cultural diversity" might be more a risk factor than an asset in the difficult context of the CEE countries. However, the integration of foreign experts with Polish background implies that current mobilities are interrelated—at least to

5. We identified three types of managers and experts with clearly diverse career prospects. This finding adds plausibility to our assumption of (increasing) segmentation tendencies even in so-called primary labour markets. The fact that foreign companies have expanded their international internal labour markets to Polish territory does not imply that managers and experts from Poland already form part of this internal segment. The international mobility of (mostly junior or middle-level) Polish managers in outlets of western companies or joint ventures is restricted both concerning quantity, quality and geographical dimensions. Redor's (1994) scenario of a balanced and reciprocal exchange of skilled personnel between east and west is a step away yet.

some extent—with transnational networks that recall migratory movements of the past.

In conclusion, by maintaining a rather strict market oriented transformation policy, Poland was successful in attracting considerable amounts of western public and private funds, though not as much as was hoped for. The priorities of the programmes and the regional allocation, however, could not be completely controlled by the national authorities. Aid of western national and international organisations, as well as FDI, contributed substantially to the restructuring of the country's economy as demonstrated by the food and information and telecommunications sectors. Mobile western managers and experts played and continue to play an important role in bringing about the transformation and the integration of the Polish economy into the world market.

However, our project could not answer a number of important questions concerning the function and dynamics of the west-east-west mobility of managers and experts. Such open questions concern the role of inter-firm networks in the transformation process, as well as in the transfer of hard and soft skills, the influence of sector-specific factors and of the "culture" of the home countries. Moreover, there is still a lack of detailed analysis on the numerous multi- and bi-national political contracts that constitute an important framework for private FDI and channel large numbers of western experts to the east. There are other open questions as well, e.g.: to what extent is the experience of early starters like Poland used as a model by late-comers among post-socialist countries? Do the corporate and personnel strategies of western companies in various CEE countries reveal what place in the new international division of labour the west is prepared to cede to the respective countries?

Notes

1. "Western" or "west" and "eastern" or "east" generally refer to western Europe and eastern Europe in the context of this chapter. The phrase "western countries" includes North America in some contexts.

2. The fact that private Polish enterprises mushroomed immediately after political and bureaucratic constraints had been removed does not contradict this statement. The manifestation of entrepreneurial spirit among the population is not equivalent to proof of market related skills, especially skills for managing large companies.

3. Most of the companies in our sample were of this type because during the first years of the transformation process foreign companies could only operate in Poland if they created joint ventures.

4. Boltanski (1990) demonstrates this process as exemplified by the modernisation of France after World War II. Lange (1995) illustrates the intricacies of this task in the case of managers in the former German Democratic Republic.

5. In total, western public assistance in the 1990s considerably surpassed the volume of the Marshall Plan for western Europe after World War II, an instrument often cited as urgently needed in order to push the transformation in the east (Winterberg 1994: 47).

6. In Poland, the official statistics of PAIZ (the Polish State Agency for Foreign Investment) only record FDI over US$1 million; it is estimated that because of this high benchmark, 60–70 per cent of German FDI in Poland is not recorded (Handelsblatt 31.8./1.9. 1996).

7. In the initial phase, major western investors (especially in the automobile industry) had successfully demanded high import tariffs in order to protect "their" markets (Clement 1995; Stankovsky 1996).

8. In the case of Germany this was not more than 0.3 per cent. A more accurate evaluation of the relevance of foreign capital would also have to include qualitative aspects, such as the criterion whether strategic sectors and/or companies are affected or not.

9. However, one should remember that most of the official data on FDI excludes investment below 1 million US$, thus underestimating the dynamics of the economic process.

10. This was underlined by the response to a postal survey of 300 Polish firms with foreign capital input: only 6 per cent of the firms returned the questionnaire with useful information, while almost 20 per cent of the letters were returned stamped "changed address," "unknown" or "undeliverable" by Polish post offices.

11. Some of the case studies were carried out in collaboration with Prof. Marek Okólski, Warsaw and Prof. Zenon Wisniewski, Torun.

12. There is no production in the computer industry in Poland yet and the technological standards of telecommunications are in the process of being upgraded.

13. As the national backgrounds of the foreign managers often were not identical with the home base of their company, the relevance of the different management development types (Ferner 1997) could not be tested: elite recruitment (Japan, France), Germanic functional career path and Anglo-Saxon generalist culture.
14. See Tzeng (1995) for similar policies of large U.S. companies concerning graduates of Taiwanese background from American universities.

Chapter 9

Immigrant Firms and Transnational Embeddedness: Chinese Entrepreneurs in Los Angeles

Yen-Fen Tseng

Transnational Economy and Immigration

Since late 1970s, the economies of major cities in the U.S. have been restructured by a new wave of immigration from Latin America and Asia. Two major economic changes have been observed as a result of the presence of a large number of immigrants in these cities: the expansion of the low-skilled labor market and the economic revitalization of certain regions by immigrant businesses (Mollenkopf and Castells 1991; Sassen-Koob 1984; Sassen 1992). First, the vast supply of cheap and powerless labor represented by immigrants from Latin America has helped to structure new industrial zones in several U.S. regions, such as California, which are emerging as alternatives to the zones in less developed countries (Sassen 1988). For example, in Los Angeles, immigrants have filled low-skilled jobs in both the high technology (aerospace, defense) and the low technology (apparel, furniture) industrial sectors (Scott 1993). Consequently, the availability of low-skilled job opportunities has further stimulated heavy labor migration from the third world, especially from Latin America. However, not every immigrant serves as a low-paid laborer. This group of new arrivals are heterogeneous in terms of their class background and their post-immigration economic activities (Portes and Rumbaut 1990). In general, immigrants from Asian NICs, namely Singapore, Taiwan, Hong Kong, and South Korea, tend to come from the middle or upper-middle classes. Many Asian migrants are college-educated, urban individuals who come to the U.S. from positions as professionals, technicians, managers, and small business owners in their countries of origin (Ong et al. 1994). They are the so-called "new Asian immigrants," characterized by their capital and skill. Entrepreneurship is one of their modes of economic incorporation. Better equipped than other immigrants with entrepreneurial resources, Asian immigrants have been able to establish their own businesses soon after their arrival.

Today, immigrant businesses are an essential part of American metropolitan life. There are Korean middleman merchants selling goods to inner city residents in Chicago and Los Angeles, Cuban entrepreneurs creating a self-sufficient little Havana in Miami, and Taiwanese businesses penetrating the suburban white communities of Los Angeles. Immigrant entrepreneurship has, to some degree, helped to revitalize the economic development of several areas (Light and Bonacich 1988). One of the important economic implications of the arrival of immigrant entrepreneurs is that they help to integrate the local economy into the international context. Rogers (1992: 247) uses the term "transnational business enclave" to refer to those economic communities with a significant proportion of economic activities involved in trade, financing, and capital flow across national borders. According to him, the emergence of this new type of immigrant community is due to two factors. First, the arrival of new immigrants with an established adaptation to urban conditions, middle-class characteristics and sometimes direct connections to transnational business. Second, the interdependence of economies in the U.S. and the homeland, which often provides immigrants with transnational economic niches unavailable to others. For example, Portes and Bach (1985) found that international finance and business between the U.S. and Caribbean economies are in the hands of Cuban immigrant entrepreneurs.

Thus far, the research on the economic consequences of immigration (from the host country's point of view) usually assumes that immigrants are independent of the economic context of their homelands. Few pay attention to the transnational economic linkages brought by immigrants in integrating different economies across borders. Although several researchers have acknowledged that international linkages between immigrant sending countries and receiving countries have affected economic activities in various immigrant communities (Kim 1981; Light and Bonacich 1988; Portes and Zhou 1992), they have not attached sufficient importance to this aspect. In their report to Congress on the effects of immigration on the U.S. economy, Bach and Papademetrious (1989: 4–5), two famous scholars in the field of international migration, argue that immigration, together with international trade and foreign investment, constitute three important dimensions integrating the U.S. into the world economy. Empirical evidence can be found to support their assertion. For example, Portes and Stepick (1994) found that Cuban immigrants are significant players in linking Latin American economies and Miami, where most Cubans in the U.S. settle. As the "Capital of the Caribbean," Miami has been turned into a major trade entrepot for goods from Latin America (Portes and Stepick 1994: 207) because of the availability of bilingual immigrants. These scholars' perspectives represent both one of the possible ways of evaluating the economic consequences of immigration and a position that I adopt in this paper. I argue that in today's global economy, although multinational enterprises and emerging systems of international subcontracting and inter-firm strategical alliances play important mediating roles between countries, population migration across countries can also facilitate the creation and maintenance of transnational economic linkages. Population movement across borders enables social networks, or embeddedness, to use Granovetter's concept (1985), to become transnational. This paper aims to provide evidence for the argument that the significant presence of Chinese immigrant businesses in Los Angeles links its economy to diaspora networks of Chinese entrepreneurs and capital.

This article is about the new types of Pacific Rim enterprises associated with the recent immigration of Chinese and their capital to Los Angeles. Since the mid-1980s, Los Angeles has emerged as the single largest Chinese business center in the U.S. Moreover, Los Angeles is a crucial node in the global Chinese economy, linking ethnic Chinese in such cities as Taipei, Hong Kong, Vancouver, Sydney, Singapore, Kuala Lumpur, Bangkok, and Manila. This Chinese "global capitalism," if we would, is brought together within a world-wide web of population migration, investment flows, and industrial linkages. This article examines the development of Chinese immigrant firms in Los Angeles as an integral part of the Pacific Rim economy, by presenting case studies on Chinese high-tech and international trading industrial activities in Southern California. Relying on transnational business networks, Chinese entrepreneurs have developed efficient forward and backward linkages based on personalistic ties that can be used to mobilize capital, locate demand and supplies, and link with other business resources across borders.

Data

The data set on which this article is based is part of a study on Chinese immigrant enterprises which I conducted between 1991 and 1994 in Los Angeles, supplemented by further interviews in 1997. Although immigrant entrepreneurs originating from Taiwan are the major players in the region, official statistics do not differentiate different subgroups of ethnic Chinese (Tseng 1995). Therefore, although my analysis is based mostly on data collected among Taiwanese immigrants, throughout the paper, I use the more general category "Chinese" to refer the subjects of this study. As a result, one has to use caution in the application of my observations to other ethnic Chinese groups such as those from People's Republic of China.

Most researchers of immigrant firms have found it necessary and indeed essential to use a combination of qualitative and quantitative methods to investigate the multiple dimensions of firm operation. Given the lack of pre-existing data on small businesses in Chinese communities, I rely on primary data collection in the form of surveys and interviews. The data were obtained from the following sources: in-depth interviews with individual entrepreneurs and organization leaders; documentation such as newsletters of business organizations, Dun and Bradstreet Report, Emigrant Express published in Taiwan, reports of Rebuild LA, etc.; and statistical data including a Chinese business survey conducted in 1992 and the 1990 U.S. census 5 per cent sample data. The Chinese Business Survey was a telephone survey conducted in 1992. The sample frame was taken from all firms listed in the 1992 Chinese Business Directory. I used a proportional stratified sampling method based on industry type in my analysis. One thousand firms were chosen from the list, but 210 firms were eliminated due to changes in businesses and phone numbers. Consequently, 790 business owners were interviewed and 352 valid questionnaires gathered. Although the response rate of 45 per cent is not considered to be a good one, it confirms the difficulty researchers of ethnic economies have previously faced (Light and Bonacich 1988). The issue of representativeness, however, requires a cautious interpretation of the survey results. While the survey covers a large number of firms and provides macro characteristics of firms and entrepreneurs, I conducted extensive personal interviews to extract complex information about firms in certain industries, for example, high-technology and international trading, two case industries I will discuss in greater details in this article. Interviews are used to provide an on-going context for interpreting survey results[1]. They also give some account of changes over time, whereas surveys are basically snapshots of one point in time.

New Chinese Immigration

Chinese emigration from East Asia to the U.S. has been a very significant contemporary trend in international migration. Among the immigrants, those from Taiwan are the most important Chinese group in Los Angeles, although they may not be the largest group numerically. According to the 1990 Census, Taiwan born Chinese account for about 20 per cent of the total Chinese population in Los Angeles County. The share of immigrants from Taiwan, however, is likely to be much larger. Since many Taiwanese are secondary migrants, meaning that they were born in Mainland China, migrated to Taiwan during the Chinese revolution, and then (usually a couple of decades later), migrated to the U.S. As a result, place of birth is not an accurate measure of immigrant origin. The Taiwanese are the most recent immigrants among Chinese subgroups, with the major surge to Los Angeles beginning only in the 1970s. The new influx was closely related to the island's political instability. Following the Kuomingtong government's retreat to Taiwan, the hostility between Taiwan and Beijing has been a major threat to the island's security and stability. Despite the economic success that has brought prosperity to Taiwan, Taiwanese have constantly worried about their country's long-term prospects. According to a 1988 survey, one tenth of the 1,400 largest business owners in Taiwan planned to migrate or have already established their immigrant status in other countries and about a quarter have at least one family member immigrating overseas (Yao 1988). In another survey in 1991, one in eight Taiwanese indicated the desire to migrate overseas. Those who expressed the desire to migrate tended to be young, urban, professional, and college educated (Hsiao 1991). Between 1985 and 1991, an estimated 50,000 Taiwanese a year emigrated abroad (Kotkin 1993). The United States was ranked as the most desirable destination for this migration, followed by Australia and Canada (Hsiao 1991).

The ways in which the Taiwanese population came to Los Angeles followed typical Asian patterns. First, they came as students to pursue advanced degrees in U.S. educational institutions. After they graduated, they became professionals working for U.S. companies. In the 1970s and early 1980s, Taiwan was the leading source of U.S. foreign student population and many of them remained in the U.S. and constitute the basis of the Chinese professional population. Los Angeles is the favored destination for Taiwanese professionals, because of its engineering jobs in high-tech and aerospace industries and its Asia-Pacific business environment. The majority of high-technology entrepreneurs discussed in next section belong to this category of students-turned-immigrants.

As part of the so-called new Asian immigration, since the 1980s, there has been an increasing number of business people from Taiwan making the move to the U.S. Those immigrants with executive backgrounds, who in 1986 accounted for 30 per cent of all Taiwanese, were likely from the entrepreneurial class (Waldinger and Tseng 1992). I argue that the relationship between the U.S. and Taiwan's economy is at the core of the process. Along with the growing international trade between these two regions, more business owners can combine their international trade, capital investment, and immigration. In other words, transnational movement of people is a phenomenon closely related to mobility of capital and commodity.

Therefore, it is no coincidence that the U.S. has been the most important destination for Taiwan's international trade, capital flow, and population migration. The economic influence of the U.S. on Taiwan began with the foreign aid to the island in 1950s. Since the 1960s, when Taiwan became incorporated into the "new international division of labor" and developed its export-oriented industrialization, the U.S. has been the number one market for exports. Later, when Taiwan's surplus capital began to search for the overseas locations for the investment and business expansion, the U.S. became the major recipient of this capital flow (Tzeng 1992). More than two thirds of Taiwan's outward foreign direct investment in all foreign countries in 1986 was invested in the United Sates (Lee and Hu 1989: 91). Many business people began to utilize their business connections with the U.S. to seek channels for themselves and their families to emigrate.

The most popular immigration channel to the U.S. among Taiwanese business people is the L-1 visa, which is reserved for intra-company transferees. Many Taiwanese business owners set up a branch office in the U.S. and qualify for L-1 status. They belong to the so-called "capital-linked migration" trend, a term used by Wong (1993: 173) to refer to the migration of capitalists which is linked to a condition which requires that a certain amount of capital be invested in the host country. The establishment of a branch office can also function both as a marketing outpost and a mechanism for capital flow.

Thus, even when Taiwan implemented a tight policy governing capital outflow before 1985, business people often managed to keep part of their foreign-exchange earnings abroad by various measures. Setting up a subsidiary overseas is a common practice. For example, if a Taiwanese manufacturer earns $1 million dollars from exports to the U.S., instead of sending $1 million back to Taiwan, he sets up a U.S. branch and employs himself and his family members/friends. By paying himself and others salaries for operating this U.S. branch office, he is able to retain a certain proportion of his earnings in the U.S. Over the years, Taiwanese business people have extensively taken advantage of this channel, sometimes to secure the money they earned by holding foreign currency. In order to operate these branches, business people and their family members often apply for L-1 visas to obtain immigrant status. This way, the capital movement begins to be linked with migration from Taiwan. Even now, with Taiwan's softening policy of capital movement overseas, the combination of trade, investment and immigration is still attractive to business owners. An advertisement in one of Taiwan's immigration magazines entitled, "How to Invest in Mexico and Immigrate to the U.S. at the Same Time?" reveals the message:

> When you are considering setting up your manufacturing factory in Mexico, you should also think about the advantages of establishing your subsidiary in the U.S. Not only can you be closer to the American market, most importantly, you can utilize the opportunity to apply for immigrant visas (L-1) for you and your family. (Emigrant Express 1993: 6)

Chinese Businesses in Los Angeles

Los Angeles has been the favorite destination for Chinese capital-linked migration (Tseng 1995; Goldberg 1985). Visitors to Los Angeles would be surprised by the extensive presence of Chinese businesses in a widespread geographical area. The Valley Boulevard, which runs through at least ten cities in the San Gabriel Valley, serves as a window to Chinese business development in the area. Along the Boulevard, there are numerous office complexes, industrial plants, and mini-malls with Chinese signs. Lots that were vacant in the 70s now look like Far Eastern marketplaces. Since the 80s, Chinese economic forces have been one of the most dynamic, vital, and influential factors affecting the regional economy. Better provided with financial resources than earlier immigrants, Chinese newcomers have been heavily investing in businesses in Los Angeles. Two indicators demonstrate these business investment activities. First, Los Angeles is now home to the largest number of Chinese-owned firms, replacing San Francisco as the nation's Chinese business center (U.S. Bureau of Census 1992a). Second, responding to the needs created by business expansion, Chinese investors have aggressively purchased commercial land in the area. According to the estimate of CB Commercial Company, the region's leading business real estate agency, in 1989, 60 per cent of the shopping/retailing property transactions handled by the company in the San Gabriel Valley, where most Chinese businesses cluster, was in invested by Chinese and, in 1991, 50 per cent of the warehouse purchases in the San Gabriel Valley were Chinese-related. The new capital and economic opportunities have transformed the local cities into a complex of offices, shops, and small industrial plants.

The Chinese are found to be well provided with resources such as financial and human capital, business expertise, and networks to begin their business ventures in the new country. The telephone survey of Chinese business owners in Los Angeles offers evidence of the availability of these resources. Immigrant entrepreneurs usually have a strong educational background, and Chinese business owners are no exception. Eighty-eight per cent of the Chinese merchants in our survey had earned four years or more of college education, while only 35 per cent of nonminority male business owners in the U.S. had a comparable level of education (U.S. Bureau of Census 1992b). Table 9.1 shows that many Chinese immigrant merchants are members of the business-owner class. Forty-three per cent were entrepreneurs in their homelands, compared to 24 per cent of Chicago's Korean business owners (Yoon 1991), another immigrant group famous for its high propensity of entrepreneurship. The mobility of the business owner class from Chinese societies offers a great supply of would-be entrepreneurs. From the survey, we also learn that Chinese entrepreneurs heavily rely on job skills which they transfer from the homeland, as evidenced by the fact that 52 per cent of respondents indicated a high correlation between their present business activities and their job skills acquired in their homelands. Business ties had been established prior to their migration. Frequent visits to the homeland are often used to strengthen these ties. A high proportion of Chinese business owners visit their homeland at least twice a year, and these visits back to their country of origin are mainly made for business purposes.

Table 9.1 Pre-migration Background among Chinese Business Owners

Characteristics	Percentage
Male	76
Urban origin	89
College-educated	88
Pre-migration occupation*	
Executive	23
Professional	21
Skill Transfer	52
Owned business in home country	43
Capital accumulated mainly in home country	57
Visiting home country at least twice a year	44
Trip to home country mainly for business	50
Cases	325

*: Occupation regardless of self-employment or employment status.
Source: Chinese Business Survey (Author's own survey in 1992).

Ethnic businesses tend to concentrate in niches characterized by the lower entry of barrier, or leftover niches of the larger economy, such as underserved or abandoned businesses that serve unstable and uncertain demands (Waldinger 1986; Zhou 1992). However, these economic niches play a much less important role in the Chinese ethnic economy of Los Angeles, as compared to Chinatown economies. Using 1980 Census data, Razin (1988) finds that industrial distribution among the Chinese in Los Angeles is more diversified than that in San Francisco. Situated in a more diversified regional economy, Chinese entrepreneurs in Los Angeles are involved in a wider spectrum of industries than their counterparts in San Francisco. Traditional Chinese businesses—restaurants, garment factories, and groceries—have been replaced by a large spectrum of both old and new industries. According to the 1990 U.S census, the self-employed Chinese were involved in a wide range of industries. Besides traditional Chinese businesses, there emerge many significant and new economic niches such as printing and publishing, computer and aircraft manufacturing, air transportation, commercial equipment (computer) wholesalers, security and commodity brokerage, hotels and motels, engineering services, accounting, computer and data processing, etc. There is a sector characterized by economic niches that either require higher and more formal training such as professional services, or larger capital investment such as hotels and motels, motor vehicles wholesale, or require both professional training and larger capital investment such as computer and aircraft manufacturing. In the following sections, I rely on data from two business sectors to analyze how transnational networks facilitated the business participation of Chinese entrepreneurs. The main reason I selected these two sectors is that they are typical of economic activities with obvious involvement of transnational linkages.

Transnational Embeddedness in Two Industries

High-Technology Industry: The Case of Aerospace-electronic Manufacturing

From 1960 to the present, the aerospace-electronics complex of Southern California has been the largest high-technology industrial region in the world. Basically three major sectors, aircraft and parts, missiles and space equipment, and electronics, represent the essential core of the region's high-technology industry. Southern California has attracted foreign capital to its thriving high-technology, capital-intensive industries. Sassen (1988) finds several advantages for Southern California to develop a high-technology economy. First, the presence of numerous, cheap, and proficient immigrant workers from all over the world, especially Asia, lowers the labor cost and at the same time provides high-quality workers which the high-technology industries require. Second, California's high-technology industries are close to various centers of technical research, control and design. Third, they enjoy the availability of industrial land which accommodates a territorial organization of production characterized by the clustering of a number of firms.

Due to the presence of a large number of Chinese scientists and engineers in California, Chinese source countries interested in high-technology ventures have invested capital in this area (Liu 1991). In 1990, California absorbed 45 per cent of all high-technology venture capital collected in Taiwan, and almost all the capital were invested in Chinese-owned ventures (Liu 1991). Information, electronics, and bio-technology were the three most favored industries. Recent figures to update the above statistics are not available, however, according to the survey conducted by Taipei Venture Capital Association (TVCA newsletter 1997), venture capital invested in the U.S. high-tech enterprises reach 14 million U.S. dollars in 1995 (with 90 per cent in California).

One might wonder why venture capitalists favor their coethnic[2]-owned high-tech enterprises. In the mid-80s, Taiwanese venture capital initially invested in non-Chinese-American high-tech companies. However, most of the companies failed to generate profit and later most of the investments were withdrawn. The director of the Taipei Venture Capital Association described the problems of investing in non-Chinese in contrast to the Chinese companies:

> Those initial investments failed mainly because there was a serious defect in communication due to language barriers and inefficient information flow. To generate a positive result, the venture capitalists need to continue to monitor as well as to assist the company invested in. In terms of these aspects, it is more difficult to achieve ideal communication with non-Chinese. On the contrary, investments in the Chinese high-tech ventures have been more successful. Later, it became a consensus among Taiwan's venture capitalists that it is better to invest in Chinese firms. From my judgment, they (capitalists and Chinese firms) can communicate better and establish more informal relationships. As a result, the investments often lead to technology transfers and international subcontracting later on. In other words, the investments in Chinese firms enhanced the industrial linkages across borders. (Interview 3/21/97)

According to the director, Chinese firms in the U.S. depend heavily upon the supply of venture capital from Taiwan. He estimated that 60 of the venture investment opportunities he handled in 1996, half were from Chinese or Chinese-co-owned high-tech firms in California. According to the director, "there is a well-known saying within our circle: 'for start-up capital in high-tech ventures, Chinese Americans can count on Taiwan, but the Asian Indians would have to collect locally in the U.S.'" The venture capital available in Taiwan mainly came from the profit made by early returnees from the U.S. who have established successful high-tech ventures in Taiwan (Chen and Joe 1996). According to Dr. Denny Ko, the founding president of the Organization of Chinese Entrepreneurial Advisory Networks (OCEAN), a non-profit Chinese high-technology consulting group based in Los Angeles, since many Taiwan venture capitalists are scientists or engineers, they mainly rely on existing networks such as former colleagues, classmates, or friends, to search for ideal investment in high-tech ventures established by Chinese.

According to the 1990 Census, in Los Angeles alone, there were 85 self-employed[3] Chinese in computer manufacturing, 65 in the aircraft and parts, 16 in guided missiles, 20 in medical and optical equipment, and 59 in electrical machinery. Table 9.2 compares Chinese self-employed with the general population. It shows that the Chinese self-employed were overrepresented in all these sectors except for guided missile manufacturing. Among these sectors, Chinese business ownership in computer, as well as in aircraft and parts, manufacturing is most significant. They respectively account for 12 per cent and 10 per cent of all businesses in these two sectors in the entire Los Angeles region. Here, I focus mainly on Chinese involvment in aircraft and parts manufacturing.

Table 9.2 Number of High-Technology Business Owners in Los Angeles County, Chinese versus Total Population, 1990

Industries*	Chinese population	All population	Index**
Computers and Related Products	85	705	384
Aircraft and Parts	65	605	342
Guided Missiles	16	748	68
Medical and Optical Equipment	20	511	125
Electrical Machinery	88	964	290
Business Owners in all industries	16,625	528,896	

*: All of the following are manufacturing industries.
**: Index=b/a x 100;
    a=Chinese business owners in all industries/ All business owners in all industries=16625/528896.
    b=Chinese business owners in specific industries/ All business owners in specific industries (for example, b=85/705 for computer and related products).
    If index=100, that means a=b.
    If index<100, Chinese business owners are underrepresented.
    If Index>100, Chinese Business Owners Are Overrepresented.
Source: U.S. Bureau of Census, Census of Population and Housing (1990: 5% public use microdata samples).

Several factors explain the emergence of Chinese self-employment in aircraft and parts manufacturing. The first has to do with push factors. This group of high-technology entrepreneurs mainly consists of scientists and engineers who obtained postgraduate degrees in the U.S. and had formerly worked for TRW, McDonnell Douglas, Rockwell, or Lockheed. During my interviews, a number of these entrepreneurs cited their disadvantage in promotion and the lack of training opportunities as the most important reasons why they left their companies and became self-employed. Many encountered a "glass ceiling" which hindered their upward mobility in American companies and a lack of training opportunities in market-oriented aspects. According to one interviewee:

> As Asian engineers and scientists, they are perceived as competent in technical-oriented tasks of research and development but weak in marketing and management. This persistent perception greatly increases their chance of being laid off when the company is not doing well. (Interview 2/21/94)

Second, small subcontract shops and input suppliers providing specialized services to high-technology producers have expanded to major proportions. These small subcontractors are manufacturers of printed circuit boards and aluminum foundry products, transistors, assembly services, and molded plastics. The subcontracting system of the aerospace and defense industries, which favors small and flexible production lines, offers an opportunity for the Chinese to establish their businesses in these sectors. According to Scott (1993: 122), one of the important characteristics of the aerospace and defense industries is that they are dominated by large systems houses embedded in dense networks of smaller, flexible specialized establishments that provide them with innumerable physical inputs and subcontract services. Large systems houses called "prime contractors" receive the primary contracts from government or the private sector and distribute the work among second-tier subcontractors who subcontract to other smaller manufacturers. Large systems are in charge of final assembly, putting together parts from smaller specialized producers. A veteran in the aerospace industry speaks of the process through which Chinese businesses cluster in this sector:

> The emergence of Chinese self-employment in the aerospace and defense industries began with a handful of Chinese entrepreneurs who pioneered in aircraft parts and the guided missiles industry during early 80s. Later they became second-tier contractors. They obtained contracts from large systems based on their previous ties established when they were employed by these companies, for example, TRW, McDonnell Douglas, Hughes, etc, and subcontract to smaller Chinese producers. The need for smaller producers in the area of specialized parts manufacturing has encouraged more Chinese engineers and scientists originally employed in the aerospace and the defense industry to set up their own companies.

Chinese engineers working in large systems also help Chinese suppliers to gain contracts. (Interview 2/3/94)

Chinese engineers and scientists are well organized. For example, in the area of aerospace, they network through the Chinese American Aerospace Engineers Association (CAAEA). They often come together to exchange information regarding the business opportunities in the aerospace industry. In a 1994 event, which the author attended, the CAAEA offered a one-day conference addressing issues regarding self-employment opportunities for components suppliers in the aerospace industry. The conference was conducted mainly in Chinese. The Chinese speakers included successful high-tech entrepreneurs and engineers from Hughes and TRW who introduced new developments of both companies and the implications for business opportunities. In attendance were more than 100 Chinese engineers, salaried as well as self-employed in aerospace industry. The capital available from Taiwan and Hong Kong provides Chinese high-technology entrepreneurs critical finance to begin their ventures, a subject we have discussed. The above factors explain the significant presence of Chinese self-employment in aircraft parts industries. Many of these companies have financial backing and production facilities within the Chinese-dominated economies of East Asia. From the membership directory of OCEAN, it is common to find companies with overseas branch offices or factories in Asia. The international division of labor occurs in different forms. Some run research and design facilities here and production lines in Asia, while others use the reverse of this arrangement.

International Trading Business: A Case of Computer Wholesaling

International trading has been one of the traditional economic niches for immigrants.[4] Trading entrepreneurs profit when gaps appear between supply and demand. The conduct of international trade requires solving basic problems relating to the regular exchange of information about the conditions of supply and demand among traders and the speedy dispatch and transport of goods. Therefore, it becomes crucial to create and maintain relations of trust between traders and intermediaries who are involved in the chain of the trade. In many instances, these technical problems are overcome when people from the same ethnic group coordinate their efforts and establish channels of communication and mutual support. Co-ethnics at strategical points along the trade route provide ready-made networks for such activity. In this way, an ethnic trading network, consisting of dispersed but highly interrelated individuals from the same ethnic group, develops.

It can be assumed that immigrants are endowed with certain transnational linkages in encouraging their involvement in international trade, especially with their sending countries. However, I argue that the active participation in transnational trade among immigrants is contingent upon the economic conditions of the sending countries. This point can be illustrated by comparing two Asian groups: Korean and Chinese. Chinese international traders are prominent in the importing and exporting of many products in which various source countries, Taiwan, Hong Kong, and China, specialize. These include computer and related products, toys, garments, electronic appliances, sports products, etc. On the contrary, only the wig business has emerged as a significant economic niche for Korean traders in the U.S. (Chin et al. 1996). Given the fact that South Korea exports a wide range of products to the U.S., Korean immigrant involvement in the import/export business is limited (Kim 1981). To account for this disparity, we need to understand the divergent pattern of business systems in South Korea, Hong Kong, and Taiwan. On of the major differences between the business systems of South Korea and Taiwan and Hong Kong lies in the industrial organization (Hamilton and Biggart 1988). Like Japan, international trading in South Korea is dominated by large affiliate groups (Chaebol), thus leaving little room for smaller traders to gain access to a supply of goods and market information. On the contrary, Chinese firms are rarely organized into such a vertical system. Rather, small or medium size firms are connected through complex and dense personal relationships. The following case illustrates that the pervasive pattern of small firms among Chinese encourages their reliance on personal networks. A second son of a watch manufacturer in Taiwan, recalled his immigration to the U.S. as part of his family's business strategy:

> My father did not think of exporting to the U.S. until there were some small orders from North America. He sensed that there were opportunities, but hesitated to set up a branch office here because he knew nothing about how to run a transnational operation. I was studying at U.S.C then, so he asked me to do marketing as a part-time job. Within only a few years, I was able to establish a solid business, so my father decided that after graduation I should settle in Los Angeles and continue the operation. (Interview 3/4/93)

Chinese entrepreneurs involved in international trading came from more diverse immigration channels than did high-technology entrepreneurs.

In some cases, they are the next generation of family firms who, as in the above situation, came as students. In other cases, they are business owners immigrating through L-1 visas. Nonetheless, with its advantage of geographical position and commercial potential, Los Angeles is the favorite destination for Chinese trading-oriented immigrants. For example, by 1994, according to Dunn and Bradstreet report (Rebuild L.A. Committee Report 1996), the largest percentage of Los Angeles' downtown Chinese firms—33 per cent of the companies and 50 per cent of the total revenues—were accounted for by the international trade industry. The Chinese-owned business services sector in Los Angeles plays an important role in facilitating Chinese participation in international trading businesses. These are business services ranging from crane operators lowering containers onto ships in the harbor to truck loaders, warehousing, forwarders, repackaging, customs brokers, insurance agents, commercial bankers, investment bankers, lawyers, and advertising companies, etc. Among these services, Chinese banks are especially important, because they are active in handing out business loans to Chinese international traders. As a matter of fact, financing international trade is one of the market specialties for Chinese banks. Chinese banks usually put special emphasis on training staff to be familiar with the financial instruments for international traders to exploit. In contrast, staff in U.S. banks have much less knowledge of such transactions (Zhou 1996). Chinese banks often use their connections in Hong Kong, Taiwan, China and Southeast Asia to run a background check on Chinese loan applicants before approving their loans. Thus, Chinese entrepreneurs who own properties and businesses or have established some credit history in their country of origin often turn to Chinese-owned banks, which can offer them a more flexible credit line. According to one Chinese banker, some of the loans handed to Chinese business owners in Los Angeles are backed by letters of credit issued overseas. He illustrates this practice:

> If you have money in Taiwan and don't want to use it to finance your business here, you want to borrow from us instead. I suggest you use your savings in a Taiwan bank as a guarantee and issue a letter of credit to us. With that letter of credit to back you up, we can give you a loan here. This way, you can transfer your credit in Taiwan to here. Even if it is not you, but rather your family members who have money or credit in Taiwan, they can do the same to finance your business. I don't know of any American bank that would be willing to do this. Some Japanese banks have followed our strategies, but they don't have the good connections with Taiwan banks that we have. (Interview 8/9/92)

Many Chinese immigrants came to Los Angeles with prior business exposure. These trading entrepreneurs establish their business base in Los Angeles, but remain heavily dependent on their networks back in their homelands and in other Chinese diaspora areas.

These regional linkages have played an important role in assisting immigrants in conducting their businesses in the host society, especially among Chinese and Japanese (Light 1972). For many Chinese immigrants who are the so called "twice immigrants" (those who emigrated to Taiwan or Hong Kong from Mainland China after 1949 and eventually came to U.S.), their set of regional networks often encompasses more than two countries. Especially in recent years, the export sector in Mainland China is dramatically expanding and many companies are seeking *"hua-qiao"*—overseas Chinese—to help them with their transnational operations. Mr. Wu, a delegate assigned from mainland China to oversee the operation of a Los Angeles based Chinese trading company, commented:

> The delegations from China will be assigned to the post for no more than three years. This is the personnel policy of most state-owned enterprises. It creates a very difficult situation for us to do business in a foreign country. Therefore, most of the time, we rely on *"hua-qiao"* traders who have been here long enough to understand business operations and accumulate channels in this country. (Interview 6/21/92)

Those *"hua-qiao"* originating from mainland China, who maintain their networks back to China, are in a privileged position to be selected as international trading partners. In the local Chinese newspapers, there are reports almost daily describing trading delegations from certain provinces of mainland China that visit Los Angeles. The reports show that the first group of people they meet are usually those *"hua-qiao"* business people affiliated with their respective regional associations (*tong-xiang-hui*). As a result of this personalized networking, Chinese international traders rarely organized formally among themselves. According to an informant in the Taiwanese Import/Export Association in Los Angeles, a trade organization with limited membership and functions, there appears to be little need for traders based in Los Angeles to network among themselves:

> Although some of them (Chinese international traders) are engaged in fierce price competition, such as garment, computer, and jewelry importers, very few have overlap suppliers. They rely on their own forward and backward networks to locate customers and suppliers. They don't need a formal organization to offer assistance. (Interview 7/7/92)

Many Chinese entrepreneurs start as sales representatives for Taiwan or Hong Kong firms in North America. The Chinese computer wholesaling business is a good case in point.

According to Zhou's (1996) investigation, many Chinese computer firms started their businesses by selling reliable products at half the market price of the name brands and still enjoying big profits. In many cases, they were allowed to pay their suppliers after they had sold the products. Consequently, much of the computers imported from Asia are in the hands of Chinese computer wholesalers in Los Angeles. According to the Southern California Chinese Computer Industry Association's estimation, at least 65 per cent of the 750 million dollars' worth of personal computer equipment imported to the U.S. in 1991 was shipped through Los Angeles and handled by Taiwanese computer importers. There are at least 350 incorporated Taiwanese computer assembly and distribution companies in Los Angeles, most companies selling or assembling portable notebooks and desktop personal computers made in Taiwan or Hong Kong. A typical computer firm will specialize in importing one or two computer parts but also might assemble and sell whole systems. Some eventually turn into manufacturers themselves, designing products and contracting with Taiwan factories. Therefore, a so-called "golden triangle" in computer industry links computer design firms in Silicon Valley, overseas Taiwan manufacturers, and assembly and distribution companies in Los Angeles. The market for Chinese computer distributors even goes beyond the U.S. and reaches Latin America, and even worldwide. Chinese computer firms in Los Angeles, therefore, act as discount clearinghouses for the thousands of independent small computer manufacturers in Asia. The Chinese computer traders in Los Angeles play an indispensable role in promoting the computer industry in Asia. This is just an example to confirm that through coethnic inter-firm market linkages, Chinese firms can operate internationally more easily.

Embeddedness across Borders

The formation of a transnational space for the circulation of capital and people migration has characterized contemporary global capitalism. This article focuses on Chinese immigrant firms and their transnational economic linkages. I have shown that the increasing economic integration between Asian countries and their emigrants in the United States plays an important role in business cooperation among immigrant firms. This article intends to contribute to two main literatures: immigrant firms and economic globalization.

With regard to research on immigrant firms, my study suggests a need for bringing the global economic structure into the study of immigrant enterprises. Previous theories of immigrant enterprises tend to focus on cultural or personal characteristics of immigrant entrepreneurs in the context of immigrant receiving countries. However this study has shown that the key to rapid growth and increasing sophistication among Chinese business entrepreneurs is their international connections. Such connections are manifest in different forms. First are financial connections, in terms of capital flow from Chinese regions. Second, the circulation of highly skilled immigrants between the United States and East Asia has brought expertise, information and connections to both sides of the Pacific. Third, immigrants often assume the role of middlemen to promote international trade between their home countries and host countries. In sum, international connections are a critical dimension that can significantly increase the resources and opportunities within the ethnic community.

With regard to research on economic globalization, much of the discussion in this literature centers on the large players such as multinational corporations, international treaties and agencies, and governments. Transmigrants, by engaging simultaneously in both the host and home countries, represent another form of globalization where the flow of capital, information, and commodity is embedded in the movement of people and governed, not by treaties or corporate hierarchy, but by a network of social relations. Such networks are thus much less visible, but more fluid than subsidiary networks of large corporations. This is especially true for Chinese immigrants whose transnational connections are generally decentralized since Chinese firms are mostly small and family-owned and have limited potential to develop a vertically integrated transnational form. Social networks across borders serve as efficient mechanisms to minimize transaction costs. Long-term relations among identified individuals in different firms across borders can greatly assist complex transactions. Therefore, via Chinese immigrants, the Los Angeles regional economy has been linked more strongly with the Pacific Rim economy. Those localities where immigrant entrepreneurs are active in international businesses are well positioned to take advantage of the growth of Chinese businesses. The decentralized networks provided by immigrants can be a significant resource for the region to gain access to the global economy.

Notes

1. Interviews were conducted in Mandarin Chinese and I transcribed them in English.
2. Coethnic refers to those who share the same ethnicity.
3. Here I use self-employed to refer to business owners, including those who employ others.
4. In his historical work on "Civilization and Capitalism 15–18th Century," Fernand Braudel (1979) cites extensive evidence showing that successful merchants who controlled international trading networks during that period often belonged to foreign minorities. For example, the Italian merchants who arrived empty-handed in Lyons needed only a table and a sheet of paper to start their business operation, because they could find on the spot their fellow countrymen who were in touch with other associates in the local market. The Jews, the Armenians, the Banyans, and the Parsees were among those foreign minorities active in international trading.

Chapter 10

Transnational Entrepreneurs and Regional Industrialization: The Silicon Valley-Hsinchu Connection

AnnaLee Saxenian

After graduating from the University of California at Berkeley, Alex Au worked for more than a decade in a series of Silicon Valley technology companies. By 1983, he felt that he had reached a glass ceiling in established firms and started the Vitelic Semiconductor Corp. in his garage. Au drew on connections in Taiwan to raise capital and later to develop the Asian market for the firm's products. When Vitelic merged with Taiwan-based Mosel in 1991, the combined business (Mosel-Vitelic) had over $150 million in sales and hundreds of employees in San Jose, Taiwan, and Hong Kong.

Kenny Liu, Jerry Chang, and David Lin all worked together at Silicon Valley-based Chips & Technologies before founding Opti in 1989. After being rebuffed by mainstream venture capitalists, they raised $1 million in seed capital from a mutual friend in Taiwan. When the company went public in 1993 it had over 200 employees in Silicon Valley (70 per cent of whom were Chinese) and over $100 million in sales. The early customers for their chipsets were all in Asia, largely Taiwanese personal computer companies; and their vendors were the leading Taiwanese semiconductor foundries, TSMC and UMC.

In 1990, Silicon Valley engineer Min Wu returned to Taiwan to start a semiconductor company. Wu, who earned a PhD from Stanford University during the 1970s, took with him dozens of friends and former colleagues as well as the contacts, technical skills, and managerial know-how he had developed from working in Silicon Valley for 15 years. Today his firm, Macronix International, is one of the largest chip companies in the Hsinchu Science Park, with over $200 million in sales and 1400 employees in Taiwan, Japan, and Silicon Valley.

Silicon Valley in California and the Hsinchu region in Taiwan are among the world's most dynamic centers of technology industry. Since its early origins as a center of semiconductor production in the 1950s and 1960s, the Silicon Valley economy has diversified significantly and its firms continue to define state-of-the-art technologies and products in sectors ranging from semiconductors and computers to communications, software, and multimedia. The Hsinchu Science-Based Industrial Park was established in 1980 and has emerged in less than two decades as one of the world's most sophisticated locations for semiconductor manufacturing. During the same period the Taipei region has became Asia's center of personal computer production. While these two regions are differently specialized and remain at different levels of development, they are among the most frequently cited "miracles" of rapid industrialization in the postwar period.

Virtually all accounts of the development of Silicon Valley and Hsinchu treat the respective regions in isolation[1]. Many scholars point to the central role of the state in spurring or guiding the rapid development of these technology regions. In the case of the semiconductor industry, for example, studies document the large and lucrative market created for Silicon Valley firms by the U.S. Department of Defense (DOD) and the promotional and resource-leveraging activities of Taiwan's Industrial Technology Research Institute, ITRI, and its Electronics Research and Service Organization, ERSO (See, for example, Harrison 1994; Mathews 1997). Other scholars focus attention on the broader institutional environment, including universities, research institutes, and local cultures that support the growth of technology industries in Silicon Valley and Hsinchu (Castells and Hall 1994). Finally, students of industrial structure stress the flexibility and learning capacities of the networks of specialist firms and supporting institutions in these localized industrial systems (or, industrial districts) (Saxenian 1994; Hsu 1997).

Each of these explanations contains important truths. The latter approach, in particular, illuminates important parallels between the decentralized industrial systems in the two regions. Both Silicon Valley and Hsinchu are dense agglomerations of technical skill that boast high levels of entrepreneurship and networks of fast-moving, intensely competitive small and medium-sized producers. These firms, by avoiding vertical integration, are flexible and focused enough to alternatively challenge or collaborate with larger, established companies. And in both regions, local institutions foster open communication and joint problem-solving among autonomous but interdependent producers. However by focusing primarily on relationships within the regional (or national) economy, these scholars have understated the importance of the growing interactions *between* these two dynamic regions.

The acquisition of foreign technology has, of course, been central to Taiwan's industrial development strategy. Scholars have documented the contribution of technology licensing arrangements, joint ventures, and foreign investment to the growth of the local electronics industry; and many have also recognized the contribution of returning US-educated engineers to the development of Hsinchu (Hobday 1995; Meaney 1991; Mathews 1997; Castells and Hall 1994). However, all of these accounts focus on *one-way flows* of technology and skill. In this updated variant of dependency theory, the key resources for development originate in the U.S. core and are transferred to industrializing, but still peripheral, Taiwan. This approach helps to explain why Taiwan is no longer a platform for low wage manufacturing investment, but it fails to capture the developmental dynamic that has been unleashed by changing relations between these two regions. In particular, it fails to appreciate that interactions between Silicon Valley and Hsinchu are often complementary and mutually-beneficial rather than hierarchical and zero-sum.

This paper argues that the growth of social and economic ties between individuals and firms in the two regions enhances the performance of *both* Silicon Valley and Hsinchu. The protagonists in this process are not multinational corporations, as much of the scholarship on globalization suggests (Dunning 1993; Sassen 1988). Rather, the key actors are a transnational community of US-educated Taiwanese engineers who have the language skills and experience to operate fluently in both regions. Their dense social and professional networks foster two-way flows of technology, capital, know-how, and information between the U.S. and Taiwan, supporting entrepreneurship in both regions while providing the foundation for formal inter-regional business relations such as consortia, joint-ventures, and partnerships.

This case suggests that collaboration between producers located in differently specialized but similarly organized regional economies can foster a positive-sum dynamic of reciprocal industrial advance. These inter-regional relationships support entrepreneurial success in both regions by supporting joint problem-solving and complementary innovation (Sabel

1989). And, like the relationships between specialist firms and their suppliers inside of the industrial districts, these inter-regional networks cannot be understood purely as market transactions or "commodity chains" linking independent firms in different locations (Gereffi and Korzeniewicz 1994). Rather, the economic ties are dependent upon a social structure and culture that foster openness and cooperation between producers in geographically distant regions. Close, trust-based relationships among the transnational community of Taiwanese engineers are thus an essential precondition for the flexible collaboration needed to adapt and survive in today's fast-paced competitive environment (Sabel 1993).

To be sure, the proliferation of business ties across the Pacific has been facilitated as well by dramatic improvements in communication and transportation technologies. This does not mean, however, that economic relations are becoming "spaceless," or that technology is undermining the importance of localities. On the contrary, as increasing global flows enhance the opportunities for entrepreneurship and interactive learning between regions like Silicon Valley and Hsinchu, they actually reinforce the advantages of those localities relative to all others. In high technology, as in other information-intensive industries like international financial services (Sassen 1997), globalization has been accompanied by intensified spatial concentration of innovation and production.

This paper begins by documenting the creation of a community among the Taiwanese engineers in Silicon Valley during the 1970s and 1980s. The focus is on the way that collective identities were constructed through the shared professional and educational experiences of these immigrants, as well as through the activities of local institutions. The middle section describes how this community became transnational during the late 1980s and 1990s when the economic opportunities in Taiwan were sufficient to reverse the "brain drain." It analyzes how this transnational community has created dense two-way flows of information, technology, skill and capital that support entrepreneurs in both Silicon Valley and Hsinchu. The following section details how the largely informal ties between the two regions are being formalized in cross-Pacific consortia, or interregional production networks, that support reciprocal learning and industrial advance between the two regions. The concluding section raises questions about the future of ties between these regions and the development of the Pacific Rim economy.

The research for this paper is part of a broader project on Immigrant Networks and the Internationalization of the Silicon Valley Workforce. The project investigates the contribution of immigrant entrepreneurs to Silicon Valley and their role in constructing ties between Silicon Valley and regions in Asia. The findings presented here are preliminary. They are based on more than 50 in-depth interviews with Chinese engineers in Silicon Valley and Taiwan (see Appendix for list of interviewees) as well as attendance at meetings of a variety of professional and technical associations in the two regions.[2]

Constructing a Community: Immigrant Engineers in Silicon Valley

There is a saying in the local technology community that "Silicon Valley is run by ICs—Indians and Chinese." While this California region is widely known for its most revolutionary product, the integrated circuit, or IC, few recognize the extent to which this California region depends on the technical skills of a large immigrant workforce. Some one-third of the professional and technical workforce is of foreign descent, largely Asian. Chinese and Indian entrepreneurs alone started one-quarter of the region's high technology businesses during the 1990s; and some 1,300 (or 17 per cent) of the region's computer and electronics companies are run by Chinese executives. The majority of the Chinese engineers and entrepreneurs in Silicon Valley, in turn, are from Taiwan. In 1990 there were more than 12,000 Taiwanese immigrants working in Silicon Valley.[3]

The community of Taiwanese engineers in Silicon Valley is known to be unusually tightly-knit. Most immigrated to the U.S. during the 1970s and 1980s to pursue graduate studies in engineering. In the words of one graduate of National Taiwan University (NTU) who earned a doctorate from Purdue University in Indiana and now works at Silicon Valley-based Sun Microsystems: "I followed what virtually all engineering graduates of NTU did at the time. I came to the United States to study, and then stayed on to work."[4] In fact, Taiwan sent more Ph.D. candidates in engineering to the United States than any other country during the 1980s. Only 10 per cent of these immigrants returned to Taiwan after graduation. The majority, lured by wages that were several times what they could earn at home, as well as a more attractive quality of life, stayed to work in research labs like Bell Labs in New Jersey or in California's fast growing technology firms. Over time, a great majority ended up in Silicon Valley because of the region's dramatic growth in the 1970s and 1980s.

Taiwanese engineers in the U.S. constructed close relationships that built on shared educational and professional experiences as well as a common language and culture. During the 1970s and 1980s, Silicon Valley became home to some 30 or 40 members of each graduating class from the leading Taiwanese Universities. Alumni relationships are very tight in Taiwan, and these classmates stayed in close touch with one another informally as well as through the frequent activities of the local Alumni Associations. In addition, a Joint Alumni Association, which unites dozens of Taiwanese campuses, holds regular meetings in Silicon Valley. Some of these engineers even report meeting regularly with classmates from high school.

This makes the Taiwanese community in Silicon Valley a very small community. Just as there are close social ties among the American engineers in Silicon Valley (Saxenian 1994), virtually all of the region's Taiwanese engineers report that their community is so tight that "everyone knows everyone else and how their businesses are doing." This can be a double-edged sword: on one hand it means that there is a tremendous amount of informal information exchange and support. Many of these engineers report that they can call on one another at any time and are always willing to help one another out. On the other hand, the fact that word spreads quickly means that reputations can be made or broken very fast as well.

This social solidarity is, of course, strengthened significantly by their status as immigrants sharing a common language and culture in a foreign country. However the trust is not based simply on the cultural or familial ties of an "overseas" Chinese community (Kotkin 1992; Seagrave 1995; Hsing 1996). These social networks are rarely based, for example, on the traditional Chinese family, village, or surname associations. In fact, most of these engineers work alongside other Chinese immigrants, yet they report much closer ties with other Taiwanese than with Chinese from Hong Kong, Mainland China, or other parts of Asia. Rather they are rooted in shared educational and professional experiences and common technological interests.

A variety of organizations were formed in Silicon Valley during the 1970s and 1980s that strengthened social ties among the region's Taiwanese community. The Chinese Institute of Engineers (CIE), a broad-based national technical and professional association, has a very active branch in Silicon Valley that meets regularly for seminars, dinners, and conferences. CIE is active in promoting ties with engineers in Taiwan (and more recently, with Mainland China) as well, and it is a bilingual association that sponsors activities in both Mandarin Chinese and English. There are also many specialist associations that Taiwanese engineers are active in, including the Chinese Software Professional Association (CSPA), the Chinese American Semiconductor Production Association (CASPA), the Association of Taiwanese Engineers of North America, the Chinese-American Computer Association, and specialist associations of Chinese engineers in various fields, from aeronautics to electronic optics to civil and chemical engineering. These Taiwanese organizations are unusually vibrant even for a region that is known for its active associational life. All of them sponsor seminars, monthly dinner meetings, annual conferences, and other social events. On a random Saturday in January, for example, there were expected to be close to 2,000 Taiwanese attending meetings of professional or political organizations in Silicon Valley, including the Annual Banquet for the Chinese Institute of Engineers and the Joint Alumni Associations of Taiwan, the Association of Chinese Computer Companies, and a meeting of a local group supporting Taiwan's independence party.[5]

Finally, social ties among Taiwanese families in Silicon Valley are supported increasingly by the Chinese schools in the region. Most Chinese immigrants in Silicon Valley send their children to Chinese schools so that they learn Mandarin and are exposed to the culture. The children are typically in the classes for several hours every week, during which time the parents have the opportunity to socialize—and, as in Silicon Valley more generally, social talk very frequently turns to business as well.

The formation in the late 1980s of the Monte Jade Science and Technology Association in response to the emergence of economic opportunities in Taiwan further consolidated the professional networks among the local Taiwanese community. A small group of Taiwanese engineers formed Monte Jade in 1989 in order to bring together Chinese technologists in the Bay Area and Taiwan and to promote business cooperation and investment between executives and companies in the two regions. They decided that the language spoken at all of the Association's functions would be Mandarin Chinese, which not only excluded most Americans but also many Chinese, such as those from Hong Kong and Southeast Asia, who do not speak Mandarin.[6] Monte Jade is an independent non-profit organization that now has branches in other regions of the United States as well. Notably, however, the Monte Jade office in Silicon Valley is located in the same office suite as the Science Division of Taiwan's Coordination Council for North American Affairs (the equivalent of a consulate) and the local representatives of the Hsinchu Science-Based Industrial Park—which supports close and ongoing interactions, if not financial support, between Monte Jade and Taiwanese government agencies.

Today Monte Jade is one of the most sophisticated and active business associations in Silicon Valley. According to the organization's brochures, its objective is to "promote the cooperation and the mutual flow of technology and investment between Taiwan and the U.S.," and it has 20,000 individual and corporate members nationwide, including the leading Taiwan and Silicon Valley-based Chinese technology companies. The 1997 Annual Monte Jade Conference in Silicon Valley drew more than 1,000 attendees (virtually all Chinese) and featured the top executives from leading semiconductor companies around the Pacific Rim. In addition to the annual conference, Monte Jade holds monthly dinner meetings, seminars, and a wide variety of unscheduled social events for members and their families.

The role of the Monte Jade Science & Technology Association in promoting business collaboration as well as social interactions among Taiwanese engineers in the U.S. and Taiwan cannot be understated. Not only does Monte Jade provide a key forum for making contacts between Hsinchu and Silicon Valley, but it also actively supports Taiwanese entrepreneurs in both regions. A special committee of the Board of Directors (made up of an earlier generation of Taiwanese engineers, most of whom came to the U.S. during the 1950s and 1960s) offers assistance to members who are considering starting companies regarding corporate formation, growth, and development. It also offers assistance to member firms on the flow of investment funds, technology transfer, and mergers and acquisitions.

During the 1970s and 1980s there were a small number of Chinese engineers who started companies in Silicon Valley. The most successful entrepreneurs and businessmen like David Lee (founder of Qume), David Lam (founder of Lam Research), Winston Chen (CEO of Solectron), and Ta-ling Hsu (investment banker of Hombrecht and Quist Asia Pacific) became important figures in the local community. In the 1990s, the number of Chinese entrepreneurs grew dramatically, with the earlier generation of entrepreneurs serving as role models and providing business advice, contacts, and mentorship to the younger group. In contrast with their predecessors, who were forced to assimilate into the mainstream because the Chinese community at the time was so small, many of these 1990s entrepreneurs started companies with other Chinese engineers.

The active social and professional networks among the Taiwanese community, in addition to the comfort provided by a shared language and culture, provided a multiplicity of opportunities to meet and discuss business. It is not surprising, therefore that many of the immigrants of the 1970s and 1980s founded companies with Taiwanese classmates and friends after having worked for a decade or so in established businesses. Some of the best known Chinese companies in Silicon Valley today, such as Knights Technology, Trident, Opti, and Integrated Silicon Solutions Inc. (ISSI), were started by teams of Taiwanese university or graduate school classmates and friends. Many of these early start-ups also got their initial financing from friends, classmates, and business contacts in Taiwan. And it is perhaps not surprising that some of these companies report that 60–70 per cent of their engineering workforces are Chinese (compared to 20–30 per cent in typical Silicon Valley firms); after all, the informal social networks are also the most important job search networks in Silicon Valley because they allow information about opportunities and reputations to spread quickly. As Opti founder Kenny Liu notes: "You hire the guys who you know because you went to school with them or you worked at the same company together or you see them regularly at church. You also hire people they recommend. Usually these are also the ones you are the most comfortable communicating with."[7]

As a result, while overseas Taiwanese engineers were known in Silicon Valley as good engineers and hard workers during the 1980s, by the mid-1990s they were increasingly recognized as successful entrepreneurs. Entrepreneurs like Kenny Liu and Jimmy Lee (of ISSI) are a far cry from the immigrant entrepreneurs of the sociological literature, which are almost exclusively located in businesses that are marginal to the mainstream economy, such as restaurants, small scale retail stores, and sweatshop manufacturing (Portes 1995; Waldinger et al. 1990; Light and Bonacich 1988). Rather than perpetuating marginality, these skilled Taiwanese entrepreneurs are building a dynamic model of high skill, high tech immigrant entrepreneurship in Silicon Valley. While during the 1980s some faced "glass ceilings" in Silicon Valley's large companies and others were rejected by the mainstream venture capital community, they were able to draw on the social and professional networks of the Taiwanese immigrant community to build dynamic high technology businesses. During the 1990s, these successes were increasingly recognized within Silicon Valley and simultaneously enhanced by internationalization of the professional and social networks.

Building a Transnational Community: Chinese Entrepreneurs Overseas

The accelerated growth of the Taiwanese economy combined with active recruiting efforts on the part of the Taiwanese government spurred a reversal of the "brain drain" in the late 1980s and early 1990s. Taiwanese government offices in Silicon Valley, such as the Institute for Information Industry (III) began to actively woo Taiwanese engineers back to Taiwan. They built databases of engineers and computer scientists that they shared with Taiwanese talent scouts. Government agencies also began to sponsor regular seminars on high-tech career opportunities in Taiwan and placed recruiting ads in the Chinese-language newspapers in the Bay Area. One such ad showed an elephant separated from its herd with the plea "Come Home." Another government agency paid the airfare of permanent returnees (and their families) to Taiwan. Finally, agencies like the Industrial Technology Research Institute (ITRI) regularly invited and financed US-educated Taiwanese engineers to return home to give seminars on their technical expertise—which served not only to transfer technology but also as recruiting opportunities. These interactions also strengthened the transnational networks among Taiwanese in technology industries on both sides of the Pacific.

Lured primarily by economic opportunities in Taiwan and by the active recruitment efforts of the government, as well as the desire to return to families and a familiar culture, engineers began returning to their homeland. Many were simultaneously pushed by the U.S. recession or by the experience of "glass ceilings" in Silicon Valley firms, and pulled by government provision of cheap housing, high salaries, and other forms of government support. The Hsinchu Science-Based Industrial Park became an especially common destination for Silicon Valley returnees because the government offered a wide range of tax incentives and R&D grants, including a five-year exemption from incentive taxes and relief from all import duties from science-based enterprises (Science Park Administration 1994: 3–6). It also provided privileged access to scarce, high quality housing and to the Chinese-American school located on the park grounds. Many US-trained engineers who had worked in (or even helped start) Silicon Valley-based technology companies saw more promising opportunities for entrepreneurship and advancement in Taiwan than the United States.

Approximately 200 engineers and scientists returned to Taiwan each year during the 1980s. By the mid-1990s some 1,000 were returning annually. In 1996 there were more than 2,500 returnees working in Hsinchu alone. Moreover, almost half of the companies in the Hsinchu Science-Based Industrial park (82) in 1996 were started by US-educated engineers. The park administration refers to these returnees as "CEOs"—or Chinese Entrepreneurs Overseas. Many of these returnees in turn continue to actively recruit their former colleagues and friends from Silicon Valley to return to Taiwan. In fact, there is now an association of Silicon Valley returnees that meets regularly in the Hsinchu Science Park (Hsu 1997).

In addition to these permanent returnees to Taiwan, a large and growing population of "astronauts" work in *both* places and spend much of their lives on airplanes. While their families may be based on either side of the Pacific (most often they stay in California because of the lifestyle advantages), these engineers travel between Silicon Valley and Hsinchu once or even twice a month, taking advantage of economic opportunities bridging the two regional economies. This includes a fast-growing group of Taiwanese investors and venture capitalists as well as executives and engineers from companies based in the two regions. Their activities are, of course, only possible because of the improvements in transportation and communications technologies, especially air travel and electronic communications. However, this does not mean they are rootless. These "astronauts," with their dense personal networks and intimate local knowledge of both regions, play a central role in sustaining and coordinating the growing economic linkages between the two regions.

Taiwan's immigrant engineers have thus created a "transnational community"—a community that spans national borders and that boasts as its key assets shared information, trust, and contacts (Portes 1996). In the words of T. Y. Wu, who worked for IBM in Silicon Valley for 18 years before returning to Taiwan to work for UMAX Data Systems: "There's a very small world between Taiwan and Silicon Valley" (cited in Hsu 1997).

As these engineers travel back and forth between the two regions, they carry technological and organizational know-how as well as contacts, capital, and information about new opportunities and new markets. Moreover, this information moves almost as quickly between these distant regions as it does within Hsinchu and Silicon Valley because of the tightness of the social networks. The creation of transnational ties has thus contributed to a dramatic acceleration in the process of learning between the regions. In the words of one Taiwanese engineer: "If you live in the United States its hard to learn what is happening in Taiwan, and if you live in Taiwan its hard to learn what is going on in the U.S. Now that people are going back and forth between Silicon Valley and Hsinchu so much more frequently, you can learn about new companies and new opportunities in both places almost instantaneously."[8]

According to Ron Chwang, President and CEO of Acer America, this continuous two-way interaction between the Hsinchu and Silicon Valley has generated "multiple positive feedbacks" that enhance business opportunities in both regions.[9] In addition to transfers of technology and product ideas, the Taiwanese returnees have accelerated the transfer of engineering skills, organizational know-how and practices, and entrepreneurial models from Silicon Valley to Taiwan. Most entrepreneurs in Hsinchu recruit engineers from among their professional networks in Silicon Valley. Moreover, these individuals bring Silicon Valley organizational models and corporate cultures back to Taiwan. According to You-wen Yau, who returned from the U.S. in 1993 and now works for Taiwan Semiconductor Manufacturing Company (TSMC), the corporate culture of TSMC is more American than Taiwanese (cited in Gargan 1994). This is true of most Hsinchu-based technology companies, which have adopted variants of Silicon Valley incentive schemes like stock options and the orientation toward entrepreneurial achievement. Finally, these Taiwanese businessmen are often far more comfortable than their counterparts from Japan or Korea in setting up R&D labs or branches in Silicon Valley because of their dense social ties in the region. As a result, most of the leading Taiwanese companies have "listening posts" or satellite operations in Silicon Valley, including Acer, Macronix, ISSI, Etron, and Winbond.

Yet the benefits of these ties are not all one way. Chinese entrepreneurs in Silicon Valley are increasingly the recipients of substantial flows of capital from Taiwan. In the 1980s, capital for start-ups was largely acquired informally through friends, family, and business contacts in Taiwan. By the 1990s, as Taiwan's economy boomed, the amount of capital available for investment ballooned as well. In fact, most Taiwanese entrepreneurs in Silicon Valley today report having been approached informally by Taiwanese investors. Moreover, a handful of Taiwanese venture capital firms are currently establishing offices in the region. Estimates place the amount of Taiwanese capital available for investment in Silicon Valley today at over $500 million.[10]

In 1996, the Mount Jade Science & Technology Association held a Venture conference that brought together several dozen potential entrepreneurs from Silicon Valley and venture capitalists from Silicon

Valley, Taiwan, and Japan. The entrepreneurs had an opportunity to present their business plans and to meet privately with the funders. A substantial proportion of the ventures were funded as a result of this conference, and many also gained important advice and mentoring. The event was so popular that it will now become an annual event.

Nor are these one-way flows. Capital also, increasingly, flows back to Taiwan. Hambrecht and Quist's Asia Pacific Venture Fund, led by Ta-lin Hsu who studied electrical engineering at UC Berkeley (Ph.D.) before working at IBM, has been active and successful in funding Taiwan-based startups, taking companies public, and supporting mergers and acquisitions.

Companies started by Taiwanese immigrants in Silicon Valley also benefit from privileged access to state-of-the-art manufacturing capabilities in Hsinchu as well as close ties to the dynamic Taiwanese personal computer industry. Taiwanese entrepreneurs in Silicon Valley can use their professional and social networks to quickly build relationships with both vendors and customers. These engineers typically have classmates and former colleagues working in the leading Taiwanese semiconductor and personal computer companies, which facilitates the rapid formation of business deals and partnerships.

Thus, while Silicon Valley and Hsinchu remain at different levels of development and differently specialized, their interactions are increasingly complementary and mutually beneficial. As long as the U.S. remains the most sophisticated market for technology products where the key customers reside, which seems likely for the foreseeable future, leading edge design and innovation will remain in Silicon Valley. Yet although Taiwanese companies still do not really do basic research, they have greatly enhanced their ability to design, modify and adapt as well as rapidly commercialize technologies developed elsewhere. More and more integrated circuit design as well as manufacturing is being done in Taiwan, for example; and the infrastructure there for manufacturing personal computers is unparalleled. In short, the community of transnational engineers has not simply facilitated a process of technological upgrading in Hsinchu; it has also enhanced business opportunities for Silicon Valley's Chinese start-ups by providing privileged access to capital and to leading Asian customers and vendors. Moreover, because these transnational entrepreneurs have not only the technology and experience, but also the ability to communicate and work effectively in both cultures, they are ideally positioned to coordinate the creation of more formal inter-regional production networks.

Creating Inter-Regional Production Networks

These transnational entrepreneurs are pioneering inter-regional production networks. The trans-Pacific networks extend the traditional model of recruiting U.S. trained engineers or setting up R&D labs as listening posts in Silicon Valley. Companies in Taiwan increasingly take new technologies from Silicon Valley and quickly integrate them into new products. While this initially entailed the simple relocation of standardized mass production, Taiwanese producers are developing increasingly sophisticated design and product development capabilities. As a result, many U.S. firms now rely on Taiwan for components and product design as well as for efficient manufacturing.[11]

What was once a one-way flow of technology and skill from the U.S. to Taiwan has now become a two-way thoroughfare as these two regions become complementary economies. Silicon Valley remains the leader in innovation, new product definition, and technology development. Hsinchu in turn offers high quality, low cost volume production capabilities, product design and improvement, and efficient integration and commercialization. In the words of Fred Cheng, Vice President of Winbond Electronics North America, who has worked in Silicon Valley for close to 20 years, "The best way to start a technology company today is to take the best from each region: this means combining Taiwanese financial and manufacturing strength with Silicon Valley's engineering and technical skill."[12]

Robert Tsao, President and CEO of Taiwan's United Microelectronics Corp. (UMC), describes how his firm is simultaneously spinning-off product divisions to Silicon Valley and establishing joint-ventures between specialist partners on both sides of the Pacific. These consortia typically pair Silicon Valley's leading edge chip design capabilities with Hsinchu's state-of-the-art semiconductor manufacturing processes. Thus, for example, UMC has established three joint ventures with "fabless" U.S. design firms.[13] The first foundry, called United Semiconductor Consortium (USC), joins UMC (with 43 per cent investment of the total US$400 million in the venture) with Silicon Valley-based Alliance Semiconductor (20 per cent) and S3 (25 per cent)—both of which were either founded by Taiwanese or have Taiwanese in key technical or managerial positions. USC, which started production in 1996, guarantees the design firms secure foundry space even in the case of industry-wide capacity shortages, while also insuring UMC full capacity utilization and the capital needed to build the fab. An even more ambitious consortium, United Integrated Circuits

Corporation (UICC), which joins more than eight Silicon Valley design firms (each with 5–10 per cent share in the $600 million fab) with UMC (40 per cent), includes Oak, Trident, Lattice, Opti, ISSI, and ESS—all of which were started by Taiwanese entrepreneurs.

The "fabless" partners in these joint ventures aggressively push their foundries to improve process technologies (because the growing complexity of chips poses more and more manufacturing challenges), while the foundries collaborate closely with their customers to help introduce innovative new products rapidly. Increasingly these relationships thus involve close communication and joint-problem solving between partners who learn from each other while avoiding mutual dependence. The collaboration required to make these partnerships work depends critically on the high levels of trust and local knowledge that exist in the overseas Taiwanese community. Trust and familiarity allow partners to respond quickly to fast changing markets and technologies without the need to precisely specify rights and responsibilities through elaborate contracts or bureaucratic rules.

The case of Platform Technology, a small Silicon Valley start-up founded by Chinese entrepreneur Paul Tien, illustrates the benefits of these cross-Pacific relationships.[14] In 1996, a Taiwanese venture capital firm called Investar invested US$3 million in Platform. Platform was several years old but was struggling to survive in spite of its state-of-the-art pc/audio chip design. The partners at Investar, who had extensive experience and connections both in Silicon Valley and in Taiwan, took Tien to meet executives at the leading personal computer companies in Taipei. Platform quickly became famous in Taiwan and received so many design awards that it became on of the world's leading producers of audio chips. Moreover, Platform was having problems with the manufacturing process at its foundry, Taiwan Semiconductor Manufacturing Corp (TSMC). As a small firm they couldn't get the attention of the giant chip manufacturer. Once again, Investar intervened. In this case, the Investar partners called their friends at TSMC and made sure that Platform's calls were returned and that its problems were addressed immediately.

One year later, Platform was so successful that it posed a major threat to ESS, another Chinese company in Silicon Valley. ESS had historically dominated the pc/audio market. In early 1997 founder Fred Chen called the Investar partner who had previously invested in ESS and asked what he could do to help. As a result, Investar arranged the sale of Platform to ESS. They coordinated a very small, simple acquisition—one that was done completely informally. There were no lawyers involved. In fact there was nothing written. This was the sort of trust-based deal that could only be made by partners who have complete confidence in each other.

The networks that link producers in Silicon Valley and Hsinchu are possible both because of the creation of transnational networks among Taiwanese engineers, and because of the complementarity of the industrial structures of the regional economies. Both are decentralized industrial systems with networks of specialized producers that depend for their success on collaboration with other specialist firms. As a result, both are organized to respond quickly and flexibly to fast changing markets and technologies. It is easier for such specialists to collaborate—even across the Pacific Ocean—than it is to work with large, integrated corporations. In the words of Winbond's Fred Cheng: "The Taiwanese in Silicon Valley can look back to their home country—to Taiwan—to do business. It is easy for small companies to talk to and work with other small companies. Japanese and Korean entrepreneurs in Silicon Valley cannot look back to their home countries because they are all big companies."[15]

This case suggests that localization is not at odds with the globalization of economic activity. Rather, they are mutually reinforcing. Globalization is increasingly a process of integration of products on an international level through collaboration. This is best viewed as a process of recombination or of repeated convergence and divergence in which the firms must first be specialists in order to successfully globalize. Once firms are specialists, they can be better partners to others because specialization facilitates mutually-beneficial collaboration. And the best environments for breeding such specialist firms are the decentralized industrial systems in localities like Silicon Valley and Hsinchu. In this case, a dynamic of reciprocal technological advance can turn the ties between regional economies into positive sum relationships that support ongoing localization of entrepreneurship and innovation.

The successes of the overseas Taiwanese engineers in Silicon Valley during the 1980s and 1990s leveraged the growing strengths of the semiconductor and personal computer businesses in Taiwan. This stage may well have reached its limit, if only because the number of Taiwanese engineering graduate students enrolled in US universities has slowed significantly. However, they were more than replaced by a dramatic increase in the flow of graduate students from Mainland China. China has sent an estimated 240,000 students overseas to study since 1980—and their presence is becoming apparent in engineering programs at places like

Berkeley and Stanford as well as in Silicon Valley's technology businesses. While the new wave of immigrants from the Mainland are, with a few exceptions, not yet well enough established to start their own companies, they are creating their own professional associations and gaining valuable work experience. Many observers predict that if the political situation in China remains stable, this new, younger generation will follow the Taiwanese in building the overseas networks that link Silicon Valley with growing regions in Asia. If this occurs, the developmental consequences could be substantially more impressive than the first wave, given the size of China's labor force and market. Moreover, the Taiwanese are ideally positioned to help orchestrate this transnational connection: like the earlier generations of Chinese in Silicon Valley, they can serve as both role models and mentors for the next generation. Having created the Silicon Valley-Hsinchu connection they are now prepared to help build the bridge between Silicon Valley and Shanghai.

Notes

1. Throughout this paper the term "Hsinchu" is used to refer to the broader region encompassing the Hsinchu Science Park and metropolitan Taipei—an industrial cluster that is roughly comparable in size to Silicon Valley.

2. All of the interviews were conducted in English. While all of the interviewees function fluently in English, I was always accompanied by a Mandarin-speaking assistant. This proved quite helpful for clarification of language and cultural differences.

3. All of the data on the ethnic composition of the Silicon Valley workforce is derived from tabulations of the Public-Use Microdata Sets (PUMS) from the 1990 U.S. Census, which documents employment, industry, occupation and other variables by national origin. The data on Silicon Valley entrepreneurship derived from a special analysis of the Dun & Bradstreet Market Identifiers data for 1996.

4. Interview by author, Shun-lung Chao, August 28, 1996.

5. Interview by author, Gerry Liu, January 22, 1997.

6. While this language requirement has begun to loosen recently, largely to allow second generation immigrants who don't speak Chinese to participate, the membership remains primarily Taiwanese.

7. Interview by author, Kenny Liu, January 22, 1997.

8. Interview by author, C. B. Liaw, August 28, 1996.

9. Interview by author, Ron Chwang, March 25, 1997.

10. Interview by author, Ken Hao, April 15, 1997. By 1994 there were 1378 Taiwanese-

funded companies in California, accounting for 53 per cent of the total amount of $2.45 billion invested by Taiwan in the U.S. Virtually all of the Taiwanese funded companies in Silicon Valley were in computer and electronics businesses. (Investment Commission, Ministry of Economic Affairs, ROC 1996).

11. This is often referred to as the shift from Original Equipment Manufacturing (OEM) to Original Design and Manufacturing (ODM).
12. Interview by author, Fred Cheng, March 25, 1997
13. "Fabless" semiconductor firms do not have their own wafer fabrication facilities (or "fabs"). They specialize in semiconductor design.
14. Interview by author, Herbert Chang, July 22, 1997.
15. Interview by author, Fred Cheng, March 25, 1997.

Appendix 10.1

Interviews in Silicon Valley

Kevin Fong	Partner, Mayfield Fund	Jun.	27, 1994
Miin Wu	President, Macronix International	Feb.	10, 1995
CB Liaw	Product Engineering Mgr., Sun Microsystems	Aug.	28, 1996
Shun-Lung Chao	Staff Engineer, Sun Microsystems	Aug.	28, 1996
Jen-Chang Chou	Director, Science Division, Taiwan Consulate	Sep.	23, 1996
Peter C. Chen	President, Crosslink Semiconductor	Sep.	23, 1996
Jerry Chang	Chairman & CEO, Opti	Jan.	6, 1997
George P. Koo Mng.	Director, International Strategic Alliances	Jan.	9, 1997
Chun P. Chiu	Chairman & CTO, Quality Semiconductor	Jan.	10, 1997
David D. Tsang	President, Oak Technology	Jan.	16, 1997
Denny T. Lee	Chairman, Wellex Corp.	Jan.	16, 1997
Chuck Chan	General Partner, Alpine Ventures	Jan.	21, 1997
Gerald Liu	VP Multimedia Marketing, Trident	Jan.	22, 1997
Kenny Liu	President & CEO, InteGraphics Systems	Jan.	22, 1997
David S. Lee	Chairman, CMC Industries	Jan.	22, 1997
David K. Lam	CEO, Lam Research	Jan.	24, 1997
Pehong Chen	President & CEO, Broadvision	Jan.	24, 1997
Sophia Chen	Manager, The InfoPro Group	Feb.	5, 1997
Peggy Liu	President & CEO, Channel A	Feb.	18, 1997
Doug Tsui	VP Marketing, Precept Software	Feb.	18, 1997
Ling-Tao Wang	President, Tao Research	Feb.	21, 1997
S. M. Jimmy Lee	President & CEO, ISSI	Mar.	5, 1997
Albert Y. C. Yu	Senior VP & Genl Mgr, Intel	Mar.	5, 1997
Fred Cheng	V President, Winbond North America	Mar.	25, 1997
Ronald Chwang	President & CEO, Acer America	Mar.	25, 1997
Pauline Alker	President & CEO, Network Peripherals	Apr.	15, 1997
Jerry Yang	Chief Yahoo, Yahoo!	Apr.	15, 1997
Ken Hao	Principal, Hambrecht & Quist	Apr.	15, 1997
Norman Wu	CEO, Avantos	Apr.	21, 1997
Edward Yang	Group R&D Mgr, Hewlett-Packard Co	Apr.	22, 1997
Jackson Hu	President & CEO, SiRF Technology	Apr.	22, 1997
Peter Lui	Manger, HK Ventures	Apr.	22, 1997

Appendix 10.2

Interviews in Hsinchu

Jeffrey Y. Tang	President, Myson Technology, Inc.	May	13,	1997
K. Y. Han	General Mgr, ISSI	May	13,	1997
Genda J. Hu	General Director, ERSO	May	13,	1997
Huey-Lin Chen	Deputy Director of Planning, ERSO	May	14,	1997
Robert C. Hsieh	Vice Chairman, MICROTEK	May	14,	1997
Nicky C. C. Lu	President & CEO, Etron	May	14,	1997
Ding-Hua Hu	Chairman, Macronix International Co., Ltd.	May	14,	1997
Eric Wang	VP, D-Link Corporation	May	15,	1997
C. S. Ho	Vice Chairman, Mitac	May	15,	1997
Miin Wu	President, Macronix International Co., Ltd.	May	16,	1997
Coe-Yen Nee	President, Highlight Optoelectronics Inc.	May	16,	1997
Kenneth Tai	InveStar	May	16,	1997
Stan Shih	Chairman & CEO, The Acer Group	May	16,	1997
Robert Tsao	Chairman, UMC	May	19,	1997
Steven C. Y. Chang	Assistant VP, Direct Investment Department, China Development Corporation	May	19,	1997
Lisa Lo	Overseas Business Department, China Development Corporation	May	19,	1997
C. David Tsao	Chairman & CEO, ALFA	May	20,	1997
C. T. Wu	President & CEO, National Datacomm Corporation	May	20,	1997
Nasa Tsai	Senior Consultant, Mosel Vitelic Inc.	May	20,	1997
Patrick H. Wang	Chairman, Microelectronics Technology Inc. (Taiyang)	May	21,	1997
Lian-Shen Tung	Director, Division of Investment Service, Science Park Administration	May	21,	1997
Ding-Yuan Yang	President, Winbond Electronics Corp.	May	21,	1997
George Huang	Sr. VP, Acer Incorporated	May	22,	1997
Matthew F. C. Miau	Chairman, Mitac Computers Group	May	22,	1997
Morris Chang	Chairman & President, TSMC	May	22,	1997

Bibliography

Abel, I. and John P. Bonin. 1994. "Financial Sector Reforms in the Economies in Transition." In John P. Bonin and Istvan P. Szekely, eds., *The Development and Reform of Financial Systems in Central and Eastern Europe*, pp. 109–126. Aldershot: E. Elgar.

Aberbach, Joel, David Dollar, and Kenneth Sokoloff, eds. 1994. *The Role of the State in Taiwan's Development*. New York, NY: M.E. Sharpe.

Aeberhard-Hodges. 1996. "Sexual Harassment in Employment: Recent Judicial and Arbitral Trends." *International Labour Review* 135: 499-533.

Abolofia, Mitchell Y. 1996. *Taming the Market*. Chicago: University of Chicago Press.

———. 1997. *Making Markets: Opportunism and Restraint on Wall Street*. Boston, MA: Harvard University Press.

Abrams, Kathryn. 1989. "Gender Discrimination and the Transformation of Workplace Norms." *Vanderbilt Law Review* 42: 447–475.

Abuza, Zachary. 1996. "Vietnam-Taiwan Relations: Convergence and Divergence." *Issues and Studies* 32(7): 109–128.

Adler, Nancy J. 1993. "Competitive Frontiers: Women Managers in the Triad." *International Studies of Management and Organization* 23(2): 3–23.

Agar, Michael H. 1986. *Speaking of Ethnography*. Beverly Hills: Sage.

Agh, Attila. 1996. "From Nomenclatura to Clientura: The Emergence of New Political Elites in East-Central Europe." In G. Pridham and Paul Lewis, eds., *Stabilising Fragile Democracies: Comparing New Party Systems in Southern and Eastern Europe*, pp. 44–68. London: Routledge.

Ahrne, Goran. 1990. *Agency and Organization*. London: Sage.

Alvesson, Mats. 1993. *Cultural Perspectives on Organizations*. Cambridge, England: Cambridge University Press.

———. 1994. "Talking in Organizations. Managing Identity and Impressions in An Advertising Agency." *Organization Studies* 15(4): 535–563.

———. 1995. *Management of Knowledge-Intensive Companies*. Berlin/New York: de Gruyter.

———. 1996. *Communication, Power and Organization*. Berlin/New York: de Gruyter.

Alvesson, Mats and Per Olof Berg, eds. 1992. *Corporate Culture and Organizational Symbolism*.

Berlin/New York: de Gruyter.

Alvesson, Mats and Yvonne Due Billing, eds. 1997. *Understanding Gender and Organization.* London: Sage Publication.

Alvesson, Mats and Ivar Björkman. 1992. *Organisationsidentitet Och Organisationsbyggande: En Studie aveu Industrifdretag.* Lund: Studentlitteratur.

Alvesson, Mats and Stan Deetz. (2000). *Doing Critical Management Research.* London: Sage.

Alvesson, Mats and Kaj Sköldberg. (2000). *Towards a Reflexive Methodology.* London: Sage.

Amburgey, Terry, Dawn Kelly and William Barnett. 1993. "Resetting the Clock: The Dynamics of Organizational Change and Failure." *Administrative Science Quarterly* 38: 51–73.

Amin, Ash and Nigel Thrift. 1994. "Living in the Global." In Ash Amin and Nigel Thrift, eds., *Globalization, Institutions, and Regional Development in Europe,* pp. 1–22. New York, NY: Oxford University Press.

Amsden, Alice H. 1985. "The State and Taiwan's Economic Development." In Peter B. Evans, Dietrich Rueschemeyer and Theda Skocpol, eds., *Bringing the State Back,* in pp. 78–106. New York, NY: Cambridge University Press.

Amsden, Alice H., Jack Kochanowicz and Taylor Lance, eds. 1994. *The Market Meets its Match.* Cambridge, Mass.: Harvard University Press.

Anastassopoulos, Jean-Pierre, Georges Blanc and Pierre Dussauge. 1987. *State-Owned Multinationals.* New York, NY: John Wiley & Sons.

Andriessen, Erik J. H. and Pieter J. D. Drenth. 1984. "Leadership: Theories and models." In Pieter J. D. Drenth, Henk Thierry, Paul J. Willems and Charles J. de Wolff, eds., *Handbook of Work and Organizational Psychology,* vol. 1, pp. 481–520. Chichester: Wiley.

Appruzzese, Vincent J. 1992. "Selected Recent Developments in the EEO Law: The Civil Rights Act of 1991, Sexual Harassment, and the Emerging Role of ADR." *Labor Law Journal* 43: 325–337.

Arrow, Kenneth J. 1974. *The Limits of Organization.* New York, NY: W. W. Norton.

———. 1998. "What Has Economics to Say About Racial Discrimination." *Journal of Economic Perspectives* 12(2): 91–100.

Asplund, Johan. 1980. *Socialpsykologiska Studier.* Stockholm: AVYE/Gebers.

Astley, Graham W. 1985. "Administrative Science as Socially Constructed Truth." *Administrative Science Quarterly* 30(4)(Dec.): 497–513.

Bach, Robert and Demetrious Papademetrious. 1989. "Chapter One: Introduction." In Demetrious Papademetrious, ed., *The Effects of Immigration on the U.S. Economy and Labor Market,* pp. 1–20. Washington, D. C.: U.S. Department of Labor.

Baker, Wayne E. 1990. "Market Networks and Corporate Behavior." *American Journal of Sociology* 6: 589–625.

Baker, Wayne E., Robert R. Faulkner and Gene A. Fisher. 1998. "The Dynamics of Market Institutions." Working Paper. University of Michigan.

Barham, K. and M. Devine, eds. 1990. *The Quest for the International Manager: A Survey of Global Human Resource Strategies.* London: Ashridge Management Guide/Economist Intelligence Unit.

Barrett, Richard E. and Martin King Whyte. 1982. "Dependency Theory and Taiwan: Analysis of a Deviant Case." *American Journal of Sociology* 87(5): 1064–1089.

Bartlett, C. A. and S. Ghoshal, eds. 1992. *Transnational Management: Text, Cases and Readings in Cross-Border Management.* Homewood, IL: Irwin.

Batson, Daniel. 1990. "How Social an Animal: The Human Capacity for Caring." *American Psychologist* 45: 336–346.

Batt, Judy. 1988. *Economic Reform and Political Change in Eastern Europe.* London: Macmillan.

Baum, Joel A. C. and Jane E. Dutton. 1996. "Introduction: The Embeddedness of Strategy." *Advances in Strategic Management* 13: 1–15.

Baum, Joel A. C. and Christine Oliver. 1992. "Institutional Embeddedness and the Dynamics of Organizational Populations." *American Sociological Review* 57: 540–559.

Baxter, Jr. Ralph H. and Lynne C. Hermle, eds. 1989. *Sexual Harassment in the Workplace: A Guide to the Law.* New York, NY: Executive Enterprises Publications.

Bazerman, Max and Margaret A. Neale. 1983. "Heuristics in Negotiation: Limitations to Dispute Resolution Effectiveness." *Negotiating in Organizations*, edited by Max Bazerman and R. J. Lewicki. Beverly Hills, Conn.: Sage.

Bell, Daniel. 1973. *The Coming of Post-Industrial Society: A Venture in Social Forecasting.* New York, NY: Basic Books.

Bello, Walden F. and Stephanie Rosenfeld. 1990. *Dragons in Distress: Asia's Miracle Economies in Crisis.* San Francisco: The Institute of Food and Development Policy.

Berend, Ivan. T. 1990. *The Hungarian Economic Reforms 1953–1988.* Cambridge, England: Cambridge University Press.

Berger, Suzanne and Ronald Dore. 1996. *National Diversity and Global Capitalism.* Ithaca, NY: Cornell University Press.

Berle, Adolf A., Jr. and Gardiner C. Means, eds. 1932. *The Modern Corporation and Private Property.* New York: Commerce Clearing House, Inc. Cited in Blair (1995).

Bernstein, Richard J. 1983. *Beyond Objectivism and Relativism.* Oxford: Basil Blackwell.

Biggart, Nicole Woolsey. 1990. "Charismatic Capitalism: Direct Selling Organizations in the USA and Asia." In Stewart R. Clegg and S. Gordon Redding, eds., *Capitalism in Contrasting Cultures*, pp. 409–428. Berlin: de Gruyter.

Blair, Margaret M. 1995. *Ownership and Control: Rethinking Corporate Governance for the Twenty-First Century.* Washington, D.C.: The Brookings Institution.

Bluestone, Barry and Bennett Harrison. 1982. *The Deindustrialization of America: Plant Closings, Community Abandonment, and the Dismantling of Basic Industry*. New York, NY: Basic Books.

Boltanski, Luc. 1990. *Die Führungskräfte: Die Entstehung einer sozialen Gruppe (Managers: The Emergence of a Social Group)*. Frankfurt a.M./New York: Campus.

Bond, Michael Harris and Geert Hofstede. 1990. "The Cash Value of Confucian Values." In Stewart R. Clegg and S. Gordon Redding, eds., *Capitalism in Contrasting Cultures*, pp. 383–390. Berlin: de Gruyter.

Bonifert, Donat. 1987. *A berszabalyozas. Hogyan Kezdodott? Hova jutott? Merre tart?* (Wage Regulation. How did it start? How far did it get? Where is it going?). Budapest: Kozgazdasag es Jogi KonyvKiado.

Bonin, J. P. and M. E. Schaffer. 1995. "Banks, Firms, Bad Debts and Bankruptcy in Hungary 1991–94." Discussion Paper No. 234. London: CEPR.

Borg, Malcolm and Anne-Wil Harzing. 1995. "Composing an International Staff." In Anne-Wil Harzing and Joris Van Ruysseveldt, eds., *International Human Resource Management*, pp. 179–204. London, Thousand Oaks, New Delhi: Sage.

Boutin, J. D. Kenneth. 1997. "Cross-Strait Trade and Investment: Economic and Security Implications for the Republic of China." *Issues & Studies* 33(12): 70–93.

Boyacigiller, N. and N. Adler. 1991. "The Parochial Dinosaur: the Organizational Sciences in a Global Context." *Academy of Management Review* 16: 262–290.

Braudel, Fernald. 1979. *The Wheels of Commerce: Civilization and Capitalism 15–18th Century*. Vol. 2. New York: Harper and Row.

Bravo, Ellen and Ellen Cassedy. 1992. *The 9 to 5 Guide to Combating Sexual Harassment*. New York, NY: John Wiley & Sons, Inc.

Bryson, Cheryl B. 1990. "The Internal Sexual Harassment Investigation: Self-Evaluation without Self-Incrimination." *Employee Relations Law Journal* 15: 551–562.

Bunce, Valerie and Mária Csanádi. 1993. "Uncertainty in the Transition: Post Communism in Hungary." *East European Politics and Societies* 7(2): 240–275.

Burawoy, Michael and János Lukács. 1985. "Mythologies of Work: A Comparison of Firms in State Socialism and Advanced Capitalism." *American Sociological Review* 50(6): 723–737.

———. 1992. *The Radiant Past: Ideology and Reality in Hungary's Road to Capitalism*. Chicago: Chicago University Press.

Bureau of National Affairs. 1988. *Corporate Affairs: Nepotism, Office Romance and Sexual Harassment*. Washington, D.C.: BNA.

Bureau of Public Health, Executive Yuan. 1995. *Yiliaoxingwei Guochengzhong Xingsaorao Shengxing Qingxing Diaocho (A Survey on the Prevalence of Sexual Harassment in the Process of Medical Treatments)*. Taipei: Bureau of Public Health, Executive Yuan.

Burns, Sarah E. 1994–95. "Evidence of a Sexually Hostile Workplace: What Is It and How Should It Be Assessed after *Harris v. Forklift Systems, Inc.*?" *New York University Review of*

Law and Social Change 21: 357–431.

Burt, Ronald S. 1992. *Structural Holes: The Social Structure of Competition*. Boston, MA: Harvard University Press.

———. 1997. "Customization or Conformity: An Institutional and Network Perspective on the Content and Consequences of TQM Adoption." *Administrative Science Quarterly* 42: 339–365.

Burt, Ronald S. and Debbie S. Carlton. 1989. "Another Look at the Network Boundaries of American Markets." *American Journal of Sociology* 95(3): 723–753.

Butler, J. S. and Robert Moffitt. 1982. "A Computationally Efficient Quadrature Procedure for the One-Factor Multinomial Probit Model." *Econometrica* 50: 761–764.

Calás, Marta and Linda Smircich. 1988. "Reading Leadership as a Form of Cultural Analysis." In J. G. Hunt et al., eds., *Emerging Leadership Vistas*. Lexington, Mass: Lexington Books.

Campbell, John L., J. Rogers Hollingsworth and Leon N. Lindberg, eds. 1991. *Governance of the American Economy*. Cambridge, England : Cambridge University Press.

Carrillo, Maria M. 1992–93. "Hostile Environment Sexual Harassment by a Supervisor under Title VII: Reassessment of Employer Liability in Light of the Civil Rights Act of 1991." *Columbia Human Rights Law Review* 24: 41–92.

Castells, Manuel and Peter Hall, eds. 1994. *Technopoles of the World: The Making of Twentieth Century Industrial Complexes*. London: Routledge.

Castles, Stephan and Mark Miller, eds. 1993. *The Age of Migration*. Basingstoke-London: McMillan.

Chandler, Alfred D., Jr. 1977. *The Visible Hand: The Managerial Revolution in American Business*. Cambridge, MA: Harvard University Press.

Chang, Ching-Feng. 1995. "Gongzuo: Maianmian Cihen, Keyoujieqi?— Nüxing Gongzuo Kunjing Zhi Pouxi" (Work: Is There Any Stop to This Long Lasting Hatred? A Thorough Analysis of the Dilemma of Working Conditions Faced by Women). In Yu-Shiu Liu, ed., *Taiwan Funüchujing Baipishu: 1995 (White Paper on Current Conditions of Women in Taiwan: 1995)*, pp. 147–180. Taipei: China Times Publishing Co.

Chao, Ai-Lan. 1984. "Funü Xingsaorao Wenjuandiaocho Chububaogao" (Preliminary Report on the Survey of Sexual Harassment Against Women). *Funü Xinzhi (New Knowledge for Women)* 25: 19–22.

Chen, Chich-Hsuan. 1994. *Xieli Wangluo yu Shenghuo Jiegou (Subcontracting Network and Life Structures)*. Taipei: Linking Publishing Company.

Chen, Dun-Sheng and Sue-Ching Joe. 1996. "Ziben yu Jishu Mijiwangluoshi Zuzhiyanjiu: yi Jitidianluchanye Weili" (Patterns of Inter-organizational Relationships in Technology and Capital Intensive Industries: The Case of Taiwan's IC Industry). Paper presented at the International Conference on Economic Governance and Flexible Production in East Asia, organized by Social Science Research Council, USA, and Institute of

Sociology and Anthropology, National Tsing-Hwa University, Oct.

Chen, Je-Chan. 1994. *Daxuesheng Xingsaorao, Qinhaijingyan Texing Zhi Yanjiubaogao (A Research Report on the Experiences of College Students on Sexual Harassment and Sexual Violence).* Taipei: Foundation of Modern Women.

Chen, Shih-Meng, Chung-Cheng Lin, C. Y. Chu, Ching-hsi Chang, Jun-ji Shih and Jin-Tan Liu. 1991. *Disintegrating KMT-State Capitalism: A Closer Look at Privatizing Taiwan's State- and Party-Owned Enterprises.* Taipei: Taipei Society.

Chen, Tain-Jy and Wen-Juan Wang. 1994. "Waizichangshang de Bentuhau: Meiri Dianzichang de Bijiaoyanjiu" (Localization of Foreign Firms: Comparative Studies of American and Japanese Electronics Factories). *Chanyejiegou yu Gongpingjiaoyifa (Industrial Structures and The Fair Trade Bill)*, pp. 231–257. Taipei: Sun Yat–Sen Institute for Social Science and Philosophy, Academia Sinica.

Chen, Xiangming. 1996. "Taiwan Investments in China and Southeast Asia." *Asian Survey* 36(5): 447–467.

Chia, Robert. 1995. "From Modern to Postmodern Organizational Analysis." *Organization Studies* 16(4): 579–604.

Chiao, Cing-Kae. 1993. "Gongzuochangsuo Xingsaorao Zai Meiguo Suo Yinqi Zhi Faluzhongyi (Shang) (Xia)" (Legal Controversies over Sexual Harassment in the Workplace in the United States (Part One)(Part Two)). *Meiguo Yuecan (America Monthly)* 8(8),(9): 101–111, 67–75.

———. 1994. "Gongzuochangsuo Xingsaorao Wenti Zai Meiguo Zhi Zuixin Fazhangqushi" (Recent Developments in Sexual Harassment in the Workplace in the United States). Laoziguanxi Yuecan (Industrial Relations Monthly) 146: 25–32.

———. 1995. "Gongzuochangsuo Xingsaorao Jiqi Fangzhizhidao" (Sexual Harassment in the Workplace and Its Prevention). In Chi-Hwa Ma, ed., *Xiandaijiating Yu Shehuifazhang (Modern Family and Social Development)*, pp. 101–111. Taipei: Chun-Hwa Association and Public Order Association.

———. 1996a. "Meiguo Lianbang Zuigaofayuan Dui Gongzuochangsuo Xingsaorao Zuixinpanjue Zhi Yanjiu" (Study on the Most Recent U.S. Supreme Court Decision on the Issue of Sexual Harassment in the Workplace). *Meiguo Yuecan (America Monthly)* 11(3): 93–105.

———. 1996b. "Meiguo Liangxing Gongzuopingding Zhidu Zhi Yanjiu" (A Study on Gender Equality in the Employment System in the United States). In Cing-Kae Chiao, ed., Oumei Liangxing Gongzuopingding Zhidu Zhi Bijiaoyanjiu (A Comparative Study of Gender Equality in the Employment Systems in Europe and the United States), pp. 85–146. Taipei: Institute of European and American Studies, Academia Sinica.

———. 1997a. *Gongzuochangsuo Xingsaorao Wenti Zai Meiguo Suo Yinqi Zhi Faluzhongyi (Legal Issues Concerning Sexual Harassment in the Workplace in the United States).* Taipei: Industrial Relations Associations of the Republic of China.

———. 1997b. "Meiguo Zuigaofayuan Dui Gongzuochangsuo Xingsaorao Zhengyi Zhi

Zuixinpanjue—*Harris v. Forklift Systems, Inc.* Yian Zhi Jiexi" (Study on the Most Recent Supreme Court Decision on Sexual Harassment in the Workplace in the United States—An Analysis of the Harris v. Forklift Systems, Inc. Case). Paper presented at Meiguo Zuigaofayuan Zhongyao Panjue Zhi Yanjiu: 1993–1995 (The Conference on Important Decision of the U.S. Supreme Court: 1993–1995), Institute of European and American Studies, Academia Sinica, Taipei, Taiwan (in draft form).

———. 1999. "Gongzuochangsuo Xingsaorao Zai Wuguo Suoyinqi Zhi Faluzhengyi—Jianlin Meiguo Zhidu Suonegtigong Zhi Qishi" (Legal Issues Concerning Sexual Harassment in the Workplace in Taiwan—Lesson from the United States). Taipei: Workers' Education Association of R.O.C..

Chin, Ku-Sup, In-Jin Yoon and David Smith. 1996. "Immigrant Small Business and International Economic Linkage: A Case of the Korean Wig Business in Los Angeles, 1968–1977." *International Migration Review* 30(2): 485–510.

China Institute of Industrial Relations. 1996. *Shishi Nannü Gongzuopingdingfa Huanjing Zhi Diaocho Yu Pinggu (An Investigation and Evaluation of the Environment for Implementing Gender Equality in the Employment Law)*. Taipei: Council of Labor Affairs, Executive Yuan.

China Petroleum Corporation. 1995. *The 1996 Annual Budget Report*. Taipei: The Execute Yuan.

———. 1996. *The 1997 Annual Budget Report*. Taipei: The Execute Yuan.

———. 1997. *The 1998 Annual Budget Report*. Taipei: The Execute Yuan.

China Steel Corporation. 1995. *The 1996 Annual Budget Report*. Taipei: The Execute Yuan.

Chu, Wan-wen. 1995. "Jinkou Tidai Yu Chukou Daoxiang Chengzhang: Taiwan Shihuaye Zhi Yanjiu" (Import-Substitution and Export-Led Growth: A Study of Taiwan's Petrochemical Industry). *Taiwan Shehui Yanjiu Jikan (A Radical Quarterly in Social Studies)* 18 (Feb.): 39–69.

Chung-Hua Institution for Economic Research. 1991. "The Evaluation of Chinese Steel Corporation Investment in Malaysian Steel Project." Research Paper Vol. 1. Taipei: Chung-Hua Institution for Economic Research.

Cieslik, Andrzej. 1996. "Foreign Direct Investment in Central Europe's Transition: Early Results." Economic Discussion Papers No. 28. Faculty of Economic Sciences, University of Warsaw, Warsaw.

Clegg, Stewart R. 1990. *Modern Organizations: Organization Studies in the Postmodern World*. London: Sage.

Clegg, Stewart R., Winton Higgins and Tony Spybey. 1990. "'Post-Confucianism' Social Democracy and Economic Culture." In Stewart R. Clegg and S. Gordon Redding, eds., *Capitalism in Contrasting Cultures*, pp. 31–78. Berlin: de Gruyter.

Clement, Hermann. 1995. "Integrations-und Desintegrationstendenzen in Osteuropa und der GUS" (Trends of Integration and Disintegration in Eastern Europe and in the Commonwealth of Independent States). Working Paper No. 186. Munich: Osteuropa-Institut.

Clement, Hermann, Richard Frensch, Michael Knogler, Wolfgang Quaisser and Alexei Sekarev. 1995. "Wirtschaftsentwicklung in den Ländern Mittel-und Osteuropas" (Economic Development in the Countries of Central and Eastern Europe). Working Paper No. 178. Munich: Osteuropa-Institut.

Clifford, James and George E. Marcus, eds. 1986. *Writing Culture*. Berkeley: University of California Press.

Coase, R. H. 1937. "The Nature of the Firm." *Economica* 4: 386–405.

———. 1991. "The Nature of the Firm: Influence." In Oliver Williamson and Sidney Winter, eds., *The Nature of the Firm*, pp. 61–74. Oxford: Oxford University Press.

Coleman, James S. 1988. "Social Capital in the Creation of Human Capital." *American Journal of Sociology* 94: S95–S120.

Collins, Randal. 1988. "The Micro Contribution to Macro Sociology." *Sociological Theory* 6(2) (Fall): 242–253.

———. 1999. "The multiple fronts of economic sociology." Guest Editorial for March 8, 1999, ECONSOC Listserver.

Comisso, Ellen. 1996. "Book Review on Peter Evans' Embedded Autonomy." *Journal of Comparative Economics* 23(71): 339–341.

Commission of the European Communities. 1996. *Consultation of Management and Labour on the Prevention of Sexual Harassment at Work*. Brussels: Commission of the European Communities.

Commerce Clearing House. 1991. *Sexual Harassment Manual for Managers and Supervisors: How to Prevent and Resolve Sexual Harassment Complaints in the Workplace*. Chicago: CCH.

Connell, Dana S. 1991. "Effective Sexual Harassment Policies: Unexpected Lessons form Jacksonville Shipyards." *Employee Relations Law Review* 17: 191–206.

Cook, Paul and Colin Kirkpatrick. 1997. "Globalization, Regionalization and Third World Development." *Regional Studies* 31(1): 55–66.

Cotta, M. 1996. "Structuring the New Party Systems after the Dictatorship: Coalitions, Alliances, Fusions and Splits during the Transition and Post-Transition Stages." In Geoffrey Pridham and Paul Lewis, eds., *Stabilising Fragile Democracies*, pp. 69–99. London: Routledge.

Council of Labor Affairs, Executive Yuan. 1996. *Maixiang 21 Shiyi Laodongzhengco Baipishu (White Paper on Labor Policies Entering into the 21st Century)*. Taipei: Council of Labor Affairs, Executive Yuan.

Crawford, Beverly. 1995. "Post-Communist Political Economy: A Framework for the Analysis of Reform." In Beverly Crawford, ed., *Markets, States and Democracy*, pp. 3–42. Boulder, Colo.: Westview Press.

Crouch, Colin and Wolfgang Streeck. 1997. *Political Economy of Modern Capitalism: Mapping Convergence and Diversity*. London: Sage Publications.

Csaba, Laszlo. 1993. "Economic Consequences of Soviet Disintegration for Hungary." In István P. Székely and David M. G. Newbery, eds., *Hungary: An Economy in Transition*, pp. 27–43. Cambridge, England: Cambridge University Press.

———. 1995. *The Capitalist Revolution in Eastern Europe*. Aldershot: Edward Elgar.

Csepeli, Gyorgy and Elte A. Orkeny. 1992. *Ideology and Political Beliefs in Hungary*. London: Pinter.

Cumings, Bruce. 1984. "The Origins and Development of the Northeast Asian Political Economy: Industrial Sectors, Product Cycles, and Political Consequences." *International Organization* 38(1): 1–40.

Czaban, Laszlo and Whitley, Richard. 1998. "The Transformation of Work Systems in Emergent Capitalism: The Case of Hungary." *Work, Employment and Society* 12: 1–26.

Dabrowski, M. 1994. "The Role of the Government in Postcommunist Economies." In Laszlo Csaba, ed., *Privatisation, Liberalisation and Destruction*. Aldershot: Dartmouth.

Dacin, M. Tina, Mark J. Ventresca, and Brent D. Beal. 1999. "The Embeddedness of Organizations: Dialogue and Directions." *Journal of Management* 25(3).

Daily, Catherine M. and Dan R. Dalton. 1994. "Bankruptcy and Corporate Governance : The Impact of Board Composition and Structure." *Academy of Management Journal* 37: 1603–1617.

Daniels, John D. and Lee H. Radebaugh. 1995. *International Business: Environments and Operations*. 7th ed. New York, NY: Addison-Wesley Publishing Company.

Daviddi, Renzo. 1993. "Discussion of Part One." In István P. Székely and David M. G. Newbery, eds., *Hungary: An Economy in Transition*, pp. 70–74. Cambridge, England: Cambridge University Press.

Davis, Gerald F. and Mark S. Mizruchi. 1999. "The Money Center Cannot Hold: Commercial Banks in the U.S. System of Governance." *Administrative Science Quarterly* 44(2): 215-239.

Davis-Blake, Alison and Brian Uzzi. 1993. "Determinants of Employment Externalization: A Study of Temporary Workers and Independent Contractors." *Administrative Science Quarterly* 38: 195–223.

Deetz, Stanley. 1992. *Democracy in an Age of Corporate Colonization: Developments in Communication and the Politics of Everyday Life*. Albany: State University of New York Press.

———. 1994. "The Micro-Politics of Identity Formation in the Workplace: the Case of a Knowledge-Intensive Firm." *Human Studies* 17: 1–22.

———. 1996. "Describing Differences in Approaches to Organization Science: Rethinking Burrell and Morgan and their Legacy." *Organization Science* 7(2) (Mar.–Apr.): 190–207.

Denzin, Norman and Yvonna S. Lincoln, eds. 1994. *Handbook of Qualitative Research*. Thousand Oaks: Sage.

Department of Labor Affairs of Taiwan Provincial Government. 1994. *Taiwansheng*

Laogongshenghuo Zhuangkuang Diaocho Baogao (Reports on Survey and Analysis of Living Conditions of Workers in Taiwan Province). Nantow: Taiwan Provincial Government.

Deyo, Frederic C. 1987. *The Political Economy of the New Asian Industrialism.* Ithaca, NY: Cornell University Press.

Dicken, Peter, Mats Forgren and Anders Malmberg. 1994. "The Local Embeddedness of Transnational Corporations." In Ash Amin and Nigel Thrift, eds., *Globalization, Institutions, and Regional Development in Europe,* pp. 23–45. New York, NY: Oxford University Press.

DiMaggio, Paul. 1994. "Culture and Economy." pp. 27–57 in *Handbook of Economic Sociology,* edited by Neil J. Smelser and Richard Swedberg. Princeton: Princeton University Press.

———. 1997. "Culture and Cognition." *Annual Review of Sociology* 23: 263–89.

DiMaggio, Paul and Walter W. Powell. 1983. "The Iron Cage Revisited: Institutional Isomorphism and Collective Rationality in Organizational Fields." *American Sociological Review* 48: 147–160.

Dobak, M. and E. Tari. 1996. "Evolution of Organisational Forms in the Transition Period of Hungary." *Journal for East European Management Studies* 1: 7–35.

Dore, Ronald. 1983. "Goodwill and the Spirit of Market Capitalism." *British Journal of Sociology* 34: 459–482.

Duan, Cheng-Pu, ed. 1992. "Waiguoziben yu Huaqiaoziben" (Foreign Capital and Overseas Chinese Capital). Taiwan Zhanhou Jingji (Taiwan's Economy after the Second World War), pp. 235–272. Taipei: Ren Jian Chu Ban She.

Dunning, John H. 1993a. "International Direct Investment Patterns." In Lars Oxelheim, ed., *The Global Race for Foreign Direct Investment: Prospects for the Future,* pp. 107–132. New York, NY: Springer-Verlag.

———. 1993b. *Multinational Enterprises and the Global Economy.* Reading, MA: Addison Wesley.

———. 1995. "The Role of Foreign Direct Investment in a Globalizing Economy." *Banca Nazionale del Lavoro Quarterly (BNL) Review* 193: 125–144.

Dyer, Jeffrey H. 1997. "Improving Performance by Transforming Arms-Length Relationships to Supplier Partnerships: The Chrysler Case." *Organization Science* (in press).

Dyker, D. A. 1990. *Yugoslavia: Socialism, Development and Debt.* London: Routledge.

Eagly, Alice H. and Blair T. Johnson. 1990. "Gender and Leadership Style: A Meta-Analysis." *Psychological Bulletin* 108(2): 233–256.

Ebers, Mark. 1995. "The Framing of Organizational Cultures." *Research in the Sociology of Organizations* 13: 129–170.

Ehn, Billy and Orvar Löfgren, eds. 1982. *Kulturanalys.* Lund: Liber.

Estrich, S. 1991. "Sex at Work." *Stanford Law Review* 43: 813–861.

European Bank for Reconstruction and Development. (EBRD). 1997. *Transition Report 1996*. London: EBRD.

European Industrial Relations Review. 1997. "Sexual Harassment at the Workplace, Part One." *European Industrial Relations Review* 287: 13-18.

———. 1998. "Sexual Harassment at the Workplace, Part Two." *European Industrial Relations Review* 288: 25-30.

Evans, Paul. 1990. "Canada and Taiwan: A Forty-Year Survey." *Transactions of the Royal Society of Canada* 6(1): 165-188.

Evans, Peter B. 1979. *Dependent Development: The Alliance of Multinational, State, and Local Capital in Brazil*. Princeton, NJ: Princeton University Press.

———. 1989. "Predatory, Developmental, and Other Apparatuses: A Comparative Political Economy Perspective on the Third World State." *Sociological Forum* 4(4): 561–587.

———. 1995. *Embedded Autonomy: States & Industrial Transformation*. Princeton, NJ: Princeton University Press.

Fama, Eugene. 1980. "Agency Problems and the Theory of the Firm." *Journal of Political Economy* 88: 288–307.

Federal Personnel Management Institute, Inc. 1989. *The Federal Managers' Guide to Preventing Sexual Harassment*. Huntsville, AL: Federal Personnel Management Institute, Inc.

Feldman, Martha S. and James G. March. 1981. "Information in Organizations as Signal and Symbol." *Administrative Science Quarterly* 26(2) (June): 171–186.

Ferner, Anthony. 1997. "Country of Origin Effects and Human Resource Management in Multinational Companies." *Journal of Human Resource Management* 7(1): 19–32.

Figyelo (Observer). 1995. *The Largest Hungarian Companies*. Budapest: Figyelo.

Filtzer, Don. 1992. "Economic Reform and Production Relations in Soviet Industry, 1986–90." In Chris Smith and Paul Thompson, eds., *Labour in Transition*, pp. 110–148. London: Routledge.

Fligstein, Neil. 1990. *The Transformation of Corporate Control*. Cambridge: Harvard University Press.

———. 1996. "Markets As Politics: A Political-Cultural Approach to Market Institutions." *American Sociological Review* 61: 656–73.

Fligstein, Neil and Robert Freeland. 1995. "Theoretical and Comparative Perspectives on Corporate Organization." *Annual Review of Sociology* 21: 21–43.

Fligstein, Neil and Iona Mara-Drita. 1996. "How to Make a Market: Reflections on the Attempt to Create a Single Market in the European Union." *American Journal of Sociology* 102: 1–33.

Formosa Cultural and Educational Foundation. 1995. *1995 Nian Taiwan Funü Dongxiang Minyidiaocho Fenxibaogao (A Report on the Analysis of Public Opinion on the Trends of Women in Taiwan in 1995)*. Taipei: Formosa Cultural and Educational Foundation.

Franko, Lawrence G. 1976. *The European Multinationals*. Stanford, Conn.: Greylock Publishers.

Fraser, Nancy and Linda Nicholson. 1988. "Social Criticism without Philosophy: an Encounter between Feminism and Postmodernism." *Theory, Culture and Society* 5: 373–394.

Free China Review. 1996. Vol. 46(11).

Freeland, Robert. 1996. "Theoretical Logic and Predictive Specificity: Reply to Shanley." *American Journal of Sociology* 102: 537–541.

Fröbel, Folker, Jürgen Heinrichs and Otto Kreye, eds. 1980. *The New International Division of Labour*. New York, NY: Cambridge University Press.

Frost, Peter. J. 1987. "Power, Politics, and Influence." In Frederic M. Jablin, Linda L. Putnam, Karlene H. Robert and Lyman W. Porter, eds., *Handbook of Organizational Communication: An Interdisciplinary Perspective*. Newbury Park: Sage.

Frost, Peter J., Larry F. Moore, Meryl R. Louis, Craig C. Lundberg and Joanne Martin, eds. 1991. *Reframing Organizational Culture*. Newbury Park: Sage.

Frydman, R. and A. Rapaczynski. 1993. "Evolution and Design in the East European Transition." In M. Baldassarri, L. Paganetto and E. S. Phelps, eds., *Privatisation Processes in Eastern Europe*. London: Macmillan.

Futo, Peter, Dylan Jones-Evans, David Kirby, Stefan Kwiatkowski and Joachim Schwalbach. 1994. "Strategic Partnering: The Development of Technical Consultancy in Hungary." Paper presented at the Conference of the European Association for the Study of Science and Technology and Change: New Theories, Realities and Institutions, Budapest.

Gabrisch, Hubert. 1995. "Ausländische Direktinvestitionen in Mittel-und Osteuropa werden unterschätzt" (Over-Estimated Direct Foreign Investments in Central and Eastern Europe). Wirtschaft im Wandel (Economy in Transition) 2: 3–7.

Gargan, Edward. 1994. "High-Tech Taiwanese Come Home." *New York Times* 143 (July 19): C1.

Garrett, Geoffrey and Peter Lange. 1995. "Internationalization, Institutions, and Political Change." *International Organization* 49(4): 627–655.

Geertz, Clifford. 1973. *The Interpretation of Cultures*. New York: Basic Books.

Gereffi, Gary. 1989. "Rethinking Development Theory: Insights from East Asia and Latin America." *Sociological Forum* 4(4): 505–533.

———. 1995. "Global Production Systems and Third World Development." In Barbara Stallings, ed., *Global Change, Regional Response: The New International Contest of Development*, pp. 100–142. New York, NY: Cambridge University Press.

Gereffi, Gary and Mei-Lie Pan. 1994. "The Globalization of Taiwan's Garment Industry." In Enda Bonacich, ed., *Global Production: The Apparel Industry in the Pacific Rim*, pp. 126–146. Philadelphia: Temple University.

Gereffi, Gary and Miguel Korzeniewicz, eds. 1994. *Commodity Chains and Global Capitalism.* New York, NY: Praeger.

Gergen, Kenneth. 1978. "Toward Generative Theory." *Journal of Personality and Social Psychology* 31: 1344–1360.

Gerlach, Michael L. 1992a. *Alliance Capitalism.* Berkeley, CA: University of California.

———. 1992b. "The Japanese Corporate Ntework: A Blockmodel Analysis." *Administrative Science Quarterly* 37: 105-139.

Gerschenkron, Alexander. 1962. *Economic Backwardness in Historical Perspective: A Book of Essays.* Cambridge, MA: The Belknap Press of Harvard University Press.

Gersick, Kelin E., John A. Davis, Marion McCollom Hampton and Ivan Lansberg, eds. 1997. *Generation to Generation: Life Cycles of the Family Business.* Cambridge, MA: Harvard Business School Press.

Ghoshal, Sumantra and Peter Moran. 1996. "Bad for Practice: A Critique of Transaction Cost Theory." *The Academy of Management Review* 21(1): 13–47.

Giddens, Anthony. 1984. *The Constitution of Society.* Berkeley, CA: University of California Press.

Globokar, Tatjana. 1997. "Eastern Europe Meets West: An Empirical Study on French Management in a Slovenian Plant." In Sonja A. Sackmann, ed., *Cultural Complexity in Organizations*, pp. 72–86. London: Sage.

Gold, Bela. 1982. "CAM Sets New Rules for Production." *Harvard Business Review* 60(6): 88–94.

Gold, Thomas B. 1981. "Dependent Development in Taiwan." Ph.D. diss., Department of Sociology, Harvard University.

———. 1986. *State and Society in the Taiwan Miracle.* Armonk, NY: M.E. Sharpe, Inc.

———. 1988. "Entrepreneurs, Multinationals, and the State." In Edwin A. Winckler and Susan Greenhalgh, eds., *Contending Approaches to the Political Economy of Taiwan*, pp. 175–205. Armonk, NY: M. E. Sharpe Inc.

Goldberg, Michael A. 1985. *The Chinese Connection.* Vancouver: University of British Columbia Press.

Goldberg, Victor. 1980. "Relational Exchange: Economics and Complex Contracts." In Louis Putterman and Randall Kroszner, eds., *The Economic Nature of the Firm*, pp. 72–77. Cambridge, England: Cambridge University Press.

Gordon, David M. 1995. "The Global Economy: New Edifice or Crombling Foundations." In Bryan R. Roberts, Robert G. Cushing and Charles Wood, eds., *The Sociology of Development*, vol. 1, pp. 352–392. Brookfield, U.S.: Edward Elgar Publishing Company.

Gort, Michael. 1963. "Analysis of Stability and Change in Market Shares." *Journal of Political Economy* 71(1): 51–63.

Gourevitch, Peter Alexis. 1996. "Squaring the Circle: the Domestic Sources of International

Cooperation." *International Organization* 50(2): 349–373.

Grancelli, Bruno. 1995. "Modernising Post-Soviet Management: A Comparative View." In Bruno Grancelli, ed., *Social Change and Modernisation: Lessons from Eastern Europe*. Berlin: de Gruyter.

Granovetter, Mark. 1973. "The Strength of Weak Ties." *American Journal of Sociology* 78(6): 1360–1380.

———. 1985. "Economic Action and Social Structure: The Problem of Embeddedness." *American Journal of Sociology* 91(3): 481–510.

———. 1993. "The Nature of Economic Relationships." In Richard Swedberg, ed., *Explorations in Economic Sociology*, pp. 3–41. New York, NY: Russell Sage.

———. 1994. "Business Groups." In Neil J. Smelser and Richard Swedberg, eds., *The Handbook of Economic Sociology*, pp. 453–475. Princeton, NJ: Princeton University Press.

Grant, David, Tom Keenoy and Cliff Oswick. 1998. "Organizational Discourse of Diversity, Dichotomy and Multi-Disciplinarity." In David Grant, Tom Keenoy and Cliff Oswick eds., *Discourse and Organization*. London: Sage.

Greif, Avner. 1994. "Cultural Beliefs and the Organization of Society." *Journal of Political Economy* 102: 912–50.

Gronn, Peter C. 1983. "Talk as the Work: The Accomplishment of School Administration." *Administrative Science Quarterly* 28(1) (Mar.): 1–21.

Guillen, Mauro F. 1994. *Models of Management: Work, Authority, and Organization in a Comparative Perspective*. Chicago: The University of Chicago Press.

Gupu, Xiao-Xiong. 1992. *Taiwan de Gongyehua: Guojijiagongjidi de Xingcheng (Industrialization in Taiwan: The Formation of the International Assembly Base)*. Taiwan: Ren Jian Chu Ban She.

Gutek, Barbara A. 1992. "Understanding Sexual Harassment at Work." *Norte Dame Journal of Ethics and Public Policy* 6: 335–358.

Hagedorn, John. 1993. "Understanding International Business: Globalization, Corporate Flexibility and Networks of Innovation." Paper presented at the EMOT workshop, Strasbourg, Oct. 1–2.

Haggard, Stephan and Tun-jen Cheng. 1987. "State and Foreign Capital in the East Asian NICs." In Frederic C. Deyo, ed., *The Political Economy of the New Asian Industrialism*, pp. 84–135. Ithaca, NY: Cornell University Press.

Halasz, G. 1993. *Alas es kozepfoku oktatas Magyarorszagon* (Basic and Intermediate Education in Hungary). Budapest: Egyetemi Konyvkiado.

Hall, John A. 1995. "After the Vacuum: Post-communism in the Light of Tocqueville." In Beverly Crawford, ed., *Markets, States and Democracy*, pp. 82–100. Boulder, Colo.: Westview Press.

Hamilton, Gary and Nicole Biggart. 1988. "Market, Culture, and Authority: A Comparative Analysis of Management and Organizations in the Far East." *American Journal of Sociology*

94: S52–S94.

Hamilton, Gary, William Zeile and Wan-Jin Kim. 1990. "The Network Structure of East Asian Economies." In Stewart R. Clegg and S. Gordon Redding, eds., *Capitalism in Contrasting Cultures*, pp. 105–129. Berlin: de Gruyter.

Handelsblatt. 31.8./1.9. 1996.

Hannan, Michael T. and John Freeman, eds. 1989. *Organizational Ecology*. Cambridge, MA: Harvard University Press.

Hardin, Russel. 1998. "Forms of Social Capital." Paper presented at the Duke Conference on *Social Capital*.

Harris, Hilary. 1995. "Women's Role in (International) Management." In Anne-Wil Harzing and Joris Van Ruysseveldt, eds., *International Human Resource Management: An Integrated Approach*, pp. 229–251. London: Sage.

Harrison, Bennett. 1994. *Lean and Mean: The Changing Landscape of Corporate Power in the Age of Flexibility*. New York, NY: Basic Books.

Hartstein, Barry A. and Thomas M. Wilde. 1994. "The Broadening Scope of Sexual Harassment in the Workplace." *Employee Relations Law Journal* 19: 639–653.

Helper, Susan. 1990. "Comparative Supplier Relations in the US and Japanese Auto Industries: An Exit-Voice Approach." *Business Economic History* 19: 153–162.

———. 1991. "Strategy and Irreversibility in Supplier Relations: The Case of the U.S. Automobile Industry." *Business History Review* 65: 781–824.

Henderson, Jeffrey, Richard Whitley, Gyorgy Lengyel and Laszlo Czaban. 1995. "Contention and Confusion in Industrial Transformation: Dilemmas of State Economic Management." In Dittrich Eckhard J., Gert Schmidt and Whitley Richard, eds., *Industrial Transformation in Europe*, pp. 79–108. London: Sage.

Hethy, L. 1983. *Gazdasagpolitika es erdekeltseg* (Economic Policy and Interest). Budapest: Kossuth.

Hillmann, Felicitas and Hedwig Rudolph. 1996. "Jenseits des brain drain: Zur Mobilität westlicher Fach-und Führungskräfte nach Polen" (Beyond the Brain Drain: Mobility of Western Experts and Managers to Poland). Discussion Paper FS 96–103. Berlin: Social Science Research Center.

———. 1997. "S(Z)eitenwechsel westliche Fach-und Führungskräfte im Transformationsprozeß Polens" (Changing Times: Western Experts and Managers in the Transformation Process of Poland). *Soziale Welt (Social World)*, Sonderband 12 (Special Issue on Transnational Migration): 245–263.

Hirsch, Paul M. 1975. "Organizational Effectiveness and the Institutional Environment." *Administrative Science Quarterly* 20: 327–44.

Hirschhausen, Christian Von. 1995. "No Privatization without Capitalization: Approaches to Post-Socialist Industrial Restructuring in Central and Eastern Europe." In Dittrich Eckhard J., Gert Schmidt and Whitley Richard, eds., *Industrial Transformation in Europe*, pp. 54–78. London: Sage.

Hirsch-Kreinsen, Hartmut. 1996. "Internationalisierung der Produktion. Strategien, Organisationsformen und Folgen für Industriearbeit" (Internationalisation of Production: Strategies, Organizational Forms and Implications for Industrial Work). *WSI-Mitteilungen (WSI- Information)* 1: 11–18.

Hirschman, Albert O. 1958. *The Strategy of Economic Development.* New Haven: Yale University Press.

———. 1970. *Exit, Voice and Loyalty.* Cambridge, MA: Harvard University Press.

———. 1982. "Rival Interpretations of Market Society: Civilizing, Destructive, or Feeble?" *Journal of Economic Literature* 20: 1463–1484.

Hirst, Paul and Grahame Thompson, eds. 1996. *Globalization in Question: The International Economy and The Possibilities of Governance.* Cambridge: Polity Press.

Hobday, Mike. 1995. "East Asian Latecomer Firms: Learning the Technology of Electronics." *World Development* 23(7): 1171–1193.

Hofstede, Geert H. 1980. *Culture's Consequences.* Beverly Hills, CA: Sage.

Hofstede, Geert H., Bram Neuijen, Denise Daval Ohayv and Geert Sanders. 1990. "Measuring Organizational Cultures: A Qualitative and Quantitative Study across Twenty Cases." *Administrative Science Quarterly* 35(2) (June): 286–316.

Hollingsworth, J. Rogers and Robert Boyer. 1997. *Contemporary Capitalism: The Embeddedness of Institutions.* Cambridge, England: Cambridge University Press.

Hollingsworth, J. Rogers, Phillipe C. Schmitter, and Wolfgang Streeck. 1994. *Governing Capitalist Economies: Performance and Control of Economic Sectors.* Oxford: Oxford University Press.

Holmes, S. 1995. "Cultural Legacies or State Collapse? Probing the Postcommunist Dilemma." Public lecture delivered at the Collegium Budapest on the 17th Oct., published as Public Lecture No. 13. Collegium Budapest, Nov.

Holtbrügge, Dirk. 1994a. *Entsendung von Führungskräften nach Mittel- und Osteuropa—Ergebnisse einer empirischen Untersuchung (The Transfer of Managers to Central and Eastern Europe: Results of an Empirical Study).* Mimeograph: Universität Dortmund.

———. 1994b. "Personalbeschaffung in Mittel-und Osteuropa-Ergebnisse einer empirischen Untersuchung" (Recruitment of Personnel in Central and Eastern Europe—Results of an Empirical Study). Arbeitspapiere des Lehrstuhls für Unternehmensführung (Working Paper of the Chair for Business Management), No. 17. Universität Dortmund.

Homans, George. 1950. *The Human Group.* New York, NY: Harpers.

Hoogvelt, Ankie. 1997. *Globalisation and the Postcolonial World: The New Political Economy of Development.* London: Macmillan Press Ltd.

Horvath, L. 1977. "Uzemi Demokracia es Vallati Strategia" (Work Place Democracy and

Company Strategy). *Tarsadalmi Szemle* 9: 72–77.

House, Robert and Aditya. 1997. "The Social Scientific Study of Leadership: Quo Vadis?" *Journal of Management* 23: 409–473.

Hsiao, Chuan-Cheng. 1995. "Zhengzhi Minzhuhua yu Taiwan de Duiwai Zhengce: Yi Ge Zhongguo Yuanze de Bengjie" (Democratization and Taiwan's Foreign Policy: The Breakdown of 'One China' Principle). Paper presented at Taiwan Minzhuhua de Huigu Xingsi Yu Zhanwan Yantaohui (The Conference of Taiwan's Democratization: Retrospect, Self-criticism, and Prospect), National Chung-Shan University, Kaohsiung.

Hsiao, H. H. 1991. *Shehui Yixiang Diaocha Baogao (Social Image Survey)*. Taipei: Academic Sinica.

Hsieh, Shiao-Chin. 1995. "Jiaoyu: Cong Fouquan de Fouzhi Dao Nüxing de Jiejiu" (Education: From Reproduction of Partiarchy to the Liberation of Women). In Yu-Shiu Liu, ed., *Taiwan Funüchujing Baipishu (White Paper on Current Conditions of Women in Taiwan)*, pp. 183–218. Taipei: China Times Publishing Co.

Hsieh, Yin-Hwa. 1984. "Cong Xingsaorao Kan Xingbaoli" (From Sexual Harassment to Sexual Violence). *Jinri Shenghu Zazhi (Today Life Magazine)* 214: 16–17.

Hsing, You-tien. 1996. "Blood, Thicker than Water: Interpersonal Relations and Taiwanese Investment in Southern China." *Environment and Planning A* 28: 2241–2261.

Hsu, Jinn-yuh. 1997. "A Late Industrial District? Learning Networks in the Hsinchu Science-Based Industrial Park, Taiwan." Ph.D. diss., Department of Geography, University of California at Berkeley.

Huberman, A. Michael and Matthew B. Miles. 1994. "Data management and analysis methods." In Norman K. Denzin and Yvonna S. Lincoln, eds., *Handbook of Qualitative Research*, pp. 428–444. Thousand Oaks: Sage.

Huntington, Samuel P. 1991. *The Third Wave: Democratization in the Late Twentieth Century*. Norman: University of Oklahoma Press.

Hwang, Fu-Yuan. 1994. "Gongzuochangsuo Xingsaorao Jiqi Yufang Zhi Yanjiu" (Sexual Harassment in the Workplace and Its Prevention). In Council of Labor Affairs, Executive Yuan, ed., *Nannü Gongzuo Pingding Luanwenji (Essays on Gender Equality in Employment)*, pp. 189–204. Taipei: Council of Labor Affairs, Executive Yuan.

———. 1995. "Funü Renshenanquan Zhengco Baipishu Yanjiu Yu Jianyi" (White Paper on Personal Safety for Women: Research and Questions). Paper presented at *Funüzhengco Baipishu Yanjiu Fabiaohui* (The Conference on the Presentation of the White Paper on Women's Policy), Central Women's Committee of the KMT Party, Taipei, Taiwan.

Hwang, Kwang-Kuo. 1988. "Zhongguo Shijiazu Qiye de Xiandaihua" (The Modernization of Chinese Family Business). In Kwang-Kuo Hwang, ed., *Zhongguoren de quanli youxi* (Chinese Power Games), pp. 233–272. Taipei: Chu-Liu Publishing Company.

Hwang, Yu-Kuang. 1993. "Woguo Shangshi Gongsi Dongshihuitexing yu Jingyingjixiao zhi Yanjiu" (A Study on the Characteristics of Board of Directors and Corporate Performance). Master's thesis, National Taiwan University.

Iacobucci, Dawn and Nigel Hopkins. 1992. "Modeling Dyadic Interactions and Networks in Marketing." *Journal of Marketing Research* 22: 5–17.

INS Statistical Year Book. 1991. *Statistical Yearbook of Immigration and Naturalization Services.* Washington, D.C.: U.S. Department of Justice.

International Labour Office. 1992. *Combating Sexual Harassment at Work.* Geneva: International Labour Office.

International Labour Office/Multinational Enterprises Branch (ILO). 1995. "Multinational Enterprises in Central & Eastern Europe—New Possibilities and Challenges for Trade Unions." Background document for discussion, Prague, Dec. 10–12.

Investment Commission, Ministry of Economic Affairs, ROC. 1996. *Directory of Taiwan/ROC Companies in North America.* New York, NY: CCNA Investment and Trade Office.

Jackall, Robert. 1988. *Moral Mazes: The World of Corporate Managers.* New York, NY: Oxford University Press.

Jaklic, Marko. 1997. "Changing Governance Structures and Work Organisation in Slovenia." In Richard Whitley and Peer Hull Kristensen, eds., *Governance at Work*, pp. 209–223. Oxford: Oxford University Press.

Jazwinska, Ewa and Marek Okólski, eds. 1996. *Causes and Consequences of Migration from Central and Eastern Europe: The Case of Poland.* Warsaw: Migration Research Center, Institute for Social Studies, University of Warsaw.

Jen-Ben Educational Foundation. 1995. Xiaoyan Jiaozhiyuangong Xingsaorao Wenjuandiaocha Jizhchui Ziliao (A Survey on Sexual Harassment by Officials and Employees on Campus). Taipei: Jen-Ben Educational Foundation.

Jensen, Michael. 1989. "Eclipse of the Public Corporation." *Harvard Business Review.* 61–73.

Joskow, Paul L. 1996. "Contract Duration and Relationship-Specific Investments: Empirical Evidence From Coal Markets." In Scott Masten, ed., *Case Studies in Contracting and Organization*, pp. 104–129. Oxford: Oxford University Press.

Juchler, Jakob. 1995. "Big Bang mit schrillen Tönen: Widersprüche und Widerstände bei der Implementierung des Balcerowicz-Planes in Polen" (Big Bang with Crazy Sounds: Contradictions and Resistance during the Implementation of the Balcerowicz-plan in Poland). In Hedwig Rudolph and Geplanter Wandel, ed., u*ngeplante Wirkungen: WZB-Jahrbuch 1995 (Planned Change, Unintended Outcomes: WZB-Yearbook 1995)*, pp. 79–93. Berlin: Edition Sigma.

Kahn, Robert L. and Mayer N. Zald. 1990. *Organizations and Nation-States: New Perspectives on Conflict and Cooperation.* San Francisco, CA: Jossey-Bass Publishers.

Kahneman, Daniel and Amos Tversky. 1982. "The Psychology of Preferences." *Scientific American* 246: 161–73.

Kalinowski, Tomasz. 1996. "Ausländische Direktinvestitionen in Polen—Anfang eines dauerhaften Wachstums?" (Foreign Direct Investments in Poland: Start of a Sustainable Growth). DIW Vierteljahreshefte zur Wirtschaftsforschung (Quarterly Journal for

Economic Research of the DIW, Berlin) 2: 248–255.

Kandel, William L. 1988. "Sexual Harassment: Persistent, Prevalent, but Preventable." *Employee Relations Law Journal* 14: 439–449.

Kaplinsky, Raphael. 1993. "TNCs in the Third World: Stability or Discontinuity?" In Lorraine Eden and Evan H. Potter, eds., *Multinationals in the Global Political Economy*, pp. 108–121. New York, NY: St. Martin's Press.

Kau, Michael Ying-mao. 1996. "The Power Structure in Taiwan's Political Economy." *Asian Survey* 36(3): 287–305.

Keesing, Rogers M. 1974. "Theories of Culture." *Annual Review of Anthropology* 3: 73–97.

———. 1994. "Theories of Culture Revisited." In Robert Borofsky, ed., *Assessing Cultural Anthropology*. New York: McGraw-Hill.

Kemme, D. M. 1994. "Banking in Central Europe during the Protomarket Period." In John P. Bonin and Istvan P. Szekely, eds., *The Development and Reform of Financial Systems in Central and Eastern Europe*. Aldershot: Edward Elgar.

Kennedy, Ruth A. 1994. "Insulating Sexual Harassment Grievance Procedures from the Chilling Effect of Defamation Litigation." *Washington Law Review* 69: 235–253.

Kim, Illso. 1981. *New Urban Immigrants: The Korean Community in New York*. Princeton, NJ: Princeton University Press.

Kleer, Jerzy. 1996. "Transformation Models: East Germany, Poland, Russia." Economic Discussion Papers No. 29. Faculty of Economic Sciences, University of Warsaw, Warsaw.

Knights, David and Hugh C. Willmott. 1987. "Organizational Culture as Management Strategy: A Critique and Illustration from the Financial Service Industries." *International Studies of Management and Organization* 17(3): 40–63.

Knorr-Cetina, Karin. 1981. "Introduction: The Micro-Sociological Challenge of Macro-Sociology: Towards a Reconstruction of Social Theory and Methodology." In Karin Knorr-Cetina and Aaron V. Cicourel, eds., *Advances in Social Theory and Methodology*, pp. 1–47. Boston: Routledge and Kegan Paul.

Kojima, Kiyoshi. 1978. *Direct Foreign Investment—A Japanese Model of Multinational Business Operations*. London: Croom Helm Ltd.

Konjhodzic, I. 1996. "The Patterns of Adjustment of Small Economies in the Process of Liberalisation." Paper presented at the Conference held at the Faculty of Economics, University of Ljubljana, Sep.

Koo, Hagen. 1987. "The Interplay of State, Social Class, and World System in East Asian Development: The Cases of South Korea and Taiwan." In Frederic C. Deyo, ed., *The Political Economy of the New Asian Industrialism*, pp. 165–181. Ithaca, NY: Cornell University Press.

Korn, Jane B. 1993. "The Fungible Women and Other Myths of Sexual Harassment." *Tulane Law Review* 67: 1363–1419.

Kornai, János. 1986. "The Hungarian Reform Process: Visions, Hopes and Reality." *Journal of Economic Literature* 24(4): 1687–1737.

———. 1996. "Paying the Bill for Goulash Communism: Hungarian Development and Macro-Stabilisation in a Political-Economy Perspective." Discussion Paper No. 1748. Harvard Institute for Economic Research.

Kotkin, Joel. 1992. *Tribes: How Race, Religion, and Identity Determine Success in the New Global Economy.* New York, NY: Random House.

Kovac, B. 1991. "Entrepreneurship and Privatisation of Social Ownership in Economic Reforms." In James Simmie and Jose Dekleva, eds., *Yugoslavia in Turmoil: After Selfmanagement.* London: Pinter.

Kozminski, A. K. 1995. "From the Communist Nomenklatura to Transformational Leadership." In Bruno Grancelli, ed., *Social Change and Modernization.* Berlin: de Gruyter.

Kraft, Evan, M. Vodopivec and M. Cvikl. 1994. "On Its Own: The Economy of Independent Slovenia." In Evan Kraft and Jill Benderly, eds., *Independent Slovenia.* London: Macmillan.

Kranton, Rachel. 1996. "Reciprocal Exchange: A Self-Sustaining System." *The American Economic Review* 86: 830–851.

Kristensen, Peer Hull. 1997. "National Systems of Governance and Managerial Strategies in the Evolution of Work Systems: Britain, Germany and Denmark Compared." In Richard Whitley and Peer Hull Kristensen, eds., *Governance at Work: The Social Regulation of Economic Relations*, pp. 3–46. Oxford: Oxford University Press

Ku, Yenling. 1984. "Xingsaorao de Zhengyixing" (Controversies over Sexual Harassment). *Funü Xinzhi (New Knowledge for Women)* 25: 17–18.

Kubielas, Stanislaw. 1994. "The Attractiveness of Poland to Foreign Direct Investors: Trends and Factors in 1989–1993." PPRG Discussion Papers No. 28. Warsaw.

Kung, Chun-sheng. 1997. "Taiwan's Offshore Shipping Center and Cross-Strait Commercial Opportunities." *Issues and Studies* 33(12): 50–69.

Kuo, Cheng-Tian. 1994. "Private Governance in Taiwan." Paper presented at the Annual Meeting of Midwest Political Science Association, Chicago, Illinois.

Kuzmanic, T. 1994. "Strikes, Trade Unions and Slovene Independence." In Evan Kraft and Jill Benderly, eds., *Independent Slovenia.* London: Macmillan

Lado, M. 1994. "Workers' and Employers' Interests—As They Are Represented in the Changing Industrial Relations in Hungary." Working Paper No. 3. Krakow: University Council for Economic and Management Education Transfer.

Laky, T. 1992. "The Reality and Potential of Autonomous Entrepreneurship." In B. Dallago, G. Ajami and B. Grancelli, eds., *Privatisation and Entrepreneurship in Post Socialist Countries.* London: Macmillan.

Lampland, Martha. 1995. *The Object of Labour: Commodification in Socialist Hungary.* Chicago: University of Chicago Press.

Lange, Hellmuth. 1995. "Qualifikation und Rolle. Führungskräfte und wissenschaftlich-technische Fachkräfte im Übergang" (Qualification and Function: Managers and Scientific-technical Experts in the Transformation). In Hellmuth Lange, ed., *Man konnte und man mußte sich verändern (One Could and One Had to Change)*, pp. 169–197. Münster: LIT.

Larson, Andrea. 1992. "Network Dyads in Entrepreneurial Settings: A Study of the Governance of Exchange Processes." *Administrative Science Quarterly* 37: 76–104.

Larson, David A. 1992. "What Can You Say, Where Can You Say It, and to Whom? A Guide to Understanding and Preventing Unlawful Sexual Harassment." *Creighton Law Review* 25: 827–849.

Law, John. 1994. *Organizing Modernity*. Oxford: Blackwell.

Lazarevic, Z. 1994. "Economic History of Twentieth Century Slovenia." In Evan Kraft and Jill Benderly, eds., *Independent Slovenia*. London: Macmillan.

Lazerson, Mark. 1995. "A New Phoenix: Modern Putting-Out in the Modena Knitwear Industry." *Administrative Science Quarterly* 40: 34–59.

Lazonick, William. 1991. *Business Organization and the Myth of the Market Economy*. Cambridge, England: Cambridge University Press.

Lee, Bi-Han. 1994. "Taiwandiqu Hou Gongye Zhuangxing zhi Guojia yu Shehui" (State and Society under the Transformation of the Post-industrial Society in Taiwan). *Zhongshan Xueshu Luncong (Journal of Sun-Yat-Senism)* 12: 45–282.

Lee, Cheng F. and Sheng-Cheng Hu, eds. 1989. *Financial Planning and Forecasting: Taiwan's Foreign Investment, Export, and Financial Analysis*. Greenwich: JAI Press, Inc.

Lee, Ming. 1996. "Woguo Wushi Waijiao de Huigu Yu Zhanwang" (The Retrospect and Prospect of Recent Pragmatic Diplomacy: the Case of Taiwan). Paper presented at 1996 Nian Woguo Waijiao Huigu Yu Zhanwang Yantaohui (The Conference of Our Diplomatic Retrospect and Prospect in 1996, National Chung-Cheng University, Chia-Yi.

Leng, Tse-kang. 1996. *The Taiwan-China Connection: Democracy and Development Across the Taiwan Straits*. Boulder, Colo.: Westview Press.

Levinthal, Daniel and Mark Fichman. 1988. "Dynamics of Interorganizational Attachments: Auditor-Client Relationships." *Administrative Science Quarterly* 33: 345–369.

Lewin, Shira B. 1996. "Economics and Psychology: Lessons for Our Own Day From the Earliest Twentieth Century." *Journal of Economic Literature* 34: 1293–323.

Light, Ivan, ed. 1972. *Ethnic Enterprise in America: Business and Welfare among Chinese, Japanese, and Black*. Berkeley: University of California Press.

Light, Ivan and Edna Bonacich, eds. 1988. *Immigrant Entrepreneurs: Koreans in Los Angeles, 1965–1982*. Berkeley: University of California Press.

Lilja, Kari and Risto Tainio. 1996. "The Nature of the Typical Finnish Firm." In Richard Whitley and Peer Hull Kristensen, eds., *The Changing European Firm*, pp. 159–191.

London: Routledge.

Lin, Nan and Karen Cook. 1998. *Introductory Remarks on Integrating Approaches to Social Capital.* Working paper, Department of Sociology, Duke University.

Lincoln, James R. and Arne L. Kalleberg. 1985. "Work Organization and Workforce Commitment: a Study of Plants and Employees in the US and Japan." *American Sociological Review* 50(6) (Dec.): 738–760.

Lindermann, Barbara and David D. Kadue. 1992. *Sexual Harassment in Employment Law.* Washington, D.C.: Bureau of National Affairs.

Linstead, Stephen and Robert Grafton-Small. 1992. "On Reading Organizational Culture." *Organization Studies* 13(3): 331–355.

Lipper, R. Nicolle. 1992. "Sexual Harassment in the Workplace: A Comparative Study of Great Britain and the United States." *Comparative Labor Law Journal* 13: 293–342.

Litz, Reginald A. 1995. "The Family Business: Toward Definitional Clarity." *Academy of Management Meeting Best Papers Proceedings* 20: 100–104.

Liu, Chih-Ping. 1991. "The Growth of Venture Capital in Taiwan." Paper presented at the Conference of Asian Venture Capital, Taipei, April.

Liu, Jing-Tian, Chi Schive and Wei-De Tsay. 1990. "Taiwandiqu Waizichangshang Chukou Xingwei zhi Fenxi" (Analyses of Export Behavior of Foreign Firms in Taiwan). *Jingji Lunwen Conkan (Taiwan Economic Review)* 18(4): 427–448. Taipei: Department of Economics, National Taiwan University.

Liu, Jin-Qing. 1992. "Taiwanzhanhou Jingjifenxi" (Analyses of Taiwan's Economy after the Second World War). Renjian Taiwan Zhengzhi Jingji Congkan Dierjuan (Ren Jian Series on Taiwan Political Economy, Vol. 2). Taiwan: Ren Jian Chu Ban She.

Liu, Jin-Qing, Zhao-Yan Tu and San-XiNan YuGu. 1993. "Taiwanzhijingji—Dianxing NIES zhi Chengjiu yu Wenxi" (Taiwan's Economy: The Achievements and Problems of Typical NIES). Renjian Taiwan Zhengzhi Jingji Congkan Dierliujuan (Ren Jian Series on Taiwan Political Economy, Vol. 6). Taiwan: Ren Jian Chu Ban She.

Lu, Pao-Chin and Li-Yeh Fu. 1993. *Taiwandiqu Gongzuochangsuo Xingsaorao Zhi Diaochoyanjiu (A Study on Sexual Harassment in the Workplace in Taiwan).* Taipei: Council of Labor Affairs, Executive Yuan

Luksic, I. 1994. *Liberalizem versus korporativizem* (Liberalism versus Corporatism). Ljubljana: Znanstveno Publicistino Sredisce.

Luo, Tsan-Yin. 1990. "Attitudes Towards Sex Roles, Sexual Harassment and Sexual Assault Among University Students." Paper presented at the 85th Annual Meeting of American Sociological Association, Washington, D.C.

———. 1993. "Sexual Harassment in the Chinese Workplace: Attitudes Towards and Experience with Sexual Harassment among Taiwan Workers." Paper presented at the Conference on Gender Issues in Contemporary Chinese Society, North American Chinese Sociological Association, Miami Beach, Florida.

———. 1995. "Xingbaoli: Jiegumisi, Duohunanye: Xingbaoli Zhi Xiankuang Yu Fangzhi" (Sexual Violence: Current Conditions of Sexual Violence and Its Prevention: Deconstructing the Myths and Taking Back the Dark Nights). In Yu-Shiu Liu, ed., *Taiwan Funüchujing Baipishu: 1995 (White Paper on Current Conditions of Women in Taiwan: 1995)*, pp. 257–308. Taipei: China Times Publishing Co.

Lydall, H. 1989. *Yugoslavia in Crisis.* Oxford: Oxford University Press.

Lyotard, Jean Francois. 1984. *The Postmodern Condition: A Report on Knowledge.* Manchester: Manchester University Press.

MacKinnon, Catharine A. 1979. *Sexual Harassment of Working Women: A Case of Sex Discrimination.* New Haven: Yale University Press.

Macneil, Ian. 1978. "Contracts: Adjustment of Long-Term Economic Relations under Classical, Neoclassical, and Relational Contract Law." *Northwestern University Law Review* 72: 854–905.

———. 1999. "Relational Contract Theory: Challenges." Working paper: Northwestern University School of Law.

Mako, Csaba and Péter Novoszáth. 1995. "Employment Relations in Multinational Companies: The Hungarian Case." In Eckhard Dittrich, Gert Schmidt and Richard Whitley, eds., *Industrial Transformation in Europe*, pp. 255–276. London: Sage.

Marcus, George E. and Michael J. Fischer, eds. 1986. *Anthropology as Cultural Critique.* Chicago: University of Chicago Press.

Markides, Constantions C. and Norman Berg. 1988. "Manufacturing Offshore Is Bad Business." *Harvard Business Review* (Sep.–Oct.): 113–120.

Marody, Miroslawa. 1997. "Polish Society from the Perspective of European Integration." In Marek Belka, Jerzy Hausner, Miroslawa Marody and Marek Zirk-Sadowski, eds., *The Polish Transformation from the Perspective of European Integration*, pp. 147–188. Warsaw: Friedrich Ebert Stiftung.

Martin, Joanne. 1987. "A Black Hole: Ambiguity in Organizational Culture." Paper presented at the Conference of SCOS, Milan, June.

———. 1992. *The Culture of Organizations: Three Perspectives.* New York: Oxford University Press.

Martin, Joanne and Debra Meyerson. 1988. "Organizational Cultures and the Denial, Channeling and Acknowledgement of Ambiguity." In Louis R. Pondy, Howard Thomas and Richard J. Boland, eds., *Managing Ambiguity and Change.* New York: Wiley.

Martin, Joanne and Caren Siehl. 1983. "Organizational Culture and Counter Culture: An Uneasy Symbiosis." *Organizational Dynamics* (Autumn): 52–64.

Masten, Scott. 1996. *Case Studies in Contracting and Organization.* Oxford: Oxford University Press.

Mathews, John A. 1997. "A Silicon Valley of the East: Creating Taiwan's Semiconductor Industry." *California Management Review* 39(4): 26–54.

Mathews, Susan M. 1991. "Title VII and Sexual Harassment: Beyond Damage Control." *Yale Journal of Law and Feminism* 3: 299–320.

Matsuura, Nanshi F. 1991. *International Business: A New Era*. New York, NY: Harcourt Brace Jovanovich Publishers.

McGuire, Patrick, Mark Granovetter, and Michael Schwartz. 1993. "Thomas Edison and the Social Construction of the Early Electricity Industry in America." pp. 213–48 in *Explorations in Economic Sociology*, edited by Richard Swedberg. New York: Russel Sage Foundation.

McKinnon, Douglas. 1972. *Money and Capital in Economic Development*. Washington, D.C.: The Brookings Institution.

McLean, Paul D. and John Padgett. 1997. "Was Florence a Perfectly Competitive Market?: Transaction Evidence from the Renaissance." *Theory and Society* (in press).

Meaney, Connie Squires. 1991. "Creating a Competitive Niche: State Policy and Taiwan's Semiconductor Industry." Paper presented at Center for Chinese Studies, University of California at Berkeley.

Meier, Thomas. 1996. "Direktinvestitionen in Mittel- und Osteuropa: Entwicklung 1995 und Ziele von Unternehmen" (Foreign Direct Investment in Central and Eastern Europe: Development in 1995 and Targets of Companies). *Wirtschaft im Wandel* (*Economy in Transition*) 3: 8–12.

Messick, David and Sentis, K. 1983. "Fairness, Preference, and Fairness Biases." pp. 61–64 in *Equity Theory: Psychological and Sociological Perspectives*, edited by David Messick and Karen Cook. New York: Praeger.

Meyer, John W. and Brian Rowan. 1977. "Institutionalized Organizations: Formal Structure as Myth and Ceremony." *American Journal of Sociology* 83: 340–363.

Miles, Robert. 1990. "Whatever Happened to the Sociology of Migration?" *Work, Employment & Society* 4(2): 281–298.

Mills, C. Wright. 1940. "Situated Actions and Vocabularies of Motives." *American Sociological Review* 5: 904–913.

Ming, Lee. 1996. "The Retrospect and Prospect of Recent Pragmatic Diplomacy: the Case of Taiwan." (in Chinese) Paper presented at the Conference of Our Diplomatic Retrospect and Prospect in 1996, National Chung-Cheng University, Chia-Yi.

Mintz, Beth and Michael Schwartz, eds. 1985. *The Power of Structure of American Business*. Chicago: University of Chicago Press.

Modern Women Foundation. 1992a. *Taibeishi Gaozhong (Gaozhi) Nüsheng Dui Xingsaorao Taidu Zhi Diaocho Yanjiu (A Survey on High School and Vocational School Female Students' Attitudes Towards Sexual Harassment)*. Taipei: Modern Women Foundation.

———. 1992b. *Taibeishi Shangbanzhu Liangxingchayi Dui Xingsaorao Jingyan Yu Dui Xingsaorao Taidu Yinxian Zhi Yanjiu (Worker's Attitudes Towards and Experience of Sexual Harassment)*. Taipei: Modern Women Foundation.

Mollenkopf, John and Manuel Castells. 1991. "Introduction." In Mollenkopf and Castells, eds., *Dual City: Restructuring New York*, pp. 3–22. New York, NY: Russell Sage Foundation.

Molz, Richard. 1985. "The Role of the Board of Directors: Typologies of Interaction." *Journal of Business Strategy* 5 (Spring): 86–93.

Morris, Jonathan. 1991. "Globalization and Global Localization: Explaining Trends in Japanese Foreign Manufacturing Investment." In Jonathan Morris, ed., *Japan and the Global Economy*, pp. 1–13. London and New York: Routledge.

Mueller, Frank. 1994. "Societal Effect, Organizational Effect and Globalization." *Organization Studies* 15(3): 407–428.

Murnighan, J. K. 1994. "Game Theory and Organizational Behavior." *Research in Organizational Behavior* 16: 83–123.

Myant, M. 1993. *Transforming Socialist Economies*. Aldershot: E. Elgar.

Nagy, Katalin. 1989. "New Technology and Work in Hungary: Technological Innovation without Organizational Adaptation." In Arthur Francis and Peter Grootings, eds., *New Technologies and Work*, pp. 88–119. London: Routledge.

National Association of Manufacturers. 1987. *Sexual Harassment: How to Develop and Implement Effective Policies*. Washington, D.C.: National Association of Manufacturers.

Near, Janet P. 1989. "Organizational Commitment among Japanese and US Workers." *Organization Studies* 10(3): 281–300.

Nee, V. and Ingram, P. 1998. "Embeddedness and Beyond: Institutions, Exchange, and Social Structure." pp. 19–45 in *The New Institutionalism in Sociology*, edited by M. C. Brinton and V. Nee. New York: Russell Sage Foundation.

Negandhi, Anant R. 1973. *Management and Economic Development: The Case of Taiwan*. Martinus Nijhoff: The Hague.

Nelson, Richard R. and Sidney G. Winter, eds. 1982. *An Evolutionary Theory of Economic Change*. Cambridge, MA: The Belknap Press of Harvard University Press.

North, Douglass C. 1990. *Institutions, Institutional Change, and Economic Performance*. New York, NY: Cambridge University Press.

Note. 1991. "Eradicating Title VII Sexual Harassment by Recognizing an Employer's Duty to Prohibit Sexual Harassment." *Arizona Law Review* 33: 383–399.

———. 1992. "Did She Ask for It?: The 'Unwelcome' Requirement in Sexual Harassment Cases." *Cornell Law Review* 77: 1558–1592.

———. 1994. "The Reasonable Woman Standard after *Harris v. Forklift Systems, Inc.*: The Debate Rages on." *Women Rights Law Review* 16: 127–137.

———. 1995. "The Forgotten Interest Group: Reforming Title VII to Address the Concerns of Workers While Eliminating Sexual Harassment." *Vanderbilt Law Review* 48: 1019–1056.

OECD. 1995. *Foreign Direct Investment, Trade and Employment.* Paris: OECD.

Oh, James J. 1992. "Internal Sexual Harassment Complaints: Investigating to Win." *Employee Relations Law Journal* 18: 227–235.

Ohmae, Kenichi. 1990. *The Borderless World: Power and Strategy in the Interlinked Economy.* New York, NY: Harper Perennial.

Okólski, Marek. 1996a. "Poland." In Tanas Frejka, ed., *International Migration in Central and Eastern Europe and the Commonwealth of Independent States,* pp. 95–110. United Nations Economic Commission for Europe. Economic Studies No.8. New York and Geneva: United Nations.

———. 1996b. *Movements of Highly Skilled Professionals from Western Countries to Poland.* Mimeograph: Warsaw University.

Ong, Paul, Edna Bonacich and Lucie Cheng, eds. 1994. *The Asian Immigration in Los Angeles and Global Restructuring.* Philadelphia: Temple University Press.

Ortner, Sherry B. 1984. "Theory in Anthropology since the Sixties." *Comparative Studies in Society and History* 26(1): 126–166.

Ost Wirtschafts Report (East Economic Report). 1996a. Jan. 19.

———. 1996b. June 6.

Paauwe, Jaap and Philip Dewe. 1995. "Human Resource Management in Multinational Corporations: Theories and Models." In Anne-Wil Harzing and Joris van Ruysseveldt, eds., *International Human Resource Management: An Integrated Approach,* pp. 75–98. London: Sage.

Palmer, Donald, Roger Friedland and Jitendra Singh. 1986. "The Ties That Bind: Determinants of Stability in a Corporate Network." *American Sociological Review* 51: 781–796.

Pang, Chien-Kuo. 1992. *The State and Economic Transformation: The Taiwan Case.* New York, NY: Garland.

Paquette, Laure. 1996. "The Republic of China's New National Strategy for the Post-Cold War World." *Issues and Studies* 32(3): 1–39.

Peng, Huai-Chen. 1989. "Taiwan Qiyeyezhu de Guanxijiqi Zhuanbian—Yigeshehuixue de Fenxi" (The *'Guanxi'* Networks' of Enterpreneurs in Taiwan and their Transformation—A Sociological Perspective). Ph.D. diss., Tunghai University.

Peng, Huei-En. 1990. *The Political Economy of Taiwan's Development.* (in Chinese) Taipei: Feng-Yun Forum Publisher.

Perrow, Charles. 1993. "Small Firms Networks." In Richard Swedberg, ed., *Explorations in Economic Sociology,* pp. 377–402. New York, NY: Russell Sage Foundation.

Petersen, Trond and Kenneth W. Koput. 1991. "Density Dependence in Organizational Mortality: Legitimacy or Unobserved Heterogeneity." *American Sociological Review* 56: 399–409.

Petrocelli, William and Barbara Kate Repa. 1995. *Sexual Harassment on the Job: What Its is and How to Stop It.* Berkeley, CA: Nolo Press.

Pettigrew, Andrew M. 1992. "On Studying Managerial Elites." *Strategic Management Journal* 13: 163–182.

Pfeffer, Jeffery. 1998. *The Human Equation: Building Profits by Putting People First.* Boston, Massachusetts: Harvard Business School Press.

Piore, Michael J. and Charles F. Sabel. 1984. *The Second Industrial Divide: Possibilities for Prosperity.* New York, NY: Basic Books.

Pisano, Gary. 1990. "The R&D Boundaries of the Firm: An Empirical Analysis." *Administrative Science Quarterly* 35: 153–176.

Podolny, Joel M. 1994. "Market Uncertainty and the Social Character of Economic Exchange." *Administrative Science Quarterly* 39: 458–483.

Podolny, Joel M. and Karen L. Page. 1998. "Network Forms of Organizations." *Annual Review of Sociology* 24: 57-76.

Pollack, Wendy. 1990. "Sexual Harassment: Women's Experience vs. Legal Definitions." *Harvard Women Law Journal* 13: 35–85.

Porter, Michael. 1990. *The Competitive Advantage of Nations.* New York: The Free Press.

Portes, Alejandro, ed. 1995. *The Economic Sociology of Immigration: Essays on Networks, Ethnicity, and Entrepreneurship.* New York, NY: Russell Sage.

———, ed. 1996. "Global Villagers: The Rise of Transnational Communities." *The American Prospect* 25 (March–April): 74–77.

Portes, Alejandro and Robert Bach, eds. 1985. *Latin Journey.* Berkeley, CA: University of California Press.

Portes, Alejandro and Ruben Rumbaut, eds. 1990. *Immigrant America.* Berkeley, CA: University of California Press.

Portes, Alejandro and Julia Sensenbrenner. 1993. "Embeddedness and Immigration: Notes on the Social Determinants of Economic Action." *American Journal of Sociology* 98: 1320–1350.

Portes, Alejandro and Alex Stepick, eds. 1994. *City on the Edge: The Transformation of Miami.* Berkeley, CA: University of California Press.

Portes, Alejandro and Min Zhou. 1992. "Divergent Destinies: Immigration, Poverty, and Entrepreneurship in the United States." Paper presented at the Joint Center for Political and Economic Studies, Washington, D.C., Apr.

Potter, Jonathan and Margaret Wetherell, eds. 1987. *Discourse and Social Psychology: Beyond Attitudes and Behavior.* London: Sage.

Powell, Gary N. 1988. *Women and Men in Management.* Beverly Hills: Sage.

Powell, Walter W. 1990. "Neither Market nor Hierarchy: Network Forms of Organization."

In Barry Staw and L. L. Cummings, eds., *Research in Organizational Behavior*, vol. 12, pp. 295–336. Greenwich, CT: JAI Press.

———. 1996. "Commentary: On the Nature of Institutional Embeddedness: Labels Vs. Explanations." *Advances in Strategic Management* 13: 293–300.

Powell, Walter W. and Paul J. DiMaggio, eds. 1991. *The New Institutionalism in Organizational Analysis*. Chicago: The University of Chicago Press.

Powell, Walter W., Kenneth W. Koput and Laurel Smith-Doerr. 1996. "Interorganizational Collaboration and the Locus of Innovation: Networks of Learning in Biotechnology." *Administrative Science Quarterly* 41: 116–145.

Prietula, Michael J. and Herbert Simon. 1989. "The Experts in Your Midst." *Harvard Business Review* (Jan.–Feb.): 120–124.

Putnam, Robert D. 1993. *Making Democracy Work: Civil Traditions in Modern Italy*. Princeton, NJ: Princeton University Press.

———. 1995. "Bowling Alone: America's Declining Social Capital." *Journal of Democracy* 6: 65–78.

Quaisser, Wolfgang. 1996. "Anpassungsprozesse im Kohle-, Stahl-, Textil- und Agrarsektor Polens in den 90er Jahren" (Adaption Processes in the Coal, Steel, Textile and Agricultural Sectors in Poland in the 90s). Working Paper No. 195. München: Osteuropa-Institut.

Razin, Eran. 1988. "Entrepreneurship among Foreign Immigrants in the Los Angeles and San Francisco Metropolitan Regions." *Urban Geography* 9(3): 283–301.

Redding, S. Gordon. 1993. *The Spirit of Chinese Capitalism*. Berlin: de Gruyter.

———. 1994. "Comparative Management Theory: Jungle, Zoo or Fossil Bed?" *Organization Studies* 15(3): 323–359.

Redei, Maria L. 1995. "International Brain Drain: Executive Research Report." In Maryellen Fullerton, Endre Sik and Judit Töth, eds., *Refugees and Migrants: Hungary at a Cross-Roads*, pp. 105–117. Budapest: Institute for Political Science of the Hungarian Academy of Sciences.

Redor, Dominique. 1994. "Les migrations de specialistes hautement qualifié entre l'Europe centrale et l'Union Européenne, analyse et perspective" (Migration of the Highly Skilled Between Central Europe and the European Union: Analysis and Perspectives). *Revue d'études comparatives Est-Ouest (Review of Contemporary Studies East-West)* 3 (Sep.): 161–178.

Reich, Robert B. 1992. *The Work of Nations: Preparing Ourselves for 21ˢᵗ-Century Capitalism*. New York, NY: Vintage Books.

Revesz, G. 1990. *Perestroika in Eastern Europe: Hungary's Economic Transformation 1945–1988*. Boulder, Colo.: Westview Press.

Rogers, Alisdair. 1992. "The New Immigration and Urban Ethnicity in the U.S." In Malcom Cross, ed., *Ethnic Minorities and Industrial Change in European and North America*, pp. 226–249. Cambridge, England: Cambridge University Press.

Romo, Frank P. and Michael Schwartz. 1995. "Structural Embeddedness of Business Decisions: A Sociological Assessment of the Migration Behavior of Plants in New York State Between 1960 and 1985." *American Sociological Review* 60: 874–907.

Rosen, Michael. 1985. "Breakfast at Spiro's: Dramaturgy and Dominance." *Journal of Management* 11(2): 31–48.

———. 1991. "Coming to Terms with the Field: Understanding and Doing Organizational Ethnography." *Journal of Management Studies* 28(1): 1–24.

Rosenau, Pauline Marie. 1992. *Post-Modernism and the Social Sciences: Insights, Inroads, and Intrusions.* Princeton: Princeton University Press.

Rus, A. 1994. "Quasi-privatisation: From Class Struggle to a Scuffle of Small Particularisms." In Evan Kraft and Jill Benderly, eds., *Independent Slovenia.* London: Macmillan.

Søndergaard, Mikael. 1994. "Hofstede's Consequences: A Study of Reviews, Citations and Replications." *Organization Studies* 15(3): 447–456.

Sabel, Charles. 1989. "Flexible Specialization and the Re-emergence of Regional Economies." In Paul Hirst and Jonathan Zeitlin, eds., *Reversing Industrial Decline?*, pp. 17–70. New York, NY: St. Martins.

———. 1993. "Studied Trust: Building New Forms of Cooperation in a Volatile Economy." In Richard Swedberg, ed., *Explorations in Economic Sociology*, pp. 104–144. New York, NY: Russell Sage.

Sachs, Jeffrey D. 1996. "The Transition at Mid Decade." *American Economic Review* 86(2): 128–133.

Sajó, András. 1994. "Has State Ownership Truly Abandoned Socialism? The Survival of Socialist Economy and Law in Postcommunist Hungary." In Gregory S. Alexander and Grazyna Skapska, eds., *A Fourth Way? Privatisation, Property and the Emergence of New Market Economies*, pp. 198–214. London: Routledge.

Salt, John. 1992. "Migration Processes among the Highly Skilled in Europe." *International Migration Review* 26(2) (Special Issue): 484–504.

Sandelands, Lloyd and Robert Drazin. 1989. "On the Language of Organization Theory." *Organization Studies* 10(4): 457–478.

Sarup, Madan. 1988. *An Introductory Guide to Post-Structuralism and Postmodernism.* London: Harvester-Wheatsheaf.

Sassen, Saskia. 1988. *The Mobility of Capital and Labor: A Study in International Investment and Labor Flow.* New York, NY: Cambridge University Press.

———. 1996. "The Spatial Organization of Information Industries: Implications for the Role of the State." In James H. Mittelman, ed., *Globalization: Critical Reflections*, pp. 33–52. Boulder, Colo.: Lynne Rienner Publishers, Inc.

———, ed. 1988. *The Mobility of Labor and Capital.* Cambridge, England: Cambridge University Press.

———, ed. 1992. *The Global City*. Princeton, NJ: Princeton University Press.

Sassen-Koob, Saskia. 1984. "The New Labor Demand in Global Cities'." In M. Smith, ed., *Cities in Transformation*, pp. 139–171. Berkeley, CA: Sage Publications.

Saxenian, AnnaLee. 1994. *Regional Advantage: Culture and Competition in Silicon Valley and Route 128*. Cambridge, MA: Harvard University Press.

Schein, Edgar. H. 1985. *Organizational Culture and Leadership: A Dynamic View*. San Francisco, CA: Jossey-Bass.

Schive, Chi. 1978. "Woguo Waizi Changshang Chukou Qingxiang de Yanjiu" (Study of the Export Predilection of Foreign Firms in Taiwan). *Taibei Shiying Yuekan (Taipei Bank Monthly Journal)* 9(11): 12–20.

———. 1990. "Waishang yu Jjishuyingjin" (Foreign Firms and the Introduction of New Technology). pp. 410–411. *Taiwan Jingyan Sishinian (Forty Years of Taiwan Experiences)*.

Schive, Chi, and Jenn-hwa Tu. 1991. "Foreign firms and Structural Change in Taiwan." In Eric D. Ramstetter and S. Naya Boulder, ed., *Direct Foreign Investment in Asia's Developing Economies and Structural Change in the Asia-Pacific Region*, pp. 142–171. Boulder, Colo.: Westview Press.

Schleifer, Andrei. 1998. "State Versus Private Ownership." *Journal of Economic Perspectives* 12(4): 133–50.

Schneider, D. 1976. "Notes toward a Theory of Culture." In Keith Baso and Henry A. Selby, eds., *Meaning in Anthropology*. Albuquerque: University of New Mexico Press.

Schoenheider, Krista J. 1986. "Theory of Tort Liability for Sexual Harassment in the Workplace." *University of Pennsylvania Law Review* 134: 1461–1495.

Schwartzman, Helen B. 1987. "The Significance of Meetings in an American Mental Health Center." *American Ethnologist* 14(2): 271–294.

Science Park Administration. 1994. *Science-based Industrial Park Administration*. Hsinshu, Taiwan ROC.

Scott, Allen. 1993. *Technopolis: High-Technology Industry and Regional Development in Southern California*. Berkeley: University of California Press.

Scott, W. Richard. 1987. "The Adolescence of Institutional Theory." *Administrative Science Quarterly* 32(4): 493–511.

———. 1998. *Organizations: Rational, Natural, and Open Systems*. New Jersey: Prentice Hall.

Sculley, John. 1987. *Odyssey: From Pepsi to Apple*. New York: Harper and Row.

Seagrave, Sterling. 1995. *Lords of the Rim: The Invisible Empire of the Overseas Chinese*. New York, NY: Putnam.

Sepler, Fran. 1990. "Sexual Harassment: From Protective Response to Proactive Prevention." *Hamline Journal of Public Law and Policy* 11: 61–78.

Shih, Tai-Cheng. 1994. "Dongshihuitexing Zhong Jiazuyingsu yu Jingyingjixiao zhi

Shizhengyanjiu" (An Empirical Study of the Relationship Between Family-related Attributes in the Board of Directors and Business Performance: Including an Examination of Institutional Director's Influence). Master's thesis, National Taiwan University.

Shirley, Mary. 1983. "Managing State Owned Enterprises." World Bank Staff Working Papers No. 577. Washington, D.C.

Shotter, John and Kenneth J. Gergen. 1994. "Social Construction: Knowledge, Self, Others, and Continuing the Conversation." In Stan Deetz, ed., *Communication Yearbook*, vol. 17, pp. 3–33. Newbury Park: Sage.

Silverman, David. 1985. *Qualitative Methodology and Sociology*. Aldershot: Gower.

———. 1993. *Interpreting Qualitative Data*. London: Sage.

Simmons, Beth A. 1994. *Who Adjusts: Domestic Sources of Foreign Economic Policy During the Interwar Years*. Princeton, NJ: Princeton University Press.

Simmons, Joe A. 1993. "Sexual Harassment—Prophylactic Measures." *Ohio Northern University Law Review* 19: 661–672.

Simon, Herbert. 1991. "Organizations and Markets." *Journal of Economic Perspectives* 5: 24–44.

Smidovnik, Janez. 1991. "Disfunctions of the System of Self Management in the Economy, in Local Terrotorial Communities and in Public Administration." In James Simmie and Jose Dekleva, eds., *Yugoslavia in Turmoil: After Self Management?* London: Pinter.

Smircich, Linda. 1983. "Concepts of Culture and Organizational Analysis." *Administrative Science Quarterly* 28(3): 339–358.

Smitka, Michael J. 1991. *Competitive Ties: Subcontracting in the Japanese Automotive Industry*. New York, NY: Columbia University Press.

Soskice, David. 1994. "Innovation Strategies of Companies: A Comparative Institutional Approach of Some Cross-Country Differences." In Wolfgang Zapf and Meinolf Dierkes, eds., *Institutionenvergleich und Institutionendynamik WZB-Jahrbuch 1994 (Comparison and Dynamics of Institutions: WZB-Yearbook 1994)*, pp. 271–289. Berlin: Edition Sigma.

Stankovsky, Jan. 1996. "Bedeutung ausländischer Direktinvestitionen" (Relevance of Foreign Direct Investments). Osteuropa, Österreichisches Wirtschaftsforschungsinstitut, Monatsberichte (Eastern Europe: Monthly Report of the Austrian Institute for Economic Research) 2: 123–137.

Stark, David. 1989. "Coexisting Organizational Forms in Hungary's Emerging Mixed Economy." In Victor Nee and David Stark, eds., *Remaking the Economic Institutions of Socialism: China and Eastern Europe*, pp. 137–168. Stanford: Stanford University Press.

———. 1992. "Path Dependence and Privatisation Strategies in East-Central Europe." *East European Politics and Societies* 6: 17–51.

———. 1996. "Recombinant Property in East European Capitalism." *American Journal of Sociology* 101: 993–1027.

Stearns, Linda B. and Mark S. Mizruchi. 1986. "Broken Tie Reconstruction and the Functions of Interorganizational Interlocks." *Administrative Science Quarterly* 31: 522–538.

———. "Board Composition and Corporate Financing: The Impact of Financial Institution Representation on Borrowing." *Academy of Management Journal* 36: 603–618.

Steier, Frederick, ed. 1991. *Research and Reflexivity.* London: Sage.

Svetlicic M. and M. Rojec. 1996. *Kolektor: Case Study of Foreign Direct Investment in Slovenia.* Faculty of Social Sciences, University of Ljubljana.

Swaan, Willem. 1993. "Behaviour and Institutions under Economic Reform: Price Regulation and Market Behaviour in Hungary." Tinbergen Research Series No. 46. Amsterdam: Thesis Publishers.

Swedberg, Richard. 1994. *Explorations in Economic Sociology.* New York, NY: Russell Sage Foundation.

———. 1997. "New Economic Sociology: What Has Been Accomplished, What Is Ahead?" *Scandinavian Sociological Association* 40(2): 161–82.

Szalai, Erzsebet. 1994. "Political and Social Conflict Arising from the Transformation of Property Relations in Hungary." *Journal of Communist Studies and Transition Politics* 10: 56–77.

Szanyi, Mikl. 1994. "Experience with Foreign Direct Investment in Hungary." Working Paper No. 32. Budapest: Institute for World Economics.

Szelenyi, Ivan. 1989. "Eastern Europe in an Epoch of Transition." In Victor Nee and David Stark, eds., *Remaking Socialism: China and Eastern Europe*, pp. 208–232. Stanford: Stanford University Press.

Sztompka, Piotr. 1990. "Conceptual Frameworks in Comparative Inquiry: Divergent or Convergent." In Martin Albrow and Elizabeth King, eds., *Globalization, Knowledge and Society*, pp. 47–58. London: Sage.

Taipei City Women Rescue Foundation. 1990. *Funü Xingbaoli Diaocho Baogao (An Investigative Report on Women Suffering Sexual Violence).* Taipei: Women Rescue Foundation.

Taipei City Working People's Association. 1996. *Taibeishi Shangbanzhu Liaodingtiaojian Yu Shenghuozhuangkuang Wenjuandiaocho (A Survey of Working and Living Condition of Working People in Taipei City).* Taipei: Working People's Association.

Taipower Company. 1997. *The 1998 Annual Budget Report.* Taipei: The Execute Yuan.

Taiwan Fertilizer Corporation. 1995. *The 1996 Annual Budget Report.* Taipei: The Execute Yuan.

———. 1996. *The 1997 Annual Budget Report.* Taipei: The Executive Yuan.

———. 1997. *The 1998 Annual Budget Report.* Taipei: The Executive Yuan.

Taiwan Salt Corporation. 1995. *The 1996 Annual Budget Report.* Taipei: The Execute Yuan.

———. 1996. *The 1997 Annual Budget Report.* Taipei: The Execute Yuan.

———. 1997. *The 1998 Annual Budget Report.* Taipei: The Execute Yuan.

Taiwan Securities. 1985. Issue 6.

———. 1986. Issue 10.

Taiwan Securities and Futures Management. 1997. Vol. 15(5).

———. 1998. Vol. 16(1).

Taiwan Statistical Data Book. 1996. *Statistics on Overseas Chinese and Foreign Investment, Technical Cooperation, Outward Investment, Outward Technical Cooperation, the Republic of China.* R.O.C.: Ministry of Economic Affairs.

Taiwan Stock Exchange Materials. 1995. Issue 403.

Taiwan Sugar Corporation. 1995. *The 1996 Annual Budget Report.* Taipei: The Execute Yuan.

———. 1996. *The 1997 Annual Budget Report.* Taipei: The Execute Yuan.

———. 1997. *The 1998 Annual Budget Report.* Taipei: The Execute Yuan.

Tayeb, Monir. 1994. "Organizational and National Culture: Methodology Considered." *Organization Studies* 15(3): 429–446.

The Abstract of MOEA. 1996. *The Cooperative Project of SOE Overseas Investment.* Taipei: The MOEA

The China Times. 1994. Feb. 7.

The Commercial Times. 1996. June 7.

The Liberty Times. 1994. March 28.

———. 1996. April 28.

———. 1996. Nov. 30.

The Twenty First Century Foundation. 1995. *Taiwan Diqu 1995 Funü Manyidu Minyidiaocho Fenxibaogao (A Report on the Analysis of a Survey on the Degree of Satisfaction of Women in Taiwan Area in 1995).* Taipei: The Twenty First Century Foundation.

The United Daily News. 1994. Jan. 10.

———. 1996. Oct. 8.

Thompson, Leigh, E. Peterson, and Laura Kray. 1995. "Social Context in Negotiation: An Information Processing Perspective." *Negotiation as a Social Process*, edited by R. Kramer and David Messick. Beverly Hills: Sage.

Tseng, Yen-Fen. 1995. "'Little Taipei' and Beyond: The Development of Taiwanese Immigrant Businesses in Los Angeles." *International Migration Review* 29 (Spring Issue): 33–58.

Tu, Jenn-Hwa. 1994. "Nanxiang Yu Xijin Zhengce de Bijiao Fenxi" (A Comparative Study on the Policies of 'Going-Southward' and 'Going-Westward'). *Guoli Taiwan Daxue Zhongshan Xueshu Luncong (Dr. Sun Yet-sun Academic Review)* 12 (Jun.): 103–142.

Tung, Chung-Ping. 1996. "Shangshi Fagui yu Zhidu Yanjiu" (An Analysis of Initial Public Offering Regulation in Taiwan). Master's thesis, National SunYat-Sen University.

Tzeng, Rueyling. 1992. "The Reverse Multinational: An Analysis of One American Factory Under Chinese Management." Ph.D. diss., Department of Sociology, State University of New York at Stony Brook.

———. 1995. "International Labor Migration through Multinational Enterprises." *International Migration Review* 29(1): 139–154.

———. 1996. "Under Taiwanese Management: A Case Study in the United States." Unpublished manuscript. Taipei, Taiwan: Academia Sinica.

U.S. Bureau of Census. 1990. *Census of Population and Housing*. Washington, D.C.: USGPO.

———. 1992a. *1987 Survey of Minority-Owned Business Enterprises: Asian Americans, American Indians, and Others*. Washington, D.C.: USGPO.

———. 1992b. 1987 *Business Owners Survey*. Washington, D.C.: USGPO.

U.S. Merit Systems Protection Board. 1981. *Sexual Harassment in the Federal Workplace: Is It a Problem?* Washington, D.C.: U.S. Government Printing Office.

———. 1988. *Sexual Harassment in the Federal Government: An Update*. Washington, D.C.: U.S. Government Printing Office.

———. 1995. *Sexual Harassment in the Federal Workplace: Trends, Progress, Continuing Challenges*. Washington, D.C.: U.S. Government Printing Office.

United Nations. 1992. *World Investment Directory 1992: Vol. II Central and Eastern Europe*. New York, NY: United Nations.

Useem, Michael. 1996. *Investor Capitalism: How Money Managers are Changing the Face of Corporate America*. New York: Basic Books.

Uzzi, Brian. 1996a. "Coase Encounters of a Sociological Kind: A Sociological Perspective on Strategy." In J. Dutton and J. A. C. Baum, eds., *The Embeddedness of Strategy*, vol. 13, pp. 419–430. New York, NY: JAI Press.

———. 1996b. "The Sources and Consequences of Embeddedness for the Economic Performance of Organizations." *American Sociological Review* 61: 674–698.

———. 1997a. "Social Structure and Competition in Interfirm Networks: The Paradox of Embeddedness." *Administrative Science Quarterly* 42: 35–67.

———. 1997b. "A Structural Embeddedness Approach to Deindustrialization and Organizational Decline." *The International Journal of Sociology and Social Policy* 17: 111–155.

———. 2000. "What Is a Relationship Worth? The Benefits of Embeddedness in Corporate Financing." *American Sociological Review* forthcoming.

Uzzi, Brian and Zoe Barsness. 1998. "Contingent Employment in British Establishments: Organizational Determinants of the Use of Fixed-term Hires and Part-time Workers." *Social Forces* 76(3): 937-965.

Van Maanen, John. 1991. "The Smile Factory: Work at Disneyland." In Peter J. Frost, Larry F. Moore, Meryl R. Louis, Craig C. Lundberg and Joanne Martin, eds., *Reframing Organizational Culture*, pp. 58–76. Thousand Oaks: Sage.

———, ed. 1995. *Representation in Ethnography*. Thousand Oaks: Sage.

Van Maanen, John and Stephen R. Barley. 1985. "Cultural Organization: Fragments of a Theory." In Peter J. Frost, Larry F. Moore, Meryl R. Louis, Craig C. Lundberg and Joanne Martin, eds., *Organizational Culture*, pp. 31–53. Beverly Hills: Sage.

Várhegyi, Éva. 1993. "The Modernisation of the Hungarian Banking Sector." In Istvan P. Szekely and David M. G. Newbery, eds., *Hungary: An Economy in Transition*, pp. 149–162. Cambridge, England: Cambridge University Press.

Voszka, Éva. 1992. "Spontaneous Privatization in Hungary: Preconditions and Real Issues." In G. Lengyel et al., ed., *Economic Institutions, Actors and Attitudes: East Central Europe in Transition*. Budapest University of Economic Sciences Sociological Working Papers, Vol. 8.

———. 1995. *Agyaglabakon allo orias: Az AV Rt letrehozasa es mukodese. (The Giant with Feet of Clay)* Budapest: Penzugykutato.

Wade, Robert. 1990. *Governing the Market: Economic Theory and the Role of Government in East Asian Industrialization*. Princeton, NJ: Princeton University Press.

Wagner, J. Ellen. 1992. *Sexual Harassment in the Workplace: How to Prevent, Investigate, and Resolve Problems in Your Organization*. New York, NY: American Management Association.

Waldinger, Roger and Yen-Fen Tseng. 1992. "Divergent Diasporas: The Chinese Communities of New York and Los Angeles Compared." *Revue Europeenne Des Migrations Internationals* 8(3): 91–116.

Waldinger, Roger, Howard Aldrich, Robin Ward and Associates, eds. 1990. *Ethnic Entrepreneurs: Immigrant Business in Industrial Societies*. Newbury Park: Sage.

Waldinger, Roger. 1986. "Immigrant Enterprise: A Critique and Reformulation." *Theory and Society* 12: 249–285.

Walker, Gordon. 1994. "Asset Choice and Supplier Performance in Two Organizations." *Organizational Science* 5: 583–593.

Walker, Gordon and David Weber. 1987. "Supplier Competition, Uncertainty, and Make or Buy Decision." *Academy of Management Journal* 29: 373–391.

Wang, Hwei-Ling. 1993. "You Liaodingfa Lun Gongzuochangsuo Xingsaorao" (Sexual Harassment in the Workplace from the Viewpoint of Labor Law). Paper presented at Gongzuochangsuo Xingsaorao Wenti Yantaohui (The Conference on Sexual Harassment in the Workplace), Council of Labor Affairs, Executive Yuan, Taipei, Taiwan.

Wang, N. T. 1992. "Taiwan's Economic Relations with Mainland China." In N.T. Wang, ed., *Taiwan's Enterprises in Global Perspective*, pp. 50–77. Armonk, NY: M.E. Sharpe.

Wang, Shu-Chen. 1993. *Pufuqianjin—Angshou de Xingsaorao (Crawling Forward—Bravely*

Combating Sexual Harassment in the Workplace). Taipei: Shu-Churn Publishing Co.

Waters, Malcolm. 1995. *Globalization*. London: Routledge.

Watson, Tony J. 1994. *In Search of Management*. London: Routledge.

Wellisz, Stanislaw, Maciej Iwanek and Marek Bednarski. 1993. "Privatization." In Kierzkowski, Henryk, Marek Okólski and Stanislaw Wellisz, ed., *Stabilization and Structural Adjustment in Poland*, pp. 171–187. London: Routledge.

Westphal, James D. and Edward J. Zajac. 1995. "Who Shall Govern? CEO/Board Power, Demographic Similarity, and New Director Selection." *Administrative Science Quarterly* 40: 60–83.

———. 1997. "Defections from the Inner Circle: Social Exchange, Reciprocity and the Diffusion of Board Independence in U.S. Corporations." *Administrative Science Quarterly* 42: 161–183.

White, Harrison C. 1981. "Where Do Markets Come from?" *American Journal of Sociology* 87: 517–547.

Whitley, Richard. 1992a. *Business Systems in East Asia: Firms, Markets and Societies*. London: Sage.

———. 1992b. "Societies, Firms and Markets: the Social Structuring of Business Systems." In Richard Whitley, ed., *European Business Systems: Firms and markets in their National Contexts*, pp. 5–45. London: Sage.

———. 1994a. "Dominant Forms of Economic Organization in Market Economies." *Organization Studies* 15: 153–82.

———. 1994b. "The Internationalization of Firms and Markets: its Significance and Institutional Structuring." *Organization* 1: 101–124.

———. 1996a. "Business Systems and Global Commodity Chains: Competing or Complementary Forms of Economic Organisation?" In Richard Whitley, ed., *Competition and Change*, pp. 411–425. Malaysia: Harwood Academic Publishers.

———. 1996b. "There Is No Alternative: The Necessity of State Coordination of East European Reindustrialisation." *Competition and Change* 1: 321–332.

———. 1997. "The Social Regulation of Work Systems: Institutions, Interest Groups and Varieties of Work Organization in Capitalist Societies." In Richard Whitley and Peer Hull Kristensen, eds., *Governance at Work*, pp. 227–260. Oxford: Oxford University Press.

Whitley, Richard and Laszlo Czaban. 1998a. "Ownership Control and Authority in Emergent Capitalism: The Case of Hungary." *International Journal of Human Resource Management* 9: 99–113.

———. 1998b. "Institutional Transformation and Enterprise Change in an Emergent Capitalist Economy: The Case of Hungary." *Organization Studies* 19: 259–280.

Whitley, Richard, Jeffrey Henderson, Laszlo Czaban and Gyorgy Lengyel. 1996a.

"Continuity and Change in an Emergent Market Economy: the Limited Transformation of Large Enterprises in Hungary." In Richard Whitley and Peer Hull Kristensen, eds., *The Changing European Firm*, pp. 210–237. London: Routledge.

———. 1996b. "Trust and Contractual Relations in an Emergent Capitalist Economy." Organization Studies 17: 397–420.

Whitley, Richard, Marko Jaklic and Marko Hocevar. 1999. "Success without Shock Therapy in Eastern Europe: The Case of Slovenia." In S. Quack, G. Morgan and R. Whitley, ed., *National Capitalisms, Global Competition and Economic Performance*, Amsterdam: Benjamins.

Whitley, Richard and Peer Hull Kristensen, eds. 1996. *The Changing European Firm: Limits to Convergence*. London: Routledge.

———, eds. 1997. *Governance at Work: The Social Regulation of Economic Relations in Europe*. Oxford: Oxford University Press.

Wilkins, Alan L. and William G. Ouchi. 1983. "Efficient Cultures: Exploring the Relationship between Culture and Organizational Performance." *Administrative Science Quarterly* 28(3): 468–481.

Wilkins, Mira. 1986. "The History of European Multinationals: A New Look." In Mira Wilkins, ed., *The Growth of Multinationals*, pp. 24–51. Brookfield, U.S.: Edward Elgar Publishing Company.

Wilkinson, Barry. 1996. "Culture, Institutions and Business in East Asia." *Organization Studies* 17(3): 421–447.

Wilkinson, Barry and Nick Oliver. 1990. "Japanese Influence on British Industrial Culture." In Stewart R. Clegg and S. Gordon Redding, eds., *Capitalism in Contrasting Cultures*, pp. 333–354. Berlin: de Gruyter.

Williamson, Oliver E. 1975. *Markets and Hierarchies: Analysis and Antitrust Implications*. New York: Free Press.

———. 1985. *The Economic Institutions of Capitalism*. New York, NY: Free Press.

———. 1996. "Economic Organization: The Case for Candor." *The Academy of Management Review* 21(1): 48–57.

Winch, P. 1958. *On the Idea of Social Science and Its Relation to Philosophy*. London: Routledge.

Winterberg, Jörg M. 1994. "Westliche Unterstützung der Transformationsprozesse in Osteuropa: Eine Analyse der bundesdeutschen Finanzhilfen und der Entwicklung der Handelsbeziehungen mit Polen, Rußland und der Tschechischen Republik" (Western Support of the Transformation Processes in Eastern Europe: An Analysis of the German Federal Financial Aid and of the Development of Trade Relations with Poland, Russia and the Czech Republic). Konrad-Adenauer-Stiftung (Konrad-Adenauer-Foundation), Interne Studien (Internal Studies) No. 92, St. Augustin.

Wolf, E. 1994. "Facing Power: Old Insights, New Questions." In Robert Borofsky, ed., *Assessing Cultural Anthropology*. New York, NY: McGraw-Hill.

Wong, Lloyd. 1993. "Immigration as Capital Accumulation: The Impact of Business

Immigration to Canada." *International Migration* 31(1): 171–190.

Wong, Siu-Lun. 1985. "The Chinese Family Firm: A Model." *British Journal of Sociology* 34: 58–72.

Wong, Timothy Ka-ying. 1997. "The Impact of State Development in Taiwan on Cross-Straits Relations." *Asian Perspective* 20(1): 171–212.

Wu, Kun-Huang. 1996. "Shangshi Gongsidong Shihui Zongcheng yu Texingduiqiye Jingyingjixiao zhi Guanlianxing Yuanjiu" (The Study of the Relationship between Board Composition and Characterstics and Corporate Performance). Master's thesis, National Taiwan University.

Wu, Linjun. 1995. "Does Money Talk? The ROC's Economic Diplomacy." *Issues & Studies* 31(12): 22–35.

Yang, Ji-Ping. 1996. "Gongsi Shangshi Shenyiweiyuan de Renzhi yu Juecexingwei" (An Analysis of Cognitive and Decision-making Behavior of Members of the Listing Review Committee). Master's thesis, National Sun Yat-Sen University.

Yao, Min-Chia. 1988. "Taiwanqiyejia de Xingxinweiji" (The Confidence Crisis of Entrepreneurs in Taiwan). *Tianxiazazhi (Commonwealth Magazine)* (May): 44–51.

Yeh, Kuang S. 1997. "Board Network Structural Change before and after Initial Public Offerings in Taiwan." *Sun Yat-sen Management Review* (International Issue): 93–114.

Yeh, Kuang S., Jen-Jsung Huang, Yunshi Liu and Hsin-Hen Peng. 1996. "Gongsishangshi de Yuanyin yu Shangshiguocheng de Zuzhibiange" (Motivations and Organizational Change Processes of Corporations' Initial Public Offerings in Taiwan). *Guanlipinglun* (Management Review) 15(1): 15–36.

Yeh, Kuang S. and Li-Chin Tsao. 1996. "Jiazu Qiye Jieban Guocheng zhi Wangluofenxi" (A Network Analysis of Ownership Succession in Family Owned Businesses). *Guanli de Xuexuebao (Journal of Management)* 13(2): 197–225.

Yoon, In-Jin. 1991. "The Changing Significance of Ethnic and Class Resources in Immigrant Businesses: The Case of Korean Immigrant Businesses in Chicago." *International Migration Review* 35: 303–331.

Yu, Hwei-Chun. 1993. "Lun Gongzuochangsuo Zhi Faluwenti" (Legal Problems Concerning Sexual Harassment in the Workplace). Paper presented at *Gongzuochangsuo Xingsaorao Wenti Yantaohui* (The Conference on Sexual Harassment in the Workplace), Council of Labor Affairs, Executive Yuan, Taipei, Taiwan.

Yu, Mei-Nu. 1984a. "Falu Dui Xingsaorao de Zhicai" (Legal Sanctions Against Sexual Harassment). *Funü Xinzhi (New Knowledge for Women)* 25: 30–35.

———. 1984b. "Falu Duiyu Xingsaorao de Zhicai Fahui Duoshao Zuoyong" (How Effective are Legal Sanctions Against Sexual Harassment). *Zhongguo Luntan (China Forum)* 18(7): 45–47.

Yukl, G. 1989. "Managerial Leadership: A Review of Theory and Research." *Journal of Management* 15: 251–289.

Zhou, Min. 1992. *Chinatown: The Socioeconomic Potential of an Urban Enclave.* Philadelphia: Temple University Press.

Zhou, Yu. 1996. *"Ethnic Networks as Transaction Networks: Chinese Networks in the Producer Service Sectors in Los Angeles."* Ph.D. diss., Department of Geography, University of Minnesota.

Zukin, Sharon and Paul DiMaggio. 1990. "Introduction." pp. 1–30 in *Structures of Capital: The Social Organization of the Economy,* edited by Sharon Zukin and Paul DiMaggio. Cambridge, England: Cambridge University Press.

Contributors

Mats Alvesson, Professor, Department of Business Administration, School of Economics and Management, University of Lund, Sweden.

Cing-Kae Chiao, Associate Research Fellow, Institute of European and American Studies, Academia Sinica, Taiwan.

Yunshi Liu, Assistant Professor, Department of Business Administration, Tunghai University, Taiwan.

Hedwig Rudolph, Director, Organization and Employment, Social Science Research Center Berlin, and Professor, Technical University Berlin, Germany.

Michael Alan Sacks, Graduate Student, Department of Sociology and J. L. Kellogg Graduate School of Management, Northwestern University, U. S.

AnnaLee Saxenian, Associate Professor, Department of City and Regional Planning, University of California, Berkeley, U. S.

Hsing-Chou Sung, Associate Professor, Department and Graduate Institute of Political Science, Tunghai University, Taiwan.

Yen-Fen Tseng, Associate Professor, Department of Sociology, National Taiwan University, Taiwan.

Rueyling Tzeng, Associate Research Fellow, Institute of European and American Studies, Academia Sinica, Taiwan.

Brian Uzzi, Associate Professor, J. L. Kellogg Graduate School of Management and Department of Sociology, Northwestern University, U. S.

Richard Whitley, Professor of Organisational Sociology, Manchester Business School, University of Manchester, U. K.

Kuang S. Yeh, Professor, Department of Business Management, and Director, Graduate Institute of Communications Management, National Sun Yat-Sen University, Taiwan.

Index

A
Abolofia, Mitchell Y. 6
Agency Theories 86
Alliance Capitalism 2
Arm's-length Ties 88-90
Asian Development Bank (ADB) 192-193
Asset-specificity 82-85, 90-92, 94, 98, 102nn. 2-3, 103n. 4
Authoritarian Regime 196, 206

B
Bach, Robert and Papademetrious, Demetrious 265
(with Portes, Alejandro) 264
Baker, Wayne E. 6, 80, 95
Banks 2, 32, 35, 67, 186, 201-202, 218, 231-232, 278: Banking System 51-52, 55, 66, 68
Basic Organizations of Associated Labour (BOAL) 54, 58-59, 61, 71
Berle, Adolf A., Jr. and Means, Gardiner C. 105
Board Composition 108, 113-114, 117-120, 125-127, 129
Board of Directors 39, 109, 111, 113, 290
Bounded Rationality 6, 31, 85-86, 102n. 2
Brain Drain 65, 286, 292
Burawoy, Michael and Lukács, János 62
Burt, Ronald S. 6, 81
Business Group 14-15, 20, 181, 190, 200-201, 206
Business System 49-50, 57, 105, 216, 277

C
Capital Flows 248, 264, 268-269, 281
Capital-linked Migration 268-269

Capital Market 106, 108, 172. See also Financial Market, Stock Market
Capitalism 2-3, 8-9, 49, 185, 242, 282n. 4: Global 1, 10, 265, 280
Central Bank 55, 65, 192
Central Eastern Europe (CEE) 239, 247, 240-241, 243-244, 246, 253-256, 259-260
Central State 54-55, 61, 67-68, 74, 77
Chandler, Alfred D., Jr. 105
Chief Executive Officer (CEO) 116, 254-255, 290, 294, 296, 301-302
China 9, 136, 146, 148, 165-166, 176-182, 186, 191-206, 208n. 14, 224, 226, 231, 237n. 2, 266-267, 277-279, 288-289, 298-299, 302. See also PRC
Chinese 10, 32-33, 113, 136, 165, 192, 196, 198-199, 204, 227, 235, 263, 265-281, 282n. 1, 283, 287-295, 297, 299, 299n. 6: Overseas (*Hua-qiao*) 112, 201, 226, 229, 279
Civil Rights Act 132, 152, 154, 158, 162-164
Collective Rationality 87-89, 92
Commodity Chains 286
Comparative Studies 11, 25, 27-28, 46
Composite Organization of Associated Labour (COAL) 54, 58-61, 71
Computer Industry 250, 261n. 12, 280, 295
Context-dependence 15, 17
Corporate Culture 40, 44, 294
Council for Mutual Economic Assistance (CMEA) 50, 53, 55, 57-60, 62, 69, 72-73, 78, 240, 242, 244
Council of Labor Affairs (CLA) 133, 137,

142-143, 145-146, 148-149, 165-166, 167n. 1
Cross Share-Holding 110
Cultural Context 21-22, 32, 37
Culture Differences 21, 135, 299n. 2
Cultural Traffic 10, 34-35
Culture 6, 11, 16, 20, 24, 29, 40, 42, 46n. 1, 79, 227, 234-237, 260, 262n. 13, 284, 286, 288-289, 291-292, 294-295: Studies 12, 15, 23, 25-26, 28, 31, 33, 36, 45; Meanings 21-23, 26-28, 30, 32, 44-45; Manifestation 10, 34-38, 43-44

D

Deetz, Stanley 14
Democratization 8, 62-63, 69, 186, 189-190, 196-198, 206-207
Dependency Theory 214-215, 285
Deregulation 2, 8, 10, 186, 215, 242, 251
Developmental State 215
DiMaggio, Paul and Powell, Walter W. 106, 115-116
  (with Zukin, Sharon) 5
Divergence 17-19, 298
Drazin, Robert (with Sandelands, Lloyd) 14

E

Eastern Europe 2, 4, 8, 49-50, 59, 64, 239, 247, 261n. 1
Economic System 1, 3, 49-50, 79, 103n. 7, 185, 212, 227
Economic Ties 101, 194, 196, 202, 204-205, 285-286
Embedded Autonomy 185
Embeddedness 2, 4, 10, 79, 103n. 5, 211-212, 263, 265, 272, 280: Approach 1, 3, 7, 82, 86-87, 89-92, 98-99, 101-102; Ties 6, 80, 87-89, 98, 103n. 6; Social 3, 8-9, 31, 242; Institutional 49; Cognitive 6; Cultural 6, 7; Structural 6, 80, 86; Political 5
Emigrants 10, 243
Employer Liability 147, 153-154, 157-158, 162

Employment Discrimination 142, 149, 154, 163
Employment Service Law 142
Entrepreneurial Capitalism 107, 114-115, 117, 126, 129
Environmental Protection 179, 183
Equal Employment Opportunity Commission (EEOC) 132, 136, 152-154, 156, 158, 163
Essentialism 38
Ethnography 23, 33
European Union (EU) 2, 135, 215, 240-241, 244, 246, 248, 250
Expatriates 227, 241, 243, 251, 253-260, 262n. 13
Export Processing Zone (EPZ) 221
Export-oriented Industrialization (EOI) 185, 200, 221, 268

F

Fair Employment Opportunity Law 153
Family Firms (Family Businesses) 9, 105, 107, 109, 111-112, 120, 122, 126-127, 278
Financial Market 3, 4, 9. See also Capital Market, Stock Market
Financial System 49
Flexible Diplomacy 189-193
Food Industry 241, 249, 251-253
Foothold Strategy 248
Foreign Capital 174, 179, 186, 189, 201-202, 219, 221, 247, 249-250, 252, 261nn. 8, 10, 272. See also Foreign Direct Investment (FDI)
Foreign Companies 194, 201, 239, 246, 248-250, 252, 259-260, 261n. 3. See also International Business, Multinational Corporations, Western Companies
Foreign Direct Investment (FDI) 170-172, 175, 178-180, 182-184, 189-191, 196, 205-206, 213-214, 218-219, 221, 224-226, 231, 235, 237n. 1, 242-243, 246-251, 256, 259-260, 261nn. 6, 9, 268. See also Foreign Capital
Forms of Business Organization 1, 4

G

Geertz, Clifford 25-26, 30, 32-33
Gender Equality in Employment 10, 131-133, 137, 143, 147-148, 150, 165, 167, 168n. 5
Glass Ceiling 275, 283, 291-292
Global Capital Market 9
Global Economy 2, 211-213, 215-216, 226, 236, 241, 265, 281. See also World Economy
Globalization 1-4, 8-9, 11, 19, 36, 127, 186, 211-214, 216, 225, 235-236, 281, 285-286, 298
Governance 3-6, 81, 85, 112, 215, 225-226, 236: Corporate 105, 107, 128; Structure 83, 92, 105, 107, 111, 113, 129
Grand Theory 15
Grandiose Storytelling 23
Granovetter, Mark 5-6, , 90, 116, 211, 265 (with McGuire, Patrick and Schwartz, Michael) 7
Guillen, Mauro F. 7

H

Hamilton, Gary and Nicole Biggart 7
Hard Budget Constraint 62, 66, 69
Helper, Susan 90
Hermeneutic Approach 30
Hierarchy 4, 15, 31, 36, 38-43, 54, 61, 281
High-Technology 172, 186, 203-204, 223, 267-268, 272-277
Hofstede, Geert H. 18, 35, 42
Holding Company 186
Hsinchu 10, 223, 283-286, 290, 292-296, 298-299, 299n. 1, 302
Human Capital 4, 6, 239-241, 243, 270
Hungary 8, 49-70, 72-74, 76-77, 241, 244, 246-247

I

IMF 64-65, 68
Immigrants 10, 34, 243, 267-269, 272, 276-279, 286, 288-289, 293, 295, 299, 299n. 6: Immigrant Community 264, 291; Immigrant Entrepreneurs 264, 266, 270, 281, 287, 291; Immigrant Firms 263, 265-266, 280-281
Import-substitution 185
Individual Investors 110-111, 114, 117, 124-126, 129n. 1
Individual Rationality 87
Industrialization 172, 184-185, 193-194, 206, 236, 268, 283-284
Informal Network Market 2
Initial Public Offering (IPO) 105-112, 114-116, 118-121, 123-128
Institutional Investors 110-111, 114, 116-117, 120, 122
Institutional Theory (Institutionalism) 31-32, 111-112, 114
Institutionalization 110, 115
Institutions 1, 2, 4-5, 7, 25, 32-33, 51-52, 66, 74, 106, 108, 110, 113-114, 212, 225, 240, 242-244, 248, 253-254, 268, 284-286: Social 26; Arrangements 49-50; Barriers 135; Change 8, 50, 62-63, 67-68, 72, 76-77, 79, 127; Constraints 127, 135; Contexts 13, 23, 50; Development 105
Intensity of Exchange 90-93
International Business 8, 181, 281. See also Multinational Corporations, Western Companies, Foreign Companies
International Division of Labour 214, 240, 259-260
International Linkages 264-265, 280
International Trading 265, 267, 276-279, 282n. 4
Internationalization 4-5, 8-9, 11, 213, 216, 223, 225, 281, 291
Interorganizational Ties 89
Interpretation 14, 21, 23, 29, 35-36, 40, 44-45, 98, 132-134, 150, 163-164, 254, 258, 266
Inverse Brain Drain 243

J

Joint Venture 81, 179, 181, 227, 242, 246, 248-251, 257, 259-260, 261n. 3, 285, 296-297

K

Kalleberg, Arne L. (with Lincoln, James R.) 18, 20-21
KMT Regime (KMT Government) 195-196, 198
KMT-owned Enterprises 185-186, 188-190, 192, 194-196, 198-199, 206-207
Kojima, Kiyoshi 216-217, 227

L

Labor Unions 132, 142-144, 148, 163-164, 166
Labor-management Relations 2
Labour Markets 66, 68, 70, 74, 254-257, 259-260
Labour System 51-52, 66-68
Large Firms 4, 8, 67, 74, 115
Larson, Andrea 90
Latin America 186, 200, 263, 265, 280
Law Firm 151
Leadership 14, 17-18, 53, 64, 132, 190, 193, 197
Legal System 51, 53, 150, 162, 165
Liberalization 8-9, 62-63, 68-69, 72, 74, 186, 189-201, 203, 206, 207n. 7, 213, 218, 221, 223-225, 242-243
Lincoln, James R. and Kalleberg, Arne L. 18, 20-21
Local 11, 13-14, 17, 24, 28, 34, 36, 38, 43, 45, 52, 54-58, 60-61, 63, 65-66, 68, 72, 75, 127, 131, 135-136, 138-139, 141-142, 146, 154, 174, 179-181, 189, 204, 213-215, 226, 231, 241, 249, 253, 255-259, 264, 270, 279, 285-290, 293, 297: Theory 15, 19, 37, 44; Business 132-133, 145, 147-149, 165-167, 205; Culture 12, 234-236, 284; Diversity 35, 211; Employers 137, 145, 149, 164-166; Firms 228-229, 234-236; Markets 182, 212, 217, 219, 221, 223-224, 227-228, 232, 234, 282n. 4; Sales 223, 228-229, 232, 234, 236
Localities 53, 59, 73, 281, 286, 298
Localization 212-213, 217, 226-229, 232, 234-236, 237n. 5, 298
Lukács, János (with Burawoy, Michael) 62

Lyotard, Jean Francois 20

M

Macro Contexts 45
Mainland Fever 190, 202
Managers 9, 15, 18, 20, 27, 36-37, 39, 41-42, 46n. 9, 54-62, 64-67, 69-72, 74-78, 105, 110, 122, 171, 205, 234-235, 252, 261nn. 4, 13, 264, 301: Professional 107, 114-117, 120, 126, 128
Managerial Capitalism 107, 114-115, 117, 126, 129;
Market Economy 2, 53, 80, 172, 239, 242-243, 253, 263, 265, 269-271, 280
Market Transactions 60, 129n. 1, 286
Martin, Joanne and Siehl, Caren 40
Means, Gardiner C. (with Berle, Adolf A.) 105
Methods 11, 16, 19, 23, 45, 64, 92, 120, 137, 143, 147-148, 160, 162, 168n. 6, 257, 266
Micro 11-12, 15, 22, 24, 33, 37-38, 46nn. 1, 6, 64
Migration 53, 80, 271
Monte Jade Science and Technology Association (Monte Jade) 289-290
Multinational Corporations (Multinationals, MNC) 10, 169, 171-172, 183, 206, 212-217, 223, 225, 228-229, 232, 236-237, 281, 285. See also International Business, Western Companies, Foreign Companies
Multiple Cultural Configuration 33-34, 36, 43

N

Nation State 211, 235-236
National Boundaries 2, 8, 10, 216
National Culture 44
Neoclassical Economic Theory 2-3, 6-7, 114
Network 1-3, 5, 7-8, 14, 25, 32, 44, 73-74, 79, 81, 86-87, 89, 98-99, 101-102, 137, 212, 217, 247, 250, 259, 265, 270, 273, 275-276, 279-282, 282n. 4, 284-285, 288, 289, 291, 294-296, 299, 301:

Bridges 6; Size 82, 90-94, Interregional 286; Transnational 10, 260, 272, 292, 298; Personal 53, 60, 277, 293
New Asian Immigrants 264
New Economic Sociology 5, 79
Norms 3, 5-6, 8, 21, 32, 35, 51, 62, 74, 103n. 7, 115, 149, 162, 216, 237, 243, 254, 259
North America 261n. 1, 277, 280, 289, 296, 301
North American Free Trade Agreement (NAFTA) 2, 215

O

OECD 55, 59, 70, 77, 240, 244, 246-247
Of Meaning 12, 15, 20, 25-26, 29, 32-34, 44-45, 46n. 2
Opportunism 31, 81, 84-85, 87, 89, 91-92, 98, 102n. 2, 103nn. 7, 8
Orders 7, 13, 16, 23-24, 29, 39, 44, 131, 140-141, 172, 175, 178, 200, 277
Organization 2, 8-11, 14-15, 17, 19, 24, 26-27, 34, 37, 39, 41, 43, 45, 46n. 1, 79-80, 86-93, 95, 101, 102n. 2, 105, 114-116, 132, 137-138, 148-150, 163, 165-166, 174, 186, 189, 192, 195, 199, 217, 226, 236, 266, 272-273, 277, 279, 284, 288-290: Boundaries 81, 83-84; Changes 1, 3-5, 7, 49-51, 69, 73, 77, 106, 110; Commitment 18, 20-21; Culture 12, 28-29, 35, 40, 44, 294; Structures 31-32, 112, 212, 227
Outside Directors 114, 129n. 5

P

Pacific Asia 180
Party-state 51, 54, 56
Podolny, Joel M. 98
Poland 10, 53, 239, 241-244, 246, 248-253, 255-260, 261nn. 3, 6, 12
Polonia 10, 249, 257
Portes, Alejandro
 and Bach, Robert 264
 and Stepick, Alex 265
Post-socialist Countries 246-247, 260

Powell, Walter W. 5-6
 (with DiMaggio, Paul J.) 106, 115-116
 Koput, Kenneth W. and Smith-Doerr, Laurel 80
Power 2, 5, 7, 12, 18, 22, 26, 29-32, 35, 42-44, 52, 54, 59-60, 62, 64-65, 67-68, 73, 75, 110-111, 139, 185, 193, 195, 206, 211-212, 214, 224, 226, 235-236, 251, 256-257
Pragmatic Diplomacy 189-190, 193, 195-196, 199-200, 204, 206
PRC 176, 191-193, 198-200, 202-205. See also China
Private Enterprises 2, 145, 170, 249
Private Firms (Private Companies) 9, 73, 76, 106, 109, 115, 129n. 1, 170, 175
Private Investors 179, 250
Privatization 2, 4, 8, 169, 183, 186, 189-190
Professionalization 127
Property Rights 4-5, 215
Public Enterprises 185-186, 189
Public Firms (Public Companies) 9, 106-107, 110-112, 114-119, 121, 123, 126-128, 129n. 1
Public Sector 2, 151

R

Random Effects Panel Probit Model 96
Reasonable Woman 157
Redding, S. Gordon 17
Regional Associations (*tong-xiang-hui*) 279
Regional Development 174
Regulation 2-3, 32, 109-110, 114, 116, 129n. 2, 142, 150, 186, 202, 204-205, 215, 236-237, 242, 250, 254: State 8, 52, 68, 213; Wage 56, 59, 62; Labor 5; Business 128; Market 225
Reify 16, 23, 27, 44
Relationships (*Guanxi*) 113, 116: Density 82, 89-90, 94; Structure 112; Interenterprise 57, 60-61, 72; Informal 33, 81, 273; Social 3, 5-6, 14, 31-32, 35-36, 42, 44, 79, 281
Remigrants 248, 257

Repeated Ties 81
Returnees 273, 292-294

S

Sandelands, Lloyd and Drazin, Robert 14, 46n. 1
Sassen, Saskia 215, 236, 272
School Systems 56
Sculley, John 38-40
Service Industry (Service Sector) 202, 212, 214, 218, 224, 226, 229, 231-232, 234, 236-237
Sex Discrimination 134, 149, 153, 155, 167
Sexual Favoritism 153, 163, 166
Sexual Harassment in the Workplace 131-137, 139-148, 150, 152, 154, 156-165, 167
Shock Therapy 64, 239, 242
Shortage Economy 55, 57, 60, 62, 69, 76
Silicon Valley 280, 283-301
Slovenia 8, 49-77
Small and Medium-sized Enterprises (SMEs) 196, 200, 216, 218, 244, 277, 284
Small Firms 4, 277, 297
Small-numbers Bargaining 82, 84-85
Social Action 12, 26, 31, 33, 43
Social Capital 6, 80, 257
Social Constellations 34
Social Science 13, 16-17, 19, 22-25, 29, 102n. 1, 103n. 6, 237n. 3
Social Structure 1, 3-6, 10, 25-26, 79, 86, 89, 92, 95, 101-102, 103n. 5, 186, 211, 243, 286
Social Ties 81, 86-88, 288-289, 294
Socialist Countries 192, 239-240, 250, 254
Societal Culture 28
Soft Budget Constraints 54, 57, 62
Soft Comparison 43
Southeast Asia 9, 180-181, 184, 194-196, 201-206, 278, 289
Southward Strategy 170, 194-196, 205-206
State 2, 4-5, 8, 10, 18, 28, 49, 55, 63, 66, 70-71, 73, 75, 96, 118, 129nn. 1, 7, 134-135, 162, 169-173, 183-186, 188, 191, 193, 198, 202, 207, 211-214, 216, 218-219, 225-226, 235-236, 242, 249-250, 279, 284: Theory 9; Structure 51-52, 54, 57, 68; Autonomy 52, 206; Control 9, 52, 54, 60-61, 68, 74, 189-190; Socialism 50-51, 57, 64, 67; Socialist 9, 50-53, 56-59, 62, 64-65, 69, 72, 76-77
State-owned Enterprise (SOE) 9, 58, 69-71, 73, 75, 169-179, 182-185, 189-191, 195-196, 205-207, 279
Stock Market 8-9, 108, 110, 118, 129n. 1. See also Financial Market, Capital Market
Strong State 219, 225, 236
Structural Constraints 82
Structuration 79-80, 89, 91, 93, 101, 102n. 1
Swedish 33, 35, 38, 40-43

T

Taiwan (ROC) 4, 7-10, 34, 105-119, 124-125, 126, 128-129, 129nn. 1, 2, 3, 131-133, 135-140, 142-143, 145-146, 149-150, 158, 164-167, 168nn. 4, 5, 169-170, 175-186, 188-202, 204-206, 207nn. 2, 4, 5, 6, 8, 208nn. 11, 12, 14, 15, 211-213, 218-219, 221-229, 231-232, 234-237, 237nn. 1, 4, 5, 11, 264, 266-269, 272-273, 276-280, 283-298, 300n. 10, 301
Telecommunications Sector 241, 248, 250, 252-253, 255, 260
Trade Block 8
Transaction Cost 31, 79, 81-89, 91-92, 98-99, 101, 103n. 8, 281
Transformation 8, 50, 64, 77, 83, 105, 186, 225, 242, 248-249, 254, 256, 261n. 5: Process 63, 65, 67, 106, 124, 126-127, 239, 243-244, 246, 253, 257, 260, 261n. 3; Economic 1, 7, 51, 53, 63, 65, 79, 101, 102n. 1, 170, 184-185, 200, 206, 213-215, 218-219, 221, 227, 240-241, 247, 251, 263-264; Societal 49, 63

Transnational Business   247, 264-265
Transnational Community   285-286, 292-293
Transnational Entrepreneurs   238, 295-296
Trust   6, 9, 51-53, 71, 80, 88, 90, 103n. 7, 276, 286, 288, 293, 297-298

U

United States (USA, America)   20, 33, 40, 109-110, 114, 117, 121, 129n. 1, 131, 133-134, 150, 153-154, 158-159, 163-167, 172, 191, 194, 197, 200, 202, 204-205, 226-227, 229, 231, 236, 267, 280-281, 287, 289, 292-293
Useem, Michael   110, 114
Uzzi, Brian   1, 6, 10, 79-80, 87, 89-91, 98

V

Venture Capital   2, 32, 122, 272-273, 291, 294, 297

W

Weak Ties   6
Western Companies   240, 242, 246, 249-250, 254-255, 259-260. See also International Business, Multinational Corporations, Foreign Companies
Westernization   10, 212
Williamson, Oliver E.   81, 83-84, 102n. 2, 103n. 5
Winch, P.   20
Women's Rights Groups   132, 136-138, 140, 142-143, 163
Wong, Lloyd   269
Work Organization   57-58, 61, 73-74
Work System   62, 75
World Bank   64-65
World Economy   169, 184, 186, 212, 214-215, 265. See also Global Economy
World Trade Organization (WTO)   2, 215, 225

Y

Yeh, Kuang S.   129n. 1
  and Tsao, Li-Chin   107
  Huang, Jen-Jsung, Liu, Yunshi and Peng, Hsin-Hen   106, 108, 115
  (with Liu, Yunshi)   9, 105

Z

Zukin, Sharon and D   5